ACTS OF WAR

ACTS OF WAR

IRAQ AND AFGHANISTAN IN SEVEN PLAYS

Edited by Karen Malpede,
Michael Messina, and Bob Shuman

Thanks so much for a great experience at LPA! Michael Messina 5-4-11

◼ NORTHWESTERN UNIVERSITY PRESS
EVANSTON, ILLINOIS

Northwestern University Press
www.nupress.northwestern.edu

Printed in the United States of America

10   9   8   7   6   5   4   3   2   1

LIBRARY OF CONGRESS CATALOGING-IN-PUBLICATION DATA

Acts of war : Iraq and Afghanistan in seven plays / edited by Karen Malpede, Michael Messina,
and Bob Shuman.

p. cm.

ISBN 978-0-8101-2732-6 (pbk. : alk. paper)

1. War stories, American. 2. War stories, English. 3. Iraq War, 2003– —Drama. 4. Afghan War,
2001– —Drama. 5. War—Psychological aspects—Drama. 6. War—Moral and ethical aspects—
Drama. I. Malpede, Karen. II. Messina, Michael. III. Shuman, Bob.

PS627.W37A38 2011

812'.60803585810443—dc22

2010045069

∞ The paper used in this publication meets the minimum requirements of the American
National Standard for Information Sciences—Permanence of Paper for Printed Library Materials,
ANSI Z39.48-1992.

CONTENTS

FOREWORD

Chris Hedges

The crisis faced by combat veterans returning from war, a persistent theme in the plays collected in *Acts of War: Iraq and Afghanistan in Seven Plays*, is not simply a profound struggle with trauma and alienation. It is often an existential crisis—for those who can slice through the suffering to self-awareness. War exposes the lies we tell ourselves about ourselves. It rips open the hypocrisy of our religions and secular institutions. Those who return from war have learned something which is often incomprehensible to those who have stayed home. We are not a virtuous nation. God and fate have not blessed us above others. Victory is not assured. War is neither glorious nor noble. And we carry within us the capacity for evil we ascribe to those we fight.

Those who return to speak this truth, such as members of Iraq Veterans Against the War, are our contemporary prophets. But like all prophets, they are condemned and ignored for their courage. They struggle, in a culture awash in lies, to tell what few have the fortitude to digest. They know that what we are taught in school, in worship, by the press, through the entertainment industry, and at home—that the melding of the state's rhetoric with the rhetoric of religion—is empty and false. And these seven plays give to our neglected prophets a voice. In exploring the psychic and physical pain of war, these plays go to places most modern theater productions will not. They have a conscience. They speak in the unfamiliar language of justice.

Corporate money, government support, and grants reward those who stay on script, who do not challenge the cruel structures of imperialism, the permanent war economy, and unfettered capitalism. This kind of insidious censorship relegates cutting-edge productions to obscurity. The words these prophets speak are painful. We, as a nation, prefer to listen to those who speak from the patriotic script. We prefer to hear ourselves exalted. If veterans speak of terrible wounds visible and invisible, of lies told to make them kill, of evil committed in our name, we fill our ears with wax. Not *our* men and women, we say, bred in our homes, endowed with goodness and decency. For if it is easy for them to murder, what about us? And so it is simpler and more comfortable not to hear. We do not listen to the angry words that cascade forth from their lips, wishing only that they would calm down, be reasonable, get some help, and go away. We, the deformed, brand our prophets as madmen. We cast them into the desert. And this is why so many veterans are estranged and enraged. This is why so many succumb to suicide or addictions.

To those who would fight it, a war is touted as the ultimate test of courage, where the young can find out what they are made of. War, from a distance, seems noble. It offers a chance to play a small bit in the great drama of history. But up close war is a soulless void. War is about barbarity, perversion, and pain, an unchecked orgy of death. Human decency and tenderness are crushed. Those who make war work overtime to reduce love to smut, and all human beings become objects, pawns to use or kill. The noise, the stench, the fear, the scenes of eviscerated bodies and bloated corpses, the cries of the wounded—all combine to spin those in combat into another universe. In this moral void, naively blessed by secular and religious institutions at home, the hypocrisy of our social conventions, our strict adherence to moral precepts, comes unglued. War, for all its horror, has the power to strip away the trivial and the banal, the empty chatter and foolish obsessions that fill our days. It lets us see, although the cost is tremendous.

The Reverend William P. Mahedy, who was a Catholic chaplain in Vietnam, tells of a soldier, a former altar boy, in his book *Out of the Night: The Spiritual Journey of Vietnam Vets*. The soldier says to him, "Hey, Chaplain . . . how come it's a sin to hop into bed with a *mama-san* but it's okay to blow away gooks out in the bush?"

"Consider the question that he and I were forced to confront on that day in a jungle clearing," Mahedy writes. "How is it that a Christian can, with a clear conscience, spend a year in a war zone killing people and yet place his soul in jeopardy by spending a few minutes with a prostitute? If the New Testament prohibitions of sexual misconduct are to be stringently interpreted, why, then, are Jesus' injunctions against violence not binding in the same way? In other words, what does the commandment 'Thou shalt not kill' really mean?"

There is a difference between killing someone who is trying to kill you and taking the life of someone who does not have the power to harm you. The first is killing. The second is murder. But in the wars in Iraq and Afghanistan, where the enemy is elusive and rarely seen, murder occurs far more often than killing. Families are massacred in air strikes and drone attacks. Children are gunned down in blistering suppressing fire laid down in neighborhoods after an improvised explosive device goes off near a convoy. Artillery shells obliterate homes. And no one stops to look. The dead and maimed are left behind.

The utter failure of nearly all our religious institutions—whose texts are unequivocal about murder—to address the essence of war has rendered them useless. These institutions have little or nothing to say in wartime because the god they worship is a false god, one that promises victory to those who obey the law and believe in the manifest destiny of the nation. And it has been left to the theater to address the moral issues that should have been the domain of our religious institutions.

We all have the capacity to commit evil. It takes little to unleash it. For those of us who have been to war, this is the awful knowledge that is hardest to digest, the knowledge that the line between the victims and the victimizers is razor-thin, that human beings find a perverse delight in destruction and death, and that few can resist the pull. At best, most of us become silent accomplices.

Wars may have to be fought to ensure survival, but they are always tragic. They always bring to the surface the worst elements of any society, those who have a penchant for violence and a lust for absolute power. They turn the moral order upside down. It was the criminal class that first organized the defense of Sarajevo. When these goons were not manning roadblocks to hold off the besieging Bosnian Serb army, they were looting, raping, and killing the Serb residents in the city. And those politicians who speak of war as an instrument of power, those who wage war but do not know its reality, those powerful statesmen—the Henry Kissingers, Robert McNamaras, Donald Rumsfelds, the Dick Cheneys, the Barack Obamas—those who treat war as part of the great game of nations, are as amoral as the religious stooges who assist them.

"In theological terms, war is sin," writes Mahedy. "This has nothing to do with whether a particular war is justified or whether isolated incidents in a soldier's war were right or wrong. The point is that war as a human enterprise is a matter of sin. It is a form of hatred for one's fellow human beings. It produces alienation from others and nihilism, and it ultimately represents a turning away from God."

The young soldiers and Marines do not plan or organize the war. They do not seek to justify it or explain its causes. They are taught to believe. The symbols of the nation and religion are interwoven. The will of God becomes the will of the nation. This trust is forever shattered for many in war. Soldiers in combat see the myth used to send them to war implode. They see that war is not clean or neat or noble, but venal and frightening. They see into war's essence, which is death.

War is always about betrayal. It is about betrayal of the young by the old, of cynics by idealists, and of soldiers and Marines by politicians. Society's institutions, including our religious institutions, which mold us into compliant citizens, are unmasked in war. This betrayal is so deep that many never find their way back to faith in the nation or in any god. They nurse a self-destructive anger and resentment, understandable and justified, but also crippling. Ask a combat veteran struggling to piece his or her life together about God and watch the raw vitriol and pain pour out. They have seen the corruption and staggering hypocrisy essential to war. Those of us who refuse to heed their suffering and their words, brought to life in the hands of these playwrights, become complicit in the evil they denounce.

ACKNOWLEDGMENTS

Karen Malpede thanks my coeditors, Bob Shuman and Michael Messina, for their careful edits of and comments about the introduction as it developed, and their good-humored judiciousness at every step on the way. Thanks, also, to Bob for his excellent theater blog: www.stagevoices.com and to Michael for his support of *Prophecy*. My thanks to the playwrights, those whose plays are here, and the others who have written about the wars, but especially: David Hare for his commitment to this project from its inception; Lydia Stryk for her comments, questions, and suggestions; and Naomi Wallace for alerting me to Simon Stephens's play. Thanks to Nicolas Kent, artistic director of the Tricycle Theatre, London, for commissioning three of the plays in this volume: *Guantanamo: "Honor Bound to Defend Freedom," No Such Cold Thing*, and *A Canopy of Stars*. Thanks to James Nicola, artistic director, and, especially, to Linda Chapman, associate artistic director, of New York Theater Workshop for offering *Prophecy* a home in their Fourth Street Theater. My most heartfelt thanks go to my immensely talented collaborators on the May–June 2010, Theater Three Collaborative, American premiere of *Prophecy*, each of whom worked with such joy, commitment, and insight toward stunning results: Kathleen Chalfant, George Bartenieff, Brendan Donaldson, Peter Francis James, and Najla Said, the wonderful actors; Maxine Willi Klein (set), Tony Giovannetti (lights), Sally Ann Parsons (costumes), Arthur Rosen (sound and music), Jonathan Donohue (production stage manager), Luba Lukova, (graphic design), Shelley Valfer (company manager), and Sara Roer (choreographer and producing assistant). The theater should always be this openhearted, collaborative, and fun. For their support over the years and for the example of their work, my deep appreciation goes to: Olympia Dukakis, Lydia Koniordou, Judith Malina, John Malpede (my twin), Kika Markham, Arsen Ostojic, and Vanessa Redgrave. Thanks to: Erika Duncan for thirty years of being my best writer-friend and closest reader, to Elsa First and Ynestra King, who offered valuable comments about the introduction, and to Martha Bragin, Sue Finkelstein, Bob Machover, Stefanie Siegel, Paul and Harriet Pitcoff with whom I have shared many hours of conversation over the years about war, trauma, art, and social action; thanks to Linda Hoaglund, Paul McIsaacs, and Gail Pellet for cocreating with George Bartenieff and me the 2004 public ritual "Iraq: Naming the Dead," the event which began the journey toward this anthology; thanks to newer friends and colleagues: Laurie Arbieter, Noam Chomsky, Laura Flanders, Norm Fruchter, Chris Hedges, and David Swanson; and to earlier colleagues Robert Jay Lifton and Charles Strozier for a decade of stimulating conversations at the now, alas, defunct Center on Violence and Human Survival, and Stevan Weine, who first introduced me to the literature on art and bearing witness. At Northwestern University Press, thanks to Susan Hahn for publishing my short story "Prophecy," and to Mike Levine for his persistence in helping shape this collection. Thanks to my mother, Doris Isgrig, for raising us to care. The air I breathe, the work I do, the plays I write are possible because of the multiple talents and sustaining love of my partner, collaborator, and most constant inspiration, actor, producer, director, George Bartenieff, and my artist daughter Carrie Sophia Hash, with grateful strokes, too, to Cleis and Hermes, for endless doggie humor.

Michael Messina would like to thank Bob Shuman and Karen Malpede for the experience of editing this wonderful and important collection with them; and Mike Levine at Northwestern University Press, whom I was lucky to meet at an Association for Theatre in Higher Education conference in New Orleans several years back. I would also like to thank the Great Recession for giving me the time to work on this project. Special thanks also to my partner, Jeffrey Soto.

Bob Shuman would like to thank Karen Malpede for her deep knowledge of our wars in the Mideast and Michael Messina for the breadth of his expertise in the publishing industry. He'd also like to thank them for their insistence on finding the finest work written during and about the contemporary Iraq and Afghanistan conflicts. Sadly, there are not many plays documenting this piece of history, much less ones that have been produced. The effect of these wars on individuals and families, subcultures and nations must be exposed artistically as well as in the press, and he is grateful to Mike Levine at Northwestern University Press for understanding this. Bob extends gratitude to our men and women in uniform and to those noncombatants caught in the fire of these engagements, whether physical or psychological. He is, additionally, indebted to the playwrights in this collection as well as to: Rosalee Abrams, Serena Brommel, Casarotto Ramsay & Associates Limited, June Clark, College of

Mount Saint Vincent, Kimberly Cottrell, The Drama Bookshop, Fred S. Bull and Stephen R. Bull and their families, Faber and Faber, Rudy Faust, Victoria Fox, Jenny Gavacs, Anne Gendler, Pam Green, Rob Jacklosky, Chris Hedges, Joyce Henry, James Hogan, Harri Hurley Jahss, Rebecca Dunn Jaroff, Nicolas Kent, Mel Kenyon, Lorraine Kornreich, Stuart Marshall, David Miller, Nancy Nelson and Randy Lanchner, Northwestern University Press, Oberon Books, Kathleen Peirce, Peter Rubie, Karen Schimmel, Marit Shuman, the Shuman and Nolan families, Rita Battat Silverman and Steve Silverman, Barbara Smith, Rachel Taylor, Dietrich and Anne von Schwerdtner, and Stephen Watson.

INTRODUCTION

Karen Malpede

Dramatic art arose as a complement to, perhaps also as an antidote to, war. Athenian democracy, Greek tragedy, and the universal conscription of Athenian citizenry (only men were citizens) are products of the same golden age, the fifth century B.C. It is nearly impossible to imagine one without the others. If Athens were to increase her hegemonic reach, conscripts had to be granted democratic rights—why else would young men leave their homes to fight? And to celebrate the muscular glory of the Athenian state, a dramatic festival was, then, created.[1] The playwrights were combat veterans (Aeschylus and Sophocles were generals, Euripides also fought). The majority of their plays are about the effects of war on its victims and, equally, on its victors.

Greek drama shows us again and again that a decisive battlefield victory will also have a deleterious effect on the psyches of the heroes. It is the fact of war itself, not its ultimate end, which alters and corrupts human character and social interaction. All the plays about the Trojan War, the defining conflict of the Greek canon, elaborate this theme. The general responsible for the victory at Troy, Agamemnon, is slain by his wife upon his return for the previous crime of having had his daughter slain as sacrifice so the Greek ships might raise the winds to sail off to fight. For Greek women, although they were not combat veterans, war is seen as equally corrupting; it steals children, turns women into chattel who are raped and sold, and ultimately changes the Greek Queen Clytemnestra and the Trojan Queen Hecuba into furious avengers. Succeeding generations are affected; Electra, Orestes, and Cassandra become crazed with rage and suffering brought on by the wars of their fathers. Athens, a warrior democracy, needed its great theater Festival to Dionysus (god of ecstasy and madness) in order to remember, reflect upon, and, perhaps, to somehow mediate if not actually redeem the multiple losses and sacrifices of its people. "Now in place of young men / urns and ashes are carried home / to the houses of the fighters / . . . Urns with ashes that once were men," Aeschylus writes in the most bitter of his great *Oresteia* choruses. ". . . and the slow anger creeps below their grief."[2]

⊗ ⊗ ⊗

Our modern theater in form and function is far removed from Greek tragedy, the argument might go. Ours is meant for entertainment. It is not funded by the state, but driven by commercial concerns. Most audiences, it's said, are looking for escape. Besides, unlike the Greeks, we have media and film able to provide real records in real time of real events. We have talk shows for airing public problems. We have the Internet to share our thoughts. Why, then, should contemporary playwrights turn their attention toward contemporary wars? Why should audiences care if they do?

The current wars are different from previous American engagements. Unlike Vietnam, when everyone's son, brother, lover was at risk to be drafted, it is easy, now, for most of the public to avoid being personally touched by the sacrifices implicit in war. The wounded and the dead are coming home to a small percentage of families; the strains of multiple deployments are being borne by a minority. Whether or not it is healthy for a democracy to employ a volunteer army is a subject not under debate by the masses who are simply glad to be spared. Nor is there much public discussion about the wisdom of outsourcing military duties to offset chronic troop shortages. More than one hundred private security companies like Blackwater or Kellogg, Brown and Root, a subsidiary of Halliburton, are funded through State Department and U.S. military contracts and employ close to 100,000 contractors in the war zones. These wars are being fought by an undersized military made up largely of the poor and an oversized mercenary army, far better paid than soldiers, but still at risk.

Also different from previous wars, more soldiers today are living through catastrophic battle injuries instead of dying on the field because of swifter evacuation to and better care at military hospitals like the medical trauma center in Landstuhl, Germany. Many more soldiers than ever return home not in caskets but bearing serious physical wounds, often debilitating brain injuries because the very helmets that save their lives rattle their brains under the force of nearby explosions.[3] Partly because of the multiple deployments of a limited fighting force, partly because of the terrifying nature of an insurgent war (in which there are no front lines, and the "enemy" is never clearly known), and partly, too, because the post-traumatic stress disorder (PTSD) diagnoses are being made, the documented psychological toll of these wars is on the rise.[4]

Rising, too, at a rate alarming to the military, is the number of post-combat suicides. "Eighteen American war veterans kill themselves every day. One thousand former soldiers receiving care from the Department of Veterans Affairs attempt suicide every month. More veterans die of suicide than are dying in combat overseas."[5] Incidents of veterans' violence against others are also on the rise—often the horrific murders of wives or lovers, sometimes strangers, and also soldier-on-soldier violence.[6] And for the majority of veterans who escape a PTSD diagnosis, or the many who refuse to be diagnosed or treated and who manage bravely to readjust to civilian life, the toll that traumatic memory exacts is still great and greatly damaging to a sense of well-being and quality of life.[7]

Then, there is the question almost never to be asked: how many Iraqi and Afghan civilians (and fighters) have these wars killed, maimed, displaced; caused to suffer the loss of relatives, stability, property; and traumatized forever? At least we know the names and number of American and British soldiers dead in the two conflicts we fight. But is it 90,000 or more than one million Iraqis killed thus far?[8] How many children were among the 147 civilian dead in the May 2009 bombing of the Afghan village whose name we can no longer recall?[9] How many Afghan civilians are yet to be killed in the escalation of that war?

These facts of life for the battle wounded become moral questions for the rest of us. How much, exactly, are we willing to know about the wars being fought in our names?

State sponsored violence impacts whether we will it or not. Though we might pretend we live in peace, it is not so. For the moment, "America's far-flung wars"[10] seem to exist separately from the economic crises of our domestic life. Yet, our wars inform our consciousness and influence our choices in ways we may not fully comprehend. Our state and federal governments slash jobs and pensions; close schools, parks, libraries, arts programs, public transportation routes; and curtail all manner of services to citizens in need rather than reduce our bloated military budget which totals 50 percent of what the entire rest of the world spends on defense.

In the contemplative place theater provides, we might become citizens of the times in which we live. It is at the intersect between public moral dilemma and the individual capacity to understand and feel that theater of war and witness enters, useful and meaningful, to create a communal gathering space in which we might consider together the sorts of societal choices, their reasons and consequences, we fail to fully grasp in isolation. The multiple tragedies of war, if left alone, numb us, or cause us to lose ourselves in meaningless pursuits.

And this is why we need stories, not sound bites, not documentary pastiches, but the tales of characters who live through a series of events both instigated by and imposed on them, and who, caught even in the worst situation, nevertheless must make a choice. This is dramatic action, revelatory of the movement of the human spirit because it shows how a self-conscious individual is changed by history, and rises or falls morally. Dramatic action traces the best of choices, and the worst, and sets for a given society the parameters of the dilemma of how well or badly one might live.

⊠ ⊠ ⊠

I was a college student and then a graduate student during the Vietnam War. It marked my education and my growing up. Nearly fifty-nine thousand Americans were killed between 1963 and 1976, and nearly three million Vietnamese. Every young man I knew was potentially a soldier: a good friend's fiancé died piloting a helicopter (those pilots had a huge mortality rate); some friends acted mad or gay at their induction physicals and came armed with psychotherapists' notes; others went to Canada or underground; the man I briefly married was drafted but was savvy enough to manipulate his orders and get sent to Germany, where he designed scenery for traveling G.I. shows. Another good friend organized his high school against the draft, burned his draft card, and was sent for a term to federal prison—an experience from which he never quite recovered. When, with hundreds of thousands, I marched on the Pentagon in October 1967, wearing a red miniskirt and high blue patent leather boots, I wondered if a certain boy I liked would be facing me behind his pointed gun. The young soldiers looked more frightened than we did as we impulsively broke through their ranks to reach the steps of the huge building, in the same phalanx, by chance, as Norman Mailer, who would memorialize the march in a famous book, *The Armies of the Night*.

In 1973, I did my first oral history interview (we know these have therapeutic as well as other value) with a former pilot who after flying fifty bombing missions over North Vietnam refused to fly the fifty-first. Several things, he said, had happened: The military, concerned about flagging morale among the fighter bomber pilots as the war dragged on, had actually played them tapes of the screams of the victims on the ground. Then, home on leave, he watched *West Side Story* on television and wept in the lap of the young wife who would soon divorce him. He realized the enemy his bombs annihilated were people. He spent several months in the brig before being dishonorably discharged; feeling principled and guilty, he needed to talk.

I spent many of the years since then teaching young people to think about the world by learning the history of the theater. Many of these students had friends and relatives serving in Iraq or Afghanistan; a number were veterans themselves. After September 11, 2001, I was again employed taking oral histories from victims and survivors of the attack. One of my interviewees was also my student; a Cuban-American veteran, he was called up to work at Ground Zero for several weeks literally packing body parts. At the same time, many of his friends, overcome by patriotic fervor, were planning to reenlist to go fight the coming wars. He, however, was done with the military. He had learned something at Ground Zero, he told me, almost in a whisper: as the firemen came toward him with their wheelbarrows full of human remains, he had seen them cry. The tears of those big, strong men saved him, he said. He saw it was all right to be vulnerable. Necessary, in fact; one could cry and do the rescuers' work. I interviewed one of the firemen. A yoga instructor also, he was teaching a yoga class at fire headquarters in Brooklyn and hopped an ambulance headed across the bridge. Because he was not suited up, he was not sent inside the buildings and, instead, did triage work outside. He managed, he told me, in a somewhat self-deprecating tone, to save "only about ten lives" by directing them to safety. He survived the collapse of both towers; bodies and debris fell all around him. In the following days, he returned to work on the pile. Detritus still sticks in his lungs. He has retired on disability from the fire department and has traveled several times to India. Did he want to bomb Afghanistan, to invade Iraq? I sat with him while he trembled as a passenger plane flew overhead. "No," emphatically not. He had no wish to do unto others what he had experienced.

These oral history interviews along with nearly five hundred others housed in the archive at Columbia University give evidence that many New Yorkers of all races and all walks of life, and in many different proximities to the towers, were united after the attacks in wishing for another way—not war. Eighty-five percent of interviewees in the Columbia study were opposed to the bombing of Afghanistan and the invasion of Iraq.[11]

Fear has been used since September 11, 2001, to fuel the wars we fight. Fear and its companion, rage. But how might we grow able to bear our fear, which is real, and rage, which is often justified, without resorting to lashing out, or acquiescing to manipulation? The tragic theater is useful here since it forces us to *be* in the presence of the huge emotions and offers communal solitude in which to take them in. The Greek dramatists knew their audience to be capable of enormous feats of watching, listening, and contemplation. Under the hot sun, on those stone benches, in view of the sea, combat veterans could sit silently and breathe.[12]

⊗   ⊗   ⊗

Here are seven American and British plays which literally attempt to bring us to our senses. Written in the midst of unfolding history, demanding to be written, their authors would say, these are plays that let the present in. Widely divergent in style, each is a bold, imaginative act of giving shape to the heretofore unimaginable—for the effects on body, psyche, and society of prolonged and extreme violence surpass our ability to know unless we are given the stories that let us feel. Each of these plays extends the imagination by using and inventing new dramatic strategies of necessity. They show surprising bursts of humor; several retain their ironic wit throughout. Their language and structures are poetic, their arguments provocative. They seek neither to glorify violence nor render violence inevitable. Instead, each play inscribes new dramatic actions which propose new moral choices about how we might become. They offer, each one, a passionate exploration of heretofore unexplored contemporary moral problems: What are the costs to the individual and to democracy of being constantly at war? Are bombing, invasion, occupation, detention, and torture the best ways to defeat extremism—or are these tactics dangerous for the extreme reactions they evoke?

The Greek playwrights carved the very notion of the individual from feats of battle. They looked at themselves, stunned that they survived, and wrote the range of their emotions for those who did not. Their plays show us how the individual emerged from collective consciousness. As the hero literally stepped out from the chorus to take action, often violent, at the extremity of being, he became a self-reflective person, capable of suffering and understanding.

The playwright of war and witness, operating at the far end of individualism, asks whether or not, under what extreme conditions, a person might be motivated or able to make a crucial self-defining choice which, at the same time, helps redefine the nature of our social interaction away from the emotional and financial costs of our addiction to violent conflict. Can we forswear violence and hone a richer notion of psyche and self and human connectedness? If the Greek plays were built on what we learn too late from inflicting suffering, might not a theater of witness, sometimes, help us to predict not our mistakes but a measured moment of reflection before the rush to action which we might regret?

Driven to enter and reveal the human stories inside the wars we fight, these contemporary dramatists have touched upon the theater's ancient source to release the theater's socially reparative power.

Naomi Wallace uses multiple nonrealistic strategies to set opposing characters in situations where they must relate. Three earlier plays about the Middle East collectively titled *The Fever Chart* imagine Palestinians and Israelis in intimate contact (based on a true story, an Israeli has received a lung transplant from a Palestinian in one play, *Every Breath We Take*). Each of her plays acts to diminish distances between characters and to offer moments of mutual recognition which result in momentary cessation of hostility.

No Such Cold Thing[13] is set in Afghanistan in 2001, at the start of the war. "The play is not about victims of war, but rather about imagination as agency. And how 'their' world and 'our' world are, in some ways, the same world,"[14] Wallace says. The three-character play was written as one of a series of short plays on Afghanistan collectively called *The Great Game* and commissioned by the Tricycle Theatre in London, where the playwright, originally from Kentucky, makes her home. We find out as the action progresses that Wallace's two Afghan sisters and Hispanic-American soldier are already dead. Conversing across barriers they could not have broached in life, Wallace lets us feel her three dead ones are more than they were let be.

"For me," writes Lydia Stryk, author of *American Tet*,[15] born in the Midwest but living now for many years in Berlin, "the Iraq war has been the seminal experience of my political awakening—and more specifically, the events leading up to the war. When literally millions took to the streets on February 15, 2003, across the world to say NO, DON'T DO THIS.

"Since 9-11 and then leading up to and during the war/s, I had listened to a number of vets—of the Vietnam, Korean, Gulf and Iraq wars speak at various gatherings and also—and perhaps most importantly—many military family members. Listening to them, I began to understand what it meant to be raised with a set of values—and I mean real values—that enabled them to take part in what I had grown up believing was a preposterous and immoral way of life. These military folk were thinking this through on their own terms and voicing deep concerns and amazing resistance from *within*. For some reason, it came to me that the only way I could write about this war was by entering their world."[16]

Entering the world of military families in *American Tet* means writing to expose the contradiction inherent in the military mythos: between the idealized heroism of the soldier and the gory realities of war, its boredom, too. There is a terrible tension throughout this sparse, moving play between the feelings of the characters and their actions, which remain controlled by military ideology.

Prophecy is at one and the same time a tragedy of a young life lost to memories of war and a story of the creation of an extended family across seemingly irreconcilable fault lines. These dual actions, one disastrous, one redemptive, proceed in parallel and interconnecting plot lines. The quality of listening is crucial here: as an absent Jewish father hears his Muslim daughter's story and his wife asks advice about the battle wounded from the woman who betrayed her, each becomes able to hear the other's truths and so to bond. It has been my fate as a playwright to connect disparate themes, generations, and wars. But these things are connected: the tensions between young and old; the wars in Vietnam/Iraq/Lebanon; the stories we inherit, with their seemingly intractable conflicts, and what we might make of them, in this case: Abraham-Sarah-Hagar and Ishmael-Isaac. In its form, the play also makes connections intended to expand consciousness by bridging modernist realism and something older and more classical.

This anthology intentionally privileges works of dramatic fiction over the documentary drama form, revealing by example the need for imaginative interventions by single artists. However, one documentary is included because the story of how the U.S. began to indefinitely detain and torture has yet to be adequately addressed in dramatic fiction.

The documentary drama *Guantanamo: "Honor Bound to Defend Freedom,"* taken from spoken evidence by Victoria Brittain, a British journalist, and Gillian Slovo, a South African novelist living in London, is a cri de coeur against the indefinite detention system instituted by the Bush administration in prisons in Iraq (Abu Ghraib), Afghanistan (Bagram), and Cuba (Guantanamo), and in hidden prisons around the world.

Like *The Eumenides,* the final part of the *Oresteia* trilogy, the theater functions once more in place of a court of law. But where the Aeschylus play commemorates and celebrates the foundation of our legal system, the right to habeas corpus trial by jury, *Guantanamo* speaks to the dismantling of justice by the abrogation of our laws.[17] In the Greek play, the momentous question before the court, is matricide or patricide the greater crime, has resulted in a hung jury of mortal men. The goddess Athena casts the deciding vote acquitting Orestes, who cut his mother's throat to avenge his father's death. Ironically, with her vote the goddess institutionalizes patriarchy, stating, memorably, we might say, tragically for women, "The mother is not parent of that which is called her child, but only nurse of the new-planted seed that grows. The parent is he who mounts."[18] Thus, justice, even at its start, is defined by and belongs to the victors.

Guantanamo must intercede. The theater, where bodies come before an audience which judges, is of use. Those who have been denied a trial might testify in their own defense—their words in the mouths of actors who become channels for censored truths.

Four of these plays about war and witness are authored by women. We might ask the gender question: Are women's plays different than men's and, if so, in what ways? Or when women come to write plays about war and witness, what do they add? Of course, they offer a woman's perspective; they look at history from a woman's head. Stryk's play includes the story of a woman soldier who is seriously wounded in combat. Although technically the women in our military serve supporting roles, in wars without front lines, women often find themselves in battle. The women playwrights' female characters will speak of female concerns: despair at a disfigured face, maternal love, abortion, infertility, female desire, eroticism, jealousies and they will bond with other women.

But, there is something more significant found in these plays by women, including the docudrama *Guantanamo,* and that is the female playwrights' insistence on materializing the physical presence of the other on the stage. In these plays by women, Vietnamese, Afghan, Arab characters appear, speak, feel, and act. If terrorism lies in our propensity to demonize, harmony and humanity arise from our ability to empathize. Empathy, first of all, requires that we are able to imagine the sentient life of another.

In *Stuff Happens,* his best-known Iraq war play, David Hare brings onstage an Iraqi refugee and a Palestinian jurist who with bold and riveting speeches counter the official narrative of George Bush, Tony Blair, and their teams. *Stuff Happens* is a Shakespearian epic history taken in part from actual words of the historical characters presented and in part from the playwright's imagination of what must have been said and decided in the off-the-record meetings as the war was planned and executed. The arguments of Hare's Arab characters have been equally well-researched. If Bush and company jar the mind with their lust for war and sappy expressions of patriotism, the anger and grief of Palestinian and Iraqi are also hard to hear.

Hare says in *Berlin/Wall,* one of his two monologues about the Israeli–Palestinian conflict,[19] that as one ages, memory becomes fantasy; when one is young, fantasy is in the future, but when older, fantasy is in the past because memory becomes the more fertile ground for imaginative play. He says he wants to put that sentiment into a play, but in his second Iraq war play, *The Vertical Hour,* it feels as if he already has—for to a large degree, since nothing actually happens on the stage aside from some very good talk between two wounded and principled people, it is the charged events surfacing in the characters' memories that determine dramatic choice and change.

As the intellectual debate about the morality of armed intervention plays out in language elegant and driven, the characters' emotional lives twist and turn underneath their belief systems until it seems that emotions and intellect exist as two separate entities inside these same conflicted souls.

9 Circles by American Bill Cain and *A Canopy of Stars* by Englishman Simon Stephens are two different plays, from two different countries, about two different wars—yet, the wars are nearly one war, Iraq/Afghanistan. "A war of choice" / "A war of necessity." Each play is written, more or less, in the lingo of each country, working class talk, male talk, war talk, although there are female characters in each. The plots are different, the characters unique, the themes resonate in different ways, yet, underneath, riven through, is *the* theme, the moral destructiveness of war on those who fight.

Aeschylus, ever the military man, when choosing how to immortalize himself, had written on his tombstone not that he was author of *The Oresteia,* and invented Greek Tragedy, but that he "fought at the Battle of Marathon."

And, there, at that miraculous battle in which the tiny Greek fighting force turned back the Persian Empire and so cleared the path for Greek democracy, what did Aeschylus see happen to men? The classical answer would be hubris. In the face of battle overweening pride took hold of heretofore ordinary youth: they began to feel invincible. They did things that set them apart from the crowd and made them the sorts of heroes the tragic playwrights would memorialize.

In his landmark book *Achilles in Vietnam: Combat Trauma and the Undoing of Character,*[20] psychiatrist and classicist Jonathan Shay writes about the changes wrought by battle on the soldier's psyche. In its extreme state, the soldier in the grip of hubris on the battlefield literally goes *berserk,* a "Norse word for the frenzied warriors who went into battle naked, or at least without armor, in a godlike or god-possessed—but also beast-like—fury."[21] Shay lets a Vietnam veteran explain: "I lost all my mercy . . . I just couldn't get enough . . . I really loved fucking killing." Shay writes, "I conclude that the *berserk* state is ruinous, leading to the soldier's life-long psychological and physiological injury if he survives. I believe that once a person has entered the *berserk* state, he or she is changed *forever.*"[22]

A Canopy of Stars has the gritty, up-close feel of film noir. Stephens's hero Jay Watkins does not commit atrocities on stage, but he is on the edge of *berserking* at every moment; the tension of his coiled body is the tension in the play. "I'm here cause I want to take the face of every single last Taliban and grind it into the rock of the desert," he tells a soldier in his command as they wait and watch.

The antihero of Bill Cain's *9 Circles* has a character which is "undone" before the play begins. Daniel Edward Reeves was granted a special "moral" waiver to join the army. The play was suggested by the true story of Steven Dale Green, a high school dropout with a troubled emotional history who was in prison on his third misdemeanor charge just days before he was allowed to enlist in an army desperate for recruits. In the last heady days before the U.S. economic crash, during the height of the insurgency in Iraq in 2005, Army recruiters were regularly granting waivers to fill their quotas.

If Green was "damaged goods" before he entered into combat, why should we be surprised when he rapes, murders, and burns the body of a fourteen-year-old Iraqi girl after murdering her family, including a toddler? The play does not alter these basic facts; Steven Dale Green is currently serving a life sentence for the crime. Cain, who wrote the play before the trial, gives his character, Reeves, the death penalty.

❊   ❊   ❊

When extremity is the topic, beauty becomes an issue—a necessary strategy, in fact, far more so than when the topic is more mundane. Language is the first place to look for beauty on the stage—a language driven by passionate idea and feeling. None of the playwrights facing the realities of current wars wish to overwhelm with violence, especially so since the violence these plays document is real and is happening to real people. You might well find more enacted brutality in plays about love relationships or family strife. Even Stephens's brutal re-creation of battle focuses on battle losses, not on violence done. Bill Cain avoids staging the rape. Though deaths in battle determine the action of *No Such Cold Thing, American Tet,* and *Prophecy,* no battle deaths are shown. Instead of violent reenactments, an image-filled language of the head and heart contains the horrors, transmits and transforms them, in a manner that is non-assaultive and leaves each audience member or reader free to feel whatever they are able.

The beauty of Eros figures, too, by powering an undercurrent of longing. Through its transgressive force between student, Jeremy, and his teacher, Sarah, in *Prophecy,* and son's fiancée, Nadia, and his father, Oliver, in *The Vertical Hour,* forbidden Eros spurs charged relationships and triggers the memories of loss from which these characters' fates are made. *Prophecy* is also informed by a deep but less disruptive erotic charge of a long marriage righting itself as the infidelities of the past are revisited and laid to rest. In *No Such Cold Thing,* their quoting the spiritual and sensuous lines of the Pakistani poet Ahmed Faiz

("He is the lord of sleep / lord of peace / lord of night") arouses desire for the erotic fulfillment the sisters have been denied by death.

The Greek tragedians set the restriction against violence on the stage. Their messenger speeches become the vehicle through which the audience sees and feels the most extreme actions. This shock of hearing comes at the audience more strongly than any pretend stage violence. Perhaps, the formal messenger speech from classic tragedy becomes in contemporary plays of war and witness the memory speech. These plays use memory in transformative ways. Normal memory is what traumatic events disrupt. Disrupted memory is where traumatic events are lodged. Violent trauma fractures the self. Extreme violence asserts its hold on character through the constant interior replay of terrifying sights and sounds, flashbacks, nightmares, and compulsive behavior, silence or deadening repetitive talk. Remembering trauma might well be reparative, at least to some degree, and is anyway the best medicine we have. Memory becomes the battleground on which characters fight for restoration of the self.

As memory asserts itself, time becomes altered. Linearity is less revealing of possibility than is a present permeated by a past. The juxtaposition of what once was with what is allows the future, the *what if* or the *perhaps now* to enter.

Characters sometimes cannot remember because they lack an empathic listener; sometimes, too, an internal prohibition (their idea of military honor, for example) forbids their speech. These characters made mute by circumstance have trouble working through their losses. They stay stuck in a limbo of pain to which they lack full access. This is the ultimate sorrow of the military family in *American Tet*, immobilized by loss, and of Jay Watkins in *A Canopy of Stars*, sleepless, drinking tea and watching Belgian football, longing to return to war; yet the audience is moved to question what the characters cannot.

Prophecy, *The Vertical Hour*, and *9 Circles* hinge their dramatic action on memory speeches. The results of such difficult memory work depend on several factors: the severity of the event or events, the inner resilience of the one who bears the memories, the empathic qualities of the listener, and luck. Bad luck can bring one down.

Cain's soldier, condemned to death, never had a chance; bad luck was all he ever knew, but in a final scene after his death, he remembers and even hears the words of his victim as she begged for life.

Jeremy, the Iraq veteran in *Prophecy*, kills himself, and yet, he has been ennobled by his need to remember the night he killed a pregnant woman and wept with her husband over the corpse. Jeremy's death is determined not by any flaw in Sarah's listening but by his own belief that the severity of what he's done has forever violated his growing awareness of how a good life must be lived. In this sense, Sarah's passionate teaching of Greek drama both awakens Jeremy and dooms him. There have been one thousand suicides among Iraq combat veterans and four thousand combat deaths. "Something is wrong," says military psychiatrist and retired Brigadier General Steven Xenakis, adding that the memories leading "somone capable of feeling guilt" toward suicide have more to do with what that soldier may have done in war than with what was seen.[23] While the U.S. combat role in Iraq may be finished, fatalities due to combat aren't.

It is to Oliver Lucas's credit, in David Hare's play, that he talks about his road accident—the memories of those he killed need to live inside him in order for his own life to be bearable as lived. "In combat medicine, there's this moment—after a disaster," Nadia Blye tells him, "after a shooting—there's this moment, the vertical hour, when you can actually be of some use." "Of use to me?" Oliver asks, and that is when they begin to tell each other the stories of their pasts. Nadia Blye appears to be Hare's somewhat ironic homage to Samantha Power, author of a major book on genocide, *A Problem from Hell,* and exemplar of the American exceptionalist doctrine that our force can make things right. "She's extraordinary," the besotted British physician tells his son, "worth a whole lifetime," though he disagrees with everything she's done.

Like the Greek messenger speech, contemporary memory speeches and scenes both distance and allow for deeper entry at one and the same time. Recalling the crucial memory, characters observe their past as relived in the present while the listener observes both speaker and self. Often a crucial memory is triggered inside the listener which is often shared. The audience witnessing these layered dynamics gains access to their own memories, too.

Moral philosopher Judith Butler in her book *Frames of War* asks which lives are "grievable" and why?[24] She points out that war limits empathy by declaring the enemy off-limits or out-of-frame.

Invoking the other, encouraging empathy for the one not quite like you, is a function of a theater of witness whose ultimate goal is a revisioning of dualistic patterns of thought. Violent conflict in service of the defeat of an enemy, who otherwise is bent on your destruction, might not be the most effective, self-sustaining, or, certainly, the most creative response to the inevitable conflicts which arise among human beings. Cain summarizes the argument in *9 Circles:* "Three thousand Americans got killed. Somebody has to pay," says Reeves, sounding like a member of the Bush-Cheney administration. "Forty thousand Americans get killed in traffic accidents every year . . . Based on your logic, we should be bombing car dealerships," responds the lawyer Swift.

Inside the family it is generally agreed, though hardly universally lived, that violence is an inadequate, emotionally stunted and stunting response to conflict. If we were to extend the concept of family out, from those who are biologically related or receive nurturance from the family group as a means of being included in that family, to include even those who require the same sorts of sustenance we require, though we might be, for many reasons, those of distance or cultural difference, for example, unable to deliver, we would arrive at an understanding of relatedness that is global, species-inclusive, and many would argue, including myself, cross-species inclusive, of animal, plant, and ocean life as well. Theater of witness fosters an understanding that here transcends its own "narrow" focus on the causes and resistance to violence to become eco-conscious, bent on supporting creation.

In the four plays by women, the other comes onto the stage as a self—a person with a unique story, individual agency, able to affect the destiny of self and others, too. The other, thus, becomes one of us—*a one like us*—needful necessarily of our concern, our empathy, recognizable as an intimate, a different same. It is an act of generation, this endowing of a separate life.

The male playwrights are also engaged in mining empathy and exploiting its limits. The shock of Simon Stephens's play lies in the loss of the ability to feel for others, not in the soldier who fights to protect "good" Afghans, but in his wife who says, "People shouldn't survive in places like that. You should let them burn. They deserve it." In Bill Cain's play, the other is not birthed as a separate entity on stage; she can exist in the mind of Reeves only after he has murdered and raped her. For David Hare, however, bringing onto the stage fully dimensional female characters, equal adversaries to his men, has long been a priority, as is confounding gender stereotypes with the dramatic actions that ensue and which unsettle, disrupt, and ultimately expand the possible.

What to make of the presence of the dead: Wallace's American and Afghan young people, their promise unfulfilled; in Stryk's play, the appearance of the dead Vietnamese child Dao to former soldier Jim Krombacher; Khorsheed's increasingly vivid presence in the mind of Reeves, her rapist, as he is injected with lethal drugs and dies? These plays land us on a boundary between life and death which we find to be permeable. By remembering the dead, by being dead and therefore becoming able to remember, in Cain's and Wallace's plays, or by receiving the dead, allowing them to be present in the minds of the living, characters recognize the moral worth of each fragile life. In *Proph-*

ecy, Sarah's memories of her lover who died in Vietnam become increasingly vivid until, at the moment her Iraq-war veteran student, Jeremy, kills himself offstage, the young Lukas appears to her. These two young men become one in Sarah's mind's eye, where she will hold them all her life—all their loveliness sacrificed to war. Hare's *The Vertical Hour* is resolutely realistic and linear, but here, too, Oliver Lucas finds an intimate relationship with death. He was once a surgeon, intervening in the most medically spectacular ways. But after killing two people in a road accident, his new mission becomes to sit with the dying and be a comforting witness at life's end. Hare's antihero has renounced heroics, and therein lies the greatness of his act.

The dead must be palpable in these plays. When the dead are not dignified by memory, the living lose their ability to feel anything but rage. If violence is glorified onstage (or onscreen) as is so often the case when witnessing is not the point, no care is paid to those who are struck down. Bodies litter the ground like things. But in the play of war and witness, the dead never cease to matter to the living who, to varying degrees, may be culpable in their deaths. Memory of the dead keeps conscience alive.

Against the destructive force of violence is only flesh—only the story survives death.

If individual characters cannot always outlast the claims of traumatic memory, the audience can and does. The audience is made stronger, more able to bear the truth, to feel with and for the sufferer and to find increased compassion for the self. Thus, the play of war and witness enlivens audiences, purifies them, provides them with clearer sight—and this is how *katharsis* is attained.

The truest function of theater of war and witness, as of classical tragedy, is to allow the audience to dwell in ambiguity—growing larger, more able to contain more of life's harshness and its wonders than before. *Katharsis,* clarity of sight, does not mean knowing one thing only; it is never doctrinaire. *Katharsis* leaves the audience alert and trembling in a vastness of being which exists as much inside them as without.

The incantatory quality of invocation—the drive to remember, to summon the dead, call forth the other—returns us to the ritual origins of the drama, origins re-evoked by a theater of witness. In Greek tragedy, the chorus performed the ritual function by allowing the audience to witness and partake in group lamentation, praise, rejoicing, and prayer. Theater of witness as an extension of psychological realism, epic, and modernist theater techniques seldom includes a chorus (though individual characters may take on a choral function). The ritual underlay shows through, with intention and intensity, in the witnessing drama's propensity to involve the audience by evoking the presence of the other and of the dead in order to provoke a combination of perceptions which might not yet be commonly assumed: That war is other than heroic adventurism and participation in armed conflict, whether as a soldier or as a noncombatant citizen even in a nation at war overseas, produces lasting, often deleterious, effects on human character; that an increase in empathic understanding of the other might serve to strengthen democracies and defeat the terrorism meme.[25] These may yet be debatable, but they are profoundly affecting and effective ideas which when given emotional force on stage do serve a ritual intent of provoking changed perception. A theater of witness is not so much rooted in a more ancient ritual action, as was Greek drama; it harks forward to a time-to-come in which age-old assumptions about the necessity of, and even the genetic inclination toward, mutual annihilatory destruction can be generally challenged.

Without the exploration of contemporary history's impact on the psyche, characters are unredeemed, and society stays mired in endless repetition of the same fatal violent sacrifice of the young that is and always has been war. With insight, new ways of being almost suddenly appear. Thus, the potentiality latent in a theater of witness must not be underestimated. Audiences who are deeply moved, whose perceptions have been altered, who are immersed in ambiguity, who recognize the other in themselves and remember the dead, and who come this far together, in the communal seeing place of theater, have been changed. They feel more alive, courageous, more affirmed in their connectedness, more able to be present in the world.

These plays of war and witness remain somehow open-ended. Each hints that there is more to come. Each play has moments when language and dramatic action transform what is to remind us that we, too, are in process of creation.

NOTES

1. Jonathan Shay, "The Birth of Tragedy—Out of the Needs of Democracy," *Didaskaslia: Ancient Theater Today,* vol. 2, no. 2, April 1995.

2. Aeschylus I, *Oresteia: Agamemnon* translated with an introduction by Richard Lattimore (Chicago: University of Chicago Press, 1953), 434–36, 444–45, 450.

3. "More injured troops are surviving the war in Iraq than any other. But because of the terrible force of IED explosions, more are surviving with brain injury than in any other war." Robert Bazell, chief science and health correspondent, *NBC News,* April 26, 2006. See also www.braintrauma.org.

4. "Last year, 140 US soldiers committed suicide, a record high, and during the first four months of 2009, 64 US soldiers have committed suicide. Military officials said a US soldier is now more likely to

commit suicide than a civilian and the Army has recently commissioned a $50 million study to explain the suicide epidemic." Also, veterans' disability claims are on backlog; it can take six months for a disability claim to be processed and up to four years before an appeal is heard in cases where disability has been denied. Jason Leopold, www.truthout.org. June 5, 2009.

5. These numbers, widely reported, on *CBS News* among other places, come from the Centers for Disease Control and Prevention (CDC). In May 2009, *CBS News* also reported that the Veterans Administration had hidden the suicide numbers from public view.

6. Bob Herbert, "War's Psychic Toll," *New York Times,* May 19, 2009. (Herbert has been writing about the toll of the wars since they began.) In May 2008, an American GI was charged with gunning down five of his fellow service members in Iraq; the same month, a former soldier who had been given an honorable discharge from the army was sentenced to life in prison for raping and murdering a fourteen-year-old Iraqi girl and killing her family, an atrocity which became the subject of the play *9 Circles.*

7. PTSD is defined by the United States Department of Veterans Affairs as "a psychiatric disorder that can occur following the experiencing or witnessing of life-threatening events such as military combat, natural disasters, terrorist incidents, serious accidents, abuse and violent personal assaults like rape. People who suffer from PTSD often relive the experience through nightmares and flashbacks, have difficulty sleeping, and feel detached or estranged, and these symptoms can be severe enough and last long enough to significantly impair the person's daily life." The military has stated that at least one in five American soldiers who were deployed overseas to Iraq or Afghanistan suffer from some degree of PTSD. (William Rivers Pitt, www.truthout.org, May 13, 2009.)

8. "We don't do body counts," said General Tommy Franks when the Iraq conflict began. Thus, we have no good idea of how many Iraqis have died because of the invasion and the occupation. The estimates vary wildly from the conservative numbers posted on www.iraqbodycount.org, which listed "documented civilian deaths from violence" as "94,243–102,835" on November 23, 2009, to the high-end medical journal *Lancet*'s study figure of 654,965 excess deaths through the end of June 2006, which was based on household survey data. Nor can we guess how many more will die from continued conflict, cluster or other unexploded bombs, birth defects from exposure to battlefield toxins, wounds, and suicide. We know upward of four million Iraqis have been internally or externally displaced. The effects of all this loss on civil society are staggering. "Ninety percent of Iraq's 180 hospitals do not have basic medical and surgical supplies . . . Iraqis also have disproportionately high rates of infant mortality, cerebral palsy and cancer. Exacerbating the problem, Iraqi and American officials [say], is that hundreds of thousands of Iraq's professional class have fled or been killed during the war, leaving behind a population with too few doctors, nurses, engineers, scientists and the like." From an article by Timothy Williams titled "U.S. Fears Iraqis Will Not Keep Up Rebuilt Projects," *New York Times,* November 21, 2009, 1, 8. The same day, the *Times* announced U.S. fatalities in Iraq hit 4,355.

9. The village was Farah. The 147 fatalities counted by the villagers on the ground, two-thirds of them said to be children and teenagers, are sharply disputed by the U.S. military, which says the death toll from the bombing was far lower (thirty civilians) and attributes some of the deaths to grenades thrown by the Taliban. The villagers have argued that the Taliban had left the region before the bombing began. Laura King, *Los Angeles Times,* May 8, 2009, and May 17, 2009. Nevertheless, "A military investigation has concluded that American personnel made significant errors in carrying out some of the air strikes in western Afghanistan on May 4." *New York Times,* June 3, 2009.

10. Mark Mazzetti, "CIA Takes On Expanded Role on Front Lines," *New York Times,* January 1, 2010. Seven CIA operatives were blown up in a suicide attack in a remote base in Afghanistan perhaps "in retaliation" because "the agency is in effect running a war in Pakistan."

11. Mary Marshall Clark, The September 11, 2001, Oral History Narrative and Memory Project: A First Report. *The Journal of American History* 89.2 (2002): 33 pars. January 4, 2010. For more on the interviews, see: Malpede, "Empathy & After" in *On the Ground After September 11: Mental Heath Responses and Practical Knowledge Gained,* edited by Yael Danieli and Robert L. Dingman (New York: Haworth Press, 2005), 560–64.

12. In this respect, it is laudable that the Department of Defense, increasingly in need of ways to treat traumatic stress, is funding a group called Theater of War to present readings from Greek tragedy to troops. And it is disheartening that plays that speak against war are hardly ever well-funded or widely produced, at least in the United States.

13. The play's title is taken from a poem by George Herbert: "Grief melts away / Like snow in May / As if there were no such cold thing."

14. Email communication with the author.

15. The play's title refers back to Vietnam and the Tet Offensive of 1968, a surprise assault launched by North Vietnam and the Viet Cong against American and South Vietnam government troops which proved the war was far from over.

16. Email communication with the author.

17. For a comprehensive understanding of what happened and how, see Jane Myers, *The Dark Side* (New York: Doubleday, 2008).

18. *The Eumenidies,* Lattimore, 658–60.

19. Asked to commemorate the fall of the Berlin Wall, Hare contrasts the united German city with the cities now walled in Israel and the Occupied Territories. The other monologue on the situation in Israel-Palestine is *Via Dolorosa.* "I don't choose my subjects, my subjects choose me," he says in *Berlin/Wall.*

20. New York: Atheneum, 1991.

21. Ibid., 77.

22. Ibid., 98.

23. Question and answer session at the Open Society Institute event *None of Us Were Like This Before,* September 13, 2010.

24. London: Verso, 2009.

25. "The American right and left reacted to 9/11 differently. The respective responses were, to oversimplify a bit, 'kill the terrorists' and 'kill the terrorism meme.' Robert Wright, "Who Created Major Hassan," *New York Times,* November 22, 2009, 11.

ACTS OF WAR

GUANTANAMO
"HONOR BOUND TO DEFEND FREEDOM"

Victoria Brittain and Gillian Slovo

Taken from spoken evidence

ABOUT THE PLAYWRIGHTS

Victoria Brittain was coauthor with Moazzam Begg of his memoir, *Enemy Combatant*, a British man's journey to Guantanamo and back. Her play, *The Meaning of Waiting*, is a verbatim work with Muslim wives of men held in Guantanamo, or in British prisons on secret evidence. She has lived and worked as a journalist in Washington, Saigon, Algiers, and London. She worked at *The Guardian* for twenty years.

Gillian Slovo is the author of eleven novels and a family memoir, *Every Secret Thing*. Her fiction includes five crime novels featuring her detective, Kate Baeier, and *Ties of Blood*, a novel set in South Africa, Slovo's mother country from which she had been exiled. Her novel *Red Dust*, a fictionalized account, followed Slovo's participation in the Truth and Reconciliation Commission hearings on the former policemen who had killed her mother, Ruth First. *Red Dust* was awarded the RFI "Temoin du Monde" prize in France and was made into a film starring Hilary Swank and Chiwetel Ejiofor. In 2007, she wrote a series of columns for the South African newspaper *The Star*. Her novel *Ice Road*, set in the Leningrad of the 1930s, was short listed for the Orange Prize. Her most recent novel is *Black Orchids*. She is currently writing a new novel as well as working collaboratively on a theater project on women, politics, and power.

PRODUCTION HISTORY

Guantanamo: "Honour Bound to Defend Freedom" was first performed in 2004 at the Tricycle Theatre, London, directed by Nicolas Kent and Sacha Wares, with the following cast:

Lord Justice Steyn	William Hoyland
Mr Begg	Badi Uzzaman
Wahab Al-Rawi	Aaron Neil

Jamal Al-Harith .... Patrick Robinson
Gareth Peirce .... Jan Chappell
Mark Jennings .... Alan Parnaby
Bisher Al-Rawi .... Daniel Cerqueira
Moazzam Begg .... Paul Bhattacharjee
Tom Clark... Theo Fraser Steel
Donald Rumsfeld ....William Hoyland
Ruhel Ahmed.. Tariq Jordan
Clive Stafford Smith.. David Annen
Major Dan Mori ....Daniel Cerqueira
Jack Straw .... David Annen
Greg Powell .... Alan Parnaby
Mr Ahmed .... Paul Bhattacharjee

CHARACTERS

Lord Justice Steyn	*Tom Clark*
Mr Begg	*Donald Rumsfeld*
Wahab Al-Rawi	*Ruhel Ahmed*
Jamal Al-Harith	*Clive Stafford Smith*
Gareth Peirce	*Major Dan Mori*
Mark Jennings	*Jack Straw*
Bisher Al-Rawi	*Greg Powell*
Moazzam Begg	*Mr Ahmed*

AUTHORS' NOTE

The transcripts used for this play are of interviews done by the authors with the individuals concerned (except for Straw and Rumsfeld—their material was taken from press conferences in which they spoke). Bracketed material in the play has been added to the original transcripts' content. Portions of letters from the detainees remain virtually unchanged.

ACT ONE

(House lights on. From the auditorium comes LORD JUSTICE STEYN, *up on stage to a podium. Written on the dot matrix.)*

F. A. Mann Lecture given by Lord Justice Johan Steyn on 23rd November 2003 at Lincoln's Inn, London.

LORD JUSTICE STEYN: The most powerful democracy is detaining hundreds of suspected foot soldiers of the Taliban in a legal black hole at the United States naval base at Guantanamo Bay, where they await trial on capital charges by military tribunals. This episode must be put in context. Democracies must defend themselves. Democracies are entitled to try officers and soldiers of enemy forces for war crimes. But it is a recurring theme in history that in times of war, armed conflict, or perceived national danger, even liberal democracies adopt measures infringing human rights in ways that are wholly disproportionate to the crisis. Ill-conceived, rushed legislation is passed granting excessive powers to executive governments which compromise the rights and liberties of individuals beyond the exigencies of the situation. Often the loss of liberty is permanent . . .

The purpose of holding the prisoners at Guantanamo Bay was and is to put them beyond the rule of law, beyond the protection of any courts, and at the mercy of the victors. At present we are not meant to know what is happening [there]. But history will not be neutered. What takes place today in the name of the United States will assuredly, in due course, be judged at the bar of informed international opinion.

The regime applicable at Guantanamo Bay was created by a succession of presidential orders. It can be summarised quite briefly. The prisoners at Guantanamo Bay, as matters stand at present, will be tried by military tribunals. The military will act as interrogators, prosecutors, defence counsel, judges, and when death sentences are imposed, as executioners. The military, however, is in all respects subject to decisions of the President as Commander-in-Chief even in respect of guilt and innocence in individual cases as well as appropriate sentences. It is an awesome responsibility. The President has made public in advance his personal view of the prisoners as a group: he has described them all as "killers" . . .

(*As Steyn leaves house lights dim.*)

(*The predawn call to prayer: sung from the stage.*)

Alaahu Akbar
Bishmillaahi-r-Rahmaani-r-Raheem
Al-hamdu Lillaahi Rabbi-i-'aalameen, etc.

MR BEGG: I will start with his childhood so you have the full picture of [Moazzam]. He was born in '67 on 5th June and he was very well looked after by his mother and by me. When he was a little bit grown up he went to a Jewish junior school. His reports were quite good. His teachers, especially the Headmaster Mr Levy, I don't know whether he's alive or not but he was very, very good. He was quite happy with Moazzam.

WAHAB AL-RAWI (*He is smoking.*): I came into the UK in '83. [My brother Bisher] came one year later. In the early '80s, my father was arrested—the Iraq secret service went to his office and arrested him and they took him and he disappeared for eight months. And we found out where he was, then he was moved from one secret service to another and he disappeared again. Eventually we found him and we used some influence at that time to just get him to go to trial. Of course he was tortured and he was abused. A year and a half he spent with the Iraqi secret service which is one of the worst in the world. Finally he went to trial. The judge found him innocent and he was released, but by then the Government had confiscated a lot of his properties and so we decided to leave Iraq for the UK. None of us ever asked for asylum. We were very well off at the time.

MR BEGG: One day Moazzam said, "Dad I want to make a society" and I smiled [because he was too young to talk about society] and said, "What kind of society are you going to make son?" He said, "A society to help older people, feeble people, and people with disabilities and all that." So, I said, "This is a very good thing, it's a noble thing. I'll not stop you doing that. I don't know how far he went."

WAHAB AL-RAWI: I was studying GCSEs at a school in Cambridge and my brother [Bisher] came to do the same thing. We were teenagers living on our own in one house. It's the first time we've ever gone anywhere, so it was a mess. Every day there was a fight. We'd make peace and then we'd go back and break the peace. So the next year, my mother split us apart. I went to study my A levels in Shrewsbury and he went to Millfield College to finish his GCSEs and then do his A levels. [Bisher] finished A levels, went to university. Bisher was very physical, he was very active—this is why he loved it in Millfield—he did all the sports, wrestling, archery, climbing.

Even he was a parachutist. He had 63 jumps. He had PPL—private pilot's licence. He studied on helicopters as well. Deep sea diving—he's got all the equipment for deep sea diving. He was a biker. Every sport you can imagine. If he's interested in something, then he takes it on completely. He absorbs it in his blood and veins. It's a profession. Then he leaves it and goes on to another thing.

Oh. No smoking? Okay. No problem. I'll put it out. (*Putting out his cigarette*) I don't like to break the law.

MR BEGG: [Moazzam] was about seven [then] I think, yes he was, because it was one year before his mother died. After one year I married again. Moazzam [was my] second born. Firstborn had a bit of a tussle with my [new] wife (*laughter*) but Moazzam never had that. He was quite all right with her and he in fact supported me that we had to have somebody in the house.

WAHAB AL-RAWI: [Gambia] was my idea. My idea was I build a mobile oil processing plant and because of . . . obviously because of the title . . . because you're mobile you need to go to where the peanuts are.

MR BEGG: I'm a banker by profession [but] I opened another business [an estate agent] and [with] Moazzam ran [it] four or five years. Without [Moazzam] I would have not done [it]. [He] was attending the college as well at that time—going to the university part time. Then, when I finished from that business and everything he said, "Dad, I want to get settled now. I want to get married." I said, "Son, I wanted you to finish these studies," as every father would think, "and after that, you may do whatever you feel like." He said, "No, it's all too tiring now, I can't do anymore." I said, "All right, take a break and next year you do what you want to do." But . . . er . . . he got married and settled down and he opened a shop, an Islamic book-shop and an Islamic clothing shop.

WAHAB AL-RAWI: And we decided for the experimental stages to go to a small country like Gambia and then there would be a stage two. We de-cided to go to Gambia because we knew somebody there. I met the first secretary for the Ministry of Agriculture and he encouraged me—I met a lot of people who encouraged me in the UK as well. I met the Gam-bian High Commissioner. He encouraged me—everybody encouraged me. And I thought what better to do? You go to Africa where there's poverty, you produce labour, you give these people wealth and at the same time you help yourself.

MR BEGG: [Moazzam] always used to pray in the midday because we pray, well, when I say we pray—practising Muslims I should say—pray five times a day. One early in the morning before the rise of sun and then mid-day, and then we pray in the afternoon at about four or five o'clock. After that, at the time of sunset and then before going to bed. So, this five times prayer is supposed to be done by practising Muslims. I never did it (*laugh-ter*) unfortunately. Apart from that we have got to keep fast—one month fast. So this is all good things. I don't have any objection to it leaving that fundamentalism aside.

WAHAB AL-RAWI: [My idea was] we buy the peanuts from the farmers. We process it. We produce cooking oil, which we sell back to the farmer and the by-product is animal feed which you can use to raise chicken or beef or whatever. So, everything is produced on the ground and everything is sold on the ground. And it is very, very profitable.

And my brother Bisher's position was that he was going to come over with us for a couple of weeks to help us just set the factory, build the fac-tory—and then he'd come back. His ticket was for one month. When I asked him what he was going to do with the extra two weeks, he said, well, I'm going to go for a walkabout, see Africa.

MR BEGG: [Moazzam prayed] at least three or four times a day [and] in mid-day he used to put the shutter down of the shop. Not just him, there were two or three persons more used to come to the prayers. So, Moazzam prayed here, in this house; in his house; in his shop; whenever he had time for prayers.

[But] when he was putting the shutter down and putting the light little, people got suspicious. What this man is doing? Why the half shutter and so forth—what is he doing? So, somebody, possibly of different faith took it that something funny was going on and informed and the shop was raided.

[The police] said that [Moazzam] must be having some connections with Taliban or somebody. He said, "I don't, I don't know what you are talking about." They raided his house. They couldn't get anything, nothing at all, but they were after his computer. They said there must be something in the computer, a code in computer and you have got to tell the code. [Moazzam] said, "There is no code in computer—whatever is there is there and you can check it. You are [the] experts have it checked."

[So] they took him to the court, I mean to the police station, questioned him and immediately released and afterwards they apologised. They said we are sorry that we bothered you but we were informed or misinformed or whatever. I don't know what reason was that, but he came out very clear and there was nothing wrong and he was running his business as usual.

WAHAB AL-RAWI: I went in advance of the party to reconnaissance, to set up the company, to lease the warehouse, to lease the house for us to stay in the city, to do the banking, to get the equipment out of the port.

When I left London at the Airport I was called into a room with two British officers and they interrogated me for about twenty-five minutes. They asked me why was I going to Gambia? What did I have business in Gambia? Did I know these people—they named a few people—Abu Qatada. Did I know any Algerians? Which mosque did I frequent? All of these questions and then they were satisfied and they let me go.

MR BEGG: I told you in the beginning [Moazzam] was very much interested to help people all the time. He somehjow had it in his mind that the Afghan people are the people in the world who are most deprived. He talked to me about it. He said, "I want to go and start some educational institutions there." I said, "Who's going to back you? Do you know how the money is going to come? Is it a big project?" He said, "No, I'll work with a small project. My wife," because Afghanis don't like mixing of woman with man or girls mixing with boys, "so I'll take my wife and my wife will be teaching the girls side of the school and I'll be teaching the boys side." I said, "Well, it's a good idea if you can do that."

JAMAL AL-HARITH: I'm Jamal Al-Harith. I went from Manchester to Pakistan and ended up in Guantanamo, can you believe it? Yes, I went to Pakistan, well if that's my crime then you'll have to arrest plane loads of people. I went to Pakistan on tableeg. That's sort of like when you want to find out about the religion like but you also visit villages and all that. But I didn't actually get there. It was October 2001 and I was told by the money changers, they said obviously that American and British wouldn't be welcome there because they were the ones who were going to be attacking, they said. Like it's 60 percent Pashtoun in that part of Pakistan so they are like the people of Afghanistan. This is what I was told.

MR BEGG: Then suddenly I received a letter—I was suffering from angina—I received a letter from the hospital that we have made arrangements for you to go to hospital.

When Moazzam heard that his father was going to have an operation, he came to me and he said, "I'll drop the idea of going to Afghanistan until you are well." I say, "No, you go. I'm in safe hands and you cannot do much here so you'd better go. I'll be all right, don't worry," But he said, "No, this is a bad time, I need to be with you, I'll not go."

JAMAL AL-HARITH: I decided to [travel] to Turkey, through Iran to Turkey [with a guy who had a truck full of people]. The truck went off and then in the journey it was stopped. I was in Pakistan and then they stole the truck and I was just handed over. Gun toting Afghanis. They didn't steal the truck to get me, they stole the truck because they wanted the truck themselves.

When the truck was being pulled over, you don't really think anything. You think, oh, they're just going to look in the truck or it's some road toll you know. That was what was crossing my mind, they were just going to check the truck or whatever. But then they just ordered everyone out and then you know me and the driver's mate were put in their jeep or whatever to take away. Then I start to think, oh well, things aren't, you know, going as I planned—there's something wrong here, something's wrong. And obviously you're scared, your stomach's turning over and you just . . .

MR. BEGG: He is a good son. He is the best son of mine. I told him, "You are wasting your time here, you are wasting your money here. They are not going to wait for you, you had better go and start the job and you can come later on, come and see me." After about a week of intensive conversations, he somehow agreed. But he had small children. I said, "I don't particularly like that area because Afghan people are very different people as compared to us or to English people. We are more like English person: how can you live with Afghans?" He said, "No, I won't live with them, I'm teaching them but as far as living is concerned I'll be confined to my wife and children."

JAMAL AL-HARITH: [I was handed over to the Taliban.]

WAHAB AL-RAWI: My brother [and my partners tried to join me in Gambia but] at Gatwick they were taken. They were held for, I think four days altogether. Our homes were searched and the whole case went in front of a judge and the judge found there was absolutely nothing, I mean he asked the secret service why did you arrest these guys and they showed him a piece of equipment, electrical equipment and our solicitor, Gareth Peirce, she said . . .

GARETH PEIRCE: [One of Mr Al-Rawi's partners Mr Al Banna had] a visit from special branch two days before he was leaving saying we know you are going. And he said do you have a problem with that? And they said no. Two days later they get to Gatwick and they're all taken off and away from embarking on the plane, their luggage searched, held on a completely false pretext for two or three days, said that there was a suspect item in their luggage, which turned out to be a battery charger so that we were able to go down the road from Paddington Green Police Station to Argos and get a catalogue saying here's the battery charger, while they were busy saying they were flying a forensic expert from Bali to inspect this thing.

WAHAB AL-RAWI: The judge dismissed the case.

GARETH PEIRCE: However, they then go to Gambia and are immediately arrested.

WAHAB AL-RAWI: All of us, my brother, my two partners, myself, my driver, my contact in Gambia, we were all arrested by the Gambian secret service.

MR BEGG: [After Moazzam] went [to Afghanistan] he was ringing me up all the time from there, telling me, "I have submitted the application to Taliban government, and I'm going and coming every day and there is little movement." He felt that they are not very keen to have English or Maths or education in the country and he started getting a bit disappointed.

One day he said that I have got another idea in my mind, to put in water pumps for people living far, far away from the water source. I think that in a week's time the water was there. He called me and said, "People are very, very happy—they are dancing, they're kissing my hands, and I'm very happy." I said, "Son, I'm happy too, that you have done that very gentle work, very high class work but what happened to your application?"

JAMAL AL-HARITH: [The Taliban took me to Afghanistan and] I was put in some building for three days and questioned, well not really questioned really—the main questioning was in another place. And then that's when I, you know, the kicking and all that. And then they took me out to the main prison, a political prison that they have. And then I was in isolation for two weeks but in that two weeks was when I was questioned. They asked me . . . where do I study, surprisingly and all this stuff. What education have I got. Then they said I'm part of some elite special forces from England obviously, some British special forces military group that was trying to enter Afghanistan and that, er, where are the rest of the other guys, you know? And what rank do I hold in the British army? Oh and, what mosque did I go to back home? Would you believe it, what mosque do I pray at back home? (*Laughs*) Even the Americans asked me that.

WAHAB AL-RAWI: They took us to the secret service HQ in Banjul and they started interrogating us. It's a routine investigation. They asked us about the business. What we were coming to Gambia to do, who did we know in Gambia, all of the stuff that were routine to the Gambians. At the end of all this two Americans came in. They introduced themselves as Mr Lee, and the other guy I can't remember what. Mr Lee said I'm with the American Embassy, we're here working with the Gambians, can I ask a few questions? I said, you can't ask me anything, you have no authority over me. I want to see a solicitor. I want to see my High Commissioner. Mr Lee turned to the other guy and said, this guy's going to be trouble and he left the room.

JAMAL AL-HARITH: The Americans had started bombing while I was in there, and after two or three weeks I'm not sure, the Taliban released me out into the normal population, the prison population that is.

WAHAB AL-RAWI: We were separated and put in different rooms in the Gambian HQ. I was in the conference room with a mat on the floor. They told me to relax and take it easy. I was very, very upset. I was shouting and screaming and being abusive. I knew that I hadn't done anything and I didn't know who had, I mean I suspected that the British authorities had ordered the arrest, but I didn't know why.

We were all moved into a house in the suburbs of Banjul. There were three or four Gambians, but I wouldn't say guarding. Don't forget this was Ramadan in Africa, so it was hot and people were fasting. It was low security. I was preparing breakfast on most occasions because the food they were bringing wasn't so tempting, so actually once I went out of the house and did some shopping on my own. Well, the guy was with me, supposedly.

[After two days] we were taken back to the Gambian secret service headquarters. [In the interrogation room] were the two Americans in front of me, and the two Gambians beside me. They went over the whole thing again and again. About the business; about who I knew. And then after they had finished about the business, they go onto fanatical questions.

About what did I think of Mr, what is his name, not the Taliban, the Qaeda guy, what's his name . . . em . . . Bin Laden. I said, I don't know Mr Bin Laden, you probably know him more than I do, you trained him. They said, do you know any terrorists? I said, of course I don't know any terrorists. They say that we think you have come here to do so, so, and so. And I say, well this is stupid because there is no basis for that.

One idea was that [we] were in Gambia to build a training camp. The division of labour as follows: I was the cover, going to run the business. [One of my partners] was to keep an eye on me just in case I did something wrong, so he was to be my policeman, and my brother, because of his skills, is supposed to be the trainer of the camp.

I said "Have you found any training equipment or military stuff?" They said no. I said, "My brother is supposed to be training these people but he only has a visa for one month. How can he set up a camp and train people in one month?"

At the next meeting they brought another theory. We were supposed to come to Gambia to blow up something. So I told him OK, name two targets in Gambia that are worth blowing up and he could only name one—the American Embassy. There aren't any targets in the Gambia. Point one. Point two is: if I was coming over to blow up something, why would I come through the airport, you have two hundred miles of porous borders—no police no nothing—I could have easily slipped through these borders. Third, where is the equipment that I was supposed to use to blow up anything? Have you found a bullet or a gun or explosives? No.

MR BEGG: When Moazzam was [putting in] the fifth water pump the American bombardment started. He rushed to his house in Kabul, took his wife and children, crossed the border, and came to Pakistan. He reached there and he telephoned me that we are all safe, children are all safe. I said, "Why don't you come back now, enough is enough." He said, "No, I've just started and I'm quite happy with it and this thing will stop in a week's time."

JAMAL AL-HARITH: When the Taliban fell and the new Afghan government came in to power, we were told we could leave and they were offering us money to travel to Pakistan with some guards . . . and I said, well, it's quicker for me to go to Kabul, thinking it would be quicker to go to Kabul, because I heard the British had an embassy there. So they got hold of the Red Cross [and the Red Cross] said, okay then you stay here and we'll be in touch with the British in Kabul and then you can, you know, make arrangements to travel.

WAHAB AL-RAWI: They told us they were going to move us to a better place. I understood later they were actually using my tools and my equipment and my timber to build a jail. You heard they were boarding the windows and blocking the doors. They were using the food we had brought with us to feed us as well. We were hooded and handcuffed and we were moved at two o'clock in the morning to this house one at a time. We didn't see each other.

At every single interview and every single occasion, whenever the subject comes along, I would ask to see the High Commissioner. Every single time they said the High Commissioner doesn't want to see you, sometimes they tell me, who do you think ordered your arrest? The British already knew you were in this situation.

MARK JENNINGS: I was working three days a week doing case work for Ed Davey, the MP for Kingston and Surbiton and Ed happened to say to me [he had a case that] turned up to one of [his] surgeries: an Iraqi guy nabbed in Gambia. I met the family and I got to know them as friends and it struck me that no way are they fanatical about anything. [What I learned about] Bisher was that, yes, he was reasonably devout but he's the sort of guy that can sleep for England—he used to sleep through morning prayers.

WAHAB AL-RAWI: There were questions that intrigued me, for example, the Americans had files on us. They were asking me about Abu Qatada and what Abu Qatada said about us.

MARK JENNINGS: [The connection to Bisher] is suspicious immediately because first of all, yes he's a Muslim, [and] there's Abu Qatada. [Bisher] also in 1998 did a pilot's licence to fly small light helicopters, little two/four seater things, it's hardly 737s if you want to get into that, and he's a bit of a speed freak, he's got a collection of seven motorbikes, well we think there's seven—they're all in different stages of disassembly in the garage and in various places and he likes parachute jumping, he likes the adrenaline thrill. But then on the other hand he's a young man with probably slightly more money than sense so I think the only connection to any al Qaeda is Abu Qatada and I mean [the British have] held Abu Qatada in Belmarsh prison for getting on for eighteen months, if not longer. We haven't been able to charge him with anything.

[With] Bisher [and Abu Qatada] certainly I think it was a friendly relationship. Bisher strikes me, from what I've heard, as being very popular with his neighbours, Muslim and non-Muslim. He's the sort of guy that's helpful. As far as I know he and Wahab, Bisher's elder brother, used to take Abu Qatada's kids swimming. I think Abu Qatada's got quite a few kids. I think the other thing they used to do was take Abu Qatada's wife to the hospital which again is hardly the stuff of terrorism.

WAHAB AL-RAWI: One day they came into my room. Mr Lee, he came into my room and he asked me if I worked for the British secret service. I said, well I really can't answer this question, you will have to go to them and ask them politely. What kind of a question is that, I mean? So I thought about it, and I thought they must have asked him to release me. If I tell you exactly what happened, you would never be able to come up with an answer to this problem. It's very, very stupid. It's dumbfounding.

JAMAL AL-HARITH: [The Red Cross took my details] and so on, so on. Then the games began. They were in contact with the British Embassy. They said oh you know the British will be sorting something out for you. I was using the journalists' phones, they had satellite phones, so I was phoning the British Embassy all the time to speak to the guy, said yeah yeah we're sorting it out, you know, we're going to get either someone down, or we are going to fly you up.

[We were] constantly in touch for about over a month [then] the Special Forces came—the American Special Forces—and they questioned us to give our stories and then the Red Cross came like the day after and said like, "Oh you're going back now" said "you're going to fly out in a plane from the American base to Kabul" and the British obviously will meet [you] there. This was arranged by them they said.

Two days before I was booked to fly out then the Americans come in and go, you know, "You're not going anywhere. We're taking you to Kandahar" to their base. They took me to their base obviously but put me in jail or in a concentration camp and they questioned us. Even though British Intelligence were there at the time in Kandahar questioning other British people that were there, they refused to see me for some reason, I have no idea what for. I spoke to some SAS guy. And then I spoke to American Intelligence—American military.

[They asked] mainly my details in England, where I lived, what jobs I had. Didn't really seem interested in anything else. Mainly just where did I work in England. At what time? My education and so on, so on. Where did I go? Where did I pray? They just seemed more interested in getting all that out than why I was here it seemed. And the SAS guy said—he interviewed me about twice, at night, cold—he said, "I can't release you." He didn't actually say, "You are going to be sent to Cuba," but, "the decision is going to be with the Americans whether you get let out or not."

WAHAB AL-RAWI: After two weeks of interrogation and threats and all of that stuff, he comes into my room, Mr Lee that is, he says, there's your passport and your ticket, you're going home, this is not a joke, we're not playing with you, you're really going home. And then he starts to relax and starts, you know, acting normally instead of the formal way. He told me that [he had freed my one partner the day before and now, he said,] we're getting rid of you, [so] I can concentrate more on your brother.

It doesn't make sense. I'm friends with Abu Qatada, why was I let go? The whole thing doesn't make sense. If it is because we know Abu Qatada, OK, I know Abu Qatada, why release me—do you see what I mean?—and take my brother. It doesn't make sense.

MARK JENNINGS: The only difference between [the two brothers] is that Wahab Al-Rawi has British citizenship and Bisher doesn't. When [they came here from Iraq] they left behind quite a large nice house plus some other assets, and they thought well Bisher is the youngest member of the family, if he keeps Iraqi citizenship, if there's ever a change in the regime—and I hasten to add they were very anti the war—if there was ever a beneficial change in the regime in the future, there's no problem for him as an Iraqi citizen for him to go back and say, we want our house back, thanks very much.

WAHAB AL-RAWI: Mr Lee asked me if he could keep my Iraqi passport—I had an expired Iraqi passport—and he said he wanted to keep it as a souvenir and I said no, you can't keep it as a souvenir. He said, can we give this to the guards—we had some brake pads and some expensive equipment, he said, can we give that to the guards? And I said, no you can't give that to the guards. You can give this to the guards—and we were trying to negotiate what I can keep and what I can't. And then again I was hooded, I was taken to the airport, I was taken into a lounge on my own with the Americans. We sat down talking normally and the Gambian security guard came in at that point and asked them about my property. Mr Lee denied ever knowing anything about it. He said what property? I said my factory, my lorries, my equipment, my cars, my generators. He said, no we don't know anything about it, so I understood it was all gone . . . Altogether about a quarter of a million dollars. [My one partner] and myself [had been held for] 27 days.

My brother and [my other partner Mr Al Banna] have been in prison ever since.

MR BEGG: One night two Pakistanis . . . two American soldiers, assisted by two Pakistani officers, burst into [Moazzam's] house [in Pakistan], took him as prisoner, threw him to the floor, bundled him up and put him into the boot of their car—in front of other neighbours and the little child, she saw that and—they took him away. I received a telephone . . . it was whispering . . . I think he had his mobile phone with him or what . . . he said—just like that.

(MR BEGG *drops his voice and whispers.*)

"Dad."

(*Raising his voice to normal*)

I said, "Who is that?" He said,

(*Dropping to a whisper again*)

"Moazzam."

(*Normal voice*)

I said, "Why you are talking like that?" "I have been arrested." I said, "By whom?" He said, "Two Pakistanis . . . two American soldiers and two Pakistanis soldiers." I said, "Where are you?" He said, "I'm in the car and they are taking me away, I don't know where. My wife and children are in Pakistan, please take care of them and don't worry," and then either somebody saw him talking or something . . .

Well, I was so shocked for ten minutes I was just looking as if something had happened to my mind—it didn't work at all. I didn't know why? How? I couldn't make out anything.

My wife got up as well and she said, "Well, you calm down, nothing will happen." I said, "In that [area] people kidnap people for the sake of money and they kill them and throw their bodies and take the money and so— that area is very dangerous . . ."

WAHAB AL-RAWI: The law in Gambia is that you can't hold somebody for more than 40 days or something like that. So, we moved immediately to get the solicitors to work on his behalf, but just before the expiry of that deadline, [Bisher] was moved with [my other partner Mr Al Banna] to Bagram airbase [Afghanistan].

MR BEGG: Moazzam said that two Americans assisted by two Pakistanis [had taken him], but who knows whether they were Americans or Pakistanis? But it comes to my mind that they could be Afghans, dressed up as Americans or something. How could I think that—that Americans will catch my son, he's from England. I couldn't think that.

WAHAB AL-RAWI: It's worse than kidnapping. It's like, if you take it from the American standpoint, we want to make sure that our people in America think that these people are terrorists. So they came not from Gambia, they came from Bagram airbase, from Afghanistan, so they must be terrorists.

We don't know exactly [how long they were held in Bagram] because Bagram everybody knows is a no-go zone for anybody—there's no human rights, nothing.

MR BEGG: I used my resources, whatever we have in Pakistan in army—because we come from army you see. For generations we have been with British army. [So] when the Foreign Officer didn't give me any answer, proper answer, I rang up one of my cousins who is Brigadier General there. I asked his help and he straight away said, "Very sorry about it, I'll do whatever I can." Then I rang up General Begg who was Chief of the Army Staff some time ago, and then I got in touch with several officers, the high ranking officers to search and find out if Moazzam is dead—but nobody could find that Moazzam is dead. They said that Moazzam is not here; he must be either as you say kidnapped by local Patans or he is with Americans.

WAHAB AL-RAWI: [We got one letter from Afghanistan.]

BISHER: Dear Mother, I'm writing this letter from the lovely mountains of Afghanistan at a US prison camp. I am very well. The conditions are excellent and everyone is very, very nice. I hope that you, my brother, my sister and all the family are well. Give my salaam to everyone and I hope we meet soon. p.s. Tell

CENSORED

that the food is very good and I can pray as much as I want. Your loving son, Bisher.

MR BEGG: I was like a madman for one month because [Moazzam] was very precious to me. After one month I receive a telephone call from a gentleman called Simon. He rang me from a province called Kandahar next to Pakistan—and said, "I am speaking from Red Cross. This is about your son. He is in the custody of Americans [here] and he sends you regards"—that's all. I said, "Tell me please more." He said, "I'm not allowed, nor I know. I can't tell you anything more."

On one hand I was happy that [Moazzam] was alive and on the other hand I was shocked that he was in custody and I thought that possibly he is there for a week or two and then he would be released. Now, Birmingham Red Cross people came down and [they] had a letter from Moazzam.

MOAZZAM: To dad,

As Salamu alaikum

I am writing this letter after around 4 wks, I am in good health and ok. I don't know what is going to happen with me, but I believe everything will eventually be ok. Please contact my wife and ask her to go back to the UK and stay with her mother. I am sorry to put you all through this, but I didn't want any of this to happen.

MR BEGG: [The letter was] from Kandahar. After about two or three weeks, he was transferred to—from Kandahar to—there's another American base which is known as Bagram. We went to the Foreign Office and they say, "Well, unfortunately we don't have any access to American military bases, they won't allow anybody, so, go to the Red Cross," and that's it.

JAMAL AL-HARITH: I actually thought I was going to be released, because they said before we left [Kandahar], they said, "You have to complete the process." The guy he said, "The process is that you are going to be [in Cuba] for one or two months and then you'll be sent home, but anyone who comes to our prison in Kandahar [has] to go to Cuba," he said. So I said, "OK then," well I didn't say "OK," but "if I have to go, then I have to go" and then they sent me.

ACT TWO

TOM CLARK: [My sister] was I think a very, very independent, capable, flexible—an enormously sort of liberal-minded person who . . . she was a very . . . it's hard to talk about someone's life without saying sort of something insipid . . . I don't know charming, attractive, sensible, intelligent person, enjoying her life in New York. We lived together for a while, for a couple of years, in New York actually, because I was studying there and my sister had a successful job and she offered to support me in my time of need. So I lived with her . . . and at first it was a kind of a convenience thing and we hadn't really spent any time together since we were kids, but it worked out really, really well. It was interesting, we never used to fight or argue, until we got home of course, you know what siblings are like as soon as you put them in a sort of domestic environment, things go tits up. But it was you know, it was absolutely, it was wonderful. It was the happiest couple of years of my life, and I was, in a way, you know I look back and know that I was very lucky to have had that—it would have been a much greater shame if I hadn't had the chance to spend so much time with her.

[I call it September 11th] not 9/11. I've always had this thing about American dates.

This is someone who worked in public relations, you know [but] she was always sort of politically minded and she studied politics at college and that's what she was always going to be sort of interested in. She got into public relations through working for the European Commission and things, that's how she got into it. But . . . and . . . it was, I don't know, I just remember thinking that [the Middle East] was something we spent so much time thinking about and that she actually genuinely cared about. And that was one of the great . . . the things that made me most sad. Aside from I mean obviously her loss was the most sad thing, but of all the sort of things peripheral to it, of all the sort of injustices and wrongs, the fact that she cared, sort of, she actually did care about the things that led some people to think that was a smart thing to do some sort of clever stunt and it was so . . . that really upset me.

(*Call to prayer—2nd. Noon. Over loudspeaker.*)

MOAZZAM: Dear Dad, Mum, Twins and Motard,

As-Salamu alaikum

I was very happy to receive your letter today, and I hope that you are all fine and well. Thank you for staying in touch with Zeynab and the children. Two letters have arrived from her and they should allow me to read them today or tomorrow. I have been extremely worried about them, and don't know even if they were left with any money. Please, help them in whatever way you can and I will repay you as soon as I can. Don't let my children want for anything due to any financial problems. I am doing well here and treatment has been good. Food, water, clothes and Quran are all provided. I am now about to complete my 7th reading of the Quran, and have memorised many chapters, praise be to Allah. The days go by slowly, but my ability to speak English has been a tremendous help. I cannot tell you much about what is going to happen, but I remain patiently hopeful and pray that soon I will see you all again. This is the hardest test I have had to face in my life and I hope I have not caused you too much distress, but I will pass this test by the will of Allah and your prayers. I love and miss you all very much. I thank you for all that I never did thank you for (both you and mum).

Your loving son, Moazzam.

(DONALD RUMSFELD *in press conference.*)

NEWSPAPERMAN 1: Mr Secretary . . .

NEWSPAPERMAN 2: Mr Secretary . . . Rumsfeld.

RUMSFELD: Let me just answer the previous question.

On September 11th the terrorists attacked the United States, killing thousands of innocent men, women, and children. Less than a month later, the coalition countries responded and the Taliban had been driven from power. This is a dangerous and determined adversary for whom September 11th was an opening salvo in a long war against our country, our people, and our way of life. Our task, our purpose must be to stop the terrorists; to find them, to root them out.

We were able to capture and detain a large number of people who had been through training camps and had learned a whole host of skills as to how they could kill innocent people—not how they could kill other soldiers. We've got a good slug of those folks off the street where they can't kill more people.

(BISHER AL-RAWI *is putting on the orange boiler suit of Guantanamo marking his transition from Bagram to Guantanamo.*)

BISHER: Dear Mother,

I'm writing to you from the seaside resort of Guantanamo Bay in Cuba. After winning first prize in the competition, I was whisked to this nice resort with all expenses paid. I did not have to spend a penny. I and Jamal [Al Banna] are in very good health. Everybody is very nice. The neighbours are very well behaved. The food is first class, plenty of sun and pebbles, no sand I'm afraid. Give my salaam to everybody and my special salaam to Wahab. I wish him the very best with his life, religion and business. I hope to see you soon if you want. Your son, Bisher.

(RUHEL AHMED *is wearing the boiler suit.*)

RUHEL: Assalamwa-alakum.

BISHER: p.s.—Please renew my motorbike insurance policy.

RUHEL: Hi, how are you all. I'm fine and well. I recieve your letters and photos. Well about my eyes u can send me contact lenses. Get them from Sandwell hospital (Eye Clinic) and solution [from] Boots [chemist]. Its call (Boston advance care) . . . and I need protein tablets to clean them . . . (Total Care tablets for hard contact lenses). Both solution and tablets for hard contact lenses. Its going to cost total of £30.00. I need 2 packets of tablets and 1 packet of solution. You don't need to worrie about me. They army cool with me and everyone. Well what can I say to u all. The solders call me by the name of Tiger and Slimshady for some reason. Im know very well. All the army know me as U know everyone me back home as I used to be centre attration where ever I went. Hope to see you very soon inshallah, assalema-laykum, love Ruhel Ahmed

(RUMSFELD *points at one of the newspaper men.*)

NEWSPAPERMAN 1: But have you determined [the detainees'] status individually, on an individual?

RUMSFELD: Yes, indeed, individually.

NEWSPAPERMAN 1: So you know which are al Qaeda and which are Taliban?

RUMSFELD: "Determined" is a tough word. We have determined as much as one can determine when you're dealing with people who may or may not tell the truth.

NEWSPAPERMAN 1: Right.

RUMSFELD: So yes, we've done the best we can.

They are not POWs, they will not be determined to be POWs.

Don't forget we're treating these people as if the Geneva Convention applied.

GARETH PEIRCE: There are a number of concepts which are deliberately confused by the American administration. It seized people for purposes that are clearly the obtaining of information and having seized those people, it transferred them to a place which it believed would be beyond the reach of courts in America. It claimed that it had seized people on the battlefield, there were frequent references to capture on the battlefield, and then, having presented it to the world in this way, found itself stuck with the immediate response, well if these are prisoners of war, they are entitled to give name, rank, and number and no more and they deserved to be treated as the Geneva Convention dictates and not to be made the subject of interrogation. So having at first flush grabbed the nearest label, finding that it meant that there were international treaty obligations to provide prisoners of war with rights, the regime very quickly had to redefine what it had, and therefore it said these were unlawful combatants who were not wearing uniform and were not conforming to the norms of warfare.

RUMSFELD: We said from the beginning that these are unlawful combatants, and we're detaining them. We call them "detainees," not "prisoners of war." We call them "detainees." We have said that, you know, being the kind of a country we are, it's our intention to recognise that there are certain standards that are generally appropriate for treating people who were— are prisoners of war, which these people are not, and—in our view—but there—and you know to the extent that it's reasonable, we will end up using roughly that standard. And that, that's what we're doing. I don't—I wouldn't want to say that I know in any instance where we would deviate from that or where we might exceed it.

MOAZZAM: Dearest Zaynab,

As-Salamu alaikum

I am writing this message late at night, which is usually when I cannot sleep, because of thinking and worrying all the time, the heat and bright lights. I have written several messages to you and it appears that you have not received any except the first one.

Please let me know exactly what messages you got (the date I wrote on the message) and I will see what has happened. These past few weeks have been more depressing than usual especially since the birth of our son, May Allah bless and protect him and all my family. Time is dragging on so slowly and things don't change here at all, if they do it is very slowly. I still don't know what will happen with me, where I will go and when, even after all this time! There is nothing here to do to occupy time, except read the Quran which I have finished so many times. There are many rules here which does not make this wait any easier. The food has been the same for 5 1/2 months, 3 times a day, first meal in the morning and last in the late afternoon, and most of the time I am hungry. I miss your cooking so much.

CENSORED

The most difficult thing in my life is being away from you and the kids, and being patient.

CENSORED

I miss you and love you as much. Moazzam

CLIVE STAFFORD SMITH: I run a [legal] charity called Justice in Exile in the US, which is devoted to representing the people in Guantanamo Bay. Guantanamo Bay is a massive diversion. It's got nothing to do with the real issues—none of [the people who they think are] the real bad dudes are in Guantanamo Bay, because the American Government would never put them there while there is a possibility that we'll get jurisdiction to litigate to get them out of there. So all of them are in Bagram air force base and places like that.

GARETH PEIRCE: There are many thousands around the world, distributed in places where Guantanamo would probably look quite humane. And there is a process of shipping people for instance to Egypt, where you know they'll be tortured. [You] torture something out of them, then get them back to Guantanamo. [It's] a grotesque international redistribution. And what are you getting out of it? Well maybe that's where the weapons of mass destruction came from. Certainly the product you'll get is bound to be complete nonsense, bound to be, once it's ricocheted off [hundreds of] people in Guantanamo, any cocktail of invention will have happened.

RUMSFELD: Anybody who has looked at the training manuals for the al Qaeda and what those people were trained to do, and how they were trained to kill civilians—and anybody who saw what happened to the Afghani soldiers who were guarding the al Qaeda in Pakistan when a number were killed by al Qaeda using their bare hands—has to recognise that these are among the most dangerous, best trained vicious killers on the face of the earth.

NEWSPAPERMAN 3: Mr Secretary, there was a debate . . .

RUMSFELD: And that means that the people taking care of the detainees and managing their transfer have to be just exceedingly careful for two reasons.

One, for their own protection, but also so these people don't get loose back out on the street and kill more people.

NEWSPAPERMAN 3: Mr Secretary, there was a debate yesterday in the British Parliament. I happened to notice—

RUMSFELD: Oh I read some of that. Just amazing.

NEWSPAPERMAN 3: —and it—well it was interesting. And one of the comments made was that [the] handling of John Walker, a United States citizen, has been different from the handling of the others, and that this demonstrated that the United States would not treat one of its own people the way that it has treated these others. And I would ask your reaction to that.

RUMSFELD: Well, it's amazing the insight that parliamentarians can gain from 5,000 miles away. I don't notice that he was handled any differently or has been in the past or is now.

NEWSPAPERMAN 3: Well, will he be put in an eight-by-eight cell that has no walls but only a roof?

RUMSFELD: The . . . just for the sake of the listening world, Guantanamo Bay's climate is different than Afghanistan. To be in an eight-by-eight cell in beautiful, sunny Guantanamo Bay, Cuba, is not a—inhumane treatment. And it has a roof. They have all the things that I've described. And how each person is handled depends on where they go. And Mr Walker has been turned over to the Department of Justice. He will go where they want him. He will not go to Guantanamo Bay, Cuba.

NEWSPAPERMAN 4: On a related question, there are British citizens at Guantanamo Bay.

RUMSFELD: Yeah.

NEWSPAPERMAN 4: Can you clarify—did the United States tell the British government about moving these detainees from Afghanistan to Guantanamo Bay? That we were taking this step?

RUMSFELD: I don't know. My—the United Kingdom is working very closely with us. They have liaison in Tampa, Florida. They are part of the coalition. They're leading the international security assistance force. People talk at multiple levels with the UK every day of the week, every day of the—just continuously. And do I know whether someone called them up on the phone and said: Gee we're thinking of doing this, that, or the other thing? I just don't know the answer to that. You could ask them.

NEWSPAPERMAN 4: Well their claim is that they weren't told, and they seem pretty upset about it. And I'm just wondering—

RUMSFELD: "They"—who's "they"?

NEWSPAPERMAN 4: —several members of the British parliament are claiming that the British . . .

RUMSFELD: They are not the government. The "they" is the UK government, and if I'm not mistaken, I read that Prime Minister Blair and the other representatives of the government said things quite the contrary to what you're saying. Yes?

NEWSPAPERMAN 5: Mr Secretary, you've said that you reserve the right to hold the detainees until the end of the war. You've also said that there won't be a signing ceremony on the *Missouri* in this war.

RUMSFELD: Right.

NEWSPAPERMAN 5: So when exactly is the end of the war? And are we talking about the war on terrorism or the conflict in Afghanistan?

RUMSFELD: Well, at the moment, we all know the conflict in Afghanistan is going on, so we're not past our deadline or our due date. I don't know how to describe it, and I suppose that will be something that the president would make a judgement on, as to when it was over.

(RUMSFELD *exits.*)

MOAZZAM: . . . When I wrote about all those insects etc.—that was in the summer; now it's well into winter. The camel spider is the only ten-legged spider in the world, and, I believe, is not an arachnid (technically not a spider). But it grows to bigger than the human hand-size, moves like a race car and has a bite that causes flesh to decay—if untreated. In the summer there were plenty here, running into the cells and climbing over people; one person was bitten and had to be treated. Apart from that, there is the usual melee of scorpions, beetles, mice, and other creepy-crawlies. Thank God it's winter!

MR BEGG: I received a telephone call from the Foreign Office, and the person in charge of the case she told me that [Moazzam] has been transferred to Guantanamo Bay from Bagram air base . . . It was a surprise yes. I was not expecting him to go there. I was expecting that he was going to be released. He's an innocent person and he didn't do anything wrong as far as we know.

[Moazzam's] oldest daughter here, she understands. She understands that her father has been taken away by Americans and they . . . she gets at times nightmares. She says at times, "My father is being beaten up, his head is bleeding."

JAMAL AL-HARITH: When I first arrived [in Cuba], they put me in a block where there was some English [people but] I was only there for an hour, because when I came in, obviously the plane journey with a mask, and everything, and goggles, I nearly fell out there unconscious from the plane. [Then they] moved me to the hospital. The guy took blood pressure and X-ray and then he just gave some tablets. Didn't say anything apart from, "How do you feel now?" said, "OK," "Now, how do you feel?" and I said, "like my muscles are just relaxed." He had given me a muscle relaxant. And he said, "Oh, your blood pressure was one of the highest I've seen here." But the reason why was cos the chains on my foot.

You had four or five different types of chains there. If they came with chains that made you sort of hunch up and have to walk like that then you knew they were going to be hard on you when you get to the interrogation. Or if the chains were where you can actually stand up, easier and walk, then they want something from you, so they're going to be nice, and they might offer you tea or something like that, or a drink of water.

GARETH PEIRCE: I think slowly the world has become aware that Guantanamo Bay is a convenience, it's a resource pool for American intelligence and even more disturbingly perhaps, the intelligence services of the rest of the world, who are deemed to be allies, or even those who are perhaps not deemed to be allies. There is a huge range of nationalities captured there.

JAMAL AL-HARITH: I found a lot of the guards were stupid. Just young coming in like they were in training, and I would say to them, especially when they said to me, "Oh, we've put your name and your picture through like Interpol, all the Intelligence Agencies of the world or whatever, first world countries, and nothing came back on you, you haven't even got a parking ticket." I said, "That's because I haven't done anything." And I said, "You know I'll walk out from here when I leave free, because I haven't done anything at all, but your problem is that you've got me here and you can't release me without having something on me."

They have these names they use. In [Delta] it was "reservation." "You're going for reservation." It means interrogation, but they didn't like to use the word "interrogation." "You're not really being interrogated, we're investigators." In Delta it was—no sorry in X-Ray it was "exhibition." "You're going for exhibition" it meant interrogation.

They use words but there's evil behind it, man. There's malice.

MARK JENNINGS: General Miller, the guy who designed the interrogation system in Guantanamo Bay, was sent over to Abu Ghraib to design their interrogation system. I'm afraid that says enough about what's happened in Guantanamo Bay.

JAMAL AL-HARITH: I got put in isolation for [the first time], because I refused to wear my wrist band. I said, "In concentration camps they were given tattoos, and now they've given us these, it's just the same really," I said, "As a matter of principle," I'd keep saying, "As a matter of principle"—I'd keep saying it, and that would easily get me into trouble. So as a matter of principle every time they gave me a wrist band, I'd rip it off. The cages [had] little bits sticking out, I'd just put the band on it until it's cut then I'd rip it off and [then] I used to throw it out. And this went on for a couple of weeks, and after a certain time they just said, "We've had enough, mate," so they put me in isolation for four days.

There was nothing in the isolation cell except bare metal—built like a freezer, AC system blowing through cold air for 24 hours, so it turns it into a freezer box, a freezer, a fridge. I had to go under the metal sheet because the cold air was blowing in. I tried to go to sleep but you can't because you're just shaking too much. I said, oh I can't do this to myself. I said I can't do this.

CLIVE STAFFORD SMITH: We have learnt shocking things. For example in the first few months at Guantanamo they had 32 suicide attempts and then suddenly the suicide attempts [stopped]. There was genuine effort on behalf of the powers that be down there to act as if, ah, everyone's calmed down now, they're taking their Prozac, there's no problem. But then we discover that far from suicide efforts stopping, they'd just been re-classified by the military into manipulative self-injurious behaviour. There were more than 40 of those in a six month period, since the re-classification of suicide attempts.

MR BEGG: It's very personal but I'll tell you [this]. I talk to [my son]. Because I love him. When you are in deep love with somebody you tend to talk to him—in your dreams, in your life, when you are alone.

At times I see that he is sitting here and I'm shouting and he puts his head down and quietly listening to me. He's a grown up man, he's a married man, he's got children, he's a responsible person and I was shouting at him—telling him off—[and he just sits there]—

WAHAB AL-RAWI: The times that are awkward are when you're on your own at night when I don't sleep and then you ask yourself what can I do, is there anything I can do, and you end up on a nightmare, and I keep getting these stupid nightmares. Just ugly ones—I'm walking in a tunnel, and I turn to my left and just near the staircase my brother is there and he's getting beaten up by four guys, and he just turns to me, and he doesn't say anything, he just turns to me and gives me this look, as if "why aren't you doing anything about it?" and I wake up sweating and angry and I just want to punch something. You tell me what can I do about it?

JAMAL AL-HARITH: I had a dream a year in that I was going to stay there for two years. And that's one of the big things in there—dreams. People had dreams and they would tell it to everyone, and raise everyone's spirits. So dreams was a big thing, and you had interpreters of dreams as well there.

In Kandahar, I [dreamed] myself back home, watching the news, with some guys about Cuba. So I said, "That's the sign for me that I'm going back home." And I would take it as a sign that's my personal sign to me that I'm going back home. But some people would say, "No, you can't take it, it's just a dream," and I'd say, "No, no." You have to hang on to something, because that was my hope. I freely admit that when I did see that dream, I said to myself, "I know I'm going back home." And I just had to keep on believing. No-one swayed me on that.

RUHEL AHMED: Assalamwal alykum How you three doing. Hope you all are behaving at home and school, Shanaz, how is ur college study going on and junel what are u doing school or not. U have'nt wrote to me so write and tell me now what u doing ok. Juber how are u doing and is ur study at school, behave at home and outside the area that's both of you listen to Mum and Dad do as they tell u to do, I miss u guys alot u have heard the US army has made a new prison. We got transfered here on 27/04/2002 and its better in some ways. We have a toilet and a bed. We hardly see the sun or moon anymore cause we are in side buildings in the old prison it used to be open air u could see different animal and stuff like that.

All of u pray all time not for me, for urselfs cause on day of judgement u all have to answer for ur own actions and deed. No one will want to know anyone on that day. Are you excesizing Shian, Junel and Juber. Keeping healthy if not start, stay in shape. Me myself excercis all day long about 4 hours a day. Got a nice pack of six pack now & looking good as always. Mom and Dad How are U. I hope u all forgive for the pain I brought too u both in these last few years. I know I haven't been a good son. Hope u can forgive me. Luv u all and miss.u. inhsallah. See U soon. Assalamwaalaykum. Luv Ruhel.

CLIVE STAFFORD SMITH: [I've done death penalty work] for the last 20 years. It's all about hatred. About how you get a huge group of people to hate a small group of people and in that way you get them to quit blaming their problems on the Government. You hate black people because that avoids you blaming the Government for your own problems and [you] hate people on death row and blame them all for the problems in the world.

[But] OK, [so] we hate people on death row. If they hate us back, it doesn't have any impact, because they have no power. Yet when we translate this onto [Guantanamo, and] the international stage, and we hate Muslims, and let's be honest that's what's going on here, despite the pathetic attempts to pretend that's not true. There are one billion Muslims around the world, and when we [hate them] we create a world which is a very, very dangerous and unpleasant place. Translated onto the international scene, it's terrifying.

WAHAB AL-RAWI: What is the difference between Saddam Hussein and Bush and Blair? Saddam Hussein did exactly the same thing to my country and that is why we came there and we came here and we end up with the same misery—ten times over—because this is supposed to be a land of freedom and laws.

I even thought about putting [on] a suicide belt, but that doesn't help [Bisher].

That doesn't help anybody.

TOM CLARK: When you mentioned you were doing this Guantanamo thing, I sort of thought, well, what do I think, what is my attitude because it changes and it swings over time. But, you know, [my sister] would have been incensed.

. . . But then, she, you know, was incinerated publicly, live on television, you know for, I don't know, an hour and forty minutes . . .

Let's say for the sake of argument among those detained at Guantanamo Bay are some of the people who led to her death—who murdered her essentially—that's a little difficult for me to, you know, it's difficult for me to say it was a bad thing that they were there.

Suicide bombing is a completely bizarre thing. It is . . . if there was such a thing as evil, I've lost the belief there is . . . but if there was, I mean, that would be the most evil thing. So yeh, lock 'em up, throw away the key.

JAMAL AL-HARITH: [I stopped talking to the guards], because I couldn't justify myself laughing and joking with them, [after] they're beating up on this guy, I turned away from them. I wouldn't communicate with them. Sometimes I wouldn't even ask for salt. And the guys through the holes in the cells, used to pass me salt and so on, because they knew that I had a principle that I was not going to back down on.

[There's one detainee] an Arab. They hate him, the guards the Americans hate him. Because he organised. Say right if someone was in trouble, say not giving medicine to someone, cos they used to do that, if you were ill they wouldn't give you medicine until you drop out or there's blood, because then it's not counted as serious. So if you're in pain, it doesn't matter, be in pain. He would, if it was in his block, then say he would organise this: "Right, no-one's taking food," or "We're not going off to showers, no-one's going to go in interrogation," and everyone would just stand firm and say right, "We're not going until this guy gets seen to by a doctor," and we had to do that quite a few times as well.

That same guy [who] organised people said right every block's got to have like an Emir (that's a "leader" in Arabic) that people you know have a question whatever you ask. So they try to implement it but anyone who was elected Emir would get put in isolation. So they were trying, and then the thing is [that guy], he read the Geneva Convention in Arabic, and it said that you are allowed to do this, I think it was Red Cross someone said you are allowed a leader. But the Americans said, "There's no law here, it does not apply."

RUHEL AHMED: ... It's getting hot again here as summer is around the corner. Bros getting married which I cant belive and Im stuck in Fucking Cuba mind my French couse it bad ... Everytime I write a letter I can't think what to write. Suppose don't do anything here except the same thing day in day out. I myself don't know how long its going to be until come home but Inshallah soon.

TOM CLARK: Part of me is like, yeah, throw away the key, let 'em rot. Who gives a shit really? Part of me wants to say it's completely fine. But what I can't understand, and cannot live with, and I think is really really wrong is why have they been detained for so long. I mean what the hell have they been doing up there? You know they, the American Government, put ridiculous amounts of resources into this, they've got so much money to spend on the war against terror I mean surely, they could have them processed quicker? Surely, they could figure out which ones are dangerous, which ones aren't and at least if they decided they needed detaining in some way, to do it in the eyes of you know either their own people or an international court or something, at least illustrate what they're doing to these people. Because, although their initial reaction I think I'm I'm comfortable with, given the sort of, the extremes, I'm furious at the length of detention of these people, furious because those who are innocent have been, have lost three years of their life, much much like you know I lost ... I've been living in a sort of private hell since my sister was murdered and although at least I've been able to sort of recover and and get over it and and deal with, and still sort of have my life, they've had theirs taken away. And that's ... and they'll never get it back and I'd, I'd, I'd buy them a drink if I met them, you know, if if in truth they had done nothing wrong, I can't imagine a worse thing for any person.

(*Call to prayer*)

ACT THREE

MAJOR MORI: [I am currently a Defence Counsel at the Guantanamo Military Commissions. My client, an Australian, will be the defendant in one of the first of four cases against Guantanamo detainees for violating the law of war.] I was working as a Head Prosecutor for the Marines [when I got this job]. It was half a challenge, half just wanting to find out if it really was going to be like they were planning.

The US Court Martial system is an efficient and fair criminal justice system [that already has] jurisdiction to try Law of War violations and its rules and procedures specifically gear to battlefield type cases. [But] all of a sudden you see this step back in time to before the Geneva Convention came into play. [These military commissions are] doing away with all the safe guards and checks and balances in the justice system that are there to ensure that innocent people aren't convicted. I don't understand it. It seems very contrary to fundamental fairnesses. In my introduction to the military, and through my legal training, these are very basic protections that are needed in the justice system. You need to have an independent judge, you need an independent review process. The system cannot be controlled by people with a vested interest only in convictions.

The problem with this system [is] it's not a justice system, it's a political system.

MR STRAW'S AIDE: The Foreign Secretary Mr Straw will not be taking questions after this statement.

JACK STRAW: Good afternoon. I am going to make a statement concerning the nine British citizens detained at Guantanamo Bay.

In July 2003, two of the British detainees were designated by the United States authorities as eligible to stand trial by the United States Military Commissions.

The British Government has made it clear that it had some concerns about the Military Commission process. Consequently, the Prime Minister asked the British Attorney-General to discuss with the US authorities how the detainees, if prosecuted, could be assured of fair trials which met international standards. Our discussions are continuing.

In the meantime, we have agreed with the US authorities that five of the British detainees will return to the UK. They are:

Ruhel Ahmed

Tarek Dergoul

Jamal Al-Harith

Asif Iqbal

Shafiq Rasul . . . Thank you

GREG POWELL: So finally Jack Straw tells us that [my client] Ruhel Ahmed is going to be released but there is no date given. So what you have is journalists ringing me up saying it's going to be whenever. Tuesday and it's going to be at Northolt Airport, and they should arrive at 8 o'clock on a plane. Well it's news to me you know, because no-one tells the lawyers. It's all been leaked out to [the] press boys, who then ring the lawyers and tell you, and then you ring the family and tell them, then you ring the Liaison Police Officer and tell him and he says, "Well, I don't know about that," then he has to then ring somebody else and find out about it. At the airport Jamal Al-Harith, who has been jailed by the Taliban and then handed over to the Americans is released.

JAMAL AL-HARITH: If I am the worst of the worst, and obviously the scum of the earth, and people should fear me, of course. Why then have I been released? After two years in there, I mean they still didn't give me a reason for being in there.

GREG POWELL: The other four, which include the Tipton three, are taken off to Paddington Green to be interviewed by the anti-terrorist squad. When we arrive at the freezing cold Paddington Green Police Station foyer, [there are] thousands of policemen outside, and they've got press and they've got barriers up and created a one-way system round the police station, high security and all that.

It was maybe half ten by the time we had finished the booking in procedure. And all the police are going to do, they tell us, is take fingerprints and DNA and that's going to be it for the night. [But first] we have this farce over fingerprinting. We go into a little fingerprint room [with] quite a large officer, who is fat and tired, and obviously hasn't taken fingerprints for a long, long time. There are no live scan computers: they are going to do it on a Victorian ink block. So he gets out the ink block and inks it all up but the block doesn't quite fit on the little spindle. It's not quite stable and it rocks. And he's got lots of bits of paper, and he's going to put fingerprints on them. He is putting the right hand ones on [when he sees] he's [using] the left hand piece of paper. He start(s) again with the left hand piece of paper and he [sees] that he has done the right hand and it isn't quite right.

The [trick is to] take the finger and roll it in a certain way,

(GREG POWELL *now using his index figure to demonstrate*)

make a certain movement with it, [but] because he had not done it for a long time, he's not very good. He [can't get] clear images. So he gets another officer to help, then [one more] officer turns up to help him [with] a fingerprint case [and a] different roller. [And all] this takes over two hours to do. The officer is getting hot, he's beginning to sweat and knowing he's having to do it again, and he feels really uncomfortable because it is all humiliation for him: there's this high-tech, top of the tree, top class, anti-terrorist squad officer taking over two hours to fingerprint somebody. Not to mention the bits of paper, you can't imagine how many bits of paper there are in this room at this point. [My client] is trying his best to help. [He's] twisting his fingers, and doing his stuff, and the officer is getting ink on his shirt, and I say to them at one point, "I'm sure I've seen something like this on [children's TV]."

It was the biggest farce really, at the end of it can you imagine two and a half years in Guantanamo Bay, you arrive back in the country, you go to Paddington Green High Security Police Station and you end up you know at 1 A.M. with this pile of fingerprint paper and this officer up to his knees in Victorian ink. The next day all four which include my client Ruhel are released, so the three boys from Tipton can finally go home.

GARETH PEIRCE: One of them, the tallest of them, has problems with his joints, real problems, because of the space in which they had to exercise. And one of the young men had problems with his eyes, a particular dislocation of his eyes, which require contact lenses, they require them to stop something horrible happens to the eyes he hasn't had them for two years. Ultimately the eye breaks if it isn't held in.

GREG POWELL: Ruhel and I get into a plain police van, we drive out, put our heads down so no-one can see that we have left, and we go from Paddington Green Police Station to Harrow Road Police Station, and we sit in the car park there, and West Midlands Police arrive in their car, and they take Ruhel to a hotel in Oxfordshire and they arrange for his [dad and his brother] to meet him.

MR AHMED: [When I first go to meet my boy, Ruhel I thinking him like] a small little boy, no hair, no beard. Now he have very long beard up to there . . .

(*gestures down almost to his waist*)

I'd like to cry but can't. He look like people you know who walk around the streets. You know dumb people, I think, I do not cry.

But my heart filling, I see my boy after about two years, I want to hold him, I want to cry myself, but I can't do it. [If somebody] hitting you, you can cry, somebody beating you, you cry—but without reason you can't cry, but when I see him in this condition I, I, surprised . . . I did what to visit. I did like to see him. But how much think he's not like this?

He said give me telephone. I say to him, I give you mobile to you and he doing this.

(MR AHMED *holds up a make-believe mobile to show how his son held his face really close to the phone—illustrating how bad Ruhel's eyes are.*)

I say what are you doing? He say I can't see.

I don't know how my cry coming out. I don't want it coming out . . . This make me so upset so he is my son, he is a young boy and I am old man. I can see . . . he could not see anything. So I am crying myself. And he said, Dad, don't cry, it will be all right.

The next night . . . we go with his mother—we crying everybody . . . He don't cry. He say, Dad, don't worry I'm OK. He's got less feeling, less feeling than before.

GARETH PEIRCE: The [boys] are three young British lads who are like all our children—they're people who are very familiar, very easy to feel immediately comfortable with. And yet the story they tell is one of terrible stark medieval horror. It's like going back in time to something unimaginable from beginning to end of what they say, of being bodies in a container suffocating to death, waking up to find everyone around you dead, to being tortured in a prison in Afghanistan, being interrogated with a gun to your head, being transported like animals to a country you don't know where you are, and being treated like animals from start to finish for two years. I think perhaps we're very calloused. We read, we watch, we hear about atrocities—we know what man's inhumanity to man consists of, we know all that, but we don't sufficiently register it. We don't have the capacity to take it in and react in the way we should as human beings. But when you have [in front of you] in a kitchen men you're getting to know and they're talking about it, not because you're interrogating them, but it's tumbling out and they're reminding each other, they're telling things that they haven't told anyone. Maybe it's a testimony of every survivor from a concentration camp or a massacre or a . . . How do you tell it? How do ordinary words tell it? But yet they do if you are realising the people who are telling it to you are the people who've survived it. It's a complete ordinariness of where they are now, suddenly, from something so extraordinary. It's as if they've come from another planet.

[There's] two contradictions. [There's] Guantanamo where there is continuous interrogation for the purposes of making people talk. [And there's] the converse [in Britain] under internment [in Belmarsh] where 16 foreign nationals have been certificated by the Home Secretary since December 2001 as requiring to be detained indefinitely without trial [and] none of the[se] people have been asked a single question, they're simply locked up.

MAJOR MORI: We are two and a half years into these peoples' detentions [and finally] the Supreme Court has said they have to have the ability to challenge their status. All that has done [is] force the powers-that-be to go back to do what they should have done two and a half years ago. The issue for someone captured during an armed conflict is really what is their status under the Geneva Convention—either prisoner of war or a civilian. The combatant status review tribunals aren't going to make that decision. They're only going to determine whether they committed a hostile act or were supporting hostile forces. It's side stepping the whole main issue that should have been done upon their capture or quickly thereafter [which] was what is their status, are they prisoners of war or civilians? The next issue that gets into the federal court again could take two and a half years to work its way through . . . and obviously, my client he's locked up. And will be locked up as long as that process takes.

GREG POWELL: The lesson I take from Guantanamo Bay is that it is about social control and it extends beyond Guantanamo into ordinary crime. [There are] many features inside the British criminal justice system which allow government to exercise very powerful social control from different areas of criminal law. Take football hooligans—football hooliganism established the right to take away your passport, the right to make you report to the police station on certain days, and the right to ban you from travelling abroad and attending some certain social functions; anti-social Behaviour Orders aimed at children on estates establish a whole series of things; anti-social behaviour can be for life, it can be that you are not allowed to speak to a named list of people or associate with them, you are not allowed to meet in public with more than two or three people at a time, and you must stay out of a quarantined area, a geographical area. Releasing prisoners on licence introduces home detention curfews and tagging, so you must stay at a certain place between certain hours. And finally prisoners staying in Guantanamo Bay and Belmarsh without trial.

It does not take a genius to add these together [and] you slightly re-invent the world. All those features that I just described can be made applicable to you, so effectively you have this fantastic level of social control by some individuals inside the community. And having done it to terrorists . . . you can just extend it to the whole population of people who upset you because they commit crimes. So you can enter a whole new era of social control.

You can't start to think like this unless something like Guantanamo exists. In a way it is an experiment but it leads you on into a much more controlling social control criminal justice system.

MR BEGG: I have quite a lot of letters [from Moazzam]. [At first] he didn't mention anything about er his life there, he talked his normal. [Then] one day I wrote, [my heart is better now] I am absolutely all right, I go to the park, I walk, I do so many things which I could not do before and . . . er there is nothing wrong with me. After this we received a letter that [is always] on my mind. Because he wrote in reply to my letter, Dad, I'm pleased to know that you're well . . . and you can do so many things, but my situation is different. I've been treated like an animal. Most of the time I'm in chains and they throw me into cells or what do you call it . . . cages . . .

MOAZZAM: Dear Dad,

As Salaam Aleikum

I received your message and am glad to hear all is well with you and the family. It is nearing a complete year since I have been in custody and I believe . . . that there has been a gross violation of my human rights, particularly to that right of freedom and innocence until proven guilty. After all this time I still don't know what crime I am supposed to have committed for which not only I, but my wife and children should continually suffer for as a result. I am in a state of desperation and am beginning to lose the fight against depression and hopelessness. Whilst I do not at all complain about my personal treatments, conditions are such that I have not seen the sun, sky, moon etc. for nearly a year!

CENSORED

since it is the same three times a day, everyday—for all the time that I've been here! My situation here is unique in so many ways—for "good" and "bad" but mostly bad. I believe it is wrong for me to be kept like this and I have more than served enough time for whatever has been perceived about me, yet I still see no end in sight.

CENSORED

and passed to

CENSORED

I hate so much to place this burden upon you, and do as a last resort to alleviate this injustice. Please remember me in your prayers. Your son, Moazzam.

MR BEGG (*wiping tears away*): [I have another letter.]

MOAZZAM: Ass-alamu alaikum

MR BEGG: That means "peace be upon you."

MOAZZAM: Eid mubarak

MR BEGG: That means "congratulations for the festival . . . and Ramadan blessings."

MOAZZAM: "Dear dad, I hope and pray all is well with you and the family. I am in receipt of your Red Cross messages and I'm glad to hear that all is sound. I have written countless Red Cross messages and letters by US mail to you Azam, Zaynab, mum and even Shobu. I expect that after this 'bombardment'. . ."

MR BEGG: Letters he means . . .

MOAZZAM: "of news, I have 'inflicted' upon the authorities here, that some may found their way to you. My experience thus far however, has left me to believe that much of my mail to and from home has been deliberately constrained.

Including even, pictures of the family. I have yet to receive any of them father. I have not received any communication that was brought over by the visiting British delegation despite the fact that they informed me that they were handed over"

CENSORED

"salaam to all the family, Moazzam"

MR BEGG: This is the last letter I received.

He wrote it in 2003.

I received [it in March 2004].

GARETH PEIRCE: We know that Moazzam Begg is in solitary confinement, we know he's been in solitary confinement since he was designated as an enemy combatant last summer. We have very good reason to think he's been driven into mental illness from oblique and unattributable comments that have been made to us—not by [the British] Government, not by the American Government, but we believe that he is in a very bad way now and that's what this letter is saying. We believe he's in a very bad way.

CLIVE STAFFORD SMITH: He has confessed, apparently, Moazzam Begg, to being an al Qaeda agent who was going to take part in a plot to send an unmanned drone aircraft from somewhere in Suffolk to drop anthrax on the House of Commons. That's the confession, right. Now what do you think? You as the jury. Do you feel that that's a credible allegation? [I say] if you believe that, you believe in the tooth fairy . . . Number one, the only people who have drone aircraft in the world are the Americans, they cost $50 million each, they don't ever hit the target anyway and if you want to drop anthrax on someone, you just stick it in the damn air-conditioning system and the whole thing is ludicrous . . . Now you think about what happened to the Tipton lads and you see the incredible good fortune that they had, because they confessed to being at the Al-Farouq training camp—every single person I've come across so far has confessed to being in the Al-Farouq training camp, they must have had millions of people in it at one time—and they confessed to being there in 2000. The Americans got very excited they put them in a solitary cell and were getting all fixed to prosecute them for being vicious al Qaeda terrorists. Well fortunately, and purely by good fortune, MI5 checked the story for the US, [and they] proved that they really weren't in the Al-Farouq training camp, they were working in Currys [electrical store] in Birmingham at the time. So the reason those kids didn't get charged with that and they got let out of the whole solitary confinement, was that purely by fortune an alibi was proven.

GARETH PEIRCE: I would like to be wrong, but with the people we represent [in Belmarsh] we don't want to mislead them. [They] want to know, can I win my appeal? [They] want to know, is there any point to me participating in the process? They want to know, our case is going to the House of Lords, is there any hope? Will I see my wife and children again in the foreseeable future, or is this it? And one has to be truthful at the same time as wanting to give hope, it isn't right to give false hope and it's that growing feeling, knowledge, not just feeling, knowledge that you're not meant to get out of this and that you might be there forever.

MR BEGG: If my son has done anything wrong he should be brought back to this country. Let him see his wife, his children and us. Let him be normal. If he is [medically and physically] all right take him to court and let the court decide whether he is guilty or not. If he is guilty he should be punished. If he is not guilty he shouldn't be there for a second. This is a human rights issue, I'm not asking for mercy from any one, I'm asking justice.

MAJOR MORI: One of my fears is that they're not going to bring someone just to testify against my client they are going to bring some document written by some investigator of what Mr Smith told him, and they are going to use this document, and I'm never going to have the opportunity to cross [examine] Mr Smith all the fundamental protections of a fair trial have been removed.

I worry about [not being able to do my duty to my client properly]. There is no independent judge in this process.

I think September 11th was an event that you can understand that the government felt there were new steps and new challenges in protecting America. Yet with those new changes in our conduct we have to be ... ensure that we don't sacrifice our traditional values of fairness and due process that we've championed as Americans throughout the world. And that's all I've been asking for [my client]: fairness and due process.

LORD JUSTICE STEYN: At Guantanamo Bay arrangements for the trials are proceeding with great efficiency. A courtroom with an execution chamber nearby has apparently been constructed. But the British prisoners will not be liable to be executed. The Attorney-General has negotiated a separate agreement with the Pentagon on the treatment of British prisoners. He has apparently received a promise that the British prisoners of war will not face the death penalty. This gives a new dimension to the concept of "most favoured nation" treatment in international law. How could it be morally defensible to discriminate in this way between individual prisoners? It lifts the curtain a little on the arbitrariness of what is happening at Guantanamo Bay and in the corridors of power on both sides of the Atlantic [...]

The question is whether the quality of justice envisaged for the prisoners at Guantanamo Bay complies with minimum international standards for the conduct of fair trials. The answer can be given quite shortly: It is a resounding No [...]

Trials of the type contemplated by the United States government would be a stain on United States justice. The only thing that could be worse is simply to leave the prisoners in their black hole indefinitely ...

The type of justice meted out at Guantanamo Bay is likely to make martyrs of the prisoners in the moderate Muslim world with whom the West must work to ensure world peace and stability [...]

It may be appropriate to pose a question: ought our government to make plain publicly and unambiguously our condemnation of the utter lawlessness at Guantanamo Bay?

John Donne, who preached in the Chapel of Lincoln's Inn, gave the context of the question more than four centuries ago:

"No man is an Island, entire of it self; every man is a piece of the Continent, a part of the main; ... any man's death diminishes me, because I am involved in Mankind; And therefore never send to know for whom the bell tolls; it tolls for thee."

(*Call to prayer: Isha: sung from the stage*)

VOICEOVER: During the past three years, nine British citizens were imprisoned in Guantanamo. In January 2005, the remaining four, including Moazzam Begg, were released. Seven British residents including Bisher Al-Rawi and Jamil Al Banna are among around 540 prisoners still being held. Most are from countries with even less power than Britain to influence events. They're being held indefinitely.

AMERICAN TET

Lydia Stryk

ABOUT THE PLAYWRIGHT

Lydia Stryk is the author of over a dozen plays, including *Monte Carlo, The House of Lily, The Glamour House, American Tet,* and *An Accident.* Her work has been seen at festivals across the United States and in Europe and produced at, among others, Denver Center Theatre, Steppenwolf Theatre Company, Victory Gardens, The Contemporary American Theatre Festival, the Magic Theatre, and in Germany at Schauspiel Essen, Theaterhaus Stuttgart, and the English Theatre, Berlin. She is the recipient of a Berrilla Kerr Playwright Award and a member of PEN American Center. www.lydiastryk.com

PRODUCTION HISTORY

American Tet had its world premiere at The Contemporary American Theatre Festival in Shepherdstown, West Virginia, in July 2005. The European premiere took place at the English Theatre, Berlin, in November 2008.

American Tet is dedicated to the military families living through these times. And to my parents, Nell and Lucien Stryk, with great love.

CHARACTERS

Elaine Krombacher
Jim Krombacher
Nhu Mai
Amy Krombacher
Danny Krombacher
Dao, a little girl
Angela Gomez
A waiter

SETTING

The backyard and a separate garden area of the Krombacher family home. And a Chinese restaurant.

TIME

American Tet takes place in the spring of 2004, the first anniversary of the Iraq War—a moment in time in the ongoing conflagration.

AUTHOR'S NOTE

Read at your own risk. It's not a pretty play. But it's not a pretty world.

ACT ONE

SCENE 1

(*The bugle call, Reveille, is heard. Lights up on the Krombacher backyard. Two reclining deckchairs.* ELAINE *and* JIM KROMBACHER *are lying back in their chairs. The scene begins with an almost languid feel. They hardly look at each other.*)

ELAINE: Carmen's girl is in pretty bad shape. They're saying.
    She took the brunt of it. Face blown off.
JIM (*shaking his head*): Whoosh.
ELAINE: That's what they're saying.
JIM: Anyone seen her?
ELAINE: Carmen's flying over.
    Lost a leg.
JIM: Oh boy.
ELAINE: Pelvis shattered. And her arm.
JIM: Those'll heal.
ELAINE: But her face.
JIM: She's alive.
ELAINE: Who are you without your face?

(*A pause.*)

JIM: A damn pretty girl, Angela.
ELAINE: She was . . .
JIM: Sweet smile.
ELAINE: Carmen said god might strike her down, but she wishes Angie'd just died. She wishes she'd just gone up in smoke. Without ever knowing it. One moment you're all here. The next you're all gone. Carmen said that's what she wishes.
JIM: I guess.
ELAINE: Sal's kid went like that. Just last week, in fact. Stepping out of a tank. Next thing. He's a pile of ash. Burned into the sand. Like some snow angel.

(*A pause.*)

    You can't live without a face.
JIM: Skin and bone and all the other stuff that makes a face a face. You know what I'm saying? That stuff. They probably get from some corpse. Some

fresh blown-up girl. Some shot-up Iraqi. Someone who died with her face on her.

ELAINE: You can't just take someone's face.

JIM: The hell you can't.

ELAINE: She saved the others. By taking the brunt. They're okay. Burns, mostly. Bones broken.

I don't think we should tell Danny.

JIM: Why not?

ELAINE: They were close for a while.

JIM: He's seen a thing or two, by now.

ELAINE: Carmen was so proud of that girl.

JIM: That girl's a hero.

ELAINE: She's got no face, for god's sake.

(*Silent for a while.*)

Carmen spoke to the nurse. In Ramstein, Germany. Turns out she and Carmen went to high school together. They weren't close or anything. But they knew each other. Funny small world. She told Carmen she better get right over. Angie's in agony. They've got her completely sedated, of course. But she screams out anyway. The agony is in her mind.

JIM: This nurse told her that?

ELAINE: What should she have done? Jim? Lied?

JIM: She'll pull through. She's come this far. That girl is a survivor. She'll get a fake leg. They work like the real thing now practically. She'll learn to walk again.

ELAINE: She can see, thank god. She's got one eye. But she can't hear.

JIM: No?

ELAINE: They don't think so. But of course, she can't speak. Without a mouth, so . . .

JIM: It's just the shock. The boom. Her hearing'll come back.

ELAINE: Carmen asked me to water the plants. And feed the cat. I could bring her—

JIM: —The hell with that. That cat stays there.

ELAINE: I feel sick to my stomach, Jim. Danny—

JIM: He's all right. He'll be just fine.

ELAINE: I think we should make the party out here.

JIM: So we'll make it out here.

ELAINE: Three weeks is all we've got.

JIM: Elaine, don't start.

ELAINE: I'm not.

JIM: Three weeks is twenty-one days. Twenty-one days is all you get.

ELAINE: Your first leave . . .

JIM: I was horny . . . !

ELAINE: I didn't mind . . .

JIM: I'll say. Did we ever get out of bed?

ELAINE: But the second leave. You went crazy. You even hit me.

(*A pause.*)

JIM: Where's Amy?

ELAINE: In her room. Why?

JIM: Don't let me alone with that girl, you hear me?

ELAINE: Why not?

JIM: She's talking nonsense. She's talking rot.

(ELAINE *looks at* JIM, *studying him.*)

ELAINE: I don't know what drugs you were on. Over there in Vietnam.

(*She looks at him. She waits.*)

Or was it the weather, hon? Huh? The food?

(JIM *says nothing. And* ELAINE *is clearly used to this. She shrugs.*)

ELAINE (*forcefully, thoughtfully*): But when you came home, you weren't Jim. Where did he go?

JIM: MIA. Never came back.

ELAINE: No.

SCENE 2

(ELAINE *is addressing a small group. She has an overhead projector. She has obviously done this routine hundreds of times before, though she uses seeming-spontaneity to glorious effect. She is animated, demonstrative, and very dramatic—using all the resources of her voice, timing, and emotional range—and breathtakingly cheerful. She pauses in expectation of laughs with a comedian's timing. Despite all the above, she appears completely natural and there is real compassion behind her words.*)

ELAINE: Welcome to the Army Family.

(*She smiles, takes the group in.*)

And welcome to the Family Readiness Group. And finally welcome to your first AFTB class. The first acronym you're going to learn tonight! AFTB. (*As if leading a cheer*) *A*rmy! *F*amily! *T*eam! *B*uilding! A volunteer program designed especially for you. The new spouses of the military. I'm Elaine Krombacher and I'm your teacher. I have volunteered throughout my spouse's career and now he's retired—I'm still here! I can't stop giving back after all the Army has given me.

I'm going to jump right in here to tell you something you may not know. *You are all heroes.* Yes, you. "The hidden heroes at home," as one wife put it. No one knows better than you what it takes to keep this nation free. We families are at the forefront of our nation's defense and security.

And there are certainly some qualities you are going to come to know and appreciate in yourself as a military spouse.

(*She turns on the projector with a flourish and projects the following concepts as she refers to them.*)

Number one: A SENSE OF HUMOR

(*She laughs, then grows serious.*)

Two: NERVES OF STEEL
Three: INDEPENDENCE And not just on Independence Day—which I think must be just about my favorite holiday . . . how about you?
Number four: PATRIOTISM We sure do love our country . . .
Five: FAITH . . . and our God, almighty.
And finally, number six: A SENSE OF HUMOR

(*She gasps, pretending to note her error.*)

Did I say that already???

Now, I did an informal poll and came up with some spouses' views as to various aspects of the military life. What I like best is how the pros way outweigh the . . . *challenges* every time.

(*She places a two-column list on the projector. PROS and CONS of the Army Lifestyle:*
UNCERTAINTY VS. A SENSE OF ADVENTURE
LEAVING CHURCH AND FRIENDS BEHIND VS. MAKING SO MANY FRIENDS AROUND THE COUNTRY—AND THE WORLD!
YOU'RE ALONE WITH THE KIDS VS. THAT SENSE OF COMMUNITY

But let's start with those challenges, shall we? In the Army, it's a fact, you never know where you will be. We call that *uncertainty*. From one minute to the next. Your life can turn upside down. And it does and it will. But isn't that better than knowing how every day is going to begin and end for the rest of your life? (*In a stage whisper*) *We tend to think the civilian lifestyle is pretty darn boring.* (*Placing her finger to her lips in a pact of secrecy, then*) And if you look at it, philosophically. Who can ever be certain of anything? Especially in these times? We're just ahead of the game.

Leaving friends behind. It's hard. There is no friendship like an Army friendship, and there are so many kinds! It is just amazing what a war does to bring people together! And the next thing you know, you're saying good-bye.

Being alone. The minute he leaves, the car breaks down. The day *she* takes off, the kid gets sick . . . There's no one to go out for that romantic dinner with, to share the fun things the kids do and say with. No one to cuddle up to, to wipe away those tears. You may be giving birth to a baby alone. (*As if catching herself*) Did I say "maybe"? Very likely's more like it! (*She nods—decisively, reluctantly.*) And chances are, you're far away from home. But that is where your *military* family comes in! *We are everywhere.* And that's the beauty of the American Army Family.

Now, I haven't mentioned "the transfer" yet. I somehow skipped that subject, didn't I? That's the part of our lifestyle that no one has a good word for. But let me try! Moving every couple of years is a great way to get rid of stuff you don't need! Find things you never knew you lost! When you move, you're free of all those old commitments. And look at it this way, no one has seen your wardrobe! (*Pausing for laughter*) Seriously, though, moving gives you the chance to start again. And get it right this time. Be who you are today. Not who you were yesterday.

And here, I would like to share my personal story.

I have lived thirty-one years as an Army spouse. I'm the proud wife of Commander Sergeant Major James Krombacher, otherwise known as Jim—unless I'm mad at him. And the even prouder mother of Amy, in school, and currently working here on base. And boy, has she got stories! And then there's my son, Danny. Currently serving bravely on the ground in Iraq.

(*She stops.*)

Danny. Mom's thinking of you. You're in my prayers, honey. Stay safe. We're waiting for you. And it's not long now . . . ! . . .

(*Back to the group*) Jim and I were small-town sweethearts who married shortly before Jim was drafted for Vietnam. After his tour of duty, when I was looking forward to settling down and starting a family, Jim comes home one fine morning and announces that he's enlisted in the Army. And that he would be leaving—in *TWO DAYS' TIME*.

I quit my job, packed up the house, and *moved*—for the first of what would turn out to be seventeen times in thirty-one years. I have lived in the swamps. The cornfields. The mountains and the desert. I've lived in the old country and in the land of the rising sun. If you were to ask me where my home has been? Fort Polk, Knox, Ritchie, Lewis, Benning, Dix, Irwin, Carson . . . the list goes on and on. I would tell you. My home has been the United States Army. And if I had to choose? I would live my life all over again.

And so we landed here. And Jim is retired from active duty. Sits at a desk a couple times a week. But mostly, he is to be found in his garden. Morning, noon, and night. In every weather and at every hour. (*In a sing-song tone*) "Where's Jim?" . . . "In the garden!"

As for me. I will keep on giving back as long as I can. So now let's get to work!

(*She starts with the first projection of an acronym on the overhead projector—reading each out loud and commenting on it as she moves through them.*)

AD. After the death of our lord, it ain't. *Active Duty.*
DEROS. *Date of Estimated Return from Overseas.* You can see why we shortened that!
KIA. (*Annoyed*) Well, how did that get in here. We'll just leave that.
MRE. That's more like it. *Meals Ready to Eat.* The main reason they like to come home!
PDQ. *Pretty Darn Quick!*
TDY. This is where we will stop today. *Tour of Duty.* I want to prepare you for the TDY as best as I can. So that's where we'll start next time.

SCENE 3

(ELAINE *is sitting in a Chinese restaurant eating lunch. She is observing the Chinese scrolls around her and then focuses in on the scroll above her booth. She gestures to a waitress.*)

ELAINE: Excuse me?

(NHU *approaches the table.*)

NHU: Everything all right?
ELAINE: Oh, yes. Delicious. A special treat.
NHU: Special day?
ELAINE: ... Maybe!

(*A pause.* NHU *waits.*)

NHU: You wanted something?
ELAINE (*a little shyly*): Well, I was just wondering. What do the words on that
    pretty scroll say?

(ELAINE *points to the scroll.*)

NHU: That one?
ELAINE: Yeah.
NHU: You really want to know?
ELAINE: I think so ...!
NHU: It says, "Buddha says. 'Life is suffering.'"
ELAINE: Oh!
NHU: You know Buddha?
ELAINE: Oh, sure. Of course. Everybody knows him. He's the happy god.

(*A pause. She considers.*)

    (*Slowly*) If life is suffering, like the Buddha says. Why isn't he? Why is he
    so happy?
NHU: He's not happy. He's very peaceful.
ELAINE: Oh! Peaceful. Huh. Huh ...

(*She smiles and* NHU *smiles back.*)

ELAINE: I bet you miss China.
NHU: I'm not from China.
ELAINE: Oh, I'm sorry. I thought, Chinese restaurant ...
NHU: No problem.
ELAINE: Where *are* you from?
NHU: Uh, Vietnam.
ELAINE (*flustered, covering*): Oh. Uh-huh ...
NHU: I'm Nhu.
ELAINE: But I'm sure I've seen you here before.
NHU: No. My name. Nhu.

(ELAINE *and* NHU *laugh.*)

ELAINE: Oh, I'm so sorry. It's so lovely to meet you, *Nhu.* I'm Elaine.
NHU: Elaine. Nice name.
ELAINE: Thanks. I never liked it, particularly.
NHU: Names are very important.
ELAINE: Are they?
NHU: In my country. Names. They have very important meaning. My name. Nhu. Peace, in English.
ELAINE: That's beautiful. I've never met anyone named Peace before. Nhu.
NHU: Elaine.
ELAINE: I hope I'll see you here again.
NHU: Sure. You will.

SCENE 4

(AMY, ELAINE, *and* JIM *are lying on reclining deck chairs.*)

AMY: Dianna went right up to the Detailer's office, marched in, and demanded Jerome be given a new assignment.

(ELAINE *and* AMY *laugh.*)

AMY: No one says no to her.
JIM: That woman is a battleship.
ELAINE: What happened?
AMY: They reassigned him. As a recruiter. Louella saw him on Broadway in New York City. Forty-second Street. Looking like a movie star.
ELAINE: Well, good for him.
AMY: I guess. Dale Jones said he'd rather take a bullet in Iraq. Than keep his recruiting job. His head won't stop pounding. He's quitting the day his enlistment's up.
   Maureen got her chaplain to vouch for *her.* So Tyrone is coming home.
ELAINE: An emergency case of "missing your man."
AMY: He got his leave.
JIM: What illness did she fake?
AMY: She had a nervous breakdown, Dad.
JIM: What the hell . . . ?
AMY: She stopped functioning, for real.
   You can't fake that. I saw her. She stopped eating, dressing, going out.

JIM: She went on strike.

AMY: That's one way to put it.

　　If men did that.

JIM: Yeah, what then?

AMY: There'd be no more wars, Dad. There'd be peace.

JIM: *Peace? Peace?* Sometimes I think I can't really be hearing what my ears are telling me. Am I really the father of a military family? I'll be in the garden.

(*He is going off to the garden . . .*)

　　Peace . . . !

ELAINE (*waiting until he is gone*): Larry's boy blew up.

AMY: Shit, shit.

ELAINE: Guard duty. Protecting the oil. Gas explosion.

AMY: That's an irony.

　　Aaron Larson tried the gun in the mouth. Left him blind.

　　And Jake. Remember him? He wrote me. He said, the rope is hanging ready. It's only a matter of time.

　　You know Sherman?

ELAINE: Betty's son?

AMY: He chopped off his thumb.

ELAINE: He did *what?*

AMY: He did. He's coming home.

　　Mirna's been stuffing Andre like a turkey. He's already heavy. But she's hoping it will keep him away from active duty. On his desk job.

ELAINE: How could he eat more than he does already?

AMY: Well, she doubled his intake. He drinks those special weight gain shakes. For athletes. Bodybuilders.

ELAINE: He'll just get stronger.

AMY: Marine material.

(AMY *and* ELAINE *laugh.*)

AMY: Donny's turned gay, by the way.

ELAINE: Amy. Don't start with me.

AMY: No, really. He's been at the gay disco. Every night for weeks.

ELAINE: And how did you find out?

AMY: "Don't ask, don't tell." Official Army Policy. So Donny's telling everybody. Everyone he meets. Cashiers at the checkout counters. Old ladies on the street. All his friends on base, naturally, including me. He's *out.*

ELAINE: And all the girls?

AMY: He's telling them, too.

ELAINE: But that hasn't stopped him . . . ?

AMY: *No.*

(*They laugh, then grow serious.*)

AMY: No one wants to go.

SCENE 5

(*The Chinese restaurant. After hours.* ELAINE *and* NHU *sit together at a booth.*)

NHU: He was the son of mighty king. Rich, powerful. The whole works. That kid was spoiled rotten.

(ELAINE *and* NHU *laugh.*)

NHU: But he had a secret.

ELAINE: What was that?

NHU: There was a little voice inside him. Like child pulling on your skirt. "This life, it said, it's not for you. You gotta go. You gotta get out of this place," like the song says.

ELAINE (*singing*): "We gotta get out of this place, if it's the last thing we ever do . . ."

(*They laugh.*)

NHU: That's right. Yeah. (*Continuing*) The boy was very restless. Now his daddy wasn't stupid. He knew something was wrong. So he sits and thinks. That boy needs air, adventure, fire in his belly. That's all he needs. Yeah. So he gives him fastest horse in the kingdom and the boy rides off. But the kingdom was inside high wall, you know? So the new freedom of the boy was an illusion. Like all freedom.

ELAINE: Freedom is an illusion, Nhu? Hmm. That's not what they taught *us* in school.

NHU (*she takes this in, goes on*): So the boy rides off on the horse, and first thing he sees is a *very* old man. Now you gotta remember that this boy was protected from everything. Every reality of life. And now he's seeing old man for the first time. And he says to his servant, "What is wrong with that man?" And the servant has to tell him. "Master, he's just old. All of us end up like that." "What?" says the boy. "Like that? . . . What kind of world is this, that we all end up like that?"

ELAINE: I know exactly how he feels.

NHU: And he turns his horse around. And he rides—like the wind—back to the palace. And he locks himself in his room. He won't come out. But next morning, off he goes again. And this time, there's a young beggar with baby on her breast leaning against the palace wall. And the boy sees that she is so hungry she has become mad. How does he know this? That is a mystery.

ELAINE (*completely involved*): Huh . . .

NHU: The boy becomes sick to his stomach.

But the next morning, he is off again. And now, it is like he can't stop, you know? But then the horse stops. It won't move. Because there is dead young soldier lying in the road. His throat is slashed and his stomach is cut open and his guts are stuffed in his mouth. And his penis has been taken away as trophy. And his face has been eaten by worms and flies. He has no face left. "Who did this?" cries the boy. "Your father's army," says the servant. "We're at war." "War?" the boy asks. "We're always at war," the servant says. "But war is glorious!" the boy says. And the servant, he just shrug his shoulders.

(NHU *stops. She looks at* ELAINE, *who is visibly disturbed by this last section of the story. There is a pause.* ELAINE *seems to recover, smiles encouragingly at* NHU.)

ELAINE: Go on.

NHU: And the boy stops there. He doesn't turn back. He feels angry. He feels betrayed. New feelings that make him very tired. He gets off his horse. He has to rest. He sits against a tree. It's a fig tree. The Bo-Tree. And he stays there, and he doesn't move. He sits and sits and sits.

At first, he sees old man and beggar woman and soldier in front of his eyes. They won't go away. And then, they are *inside* him, you understand? Inside his body. *He* is old, and hungry. He feels terrible pain caused by soldier's torturers. He suffers. But he doesn't move. He sits.

He sits for seven weeks and by fifth week, he is no longer separate from the earth or the tree. He is the earth. He is the tree. He is his breath.

And by the seventh week, he is the Buddha.

ELAINE: Does he go home?

NHU: He never goes home. Home?! He never gets up! If he gets up, he will step on an insect or blade of grass. He sits.

So, that's why the Buddha is so peaceful.

ELAINE: Danny's coming home. From Iraq. On leave. It's only three weeks, but that's all you get. So, we're celebrating.

SCENE 6

(DANNY, *alone, in uniform. He stands at attention. He answers to an imaginary tribunal.*)

DANNY: Fort Leonard Wood Military Police School, class of 2002. Sir!

In March of 2003 I was assigned to the 372nd Military Company attached to the 320th MP Battalion of the 800th Military Police Brigade, sir. Mission: Iraqi Freedom. As a subordinate unit of the Coalition Forces Land Component Command, sir, our unit had command and control of theater-level EPW operations.

(*Short pause, as if answering.*)

Enemy Prisoners of War, sir. In strict accordance with the Geneva conventions.

(*Very short pause.*)

Sir, we were tested on these conventions in the classroom, but I couldn't offhand recite them for you.

At any given time, our brigade was responsible for 7,000 EPWs, sir.

After carrying out our mission with the cessation of major combat on the ground in May of 2003, sir, our unit was scheduled to return home. But instead of sending us home, sir, we were given a new mission. The management of the Iraqi Penal system . . .

At that time, sir, morale was very low. We were on our way home . . .

(*He shows his arm patch.*)

The unit patch of the 800th Military Police Brigade is an axe-head with a sword encased in an oak leaf. The axe-head denotes authority and security. The sword stands for duty, military strength, and law enforcement. The oak leaf symbolizes the trees at Fort Ord, California, where the unit was first activated, sir.

One day, I hope to visit Fort Ord and sit under one of those oak trees, sir. And if at all possible, I won't get up, sir, until I understand the meaning, sir. Of everything I have seen and done.

SCENE 7

(*The backyard.* ELAINE *and* JIM, *in their reclining deck chairs.*)

ELAINE: Darlene is flying home. With Kevin's coffin. She wants him buried in Arlington. With full military honors.

She says he's at peace now.

JIM: That word again.

(*A pause.*)

ELAINE: Do you think the world will ever be at peace, Jim?

JIM: No, I don't.

ELAINE: You'd be out of a job.

JIM: You'd have to get one.

(*A pause.*)

ELAINE: You know what's funny?

JIM: What is funny?

ELAINE: One of the new wives asked me, would I really do it over again.

JIM: And?

ELAINE: Someone always asks me that. So I wrote it into the lesson plan. I say, "And if I had to choose, I would do it all over again."

JIM: Well, would you?

ELAINE: I told her. I told her, I don't know. I told her I don't know.

(JIM *lets out a laugh. There is a long pause.*)

ELAINE: The home called.

JIM: And?

ELAINE: Dad's talking German again. Calling out the name of you-know-who.

JIM: Shit, shit.

ELAINE: *Sieg Heil.* The whole bit. Clicking his heels. The whole nine yards. You know what happened last time around. Right square in the middle of the food court. Thank god it was emptying out.

JIM: Can't take Dad to the mall. That's all. That's all there is to it.

ELAINE: The war set him off. The war on TV. He sees a soldier in a tank in Iraq. And then he's off.

JIM: Ernie is back in his memory. Back in his little town square. Reporting for duty.

(*He laughs.*)

ELAINE: I don't think it's funny.

JIM: He was just a soldier.

ELAINE: Following orders, right, Jim?

(*A pause.*)

Danny's almost here. He's almost home.

(*Another pause,* JIM *says nothing.*)

ELAINE: The housing on base is a shambles. Pipes backed up. Toilets stopped. The walls are like paper. Thank god, though. Jenny Flynn heard Tobias strangling Jane last night.

JIM: She heard him strangling her?

ELAINE: She was gasping for air.

(*She imitates gasping for air several times.*)

Thought it was sex, at first. But then she knew.

JIM: How's that?

ELAINE: A woman knows these things.

So, she banged on the wall. And she ran next door. And she banged on the door.

JIM: Did he open it?

ELAINE: Sure. Like nothing was wrong.

(*Pause.*)

It's always like that.

JIM: Like what?

ELAINE: Like nothing is wrong.

JIM: Is something wrong?

(*A pause.*)

ELAINE: No.

SCENE 8

(ELAINE *with her class. Overhead projector.* TDY *is projected in large letters and below it in somewhat smaller letters:* PREPARATION / DEPLOYMENT.)

ELAINE: An army marriage is a strong marriage. It better be! It's based on openness. And honesty. So before he takes off, take care of that "unfinished business." You won't regret it.

Because the golden rule of TDY remains: preparation for the storm. I refer you to your packet, page four: "Before He Deploys?"—*Get your wills in order.* Enough said. *Learn the basics of car maintenance!* You think we're kidding, don't you?

"What is Deployment, Anyway?" Same page. Anything that takes him—or her—away! And there will always be another deployment as long as your spouse is in the military. Most asked question: How do you survive those continued separations? Well, you've heard the saying, God provides. And God has angels everywhere.

(*She puts a new page up on the overheard projector. In big letters:* SEEK PROFESSIONAL HELP.)

You will feel stress. Seek professional help.

(*She puts the next page up, a list. She smiles widely at the group while giving them time to read it through:* STOMACH CRAMPS, HEAD ACHES, TROUBLE SLEEPING, NIGHTMARES, TROUBLE LAUGHING, IMPATIENCE, IRRITABILITY, CHEMICAL AND ALCOHOL ABUSE, ONE STEP AWAY FROM FALLING OVER THE EDGE.)

These are symptoms of TDY stress. They may be even worse when it comes to the kids. The stress of military life can hit them the hardest. Be prepared. Be patient. Do fun things!

(*New page:* WHILE THEY ARE GONE: *Do's and Don'ts for Deployment.*)

While they are gone. You've got some "do's and don'ts" in your readiness packets. Let's just take a look at a few.
Don't
... be negative.
Don't
... spend time alone with the opposite sex. (*She nods with a big, knowing smile.*)
Don't
... buy a new dining room set.
And *don't* overdose on CNN! *News is not healthy.*
Do
... learn new skills—become independent, for goodness sake!
... exercise!
... write poetry!
... volunteer! I'll be talking a lot more about *that* later ...

(*She turns off the projector.*)

Memorize this, now on page six: If it weren't for their mission, we wouldn't be free. If it weren't for your sacrifice, we wouldn't be America. Trust God with your spouse's safety. *There is no reason to worry.*

SCENE 9

(*The backyard.* AMY *and* ELAINE.)

AMY: She can't stop eating. She's okay 'til she starts. So she has breakfast for dinner. But it doesn't really help. 'Cause then she stays up all night. Eating. She's just exhausted all the time. Wendy's started drinking. Cheap port wine, mostly. Can't get out of bed sometimes. She calls in sick. And me . . .
     I'm just . . .
ELAINE: You're just what . . . ?
AMY: I'm just gonna hurt someone.
ELAINE: Amy?
AMY: It's like bombs are going off. Inside of me.
ELAINE: Honey.

(*A difficult pause.*)

I know this war on terror isn't easy.
AMY: Who's spreading the terror?
ELAINE: Amy.
AMY: Answer.
ELAINE: Well, we're fighting for peace and security. Over there. If that's what you mean.

(*Pause.*)

We brought freedom. To the Iraqis.

(*Pause.*)

And we'll keep spreading it everywhere. Everywhere. Everywhere necessary. Until we've won. And the war on terror is over. And there's peace.
AMY: What's gonna happen when it never comes? Then we bomb again? Just keep on? Bombing. Bombing. Bomb—
ELAINE: Shh! *Stop* . . . stop.
     It'll be okay. We just have to trust in what our leaders say. It'll be—
AMY: Trust *who*? When all we hear is lies?

ELAINE: Oh, honey.

(*A pause.*)

On a brighter note. We stopped those Taliban.

AMY: The Taliban have not gone away.

ELAINE: We certainly tried.

AMY: We funded them.

ELAINE: Should we have let the Afghanis fall to communism?

AMY: If it were my choice. I'd have taken communism.

ELAINE (*aghast, looking around to make sure no one has heard this, in a whisper*): *Communism?*

AMY: Yes, Mom. (*Shouting*) COMMUNISM!!! COMMUNISM ROCKS!!!

(ELAINE *gets up.*)

ELAINE: Amy, I don't think that's funny.
Your father put his life on the line to bring communism down. And he almost lost it. And he is not well now. And thousands died. But we won, thank god.

AMY: We were fighting the wrong enemy.

ELAINE: We'll never get it perfect, Amy.

(*Pause.*)

If your dad could hear you.

AMY: He doesn't listen to me, anyway. He thinks I'm crazy.

ELAINE: That's not true.

AMY: Don't lie to me.

ELAINE: Okay. He thinks you're crazy.

(*A pause. They laugh. The air seems to clear.*)

AMY: Communism was not the enemy is all I am trying to say. And terrorism isn't either.

ELAINE (*holding her chest*): Terrorism isn't the enemy either? Terrorism isn't—!
—the enemy. (*Slowly*) Okay. And who *is* the enemy, Amy?

AMY: The enemy's inside, Mom.

(ELAINE *looks toward the house, confused, dismayed.*)

AMY: Inside of *us.* (*Pointing her finger to her head, like a gun*) In here. The enemy's in our heads, Mom. It's ignorance.

ELAINE (*exasperated now, finally turning on her*): This is not a pretty world, missy. You have to stand for something. If they win. We lose. Is that what you want to happen? Do you want to live in their world?

(AMY *doesn't answer, she looks away.*)

ELAINE: Well, do you?

(AMY *does not respond.*)

ELAINE (*shouting the question*): *Do you???*
> This is my world, Amy. And I'm looking around it. And it's not so bad. This is *our* world.
> You couldn't say those things in China. You couldn't wear those clothes in Iran. You'd be covered in a veil with slits for eyes. You couldn't even drive. You do not know, little girl, how lucky you are, how lucky. To wake up in this land, free. You'd be married off by age six. You'd be locked in a dungeon with that mouth of yours. You'd never even see the inside of a school. But freedom isn't free. Someone's got to pay. This is not a pretty world. You've got to stand for something. I am so proud of my country. I'm so proud and grateful. I pray for it every day, and I know you think that's crazy. The tired and the poor from the world over, they want to get here. No matter what they say. Everyone wants to be an American. Everyone wants what we have. This is paradise, honey. These are sacred shores. You wake up free, little girl. Do you know what that means? These terrorists. They hate us because they hate freedom. If they win. We lose. Is that what you want to happen? Do you really want to live in their world?
> Do you, Amy?

AMY: It's one world, Mom. And it's going up in flames.

(*A pause.* ELAINE *looks at* AMY. *She seems to be about to answer. She sighs. She looks around the yard, studying it.*)

ELAINE: We're going to need a lot of balloons. And a big old "Welcome Home" sign . . .

(AMY *looks at her mother, she shakes her head. She gets up, slowly.*)

AMY: Danny's going to die.

(AMY *leaves.*)

ELAINE: A big old "Welcome Home" sign. Or paper cutout letters . . .

SCENE 10

(AMY, *alone. She imitates her mother's cheerful teaching style.*)

AMY: *How to Make a Revolutionary.* Lesson One. I refer you to your Readiness Packets, page two?

Silence her dissent, whatever else you do. This can be accomplished in a number of bloodless ways. It's simple! Don't listen to what she says. Ignore her. Dismiss her. Make sure that she is powerless to reach you by any normal means. Try blackmailing her emotionally! Above all, do not take her seriously. *Laugh at her!* This is *essential* for her revolutionary development. Meanwhile, show by your example that everything you say is hypocrisy and the cynical manipulation of the truth. Stir well. And let her simmer for a generation or so.

SCENE 11

(JIM *alone in his garden.*)

JIM: The thing about nature is. That nothing dies. Or death—being dead—just doesn't apply. Nothing dies. You can kill it. Starve it. Drown it. Torture it. But it comes back to life. Or forget life. It just comes back. It's there again. Forget then. It's here.

That's why gardening reminds me of war. Fighting a war. They're that close. Feeding, starving, nurturing, poisoning, raising, cutting down.

I would basically be considered a killer. If you would ask my daughter. A lifelong professional killer. For thirty years I got paid for organizing and implementing effective destruction of a given enemy.

And now I'm a gardener.

I've killed men, women, and children. In cold blood. From no further away than I am standing from you. I've scorched fields and defoliated forests. And I have all kinds of medals to prove it. Life is not a value I believe in personally. Life is in fact without value. It's just a force. Everything lives to live. That's all.

Last year, Elaine and I stopped moving. Finally. Neither of us comes from here. Neither of us likes it here, particularly. But neither of us could stomach ever moving again. I'm still young. But I'm sick. So I took a part-time desk job. The misty winds of Agent Orange have destroyed my lungs.

Elaine thought it would be good for me—therapeutic, she would say—to make myself a little garden. So I did. Here in the backyard next to the shed. I have my corpses lined up here. My seeds here. Sometimes when I am gardening I think of the past. Or my family. That crazy daughter of mine. Of Danny over in Iraq. But mostly, I tend to stop thinking. Which is why gardening is such good therapy.

You've got one bare hand in the cool wet soil. The other around the root of a tree. You lay it in there. Fill that hole up. The bed? The grave? Or you're pulling up a weed with strong, deep roots. And there's a moment, when it gives in, gives up, and then you have the whole damn thing in your hand, you can feel it trembling.

Is it alive in that moment, or dead? That's the mystery. And the fact is. I don't know if I'm alive or dead. This is my little secret. No one knows this.

The confusion of the gardener. And the soldier.

SCENE 12

(ELAINE *and* NHU. *The restaurant.*)

NHU: They drove very slowly. And then they stopped. At very busy intersection of the city. Right in the center of Ho Chi Minh—but at that time it was Saigon. The car was followed by more monks—and nuns. And then the car stopped and the monks inside got out. And the others made big circle on the street. And then, the monks from the car walked into the center.

It was very hot day. June 16th. 1963.

ELAINE: My god, was it that long ago.

NHU: June can be very, very hot in Saigon. And then, the monk, Thich Quang Duc, sat down. And another monk took can of gasoline and poured it over Quang Duc. Until his robe was soaked. He was glistening in the sun.

The monks and nuns were chanting. And you could hear sobbing of the nuns in between. And then, Thich Quang Duc took box of matches out of his robe.

ELAINE: I remember. Watching on the news. Thinking, how could anyone do that to themselves? And we were sitting there on the couch in front of the TV. Eating our TV dinners. Watching that man go up in flame and smoke. No one spoke.

How could anyone do a thing like that? Nhu? He must have been in such despair.

NHU: No, no. No, Elaine. He wasn't suffering. He was a cheerful guy! He had twinkle in his eye, they say. And an eye for the ladies. He did this to stop the *world* from suffering. You understand? He did this with a great strength. With hope, too. (*She shrugs.*) He had hope.

He was flames and whoosh! He was heavy black smoke. He never moved. Not a finger. He did not cry out. The look on his face, it never changed. His expression, they say, was like a stone Buddha. Full of peace.

And then his face was burned off and was gone. But his heart didn't burn. It's kept in Vietnam. In carved wooden box. Quang Duc's sacred heart.

He was seventy-three. An old man already. But there were more. And some of them were very young. And Buddhist nun. She burned herself to death.

ELAINE: A woman!

NHU: Yeah. That's right. She burned herself to death.

Quang Duc, the old monk. He was from Khanh Hoa province in central Vietnam. This is where my family comes from. He came from same village!

ELAINE: The same one!

NHU: The village was destroyed. Burned to the ground. And the forests and the fields. All the countryside. With that poison.

ELAINE: Agent Orange.

NHU: That's right. That's what the Americans called it.

ELAINE: Jim got sick from using that stuff. They called it the War of the Rainbow Herbicides. Agents Orange, blue, white. Purple, green, pink. Because of the color-coded stripes on the barrels.

NHU: First they flew over and destroyed the forests and the crops, "using that stuff," like you say. And then they came back with their bombs. My sister, little baby sister. She was playing outside. She was burned alive. And then they came for my father. Took him prisoner. He disappeared. And we fled.

(*A pause.*)

ELAINE: Nhu—

NHU: My sister's name was Dao.

ELAINE: Dao. How beautiful. What does it mean?

NHU: Dao means Peach Blossom. She was as sweet as peach. And my father used to pinch her bottom. And say, Little Dao, are your peaches ripe, yet? And she would laugh and laugh. She was always laughing . . .

I have no one here. No family. When you lose them, you have nothing. You don't want to live, you understand. You had me read to you, the saying on the wall, remember, "life is suffering." What are you gonna do? Here I can make money. And send it home. I serve Chinese food to people from military base. Some are so kind and gentle. Others, well. I have my favorites, that's for sure. The money I make here rebuilt my family's house. The house your Army burned down. I don't hate them. But now—

(*She catches a cry of pain.*)

ELAINE: Nhu—

NHU: It's okay. I'm sorry, Elaine. Only. Now. Again. War. Why can't they stop? It's only death and destruction. No winning. (*Tearful*) Killing. Destroying. What for, can you tell me?

(NHU *is sobbing now, quietly, but intensely. The following comes out of a breakdown of all learned decorum and control in* ELAINE—*from sudden, desperate emotion. It is painfully embarrassing to watch.*)

ELAINE: Nhu. What can I do, Nhu? Help me? Nhu. Help me, please. Help me. Help you. Forgive Jim. Forgive my country. For what they did to you . . . Forgive me . . .

NHU: I can't, Elaine. I can't forgive you . . .

ELAINE: Nhu. Nhu. Nhu. If you could hold me. Just hold me in your arms and tell me it will be all right.

NHU: I can't. I can't comfort you with lies. It's going on and on. Your people don't stop.

ELAINE: Nhu. Nhu. I'm sitting here in front of you. Let me fall onto my knees.

(ELAINE *is getting out of her chair.*)

NHU: Elaine, stop, sit down.

(ELAINE *is dropping to her knees.* NHU *catches her by the arms. She holds her up.*)

ELAINE (*repeating, over and over*): I'm sorry. I'm so sorry. I'm so sorry. I'm so sorry. I'm so sorry.

(NHU *shakes* ELAINE.)

NHU: Stop it!

(*The strength of* NHU'S *words startles and quiets* ELAINE. *She waits, fixed on* NHU. NHU *lifts her up and holding her at arm's length, studies her. She shakes her head. Then she gently brushes the hair from* ELAINE'S *eyes.*)

NHU: I cook for your son's party.

SCENE 13

(ELAINE *and* JIM *in the backyard.*)

ELAINE: Carmen called. The first operation was a success. The reconstructive surgery. Of course, it's just a start. But they made her a really nice pair of lips, she says. And nostrils. Cartilage is what they use for that.

JIM: And the lips? What are they made of?

ELAINE: I think they're made of flesh.

JIM: You think? You think? You didn't ask?

ELAINE: The lips are made of flesh and blood. Okay? Jim? It's skin. That's all.

JIM: They're made from your ass. I happen to know this.

ELAINE (*ignoring him*): But getting the jaw right. That's the tricky part . . . When Daryl broke Lisa's. After he came home—

JIM: It's a hinge, for Christ's sake. Any carpenter could get that right.

ELAINE (*stopping, taking him in*): The face. It's like a house, Jim, that's true. You've got your eyes. They're the windows. And the mouth. That would be the door, wouldn't it?

Amy made a good point, Jim. For so many years, it was fun. Life in the Army. I mean after Vietnam. Germany, now *that* was the life of Reilly.

JIM: The beer was excellent.

ELAINE: But this new war'll go on and on. The war on terror. For generations, I think. What could possibly end it, Jim, huh? A nuclear holocaust maybe. A meteor strike? I really don't mean to sound gloomy. "Someone's got to do it." That's what I'm telling them now. I just want to have us all home . . .

Carmen's flying back with Angela. Just in time for Danny's leave. She's sitting up.

JIM: I knew she'd pull through.

ELAINE: But . . .

JIM: But, what?

ELAINE: Carmen said. She wanted to warn us. Prepare us.

JIM: For what?

ELAINE: She's wearing a veil. Over her face. Like a woman under the Taliban. Carmen says it's awful. She doesn't know what they're going to do.

The surgeons make a lot of promises.

JIM: Can she hear?

ELAINE: She can hear.

JIM: Told you so.

ELAINE: She can hear and she can see. She can hear gasps and see the shock on people's faces.

She wants to see Danny.

SCENE 14

(DANNY, *alone, in uniform. He stands at attention, answering the imaginary tribunal.*)

DANNY: Explain it, sir? The first thing you have to understand is that this is someone who wants you dead, sir. This is a terrorist. A terrorist is not human, sir. They don't deserve to be called human, sir. Or to be treated as such. Your heart gets filled with hate.

(*Short pause, as if answering.*)

Hate is a kind of white heat, sir. It is burning hot and ice cold at the same time. Burning and frozen. That's what hate is like, if I had to describe it.

One thing I learned early on, sir, was never to look them in the eye. Never. And best of all is not to look at their face. Faces can be deceiving, sir. So we blindfold them and put hoods on them. To cover those faces. Then you're in no danger, sir, of looking into their eyes.

So then it's just a body, sir. It's flesh. Like a corpse that's still alive. I had no problem, sir, in kicking a terrorist until he stops. He has to be made to stop. He has to be made to obey. To listen up. To do what I say.

It's funny what a body can take. Take the penis, sir. Or the balls. Take a simple finger, sir. For that matter. Or toes. You strip a body of clothes. Clothes conceal weapons. You don't know what they are hiding. Bodies are weapons. You strip them down. You search inside. Deep inside them, sir. Because you don't know what they are hiding.

(*Short pause, as if answering.*)

That's our job, sir. To find what they are hiding. Make them talk. Sometimes the secrets have to be pulled out from the deepest places. This can be tricky. Because you never draw blood, if you can help it. Blood is messy and has to be cleaned. And it leaves traces.

When a man is hanging from his feet, sir. Everything rushes down and out. Which is convenient. But the screams are too loud. So you stuff a rag in the mouth. The hands are tied behind the back. It doesn't take them long to choke to death. So you have to watch out. It's a fine art. Sir, not to let them die. Because that's what they want. A lot of the time. Just to die and get it over with.

(*Answering*) If it were me, sir? . . . Sir, if I thought like that. I couldn't do my job. I'm paid to do my job. I didn't start this war, sir.

SCENE 15

(JIM *in his garden.*)

JIM: When I can't listen to another word, and that tense thing happens like a flash in my forehead, in my shoulder blade. Then I come out here into my garden. I look around at my trees, bushes. My flower beds. Ask of each: Are you thirsty? Strong? Do you need a little trim? Are you growing? By how much? Are you blooming? Ripe yet?

Who else can you ask questions like that?

What have you grown to surprise me? New leaves? A fruit? A new branch? You amaze me, snow tree. With your fists of white blossoms. So delicate, the slightest wind sends you floating down. I love you for your strength, little daisies. Your tree-like roots and sunny faces. I am so proud of you, Tomato Joe. I took you for dead but you sure fooled me. Sprang back into action.

To the garden with my troubles! To the garden!

I can't wait to show Danny. I'm going to teach him so he knows. All the knowledge of the world's right here.

This is my fuchsia bush, this is my plum tree. Here are the zucchini, squash, and yellow beans. These are the marigolds, pansies, lilies. My lavender and primrose. And these are my roses. Amber Queen, Fragrant Cloud, Pretty Polly. Isn't she beautiful?

And this is the compost. Everything lands here. Everything.

(*Saluting*) 2,4-D and 2,4,5-T. Agent Orange reporting for duty. Change the structure. Alter nature. Yes, sir. On the double. And then fill the lungs of that sergeant major. So that he remembers you later. Dioxin in the lungs and in the liver.

(*As if giving military orders*) There are three P's of gardening. Planning, preparing soil, and planting. Your garden should be well planned in advance. Nothing can replace sunshine and a fine mesh fence. To keep out dogs, chipmunks, and cats. Especially cats. A mole, on the other hand, must be trapped. For the voles you dig a trench. One foot deep. Run your rows east/west. Tallest crops on the north end. Plant stakes. Build pathways. Be vigilant against all insect pests. Destroy them.

There will be a next spring. An American spring is like no other in the world.

SCENE 16

(ELAINE *with her class. On the overhead: THE RETURN.*)

ELAINE: Finally. *The Return.* Page nine. You will have pictured it in your mind. A thousand times. But do yourself a favor. Be prepared. *Expect the unexpected. Every time.* (*Mock-gravely*) It is never going to be what you thought it would be. (*Impishly*) But it just might be better!

SCENE 17

(AMY *and* DANNY. DANNY *is in uniform.*)

DANNY: I've got six more months. Then I'll enlist for real. Make a career like Dad did. I'm not college material. You're the egghead.

(*A pause.*)

Someone's gotta do it, right?
AMY: Why?
DANNY: Why, what?
AMY: Why has someone gotta do it?

(*He thinks awhile.*)

DANNY: I don't get what you mean.

(*Pause.*)

I'm a soldier.
AMY: Do you want to go back there, Danny?

(DANNY *shrugs.*)

AMY: Answer.

DANNY: Do I want to? Want . . . ?

(*He shakes his head, at first as if he is trying to free himself from the confusion of the question. And then the shaking becomes a no. And finally he speaks as if articulating a thought he never knew he could entertain.*)

When I go back there.

AMY: What?

DANNY: Something bad is going to happen.

AMY (*slowly*): That's very possible.

DANNY: Like it's hell. It's like what they told us hell was in Sunday school, remember? Like being dropped down into a pit of fire. It's like you joined the Devil and he gets inside you. I never had one good, proud day over there. I swear to God, Amy, when I get back there, I will stand in front of a gun and help them pull the trigger.

(AMY *gets up and goes to* DANNY. *She strokes his head, his arms. He begins to tremble under such gentleness.*)

AMY: What happened, Danny?

(*He shakes his head. He can't answer.*)

AMY: What happened over there?

(*Again, he can't respond. He turns away.*)

AMY (*something dawning on her*): *What did you do?*

(*He looks at her, says nothing, shakes his head. He begins to sob. She holds him until he stills.*)

AMY: You don't have to go back.

(*A pause.*)

DANNY: I don't?

AMY: No one has to go back.

ACT TWO

SCENE 1

(DANNY'S *Home on Leave party. Lawn chairs, balloons, a table for the food, a grill,* WELCOME HOME DANNY *is spelled out in colored paper letters on the washing line.* DANNY *and* AMY *are preoccupied with barbecuing.* JIM *is sitting with* ELAINE *when* NHU *arrives, carrying a pile of covered pans.*)

ELAINE (*getting up and going to her*): Nhu! You made it. I'm so glad.
NHU (*smiling, taking them all in*): Yeah. I made it, Elaine.
ELAINE: So much, Nhu. You shouldn't have.

(*She relieves* NHU *of some of the pans.*)

   Jim!

(JIM *comes over.*)

ELAINE: Nhu, this is Jim, my husband. Jim, this is Nhu.
JIM: I've heard a lot about you. All good. So glad you could make it. It's a special day for us.
NHU: Yes, I know.
ELAINE: Nhu's brought us special treats from Vietnam. I just wanted her to come. And relax and celebrate with us. But she insisted.
JIM: That's terrific.

(ELAINE *helps* NHU *place the pans on the table and is preoccupied with this as* NHU *moves away.*)

NHU: Enjoy it. I wish you wonderful party.

(*She appears to be leaving.*)

ELAINE AND JIM: Nhu!
JIM: Nhu. You're not going, are you? Please don't go! You just got here. Please stay and eat with us. Celebrate.

(JIM *begins to speak to* NHU *in Vietnamese. She is taken aback. He is clearly asking her to stay.*)

JIM: *Toi raf han hanh va vui mung neu Nhu, o lai choi.*
NHU (*answering him*): *Cam on.*

So sorry. I really can't stay. (*To* ELAINE) Elaine. I only wanted to bring—

ELAINE: Oh, Nhu, no—

(DANNY *comes over, wiping his hands on his barbecue apron.*)

DANNY: All *right*! Who's ready for barbecue?

ELAINE: Honey, this is Nhu. Nhu. This is Danny.

DANNY: Great to meet you, Nhu.

NHU: Welcome home. Danny.

DANNY: Thank you. It sure feels good to be here. So, can I get you that burger?

NHU (*she looks from one to the other and gives in*): Okay, thank you . . .

DANNY: Medium rare?

(NHU *nods, yes.*)

DANNY: And well done for you, Mom?

ELAINE: That's right, hon. Burn it.

JIM: And I'll get the beer. Excuse me, ladies.

(DANNY *returns to the grill.* JIM *goes into the house.*)

NHU: He's handsome boy, Danny.

ELAINE: He is.

(*They laugh, watch him.*)

ELAINE: We're pretty proud of him. Let me introduce you to my daughter.

(ELAINE *calls for* AMY *who has gone inside the house.* AMY *comes out.*)

ELAINE: Amy. Nhu's here.

AMY: Hi. It's so good to meet you, finally.

NHU: You, too, thank you.

ELAINE (*taking the covers off the food and gasping*): Nhu. This is just amazing. Amy, look at this. (*Calling out*) Danny! You have to see this. Get over here. This is so beautiful.

(DANNY *joins them. They stand around the table.*)

NHU: In Vietnam, the New Year is also start of springtime. We celebrate with big party. Big New Year party called *Tet*. We say, *An Tet*. This means *to eat* the *Tet*. To eat the New Year, you understand? Eating is very important.

Yeah. We come together. For special meal. All the family. The family come home from everywhere. And the ancestors, too. We welcome them back. All the dead come back to visit.

> *Tet Nguyen Dan. Tet.*

ALL (*repeating*): *Tet.*

NHU: Good. Very good!

(*They laugh.*)

NHU: And so, I thought, today is first day of spring here. In America. So I prepare a few little specialties . . . These special dishes, yeah. For *Tet.*

ALL (*repeating again*): *Tet.*

NHU: Just a few special dishes. Yeah. For Tet.

AMY: They look too beautiful to eat.

NHU: In my country. It must look beautiful. You don't eat it if it is not beautiful.

AMY: Uh oh, Danny. You better work on those burgers . . .

(*They all laugh.*)

DANNY: Yes, sir, sister.

(*He salutes and goes back to the grill.*)

NHU: It's spring. Danny is home. So, you celebrate. *American Tet.*

ELAINE: *American Tet.* I like that.

AMY: My god, these fruits. They are gorgeous.

NHU (*pointing*): This. *Dao.* Peach, in English.

AMY AND ELAINE (*repeating*): *Dao.* (ELAINE *acknowledging* NHU*'s sister as she says "Dao."*)

NHU: This. *Mai.* Apricot.

AMY AND ELAINE (*repeating*): *Mai.*

(NHU *nods, impressed, laughs, then moves on to another dish.*)

NHU: This. *Banh Chung.*

AMY AND ELAINE (*repeating*): *Banh Chung.* (*Amid laughter at their efforts.*)

NHU: Yeah. Very popular. Special dish for New Year. Very nutritious. Green leaves, sticky rice, and pork. Green peas and pepper. Very healthy.

ELAINE: The smell is to die for.

NHU: Good for everything. Blood. Liver. And the stomach. Heart. Brain. Good for brain!

(*They all laugh.*)

NHU: And this. *Banh Tet.* Rice cake. Yeah. From Hue, imperial city of Vietnam.

(*From* ELAINE *and* AMY, *expressions like "wow," "huh!"*)

NHU: And here. My favorite. Ginger. Ginger grows on the hills. Around Hue. Ginger is very healthy. Long life.
AMY: Let's make sure Danny gets some of that.
ELAINE: Don't joke around, hon.
AMY: You know what's funny. The war started a year ago today. On the eve of spring.
ELAINE: Is it okay if we don't mention that today? Amy? In front of your brother? Or Jim? Okay?
AMY: Okay, Mom. Whatever you say.

(DANNY *comes over with a plate of burgers.*)

DANNY: Let's rock 'n' roll! Where's Dad?

(*They sit down to eat together during the following.*)

ELAINE: Getting the beer.
AMY: What's taking him so long?
ELAINE: If I had to bet, I'd say he stopped off in his garden.

(*Repeating their little joke, mock-calling:*)

    Where's Jim?
AMY AND DANNY (*sing-song answer*): In the garden!

(*Lights up on* JIM *in his garden. The others carry on laughing, serving each other from the dishes, talking. The following dialogue goes on quietly under the scene in the garden with* JIM.)

ELAINE: Sit down, Nhu. We're serving you, for a change.
NHU: Oh, nice. Okay. It's nice to be served.
AMY: For a change, right?
DANNY: One medium rare, one burned to the crisp, one Amy burger.
AMY: And what is that, pray tell?
DANNY: Lettuce on a bun.

(*They all laugh.*)

NHU: You vegetarian?

AMY: Vegan, actually.

NHU: Oh. So sorry.

AMY: No, my god, why should you be?!

ELAINE: This is all so delicious.

AMY: This, what is this called again?

NHU: *Banh Tet.*

(AMY *repeats "Banh Tet."*)

AMY: Oh, my god, is this good!

DANNY: This is *really* good. I'm hiding those burgers.

NHU: No. No. They are excellent.

DANNY: And beautiful, too, right?

(*They all laugh.*)

ELAINE: And this, which was this, Nhu?

(NHU *repeats the names of the dishes, and they try to say the names again. . . Meanwhile, in the garden, a little Vietnamese girl appears behind the thick fuchsia bush. We might only see her head and upper body. Or perhaps she comes skipping by and ends up behind the bush. In any case, she startles* JIM.)

JIM: Hey! Little girl . . . ? Hey. Where did you come from? Out of nowhere like that. Who are you? Are you Nhu's daughter? I didn't see you come in. You scared me.

(*She looks frightened.* JIM *notes this, mimes being scared to ease her fear.*)

JIM (*pointing from her to him*): You. Scared me. I'm scared.

(*His antics make her laugh a little. She observes him the way a child does an adult who is clowning—with a certain curiosity and withholding of judgment.*)

JIM: Nhu? You come with Nhu?

(*She nods, yes, and begins to cry.*)

JIM: Hey, hey, don't cry. She's here. I'll fetch her. What's your name? (*Pointing at himself*) Jim. (*Pointing at her*) And you?

LITTLE GIRL: Da'o.

JIM: Da'o. Now that is a very pretty name. Da'o, you come with me, okay? We'll go find Nhu.

(*He holds out his hand, but she shakes her head, refusing to come with him or to move from the safety of her position.*)

JIM: Okay. Tell you what. I'll go get her for you okay. I go. For Nhu. Bring her here. Okay? A deal? You wait here.

    Xin doi mot lat.

(*She seems to take this in.* JIM *turns away and then turns back, but she is gone. She has disappeared. He comes back, looks behind the bush, looks around the garden, starts off, turns back. Lights back up on the group and their conversation which now increases to full volume.*)

DANNY: Do the ancestors really come back from the dead, Nhu?
NHU: Yeah. They do.
DANNY: You see them?
NHU: Sometimes. We talk to them. We discuss memories. We tell stories about them. Funny stories. Sad. We do have many memories . . .

(JIM *approaches them.*)

ELAINE: Well, here he is!
AMY: You're in for a treat, Dad.
DANNY: Is something wrong, Dad? You look like you just saw a ghost or something? Hey maybe he did! It's Tet!

(*Laughter, from everyone except* NHU *who seems to sense something is wrong.*)

JIM: I'm okay. I'm fine. I'm hungry.

(*Chatter and laughter from the others.* NHU *rises. She and* JIM *look at each other.*)

SCENE 2

(DANNY *and* ANGELA. ANGELA *is in a wheelchair. Her lower body is covered by a blanket. She wears a veil underneath a baseball cap, so that her face is covered. She is crying.* DANNY *sits facing her. His head is bowed. This excruciating crying goes on for some time. Finally she quiets.*)

DANNY: I would have taken that bomb for you.
ANGELA: I know.
DANNY: You're a fucking hero, though.
ANGELA: Yeah, they gave me some medals.

(*She lets out one long, extended moan of pain which begins quietly and then builds in intensity and volume until it is unbearably loud and disturbing. This unbroken sound of existential grief and physical agony should last a very long time.*)

DANNY: What's wrong? Can I do something?

ANGELA: No, man.

DANNY: Can I get you something?

ANGELA: Yeah, a new face.

DANNY: Angie.

ANGELA: A new body, man. A new life.

(*A pause.*)

You gotta go back there, man?

DANNY: Yeah. Three weeks.

ANGELA: I guess that makes me the lucky one. Hey . . .

DANNY: Yeah?

ANGELA: Don't tell anybody, okay? About me?

DANNY: They all know, Angie. They're all rooting for you, man.

ANGELA: I can't stay here anyway. They want to send me back for more surgery.
On what used to be my face. Man . . . ?

DANNY: What?

ANGELA: If I asked

DANNY: What?

ANGELA: If I asked you

DANNY: What? What, Angie?

ANGELA: To do something for me?

DANNY: Anything.

ANGELA: Anything? You swear it?

DANNY: I swear it.

ANGELA: Get me a gun, Danny.

DANNY: Shit.

ANGELA: You swore it.

DANNY: Shit, shit.

ANGELA: Loaded, man.

SCENE 3

(AMY, JIM, *and* ELAINE *in the backyard.*)

AMY: He doesn't want to go back.

JIM: You can't not go back.
AMY: He's not going back.
JIM: Where is he?
AMY: And he doesn't want to talk. He's not talking.

(*A pause.*)

JIM: He'll go back.

(*He gets up.*)

You did this. You put this in his head. You and your commie psycho homo
friends. You and those terrorist scum of the earth . . .

(JIM *leaves them.* ELAINE *puts her hand on* AMY's *arm. They sit for some time.*)

AMY: He's not going back.
ELAINE: Your dad—
AMY: Fuck him. *Fuck him.*
ELAINE: Amy. Please . . . (*with difficulty*) . . . Did he say why? . . . Did Danny
say, why?
AMY: He won't say. He won't talk.
ELAINE: It's only six months more . . .
AMY: "*Only* six"?

(*She covers her face with her hands.*)

You can't mean the things you say.
ELAINE: He'll sit in prison.
AMY: We'll get a lawyer.
ELAINE: Your father. He'll never—
AMY: What do *you* think, Mom? *You.* Not him.
ELAINE: He'll kill him first.

(*A pause. She gives in.*)

Where are we going to find this lawyer?

(AMY *takes this in with wonderment.* ELAINE *shrugs.*)

ELAINE: It's the end of his career, just like that.
AMY: It's the end of his life, if he goes back. That's what he said.
ELAINE: Amy. Don't—
AMY: He'll apply to become a conscientious objector.
ELAINE: *My* son . . . !

AMY: We're the army, Mom. Nothing can change that. He's going to ask for an honorable discharge. Based on a diagnosis of psychological distress. And if it fails—

ELAINE: Then, what?

AMY (*with despair*): He'll go AWOL. He'll hide out. He'll turn himself in. Or he'll go back.

ELAINE: NO.

(AMY *looks at her mother with astonishment. There is a long moment of recognition.*)

ELAINE (*turning away, to something that has obviously been preoccupying her*): Imagine, Amy. The first person to burn themselves to death to protest the war in Vietnam in this country was a woman.

AMY (*taken aback, eyeing her mother*): I didn't know that, Mom.

ELAINE: She was eighty-two years old. This was in Detroit. In March of '65.

AMY: Wow.

ELAINE: It's amazing what you learn when you do a little research.

She was a Quaker. A pacifist.

(*A pause.*)

I always thought that pacifists were cowards . . .

There were others. Norman Morrison. And Roger LaPorte. He was twenty-two years old. Set himself on fire in front of the U.N. One week after Morrison did the same outside the Pentagon. LaPorte was a Catholic kid. They managed to put the fire out on him. By beating the flames. And in the ambulance to the hospital, he was conscious. And he explained why he had done this. He said "I'm against all wars." Ninety-five percent of his body was covered in burns.

AMY: Mom—

ELAINE: No. Let me finish.

At the hospital, the psychiatrists asked him if he wanted to live. Guess what he said?

AMY: I don't know.

ELAINE: *Guess.*

(AMY *shrugs and looks away, pained.*)

ELAINE: He said, "Yes." He said, "Yes," and then he slipped into a coma and he died.

AMY (*quietly*): Where's Dad gone?

ELAINE: Oh, I expect he's in his garden.

AMY: It's getting real pretty.

ELAINE: He cares for it like it's his little baby.

AMY: Well, it's not like when we were growing up. He's got nothing but time on his hands.

ELAINE: And blood.

AMY: Did you say, blood, Mom?

ELAINE: Did I say that?

AMY: Yes. You sure did.

ELAINE: I meant dirt, Amy. Dirt and memories.

SCENE 4

(ELAINE *stands before her class. The overhead projector is on with a heading that reads* CUSTOMS AND COURTESIES OF MILITARY LIFE.)

ELAINE: Every morning of Army Life starts with the custom of Reveille. This is when the American Flag at your installation is raised—usually at six A.M. While the bugle call, Reveille, is played. I know you all know that tune.

(*She toots a few bars, miming a bugle.*)

But I should leave that to the bugle, shouldn't I? Now if you are crazy enough to be up at six A.M. and you are in a moving car, you must stop. If you are outside, you must stand silently, facing the direction of the flag.

And if you have a sense of direction like me, this may give you some problems.

(*She spins around like a top, merrily, dizzily, recovers. Then she grows serious.*)

But seriously, the flag is why we fight and die.

(*She pauses for effect, but something else about these words is giving her pause as well. She goes on.*)

And finally today, page twenty in your packets, please. I'm going to talk to you about celebrating community and what that means as a military family. I am talking about *volunteering*. And if I do nothing else, I hope I can convince you to join me. (*Stage whispering, as she always does at this point in her lesson*) I'll bet you didn't know this. 'Cause it's a well-kept secret. But it's a fact . . . The military depends on us volunteers to keep the programs running. If we all stayed home and put our feet up, well the Army would just fall apart!—

(*She stops herself. She is realizing the meaning of what she has been saying for the first time in her life.*)

The military would cease to be . . . without our often unrecognized support. And then where would we be . . . ?

Well, we wouldn't be fighting this damn war, that's for sure!—

(*She catches herself.*)

I didn't just say that.

(*She smiles widely, trying to regroup.*)

Volunteering . . . Volunteering . . . The life blood of our community. Take—*Unit Coffees*! Volunteer to host one! Pick a theme and get creative!

(*She places a new sheet on the projector with the words,* UNIT COFFEES. *The list begins in her normal tone but becomes increasingly manic.*)

You might try an "international" theme with potluck from everyone's country of origin. Or how about a tacky coffee? Where everyone comes dressed up real silly? Arts and crafts? Go home with something! Sock-puppet parties are a favorite of mine. You bring the socks, I've got the buttons! Yarn for lips . . .—

(*The image of* ANGELA*'s blown-off face stops her, she puts her hand over her mouth, she seems unable to go on, but then she does—relentlessly, now.*)

Or how about a cupcake decorating party with— . . . ???
Chocolate chips— . . . !!

(*She stops. She can't go on. She tries again.*)

Chocolate chips. Sugar flowers. Sprinkles. Sprinkles. Sprinkles. Sprinkles . . .

(*She covers her face with her hands and lets out a sob.*)

I'm sorry.

SCENE 5

(ELAINE *sits in her regular booth at the Chinese restaurant. A* WAITER *comes up from behind. A comedy of miscommunication ensues.*)

WAITER: You ready to order?
ELAINE: I'll wait for Nhu, thanks.

WAITER: She not here.

ELAINE (*looking around, surprised*): Not here yet?

WAITER: No. Not here.

ELAINE: She's coming in late?

WAITER: No, not late.

ELAINE: She's not coming in?

WAITER: No. Not coming.

ELAINE: Is she sick?

WAITER: No. No. Not sick.

ELAINE: She took the day off?

WAITER: No. No day off. No.

ELAINE: Well, if she's not sick and hasn't taken the day off, can you tell me where she is, please?

WAITER: She left.

ELAINE: She what? You mean, she went home early?

WAITER: No. She not here anymore.

ELAINE (*slowly*): She's not working here anymore?

WAITER: That's right. Yeah, she left.

ELAINE (*holding off shock*): Where is she? I have to find her. She's a friend of mine.

WAITER: You don't find her.

ELAINE: Why? Where did she go?

WAITER: Home.

ELAINE: Home . . . (*incredulous*) To Vietnam?

WAITER (*jubilant that she finally understands*): Yeah. Right. To Vietnam. She left.

ELAINE (*with a sense of dread*): Do you know when she'll be back? Something must have happened. In the family. To her mother, grandmother. Did she say when she'll be back?

WAITER: Not coming back.

ELAINE: Not coming back . . .

WAITER: She moved. Apartment empty. She gone home to Vietnam. Forever. No coming back.

(ELAINE *is in a panic and trying to figure out what to do.*)

WAITER: You want to order?

(*Someone from the kitchen calls the* WAITER.)

WAITER: Excuse me, one minute.

(*He goes off, talks to the others, then comes back with a little box. He hands the box to* ELAINE.)

WAITER: You Elaine, right?

(ELAINE *nods.*)

WAITER: She left this for you.

(ELAINE *takes the tiny box from the* WAITER.)

WAITER: You need some time?

(ELAINE *nods.*)

WAITER: You call me when you ready to order, okay?

(ELAINE *nods.*)

WAITER: I come back when you are ready.

(*She nods.*)

WAITER: You just call me.

(*She gives him a pleading look. He nods, lifts his hand in an understanding gesture. But he wants to say something.*)

WAITER: Sorry, for you.

(ELAINE *acknowledges his gesture as best she can. He seems to be going, but doesn't.* ELAINE *turns her attention to the box. She studies it like a lifeline. She opens it. Inside there is a small ivory Buddha. She holds it in her hands. She places it on the booth in front of her.*)

WAITER (*unable to resist*): The Buddha.
ELAINE (*quietly*): Yeah.
WAITER (*impressed*): You know the Buddha?

(ELAINE *looks at him.*)

ELAINE: Maybe.

(*She looks back to the Buddha.*)

ELAINE: Maybe.

(*Lights fade on the scene, leaving a light on the Buddha, which if possible, casts a huge shadow.*)

SCENE 6

(ANGELA *and* DANNY *together. They have been drinking.*)

ANGELA: Man, would you give your life to save the world?

DANNY: No one can save this fucking world.

ANGELA: I know, man. But if you could. Let's say, God calls down to earth, right?

DANNY: Yeah, right.

ANGELA: Hear me out. God calls down and points at you and says, "I need you and you"—like fucking Uncle Sam—"I need you and you and then I'll save the world . . ."

That's how they did it in the old days. They would choose someone. Drain their fucking blood. And drink it.

DANNY: Shit.

(*They laugh.*)

ANGELA: No shit, man. And the person was still alive. And then they would burn them. And that would be the sign, you know, that God was waiting for. And then the world was saved.

DANNY: To save the world, man. Shit.

(*She lets out a terrible extended moan of pain which lasts an unbearably long time, as in the first scene.* DANNY *bows his head. She quiets.*)

ANGELA: If only it meant something, man. If only life meant something. Like that. Like you could save the world.

(*She pulls away, wheels her wheelchair back from* DANNY *so there is a space between them. She takes off her cap and removes the veil from her face.* DANNY *looks away in horror, instinctively.*)

ANGELA: No, look.

(*A pause. He looks. They look at each other for a long time.*)

ANGELA: It's waking up that's the worst.

You promised me something.

(*He shakes his head. A long pause, and then he goes to her and hands her something wrapped in a bag.*)

ANGELA: Now go on, man. Get out of here. And thanks, man.

(*He doesn't go. He kneels down in front of her chair. He kisses her on the mouth—very gently, yet there is something deeply passionate between them. She looks at him, steadily.*)

ANGELA: Go on. Go save the world.

(DANNY *gets up. He takes her in. But* ANGELA *has lain back in her chair, smiling with relief, and closed her eyes. He leaves. Lights go down and up.* ANGELA *is somewhere else with* DANNY. *She is no longer disfigured, or injured—is in fact, the healthy boyish young woman she was before the war. She is exuberant, vibrant.* DANNY, *too, is relaxed and free. This is* ANGELA's *dream.*)

ANGELA: This is such an awesome dream I don't want to ever wake up. Have you heard that stuff about people blowing up?
DANNY: Yeah. Do you believe it?
ANGELA: It's hard to believe, right?
DANNY: I don't believe it.
ANGELA: Propaganda put out by the other side.
DANNY: That's right. That's what I think.
ANGELA: Nothing bad, nothing bad, can ever happen to us, Danny. We made it, man. It is all over. That war, it is over. Mission accomplished.

(*They slap hands.*)

ANGELA: What are you going to do, now, man? With the rest of your life?
DANNY (*shrugging*): Party.
ANGELA: Party is right.

(*Lights fade on* DANNY. *Deeply sensual party music with a Middle-Eastern feel comes up, and* ANGELA *begins to dance ecstatically with her whole body and being for some time. The lights fade and then come up on* ANGELA, *alone, in the present, in her wheelchair. A pause. She handles the package* DANNY *has given her, and with an effort which takes her breath away and through which she is crying, she begins to open it.*)

SCENE 7

(DANNY *is alone on a reclining chair in the backyard. He appears to have awoken from the same dream. He stares straight ahead.* ELAINE *comes out to join him. They sit in silence for some time.*)

DANNY: This is the life.
ELAINE: That's right, Danny. It sure is.
DANNY: Peaceful.
ELAINE: Mmm.

(*She looks at him. He looks anything but peaceful.*)

ELAINE: Are you all right?

(DANNY *is shaking.*)

ELAINE: Are you cold?

(*He is shivering, but he shakes his head, no.*)

ELAINE: You *are* cold. Let me get you a—
DANNY: —*NO!*

(*A pause.*)

DANNY: Cold and hot.
ELAINE: Do you have a fever?

(*She reaches over to touch his forehead; he stops her brutally.*)

DANNY: *DON'T* . . . touch me! . . . Stop . . .
ELAINE: Okay, okay. I'm not. It's okay.
    Spring is funny that way. The body . . . needs time to adjust.
    (*A pause, carefully*) We found a lawyer, Danny. He's willing to help. To
    write up your appeal. You only have to sit down with him. Tell him what
    you've seen, where you've been. Why you just refuse. You refuse. (*As much
    to herself as to him*) You can't. You can't go back. You're hardly more than a
    boy. You hadn't thought this through. You're military. You're a good Ameri-
    can. You believe in all the things this country stands for and has always
    been. But now, after careful examination, you find yourself. You find your
    conscience, that's the word you'll want to use—

(DANNY *gets up abruptly.*)

ELAINE: Where're you going?
DANNY (*turning to her, sharply*): I'm going (*he struggles*) to the garden.

(*He leaves* ELAINE *alone.*)

SCENE 8

(DANNY *and* JIM *in the garden.*)

JIM: The earth was heaving. Heaving. Up and down. And then it stopped. And they dug him out. Unconscious. Poured water on him until he came to. Choking up earth. But still he wouldn't talk.

DANNY: And then?

JIM: They buried him again. And they pulled him out again. Unconscious. Came to. Wouldn't talk.

DANNY: Then, what?

JIM: Same thing. They buried him. The earth rose and fell. Stopped. They dug him out.

DANNY: He wouldn't talk?

JIM: They dug a deeper hole. And they showed it to him. That's what I heard.

DANNY: Did he talk?

JIM: Not a word. They sat him in that hole. Chained up. Naked. No water. No food.

DANNY: He wouldn't talk?

JIM (*he shakes his head*): No. And then they buried him alive. I got there six weeks later. (*Pause*) We were force-marched through the jungle to get there.

This is not something I ever told your mother.

She says, "When you got home. You weren't Jim. Whatever happened to him?"

DANNY: What did, Dad?

JIM: I wanted to show you the garden, Danny.

Before you go back.

(DANNY *turns away. He turns back.*)

DANNY: What happened to you?

JIM: You didn't live if you didn't talk. No one survived, who didn't talk.

They buried me.

They pulled me out.

I told them what they wanted to hear. I wrote it down.

DANNY: They did bad things to you. You had no choice.

JIM (*shaking his head*): There's always a choice.

DANNY: You were a hero.

JIM: They paid for it later. Someone always pays.

I'll teach you to garden, Danny.

When you get back.

(*A pause.*)

DANNY: Can I ask you something?

JIM: Shoot.

DANNY: Did they blindfold you?

JIM: What kind of a question is that? Of course, they did. Fucking cowards.

DANNY: Did they cover your head?

JIM: They used rice sacks. Why?

(DANNY *shrugs.* JIM *looks at him.*)

DANNY: Just wondering.

SCENE 9

(*The bugle call, Taps, is heard. Lights up on* JIM *and* ELAINE *in the backyard.*)

ELAINE: The home called, Jim. Dad's all right. But he won't take his coat off. Even at night. It's the middle of spring. That's not healthy.

JIM: He's on the Russian Front.

ELAINE: He's what?

JIM: Ernie's on the Russian Front, readying for battle. The battle that will only end with his death.

ELAINE: And us, Jim. You and me.

When will our battle end? The same way? (*A pause.*) I think they should be buried together. Angela. And Danny.

And maybe I will jump in the grave with them and have the earth cover me, too.

(JIM *looks at her. He gets up.*)

ELAINE: Where are you going? Don't leave.

All your life you've been leaving. Leaving me.

Stay. Talk to me.

(*A pause. He sits back down.*)

JIM: So what shall we talk about, Elaine? The fact that I sent him back there.

ELAINE: You didn't send him back. Maybe you wished it. But that's not why he went.

JIM: Why did he go, then?

ELAINE: I don't think he knew. Why.

(*A pause.*)

JIM: It's Danny's garden.

ELAINE: What, hon?

JIM: It's not mine. It's Danny's. I stopped gardening. I'm letting nature wage its own war. Fend the others off. Attack. Destroy. Gain ground. I'm letting the creatures come. Tore down the mesh wire. Let them land, gorge, plunder. And the plants and bushes and trees and flowers, they're reaching up against each other. Stems, leaves, branches, vines twisting their way up toward the sun. Every damn one. Surging up. Like some church spire, some temple. Some holy fuckin' shrine.

(*A long pause.*)

Where's Amy?

ELAINE (*surprised, cautious*): She's inside. In her room. Why? Should I get her?

JIM: (*He nods, then speaks.*) Yeah. Ask her to come out here.

(ELAINE *goes into the house.* JIM *waits. He seems nervous. Like he is preparing himself to talk to* AMY *in some new way. After some time,* ELAINE *comes out, alone.*)

ELAINE: That's funny. She's not in her room.

(*She joins him again, sitting.*)

ELAINE: She'll be home soon.

(*There is a pause. Lights up on* AMY *somewhere else.*)

AMY: I'm leaving home. Without a suitcase. Without a gun. I'm going somewhere. Far. Beyond my backyard, what is known. It's scary. This journey. But I'm not scared.

It's like I've sawed off the top of my head. The scared part. The part that holds it all in. And at the same time. It's like my heart has reached up like a hand and grabbed my mind. And suddenly, my mind is so light and so clear. Being held by my heart.

I'm going somewhere. Without a map. But I know the direction.

And if I don't find it. Well, I've got a can of gasoline. And some matches.

(*Lights out on* AMY.)

ELAINE: Let's just sit. Let's just sit here. Let's not go. Anywhere. Let's not get up. Ever. Let's just sit here, together. Nhu said, life is suffering. On the other hand, there will be another spring. Let's sit. And maybe. Eventually. The pain . . . will go away. We'll figure it out. We'll know what to do.

(*Lights to black. Silence. Then the sound of fire burning is heard and grows progressively louder.*)

THE VERTICAL HOUR

David Hare

We need, in love, to practice only this: letting each other go.
For holding on comes easily; we do not need to learn it.
  —Rainer Maria Rilke

ABOUT THE PLAYWRIGHT

David Hare was born in Sussex in 1947. Sixteen of his plays have been produced at the National Theatre, including a trilogy about the Church, the Law, and the Labour Party—*Racing Demon, Murmuring Judges,* and *The Absence of War*—which played in repertory in the Olivier Theatre in 1993. Ten of his best-known plays, including *Plenty, The Secret Rapture, Skylight, The Blue Room, Amy's View, The Judas Kiss, Via Dolorosa*—in which he performed—and *The Vertical Hour* have also been presented on Broadway. His most recent screenplays are for the films of *The Hours* and *The Reader.*

PRODUCTION HISTORY

The Vertical Hour had its world premiere at the Music Box Theater, New York City, on 30th November 2006. Julianne Moore played Nadia Blye, Bill Nighy played Oliver Lucas, and Andrew Scott played Philip Lucas. The production was directed by Sam Mendes. The British premiere was at the Royal Court Theatre in London on 17th January 2008. Indira Varma played Nadia Blye, Anton Lesser played Oliver Lucas, and Tom Riley played Philip Lucas. The production was directed by Jeremy Herrin.

CHARACTERS

Oliver Lucas
Nadia Blye
Dennis Dutton
Philip Lucas
Terri Scholes

ACT ONE

1.

(OLIVER LUCAS, *alone. He is English, undemonstrative, casually dressed, in his late fifties.*)

OLIVER: I'd known for a long time I was going to have an accident. That's how it felt. The effort of concentration becomes impossible. For so many years you haven't made a mistake. Then you make one. It feels inevitable. You signal right, intending to go left. And you pay the price.

2.

(NADIA BLYE *is sitting at the desk in her office. She is American, pale, poised in her mid-thirties, her style casual. Opposite her is* DENNIS DUTTON, *in his early twenties, also American. He is unusually dressed for someone of his age, in suit and tie, with floppy hair and trainers.*)

NADIA: This is not a bad essay.
DUTTON: Thank you.
NADIA: It's not bad.

(DUTTON *waits.*)

This is our last class together. Clearly, I haven't persuaded you to my view of politics.
DUTTON: I know your view.
NADIA: It's competing claims, isn't it? If I had to sum it up.
DUTTON: That's your view.
NADIA: That's right. People want different things. The things they want can't be reconciled. Not everyone can *have* what they want. So the mediation between the groups, between the interest groups, the groups who want different things, to that process we give the name "politics."

(NADIA *waits, but there's no reply.*)

Ultimately, you could say, politics is about the reconciliation of the irreconcilable.
DUTTON: I don't see it that way.

NADIA: No.

DUTTON: For me, politics is about the protection of property and of liberty.

NADIA: Yes, that's what you seem to be saying in this essay.

DUTTON: It *is* what I'm saying. It's about peoples' rights to live their own lives. It's about absolutes.

(NADIA *thinks, considering how to go about this.*)

NADIA: Yes. Yes, but there's a problem, isn't there?

DUTTON: Is there?

NADIA: We know for a fact that human life by its nature tends towards unfairness.

DUTTON: Do we know that?

NADIA: So: checks and balances have to be introduced. By human agency. The state, in any system yet proposed by man—be it communism, be it capitalism—has to intervene to balance things out.

DUTTON: I don't accept the term.

NADIA: What term?

DUTTON: "Capitalism."

(NADIA *frowns.*)

NADIA: You don't accept the term?

DUTTON: No.

NADIA: You don't accept it?

DUTTON: No.

NADIA: Meaning? Meaning what?

DUTTON: I don't think there's any such thing.

NADIA: No such thing as capitalism?

DUTTON: Correct.

NADIA: So what name do you give it then? The system we live under today? The system we call "consumer capitalism," "liberal democracy"—characterised by political parties and—I don't know—huge corporations, massively powerful industrial and military interests? The system as evolved by the West, by Western democracies? What do you call it?

DUTTON: Life. I call it "life."

(NADIA *nods slightly.*)

NADIA: No offence, but do you think Political Studies was a good choice of subject for you?

DUTTON: My father wanted me to do it.

NADIA: He's important to you?

DUTTON: Very much so. I admire him more than anyone in the world.

(NADIA *looks a moment, thoughtful.*)

NADIA: It's just . . . how do I put this? . . . basic to Political Studies is the notion of comparison.

DUTTON: Sure.

NADIA: We compare.

DUTTON: Sure.

NADIA: That's what we do. We say, "Here's one way at looking at things, now here's another."

DUTTON: So?

NADIA: Well, such comparison becomes difficult if we start out with the idea that there's only one system—there's only one way.

DUTTON: But there is.

NADIA: Is there?

DUTTON: I know it's inconvenient to ask, but why do you think America has triumphed?

(NADIA *is slightly thrown.*)

NADIA: Inconvenient? Is "inconvenient" the word for America's triumph? And I'm not sure I'm going to go with "triumph" either.

DUTTON: Why not? Why not "triumph"?

NADIA: Listen. Listen. This is a school. It's not a madrasa. We're not teaching one path. We're teaching many paths. You say you admire liberal democracy. Well, basic to liberal democracy is the idea of free discussion. The free exchange of ideas. *Comparison.*

DUTTON: You telling me I'm wrong to love America?

NADIA: I'm not.

DUTTON: I'm wrong to love my country?

NADIA: No. I'm not telling you any such thing. I'm telling you not to be blinded by love, that's all. Not to be made stupid by love.

DUTTON: Stupid?

(NADIA, *embarrassed, picks up his essay and walks to the other side of the room.* DUTTON *is seen to pluck up courage.*)

The fact is—I haven't wanted to say—I've come here to say this today—it's you I'm in love with.

NADIA: It's me?

DUTTON: I don't eat. I don't sleep. Ever since we met. Ever since—you must have noticed.

NADIA: What, that—

DUTTON: I've lost weight alarmingly. Have you noticed?

NADIA: I haven't.

DUTTON: I'm sick. I went to a barbecue on the weekend. The smell repelled me.

(NADIA *is lost for a response.*)

I think of you all the time. I find the idea of you incredibly exciting. Of who you are.

NADIA: Who I am? Say. If you imagine . . . For goodness' sake. Let's be serious! Tell me. Who am I?

DUTTON: This woman out there in the world.

NADIA: What woman?

DUTTON: On television.

(DUTTON *immediately holds up a hand.*)

All right, that was a foolish thing to say.

NADIA: A tad.

DUTTON: It's not what I meant . . .

NADIA: You have feelings for me because I've been on television?

DUTTON: A woman in the world. That's what I mean. A woman in the world.

(*After the shock,* NADIA *is now angry.*)

NADIA: Dennis, Dennis, I have to tell you there are now quite a lot of women in the world. As you put it. Quite a lot. In fact, the whole assumption dismays me. How old are you?

DUTTON: Twenty-two.

NADIA: I'm a feminist and what you're saying dismays me.

DUTTON: Why?

NADIA: Because the purpose of women taking part, the purpose of women being intelligent or public or in any way *represented* even, the purpose of women talking on television about international politics is not to turn men on!

(*There is a silence.* DUTTON *is very quiet.*)

DUTTON: You didn't know? You had no idea?

NADIA: I'm going to ignore what you said. I'm going to forget it.

(*There is a brief silence.*)

DUTTON: Can I say something?

NADIA: If it's about politics, yes.

DUTTON: It's all nonsense, isn't it?

NADIA: I don't know what's nonsense. You tell me.

DUTTON: The study of international relations.

NADIA: In what way is it nonsense, Dennis?

DUTTON: I took this course—as you know I'm a business major, my interest is start-up—but my father wanted me to broaden my mind. I don't know why. Dad's own mind is about as narrow as it's possible to be.

NADIA: Narrow, how?

DUTTON: He wants wealth. He wants power. He wants position. That's all he wants.

NADIA: Well?

(DUTTON *sits forward.*)

DUTTON: This is my point: America wins. It always wins. You can do all that historical perspective stuff, you can say it's an empire and like any empire it's going to fall. But not yet it isn't. Not in my lifetime. So. Say there's a runner—the runner wins the race—then the other runners, if they're at all intelligent, they ask, "How did he do that?" They look at the winner, they look at his methods, they analyze, they say, "OK." And that's the way other countries are going to prosper. They'll prosper by imitating America. And to me that's Political Studies. "What does America do? And how can anyone else get close?"

NADIA: Well I'm glad my year of teaching hasn't been entirely wasted.

DUTTON: It hasn't been wasted.

NADIA: Good.

DUTTON: In fact . . .

NADIA: Dennis . . .

DUTTON: That's what I wanted to say. I didn't want you to think I took this course—well, for any other reason but in order to learn. The last thing I want is to upset you.

NADIA: Thank you.

DUTTON: You're a brilliant teacher.

(NADIA *looks wary, fearing what comes next.*)

However, we can't—face it—the other thing happened to me.

NADIA: Dennis . . .

DUTTON: It happened. I can't pretend it didn't. I fell in love. In fact, the other day, I might as well tell you, I was talking things over with my fiancée . . .

NADIA: I'm sorry? Your fiancée? *I'm sorry?*

(NADIA *throws up her hands, exasperated.*)

DUTTON: Look, just so you understand . . .

NADIA: I don't have to understand. In fact, I don't want to understand.

(*Now it is* DUTTON'*s turn to get up, agitated.*)

DUTTON: It's not—it's hard—listen! *listen!*—I don't know if you don't—if you know Maine—anyway, two big families. In our part of the state. Big families. Both—whatever. And for many years, it's been assumed, if you like. Everyone takes it for granted. I will end up with Val. Understand.

NADIA: I just said: I don't want to understand.

DUTTON: But just so you know. So you know the context. Let me say, Val is not just my fiancée, she's also a friend. Val is my best friend.

NADIA: And Val has no problem juggling these two roles?

DUTTON: Val—talking to Val is like talking to someone—someone objective. And it was Val who said, she said, "Look, Dennis, you're suffering. You have been suffering. For a long time. For your own sake, you must speak to her." It was she who suggested it. Not me.

(NADIA *looks at* DUTTON, *trying to work him out. Then she goes and sits on the far side of the room, as if defeated.*)

I wouldn't be saying this. I wouldn't be saying it if it were up to me.

(*There is a silence. When* NADIA *answers she is hesitant.*)

What are you thinking?

NADIA: I suppose one imagines—I imagine—the world moves forward. Slowly, the world moves forward. My assumption has always been that society would progress. I work on that assumption. Old attitudes die out. But what can you say? They don't. They don't.

DUTTON: I'm not sure I understand you.

NADIA: As you know, I spend a lot of time in war zones—in Bosnia, in Serbia. In many ways I can only say I prefer it there. I prefer being there because here people—

(NADIA *changes tack, not finishing her thought.*)

Put it another way: I am so far from regarding myself as somebody available to a twenty-two-year-old as not to recognize myself in the description.

DUTTON: But that's good, isn't it? Isn't that a good thing?

(*There is a silence.*)

NADIA: This has been a profoundly depressing few minutes.

(DUTTON *looks at her a moment.*)

DUTTON: I hear you.

NADIA: Good.

DUTTON: But nothing you say convinces me. As it happens, before I took politics, I took psychology . . .

NADIA: Oh Christ!

DUTTON: Briefly. Freud.

NADIA: How many weeks? How many weeks did you study Freud?

DUTTON: Three. Intensely.

NADIA: Sure.

DUTTON: Actually you can understand quite a lot in three weeks.

NADIA: You can also misunderstand quite a lot in three weeks.

DUTTON: Do you know this?

NADIA: Try me.

DUTTON: Freud has a theory that we aren't who we claim to be.

NADIA: Really?

DUTTON: Freud says we're all somebody else. Underneath. Underneath.

NADIA: I would have thought that was self-evident. I would have thought that was obvious.

DUTTON: Maybe it is obvious, but have you considered what it means?

NADIA: Clearly, you're going to tell me I haven't.

(DUTTON *leans forward, intent.*)

DUTTON: Think: The real person—the person concealed—is quite different, has quite different feelings from the person on the surface.

NADIA: Well, it's a highly convenient theory. But that's all it is. A theory.

DUTTON: So what I'm getting at is this: you don't convince me. And something tells me—my own instincts tell me—that underneath you don't even convince yourself.

(NADIA *tries not to be angry.*)

I think this has happened before. I'm not the first student, am I? I know. I know you won't tell me. But I'm guessing it happens all the time. I don't see how it can't. It must. And yet for some reason you pretend it doesn't.

(NADIA *just looks at him.*)

I've got a feeling that's part of your attraction.

(*This is the last straw for* NADIA. *She goes to open the door for him to leave.*)

NADIA: That's it. That's the end of the course. Here is your essay.
DUTTON: Is that it? Are we finished?
NADIA: We're finished.
DUTTON: Thank you very much.
NADIA: No. Thank *you.*

(NADIA *has given him the essay at the door, and now they have shaken hands.*)

I believe I began by saying politics is about irreconcilable differences. So, by that standard, we've just had a terrific political discussion.
DUTTON: Yes.

(DUTTON *waits a moment.*)

What are my chances of seeing you again?
NADIA: They're zero.

(DUTTON *nods, accepting.*)

Up until now I would have dismissed you as a sort of throwback, Dennis.
DUTTON: Would you?
NADIA: In all sorts of ways.
DUTTON: I don't see why.
NADIA: You're going into the world of money, is that right? The world of finance.
DUTTON: I'm going into my father's business.
NADIA: Maybe it's my ignorance but I don't believe that world will be different from any other. The most important thing you can take into it is an open mind.

(DUTTON *looks at her a moment.*)

DUTTON: Why? Why would I want an open mind?
NADIA: Why would you not?
DUTTON: Our enemies don't have open minds.

3.

(NADIA, *alone.*)

NADIA: It's a choice, isn't it? How you live. How you behave. You make a choice. At some point in your life you think: there must be an intelligent way to live. And you make your choice. Maybe you don't even remember. Everything conspires to make you forget. But the choice is there. You made it.

4.

(*A lawn looking over the Welsh and English countryside. A tree. A blissful, sunny day. There are canvas chairs. The remains of breakfast. Both* OLIVER *and* PHILIP *are in shirtsleeves.* PHILIP LUCAS *is English, in his early thirties, notably handsome.*)

OLIVER: So tell me, tell me a little, so I know something about her before we meet.

PHILIP: Aside from beautiful and brilliant?

OLIVER: Aside from that, yes.

(PHILIP *smiles, thinking of her.*)

PHILIP: Formidable, certainly. Committed. Articulate. Passionate. Full of strong feeling.

OLIVER: OK. Enough of her faults, now tell me her virtues.

PHILIP: Well, the first time I met her she was carrying a book. "Pas de psychologie, pas de psychose."

OLIVER: What did that mean?

PHILIP: No psychology, no psychosis.

OLIVER: No, I know what it means. I know what it means. I'm not an idiot. Choosing that book.

PHILIP: All right, Dad.

OLIVER: That's what I'm asking. What did that mean?

(PHILIP *thinks a moment.*)

PHILIP: Well. As you know, Nadia teaches at Yale . . .

OLIVER: I know that . . .

PHILIP: Obviously what she was trying to say is that she isn't keen on the psychological.

OLIVER: I see.

PHILIP: She has a horror of it. I thought: that's refreshing. That's such a refreshing approach.

OLIVER: Why? Why did you think that?

PHILIP: Oh. Because the first thing you notice, it becomes a way of life. People
are taught to say "I think, I feel." They talk all the time as if there were no
such thing as reality.

OLIVER: Really?

PHILIP: Or rather: They know reality exists, they know it's there, but they can't
help believing that what they feel about it is somehow more important
than reality itself.

OLIVER: You're talking about Americans?

PHILIP: Not only. But obviously. Having spent time there.

OLIVER: It's something you've noticed?

PHILIP: Say you have an experience. Any experience. You're walking along the
street and a man drops dead in front of you. And peoples' first response is
"Really? A man dropped dead in the street? How did that make you feel?"

OLIVER: That's funny.

PHILIP: Yeah, but it's decadent, isn't it? As if it's not the world, it's not the
world you're interested in, it's just your own reaction to it.

(OLIVER *looks at him.*)

OLIVER: Huh.

PHILIP: I'll give you another example. This is an interesting example. Take the
former Yugoslavia, if you remember just a few years ago . . .

OLIVER: I do remember . . .

PHILIP: Yugoslavia falling apart, on the verge of collapse. But Nadia told me
that before she first went out there, she mentioned to someone, "You know,
I think this is really important." Whereupon the person looked at her and
said, "Have you noticed, you seem quite emotional, Nadia? Have you ever
stopped and asked yourself *why?* Why you're so worked up? All this fascination with foreign trouble-spots, have you ever considered there might
be a reason? Has it occurred to you, you may just be running away from
problems in your own life?"

(PHILIP *smiles at the absurdity of the question.*)

OLIVER: Well?

PHILIP: Well, what?

OLIVER: How did Nadia reply? *Did* Nadia have problems?

PHILIP: No, I don't think so. Not that she's told me about.

(*They both smile.*)

No, on the contrary. Nadia replied, "I'm not going to Yugoslavia because there's anything wrong with me. I'm going because there's something wrong in Yugoslavia. It's called ethnic cleansing. And it exists."

(PHILIP *laughs.*)

It's crazy. It's ridiculous, isn't it?
OLIVER: To be honest, I can't imagine.
PHILIP: Why not?
OLIVER: Because the people who need me so obviously need me.

(NADIA *comes out onto the lawn.*)

PHILIP: Ah there you are.
OLIVER: Good morning.

(NADIA *reaches out a hand.*)

NADIA: Hello.
OLIVER: Oliver.
NADIA: I'm sorry, Philip. I overslept. I didn't realize you'd got up.
PHILIP: I got up.
OLIVER: Good. Well this is charming, charming.
NADIA: Good morning.

(NADIA *kisses* PHILIP. *They all stand a moment, embarrassed.*)

OLIVER: So. Let me—right—to give you the idea, has anyone explained?
NADIA: No.
OLIVER: This is border country. That way, the sea. That way, the south.
NADIA: Toward the sun.
OLIVER: Precisely.
NADIA: Goodness, I really did oversleep.
PHILIP: It's not like you.
NADIA: It isn't.
PHILIP: You always wake so early.
OLIVER: You drove through the night, so I don't know how much you saw. Philip said you'd only been to England once before.
PHILIP: For a conference.
NADIA: At Chatham House. International relations. It was brief.

(OLIVER *smiles formally.*)

OLIVER: It's rare as you know for Philip to visit me at all, let alone in company.

NADIA: Actually it was an impulse. It was an impulsive thing.

OLIVER: Whose impulse?

PHILIP: Both of us.

OLIVER: Hence the short notice.

PHILIP: We got cheap tickets.

NADIA: Some of the happiest times we've had together, doing things on the spur of the moment.

PHILIP: Very much so.

(*They both smile.*)

NADIA: We simply got up one morning and decided we needed a vacation. Please don't read anything into it.

OLIVER: I haven't.

PHILIP: God forbid.

NADIA: Philip and I had both been working very hard.

PHILIP: It's something that happens over there. It's in the culture. You find yourself working every day of the year.

OLIVER: Really?

NADIA: And Philip said it was silly that I'd barely visited the country where he was born.

OLIVER: Or the people he was born to?

NADIA: Those too.

OLIVER: You're meeting both of us?

PHILIP: Yes.

OLIVER: Better and better. The grand tour.

(*Again,* OLIVER *smiles icily.*)

I'm being very rude. Let me get you some breakfast.

NADIA: In a moment. Yes. Thank you.

PHILIP: Or shall I do it?

OLIVER: Philip has actually tried to tell me what you do. I can't say I understand it entirely.

PHILIP: Oh, Dad . . .

OLIVER: What?

PHILIP: For God's sake!

NADIA: I'm not sure I do either.

PHILIP: Putting Nadia on the spot.

OLIVER: I'm not putting her on the spot. I'm making conversation.

PHILIP: That's even worse!

OLIVER: Even: I'm *interested*.

PHILIP: She's only just got up.

NADIA: I can't believe you want a lecture from me.

OLIVER: I'm not asking for a lecture. I'm asking for enlightenment.

NADIA: OK.

OLIVER: Thank you.

(*They all smile. It's easier.*)

NADIA: I teach politics. That's what I do. It's what I always wanted to do.

OLIVER: From when you were young?

NADIA: Exactly. In fact, I remember—

OLIVER: Yes?

NADIA: Even at school, I remember being bewildered. So much time spent reading—I don't know—medieval literature, doing trigonometry when meanwhile, all the important things were being ignored.

OLIVER: What were they? What were the important things?

NADIA: All right: Why so many people live in such poverty. And so few live well. And what can we do about it? These huge facts, these enormous facts not up for study. Ignored. You'd think that to be alive would mean to want to find out.

(OLIVER *looks at her a moment.*)

OLIVER: But specifically . . .

NADIA: Yes?

OLIVER: Philip had suggested . . .

NADIA: Yes?

OLIVER: Your area is now international relations?

NADIA: That's right.

OLIVER: Your specific concern.

NADIA: My field.

OLIVER: With a particular interest in terror.

NADIA: Oh, no, not "particular."

OLIVER: I read on the internet: you're known as the professor of terror.

PHILIP: That's what she has to put up with.

NADIA: Only in the media. And among a few of my students. The dumber ones.

OLIVER: Do you have stupid students?

NADIA: I'm afraid I do. Or at least I was thinking before I left.

OLIVER: Why? Why before you left?

NADIA: Oh. Something that happened. A student. My God. Made me think.

(NADIA *smiles.*)

PHILIP: Excuse me. I'm going to get coffee.

(PHILIP *goes out.*)

OLIVER: But you have written about terror?

NADIA: Of course. Everyone does. You can't do what I do and not be fascinated by it.

(OLIVER *waits for her to go on.*)

All right, crudely, if you're asking, you can say, if you want to put it this way, that terrorism may be the wrong answer to the right question.

OLIVER: What question is that?

NADIA: Well, I'd have thought terror's an attack on modernity, isn't it?

OLIVER: I'm never sure. Tell me what "modernity" means.

NADIA: Usually it means that human beings feel themselves discontent, they feel lost in the world—if there's nothing *but* the world—and they imagine that materialism must therefore be at fault.

(NADIA *shifts.*)

Of course—look, not to insult you—it's much more complicated than that . . .

OLIVER: Of course . . .

NADIA: And the actual *motivation* . . .

OLIVER: Yes . . .

NADIA: . . . the moment at which an individual picks up a gun, or straps on explosives—that moment is still deeply obscure. People claim to understand it, but do they? I certainly don't. But underlying that desire you'll often find the same discontent: namely, the conviction that materialism isn't enough.

OLIVER: And is that what you think?

NADIA: People blame materialism because they feel it doesn't nourish them. And you could say, it's true: materialism, by definition, isn't heroic. In the West, you no longer become famous for what you do, simply for what happens to you. We celebrate victims, not heroes. We're infantilized by fear to a point where all we want is to live as long and comfortably as possible. And so this Western ethic of survival, merely surviving as a human being—as though the world were everything, and the manner in which you live in it unimportant—seems to other people, other cultures, well . . . ignoble.

OLIVER: Do you agree?

NADIA: Me?

OLIVER: Is that your own view? Do you feel that?

(NADIA *looks at him a moment.*)

NADIA: I don't know. But, whether it is or not, the answer isn't violence.

(PHILIP *appears on the lawn.*)

PHILIP: I'm assuming you want toast.

NADIA: Yes, please.

PHILIP: Honey or jam?

NADIA: Honey. No, jam. Honey.

PHILIP: I'll bring both.

(PHILIP *goes.* NADIA *remembers after he's gone.*)

NADIA: Thanks, babe!

OLIVER: In fact, I must admit when I went to your website . . .

NADIA: Oh, that . . .

OLIVER: It lists subjects about which you're available to speak.

NADIA: It's a fancy piece of publicity. Shaming, but you have to do it.

OLIVER: Do you?

NADIA: Sure.

OLIVER: Why's that?

NADIA: Being an academic isn't quite what it was. We find ourselves doing all sorts of things.

OLIVER: I see.

NADIA: Inevitably, yes, I talk to the media.

OLIVER: You make a point of it?

(NADIA *looks a moment, detecting criticism.*)

NADIA: My special privilege has been to define my job as I go along. The university's been very generous.

OLIVER: You're free?

NADIA: That's it.

OLIVER: Free to do what you choose?

NADIA: More or less.

OLIVER: Because of your status?

NADIA: If you choose to put it like that. I barely teach. Mostly, I write.

OLIVER: Philip said there was a book.

NADIA: There is. And I'm writing another. This is a relatively new study. Or rather it's an old study which has been transformed. Am I boring you?

OLIVER: No.

NADIA: You'll let me know if I'm boring you.

OLIVER: You're not.

NADIA: As long as we had two great powers, two superpowers in some sort of balance, then there seemed to be a procedure for determining the world's affairs.

OLIVER: Now there's only one.

NADIA: Exactly. So my area of study becomes more vital.

OLIVER: Especially after Iraq.

NADIA: As you say. Yes. Especially after Iraq.

(NADIA *looks again, trying to gauge his agenda. Then she gets up and moves to look out over the hills.*)

I didn't get much of a look last night but this wasn't what I was expecting.

OLIVER: This spot?

NADIA: Yes.

OLIVER: In what way?

NADIA: I knew you were alone. But still.

OLIVER: I am alone.

NADIA: Is that a choice?

OLIVER: Well, this place would hardly be chance, would it?

NADIA: How do you pronounce it?

OLIVER: Shrewsbury.

(*They smile together.*)

I came here over ten years ago.

NADIA: As long as that? And you don't mind? You don't mind the isolation?

OLIVER: Philip was already practicing. He'd gone, he'd left home.

NADIA: His mother brought him up?

OLIVER: Officially, yes. But I did my share. You haven't met her yet?

(OLIVER *gestures round.*)

There aren't many spots left where you can turn three hundred and sixty degrees and see barely a single building.

NADIA: You went out of your way?
OLIVER: In France they have this expression. "France profonde."
NADIA: I'm embarrassed. I don't speak French.
OLIVER: No? I'm surprised.
NADIA: Why? Why does that surprise you?
OLIVER: Oh. Something Philip said.
NADIA: What was that?

(OLIVER *is reluctant.*)

No, say.
OLIVER: "Pas de psychologie. Pas de psychose."

(*There is a moment.* NADIA *seems displeased.*)

NADIA: He told you that? Why did he tell you that?
OLIVER: I'm sorry, have I crossed some sort of line?
NADIA: No, no, no.
OLIVER: Please, I didn't mean to upset you.
NADIA: You haven't upset me.
OLIVER: I happened to ask him how you met, that's all.

(NADIA *turns away.*)

NADIA: It's silly. Why do I want private things to be private?

(PHILIP *returns with coffee and toast for* NADIA.)

PHILIP: You two all right?
NADIA: We are. Thank you.
OLIVER: Fine.

(NADIA *takes her breakfast from him.*)

NADIA: Obviously you and your Dad were talking while I was asleep.
PHILIP: Oh, not much.
OLIVER: No, no, no.
PHILIP: Very little, in fact.
OLIVER: Philip's one of those people who's always been at peace with silence.
PHILIP: Silence never bothered me.
OLIVER: If the world can be divided into those who need to speak and those who don't.
PHILIP: People only talk because they're nervous.

OLIVER: It's funny. There's a doctor at the hospital who's notorious for his pauses. Ear, Nose, and Throat. "What are my chances, doctor?" "Well . . ."

(OLIVER *pauses elaborately.*)

If the patient doesn't die of the disease, they die of suspense.

NADIA: And you?

OLIVER: Me?

NADIA: How's your manner?

OLIVER: Oh, reasonably sympathetic, I hope. Early on, they taught me something I try not to forget.

NADIA: What's that?

OLIVER: The definition of a doctor.

NADIA: I've never heard it. Tell me.

OLIVER: A doctor is someone who tells you the truth and stays with you to the end.

(NADIA *stops eating and looks directly at him.*)

Not bad, eh?

NADIA: No. Not bad.

OLIVER: It's pretty good, isn't it?

(PHILIP *shifts, not sure what's going on.*)

PHILIP: Are we going into town? I'd like to show Nadia the town.

(OLIVER *takes no notice.*)

OLIVER: Nadia's been explaining how things have changed for the academic. The public role.

NADIA: Your father sounds as if he disapproves.

OLIVER: Not at all.

NADIA: As if it were vulgar.

OLIVER: Not vulgar, no. But I have my own idea of what it is to be a professional. The two requirements: to be objective and to be discreet.

NADIA: I'd hope I was both of those.

(OLIVER *looks at her a moment.*)

OLIVER: Philip mentioned . . . Philip did mention that the president asked for you.

NADIA: He did. Believe it or not, he did.

OLIVER: You went to the White House?

NADIA: I did.

OLIVER: Goodness.

NADIA: I know.

OLIVER: What did he want?

NADIA: Oh, you can imagine.

OLIVER: Actually, no. I have no idea.

NADIA: He wanted briefing. He wanted advice.

OLIVER: Which you were able to give?

(NADIA *doesn't answer.*)

About Iraq?

NADIA: Yes. He knew I'd written about Iraq.

OLIVER: Clearly you were in favour? You were in favour of the invasion?

NADIA: The liberation, yes. Yes, I was in favour. I don't think the president would have asked me if I wasn't.

OLIVER: No.

(*They both smile.*)

NADIA: Whatever you think, whatever your view, I'd have to say, it is undeniably something.

OLIVER: For you?

NADIA: No, I'm not talking personally. I'm talking about entering. Walking in. It's impressive. You're picked up at your hotel in a black car, with blacked-out windows. Five minutes later you're standing on the carpet in the Oval Office.

OLIVER: It's theatre?

NADIA: That's right. Theatre.

(NADIA *looks down, slightly embarrassed.*)

Also in our country, it isn't just the person, it's the office.

OLIVER: He's the president.

NADIA: In America . . . in America that still means something.

OLIVER: Quite.

NADIA: It really does. Do I sound naïve?

OLIVER: I don't think so.

NADIA: Because from what people tell me, it's not the same here.

OLIVER: Not in the smallest degree.

NADIA: Why is that?

OLIVER: It's hard to explain. But I'm probably typical.

PHILIP: Dad is absolutely typical.

NADIA: How?

(PHILIP *smiles, dodging the question.*)

PHILIP: I left this country, remember?

OLIVER: No doubt you feel that if your president calls, you have to answer that
   call. If my prime minister called, I'd let it ring. That's the difference.

PHILIP: It's true.

OLIVER: And what's more, *what's more*, politics being what it is in this country—i.e., everything, *everything*—my prime minister wouldn't call me in
   the first place.

PHILIP: That's definitely true.

NADIA: Do you—I don't know how to ask this—am I ridiculous for asking
   this?

OLIVER: Ask.

NADIA: Does no-one here have any concept of national loyalty? Of being part
   of a nation?

OLIVER: Oh.

NADIA: Well?

OLIVER: I don't know how to answer. Like most people, I do have a button marked "patriotism." But—let's say—I'm choosy about who I allow to
   press it. Certainly not politicians. And certainly not the Queen.

NADIA: Who then?

OLIVER: Oh you know. Blake. Wilfred Owen.

PHILIP: They're poets.

NADIA: I know.

(*There's a silence. Nobody moves.*)

OLIVER: An appeal to patriotism is a contradiction in terms. Especially when
   made by politicians. You can no more appeal to patriotism than you can
   appeal to love. You may feel it, but you can't demand it. Wilfred Owen, yes.
   Fifty-seven thousand British casualties on the first morning on the battle
   of the Somme, young men sent into a murderous war by the ruthless, out-
   of-touch political class of the day. People with no direct experience of war,
   and no knowledge of its reality, send ordinary working men to die on their
   behalf. They stay at home. The men die. Hello? Hard to explain, impossible
   to justify. And one man—one great man—adequate to describe the event.

(PHILIP *smiles to himself.*)

PHILIP: Dad liked the Sex Pistols as well.

OLIVER: I admit it.

PHILIP: Same reason.

OLIVER: Similar.

PHILIP: All right . . .

OLIVER: Not the same.

PHILIP: OK.

OLIVER: Don't make me sound stupid. But I did like the Sex Pistols.

(OLIVER *sits back, expansive.*)

> The only patriotic outfit still operating in this country is the awkward squad. In the United States, you're building an empire. Remember, we've dismantled one. When Philip was young I remember him saying he'd like to be gay or an immigrant because then he'd belong. He wanted a tribe.

NADIA: Isn't medicine a tribe?

OLIVER: Used to be. Now it's freelance. We've been—what's the word?—outsourced. The politicians dismantle communities, then complain that community no longer exists. They incubate the disease, then profess to be shocked when people catch it. "Oh, why can't people behave?" Well, why can't they? It's a good question. When the people who make the law become lawless themselves, what can you do? How can politicians lead except by example?

(NADIA *smiles, giving up.*)

NADIA: You have a high standard.

OLIVER: Not that high.

NADIA: If you're talking about what I think you're talking about.

PHILIP: I don't think there's much doubt, is there?

OLIVER: I don't think there is.

PHILIP: It's a fair chance, one way or another, Dad's returned to the subject of Iraq.

OLIVER: Gosh. How did you know?

PHILIP: He usually does.

OLIVER: "Usually"?

PHILIP: All right . . .

OLIVER: I don't think, Philip, you're in a position to say "usually."

PHILIP: I agree. I'm not.

OLIVER: "Usually" when you never see me?

PHILIP: OK . . .

OLIVER: Not just don't see me, barely ever talk, don't even talk to me.
PHILIP: Whose fault is that?
OLIVER: I know. I'm just saying. For all that.

(*An edgy silence.* NADIA *puts her plate aside.*)

NADIA: Good, well, maybe this is the moment to set off for Shrewsbury.
OLIVER: Maybe it is.

(*They smile at one another.*)

NADIA: Believe me, if it's what you want, I'm happy to have the Iraq discussion.
OLIVER: I'm not asking for it.
NADIA: I'll have it tonight if you want.
OLIVER: I'm not insisting.
NADIA: I've had it every day for the last three years. I never supposed a vacation in England would be a vacation from the argument.
OLIVER: Quite.
NADIA: Why should today be different?

(NADIA *gets up and turns, formal.*)

No doubt, you can imagine, I've taken a huge amount of flak.
OLIVER: I'm sure.
NADIA: In liberal Connecticut defending the war has not been a popular position.
OLIVER: It's not been big in Shropshire either.
NADIA: If you're interested: I was quite clear about why I supported it. I'm also clear about what's gone wrong. And I don't think the extraordinary incompetence of what's followed invalidates the original decision. I've always supported humane intervention in countries where terrible things are happening. I still believe in it. With all my heart. If the choice is between stepping in or staying put and watching dictators let rip, then I'm for stepping in. I was a reporter before I was an academic. I've been in these places. And I've been present in situations in which the West did nothing. I've seen the results of our indifference. So. If you want me to pass my evening defending the right of Western countries to use their muscle to free Arabs from systematic murder, believe me, I'm up for it.
OLIVER: I'm sure you are.
NADIA: I take it you were against?
OLIVER: Passionately.
NADIA: From the beginning?

OLIVER: Let's just say, I knew who the surgeon was going to be, so I had fair idea what the operation would look like.

(OLIVER *gets up.*)

Please. Don't take it amiss. I'm not being rude.

NADIA: I know that.

OLIVER: Least of all to you, to you of all people, Nadia. I'm thrilled my son has brought somebody home. Even if it isn't home. In the proper sense.

(*There's a moment.* OLIVER *speaks quietly.*)

All I want is Philip's happiness.

NADIA: We want the same thing.

OLIVER: And if you can contribute to that happiness, then believe me nobody could be more welcome.

(*There's a brief silence.*)

NADIA: However.

OLIVER: I'm sorry?

NADIA: I sense a "however."

OLIVER: No. There is no "however."

(*They look at each other a moment.*)

NADIA: Excuse me. I'll get my things.

(*She goes off into the house.* PHILIP *moves away,* OLIVER *doesn't move. A few moments go by.*)

PHILIP: Can I just say: this is an act of trust. I trusted you!

OLIVER: Well?

PHILIP: Dad, I didn't have to do this. I did it because I wanted to.

OLIVER: So?

(*There is a silence.* OLIVER *says nothing.*)

PHILIP: It's my own fault. I have this ridiculous need for family.

OLIVER: Why ridiculous?

PHILIP: Apart from anything, because I'm the only person in my family who has it.

OLIVER: Your mother has it.

(PHILIP *throws him a mistrustful look.*)

PHILIP: Just look at Nadia. You see what she is! You can tell what she is! This is the best piece of luck in my life! Meeting her! What, I'm not to marry her because you don't approve of her position on Iraq?

OLIVER: Come on, nobody said that.

PHILIP: Didn't they?

OLIVER: Nobody put it like that.

PHILIP: They didn't need to, did they?

OLIVER: And maybe I wasn't listening but I didn't hear anyone say "marriage" either.

(PHILIP *is silent.* OLIVER *is amused.*)

What am I meant to say? What have I done wrong?

PHILIP: You know full well.

OLIVER: Do I?

PHILIP: You could be a little more welcoming.

OLIVER: Welcoming?

PHILIP: Yes.

OLIVER: Come on, it's been a good old Welsh borders welcome. What was missing? Conjuring tricks?

(*But* PHILIP *has already moved away.*)

PHILIP: She said "I'd be fascinated to see a little family background." It's not very easy, is it? to explain, "Oh you can meet my father, but bear in mind, this is a man who destroyed my mother's life."

OLIVER: Did I?

PHILIP: And now—for reasons I'm not going into—he lives alone on a hillside, repelling boarders. Or rather, repelling male boarders.

(OLIVER *smiles, unperturbed, enjoying himself.*)

OLIVER: Philip, this is a tense and unnatural situation.

PHILIP: You could say.

OLIVER: Of course it is. It will test both of our characters to the limit.

PHILIP: Very funny.

OLIVER: Neither of us—all right?—has too much experience of conventional family life.

PHILIP: To put it no higher.

OLIVER: But, in my opinion, I think you're letting it get to you.

(OLIVER *sits back, content.*)

You say she's the greatest piece of luck in your life.

PHILIP: She is.

OLIVER: In that case, you might ask, why risk your luck by bringing her here to meet me?

PHILIP: I'm beginning to ask that myself.

OLIVER: Well, then, why did you?

(PHILIP *just looks at him.*)

All right. In fact, take one step back and I think you'll find the whole thing is going remarkably well.

PHILIP: You think so?

OLIVER: She's enjoying my company and relishing the chance to talk to someone who's almost as clever as she is.

PHILIP: You mean as opposed to me?

(OLIVER *looks at him reproachfully.*)

OLIVER: Look, Philip, if you'd like a piece of advice . . .

PHILIP: Advice from you?

OLIVER: . . . then I'd say—just from my experience—I have some experience of this—strategically it wouldn't be very clever when in Nadia's company to show self-doubt. Trust me. It would not be advantageous. Because—I admit, you know her better than I do—but my guess is that Nadia Blye is not someone who easily tolerates weakness. She doesn't *like* it. Am I right?

(PHILIP *doesn't answer.*)

Anyone who announces that psychology's a load of rubbish—well, you choose to call that attitude "refreshing." I think a better word for it might be "dangerous." That's all I'm saying.

PHILIP: You've said enough.

OLIVER: Take one look at her: she's someone who'd have very little trouble attracting any man on campus.

PHILIP: So?

OLIVER: So my guess is, she's picked you out because you appear to be strong. Well then. Be strong. Why disappoint her? As our government instructs us, be alert but not alarmed. Face it: nothing serious is going to go wrong unless you let it go wrong.

(*There is a mistrustful silence.*)

PHILIP: We're here till tomorrow. We're here till tomorrow night.

OLIVER: Good. Then we'll all take it step by step and see how it goes.

(OLIVER *examines his nails, smiling.* PHILIP *is annoyed with himself.*)

PHILIP: And I don't feel self-doubt when I'm in America.

OLIVER: Good.

PHILIP: I like American life.

OLIVER: I'm sure you do.

PHILIP: I like the feel of it. The look. It suits me. In America, I stand with a gin and tonic, I look out of the window, people are going out to the mall and I feel hopeful. Explain that.

OLIVER: I can't.

PHILIP: The landscape moves me. Crazy, isn't it? When there's a road across the desert and nothing in sight. When it snows in New England. Sobbing like a child about a place which isn't even home.

(OLIVER *looks down, mischievous.*)

OLIVER: Well it's always nice, isn't it? to get away from one's parents.

PHILIP: In my case very much so.

OLIVER: And what's more with an American girlfriend. Though from what I read in the magazines American women can be quite exacting.

(PHILIP *turns, half-amused, half-exasperated.*)

PHILIP: Oh God, are you off again?

OLIVER: Am I?

PHILIP: Why do you do this? My whole life, you did this stuff. Did nobody tell you? Kids aren't meant to be objects of satire, you know. That's not why most people opt for parenthood.

OLIVER: No, you're right.

PHILIP: Most people don't use their children to refine their jokes on.

OLIVER: I know. Absolutely.

PHILIP: Well?

OLIVER: You're right. Of course you're right.

PHILIP: You're fifty-eight. It's unbecoming.

OLIVER: I'll stop.

(NADIA *returns.*)

PHILIP: Good, you're ready. I'll get the car keys.

NADIA: I've got them here.

(NADIA *holds them out.*)

Are you coming with us?

OLIVER: I'm not. You enjoy yourselves.

(NADIA *hesitates, about to go.*)

NADIA: I was thinking, something about this situation reminds me of J. Paul
Getty. Do you know who I mean?

OLIVER: Of course.

NADIA: Richest man in the world. I've always liked him for one thing.

OLIVER: What was that?

NADIA: I read, before he took a girl on their first date, he insisted she submit
to a full medical examination by a doctor of his choosing.

(OLIVER *and* NADIA *smile.*)

Now that's what I call romantic.

OLIVER: Me too.

NADIA: Great start to an evening, isn't it?

OLIVER: And good business for my profession too.

NADIA: Yeah. Yeah, that's what I was thinking.

(*The two of them stand, amused by each other.*)

See you later.

OLIVER: And you.

5.

(OLIVER, *alone.*)

OLIVER: I used to go to the football when I lived in London. I thought, why's
everyone shouting at the referee? He's doing his best. In fact I'm the only
fan I know who ever took the referee for a meal. I ran into him as he was
leaving the ground—and we fell to talking. I told him I'd liked the way
he'd handled things. We went on to a restaurant and I bought him dinner.
There's a part of me that likes a well-ordered game.

6.

(*The lawn again. The remains of meal. A CD player is on in the house.* NADIA, PHILIP,
and OLIVER *have been eating at a table under the stars. It looks enchanted.*)

NADIA: It seems so long ago, it seems like such a long time ago. I suppose I wasn't there more than eight months . . .

OLIVER: That's all?

NADIA: Probably. But it seems like half a lifetime. When we were in Sarajevo.

(*There's a moment's silence.*)

Maybe there was something about my being so young. Most of us were. By the time you've got a family, it's tough, unless your partner's willing to accept you might get a bullet in the throat.

(OLIVER *refers to the scene around them.*)

OLIVER: You couldn't sit under the stars. You couldn't eat out?

NADIA: You couldn't *eat*. Most nights I was looped, all of us were.

OLIVER: Looped? What does looped mean?

(*There is a sudden silence. She looks at him.*)

NADIA: Looped? Looped means drunk.

(*Everyone is still,* PHILIP *watching intently.*)

You'd go out all day in what we call "soft skins" . . .

OLIVER: Say again.

NADIA: I thought it would amuse you, that's why I said it.

OLIVER: All your correspondents' slang.

NADIA: Yeah . . .

OLIVER: You're a tribe.

NADIA: Hmm.

OLIVER: So, "soft skin"?

NADIA: "Soft skin" meaning a car with no armour. An unarmoured car. A regular car.

OLIVER: So you went into Shrewsbury today . . .

NADIA: Yeah . . .

OLIVER: In a soft skin.

NADIA: That's right. Only in Sarajevo you felt it, you really felt it, because you knew there was just a thin layer of tin between you and everything outside. Back at the hotel you were sharing rooms, maybe even sleeping on the floor, you had relationships—these were people you're never going to forget.

(PHILIP *looks thoughtful,* OLIVER *notices.*)

OLIVER: But you stopped?

NADIA: Oh, yes.

OLIVER: You no longer do it. Why?

NADIA: The whole thing. The anger. I found myself addicted.

OLIVER: Which? To the anger or the way of life?

NADIA: Both.

OLIVER: Anger against what?

NADIA: Anger against the world. The world, for standing by, for knowing and not intervening.

(NADIA *shakes her head, remembering.*)

Endless days, days lying on a floor in a blackout, watching people die for no purpose, for no reason, except the world's laziness, its fat spoiled sense of itself, its stupid fascination with handbags and losing body weight and who won the Open and who takes an iron to the green. Who cares? Who the fuck cares? The first great war in Europe since 1945 and nobody's able even to remember which country is which. Which one's Milosevic and which one's the other guy? And which is Croatia, remind me? Is that the one full of Muslims? Or is that Bosnia? I mean, who are we? Who the fuck are we?

(*There's a moment's silence. Is she drunk?* OLIVER'S *gaze is steady.*)

Three hundred thousand people killed in Europe.

(NADIA *shakes her head.*)

There were nights so cold, so pitted from the trace of machine gun fire, I didn't know concrete could have so many holes and still stand. Like lattice-work. There were bodies—every shape, every colour, bodies rotting in the woods, on building sites—violence, dinning in your head so you wanted to scream. And three hundred miles away there were people going to the opera and hailing gondolas and laughing, not wanting to know, not needing to know. Because they didn't believe the war would come anywhere near them.

(OLIVER *reaches tactfully for the bottle and refills her glass.*)

Well, now they have their war, and good luck to them.

OLIVER: You still feel it.

NADIA: Yes. I feel it. When I've had a few drinks.

(NADIA *acknowledges the glass in her hand.*)

Philip's heard it before.

PHILIP: I don't mind.

(PHILIP *smiles a little, reassuring.*)

NADIA: Forgive me. It's a drug. The anger's a drug. I don't like that part of myself.

OLIVER: You think it's unattractive?

NADIA: I don't give a fuck if it's attractive. I only care what it feels like, and it doesn't feel good.

OLIVER: Because?

NADIA: For the obvious reason.

OLIVER: What's that?

NADIA: What, I'm supposed to spend all my time believing that everyone's wrong except me? The world is uncaring and ignorant except for me? Please!

OLIVER: I understand.

NADIA: No, walking around feeling *that* all the time doesn't make anyone happy—unless of course they're a psychopath, or—I don't know—one of your poets.

(NADIA *stares a moment, the anger unabated.*)

OLIVER: And that's the reason you stopped?

NADIA: I went out a reporter. I came back an analyst.

OLIVER: Maybe your temperament was wrong.

NADIA: Maybe.

OLIVER: Psychologically.

(NADIA *looks up, sharply.* OLIVER *smiles.*)

To use that word.

NADIA: Look, it was simple. It was a simple thing.

OLIVER: Was it?

NADIA: Yes. Don't make it out to be complex. At the end of it all, when I wasn't plain scared or exhausted, I just felt, shit, I'm spending too much of my time feeling self-righteous.

OLIVER: Why? Why self-righteous?

NADIA: Oh look—whatever—half self-righteous, half confused. "Oh you're a foreign correspondent. How fascinating!" Well yes, it would be fascinating if anyone took any notice of what we wrote . . .

OLIVER: Yes.

NADIA: If anyone listened! If anyone did anything because of what we reported!

(OLIVER *waits, tactful.*)

OLIVER: But actually you were right. You were right to be angry. Why should you be ashamed? Those people *did* die. And nobody *did* care. Why to apologise?

(NADIA *looks at him a moment, thoughtful.*)

NADIA: People have forgotten. They've forgotten already. All they think about is terrorism. The truth is there was far more terrorism in the 1980s when nobody thought about it than there is today when nobody thinks about anything else. It's just a fact.

(NADIA *smiles, relaxing at the irony. She reaches for* PHILIP's *hand.*)

In fact we went—didn't we? we went to a conference . . .

OLIVER: Where was this?

NADIA: Helsinki.

PHILIP: Helsinki was interesting.

NADIA: Philip came.

PHILIP: Just for fun. I was Mr. Blye.

NADIA: A man got up, very early on, said, "Nobody in this room is going to die of terrorism. You're more likely to die from swallowing a wasp."

PHILIP: That's what he said.

NADIA: He didn't make himself popular. Not in that company.

(*They both smile at the memory.*)

PHILIP: Actually I talked to him later in the bar.

NADIA: You did. I remember.

PHILIP: We had a beer. "The point of a conference," he said, "is to be the person who says the stupidest thing."

(PHILIP *smiles, anticipating* NADIA.)

All right, maybe he didn't say "stupid" . . .

NADIA: Ah well no . . .

PHILIP: Maybe he said "provocative." "Memorable," I don't know.

NADIA: "Memorable," "stupid"—there is a difference.

PHILIP: Anyway, we know what he meant. He said, "That's intellectual life in the West." He was Egyptian. "That way you make a reputation," he said. "It's a game."

(NADIA *is looking disapproving.*)

It's not what I think, sweet one, it's just what he said.

(NADIA *laughs, forgiving* PHILIP.)

NADIA: It's funny. It was a funny weekend to begin with. I made this stupid mistake . . .
PHILIP: I didn't mind.
NADIA: I've promised Philip I'll never do it again.
PHILIP: It's just those people. They have no idea.
OLIVER: Which people?
NADIA: I happened to mention to someone what Philip did for a living.
PHILIP: Yeah.
NADIA: Well . . .
PHILIP: Who'd have thought so many intellectuals had such bad backs?
NADIA: And such a poor idea of how to behave. Not a single one of them didn't sneak up to Philip at some point in the weekend.

(NADIA *is gathering pace, excited.*)

People—can I say this?—
PHILIP: Sure . . .
NADIA: They have this idea of physical therapy as if it were some kind of trade. As if it were plumbing. They treat him as if he's some kind of natural resource.
PHILIP: It's ignorance.
NADIA: I'd never met a physical therapist till I met Philip, but even I knew they're not the kind of people you press sweaty bills into their hands. In fact, I tell you, there was one woman there . . .

(PHILIP *rolls his eyes.*)

PHILIP: Oh Jesus!
NADIA: Well it's what happened . . .
PHILIP: Nadia doesn't care for my female clients anyway.
NADIA: I don't think that's true. I don't think that's true at all.
PHILIP: Don't you?
NADIA: No. As a matter of fact, I don't. And I don't know why you say it. I really don't.

PHILIP: All right, let's say—how do I put this—

NADIA: I don't know. How *will* you put this?

PHILIP: All right. At the best of times, Nadia distrusts my female clients of a certain age, of a certain appearance . . .

NADIA: Some of them aren't in quite as much pain as they pretend.

(*It's badinage, but it's spiked.* OLIVER *observes closely.*)

PHILIP: Anyway, one way or another, this woman's Italian.

NADIA: Attractive.

PHILIP: Sort of good-looking. Full-figured.

NADIA: Expert on early jihad.

PHILIP: She says, "Can you possibly just pop up to my room and attend to my grinding discs?"

(PHILIP *raises his voice to preempt their reaction.*)

I would like to say, can I just say, this woman is one of the foremost academics in Italy? One of the cleverest women in Italy.

OLIVER: What did you say?

PHILIP: I said, listen, signora, as a matter of fact, you may not believe this but in the United States of America, I get two hundred and fifty dollars an hour for what I do. And I deserve it. And anyway I'm on vacation, learning about the pathology of terrorism.

OLIVER: What did she say? What did she say to that?

PHILIP: I think she was surprised.

(*He grins, but* NADIA *is already continuing.*)

NADIA: I'd already gotten the hang of this fucking woman.

PHILIP: You'd taken against her. Big-time.

NADIA: Oh forgive me, but she was one of those self-hating liberals.

OLIVER: Oh, one of those.

NADIA: "It's our fault. They're right to hate us. If I were them, I'd hate us too." You know the type.

OLIVER: I do.

NADIA: It's dressed up. It comes all wrapped up in fancy talk, but underneath.

(NADIA *puts up a hand to forestall him.*)

Be clear: if what people are saying is that it's our duty to try and understand things from the other point of view, then—believe me—I'm with them. 100 per cent. But.

OLIVER: But?

(OLIVER *waits.* NADIA *doesn't want to spell it out. She sips her wine.*)

But?

NADIA: But that doesn't mean forgetting what we believe in. Does it? We be-lieve in something. We stand for something too. Don't we?

(NADIA *is appealing directly to* OLIVER. PHILIP *shrugs.*)

PHILIP: I don't know. I really don't know. Maybe she just had a bad back.

NADIA: Maybe.

PHILIP: The fact is, in America, it's true, I do all sorts of things which aren't strictly medical.

OLIVER: What sorts of things?

PHILIP: More, well, what people want.

OLIVER: What they want?

PHILIP: It's not strict medical practice. It's not orthodox medicine.

OLIVER: What are you saying?

PHILIP: You have to understand: In the States they're really keen about fitness.

OLIVER: Fitness?

PHILIP: You must know that. Fitness is seen as a vital component of health. That's what my clinics offer.

OLIVER: Clinics?

PHILIP: Sure.

OLIVER: I thought you had one. One clinic.

PHILIP: I did. I did have one. Didn't I tell you?

NADIA: Now Philip has three.

OLIVER: Three?

NADIA: Three, and counting. He's doing really well.

(NADIA *grins, provocative.* OLIVER *throws her an uncharitable look.*)

PHILIP: Anyway, there's a fine line between formal physiotherapy and—I don't know—providing the client with a general sense of wellbeing.

OLIVER: What does that mean?

PHILIP: I've just explained what it means.

OLIVER: It's not strict medical practice, you say. It's not orthodox medicine. Well, then, what is it? What do you offer? Give me an example. Beyond physiotherapy?

PHILIP: All right, I have various people on the staff.

OLIVER: People? People of what kind?

PHILIP: Therapists, osteopaths . . .

NADIA: Personal trainers.

OLIVER: Jesus Christ, what are you saying, do you send people out for a run?

PHILIP: Dad . . .

OLIVER: I'm asking. I'm asking a question.

PHILIP: What's so special about running? What's so demeaning about running?

OLIVER: Do you go running?

PHILIP: No. Not personally. I don't go running. I employ people. Jesus!

(PHILIP *turns away, appealing to* NADIA.)

Didn't I warn you? Isn't this what I said?

NADIA: It is, but I don't see why you need to take it so hard.

(NADIA *grins, enjoying herself.*)

OLIVER: Well I must say, if you want to know what I think . . .

PHILIP: I can guess what you think.

OLIVER: If you want my opinion, I've done a lot of interesting things with my patients, but I've never taken the fuckers out for a jog. I mean, are you serious?

PHILIP: This is a mistake. I should never have raised the subject.

OLIVER: I'm just saying, putting in all that effort, years of study, education, hard work, and at the end of it all, what are you doing? Handing out those ridiculous little bottles of water and lifting weights?

(PHILIP *shakes his head, keeping steady.*)

PHILIP: Dad. Dad, you know as well as I do as that there are cultural factors in medicine. You yourself used to teach me. There is no such thing as pure medicine.

OLIVER: No. But there is such a thing as charging two hundred and fifty bucks to take obese Americans for a spin in the park.

PHILIP: Do you think that's what I do?

OLIVER: And there's a word for it too.

PHILIP: Jesus, do you really think that's what I get up to?

OLIVER: I don't know what you get up to. I'm a doctor, I'm not a personal healer.

PHILIP: They're personal trainers, Dad. Personal *trainers,* not personal healers.

(NADIA *smiles, having a good time.*)

Dad, I take on people. Ordinary people. You say, "Tell them the truth and stay with them to the end." How about "delay the end?" That's not ignoble, is it?

OLIVER: No, it's not.

PHILIP: That's not wrong?

OLIVER: Certainly not.

PHILIP: "Put off the end." Why not? Get fit, feel better, sort out your problems.

OLIVER: "Sort out your problems?" God, don't say you talk to the bastards as well!

PHILIP: Isn't it called preventative medicine, Dad, and wasn't it something we were all brought up to believe in?

OLIVER: Of course.

PHILIP: So?

(PHILIP *waits.*)

So?

(*Still* OLIVER *says nothing.*)

PHILIP: We work to stop you getting ill, rather than treating you when it's too late. What's wrong with that? It's the future of medicine, Dad. Or did nobody tell you? Word not reached you? It's all a damned sight more useful than writing prescriptions for a living.

OLIVER: Don't worry, there's no need to worry about it.

PHILIP: I shan't.

OLIVER: There's no need to be defensive.

PHILIP: I'm not defensive. I'm aggressive. You're living in the past.

OLIVER: It's your business. And it's not as if I have such a high opinion of doctors myself.

NADIA: Why not? What's that based on?

OLIVER: I've met a lot of them, remember?

(OLIVER *smiles, convinced.*)

If you think you're cleverer than your doctor, you're probably right. A degree in medicine is proof of not very much. It's amazing how many people will feel twelve peaches in the supermarket before choosing the one they want, yet they go to the first doctor without a moment's thought. Nothing depending on it, of course, except their life. "Sorry, doctor I didn't want to bother you." I watch them come through my door: the more modest the manner, the more deadly the disease.

(OLIVER *smiles, at ease.*)

They look at you all the time as if you could help.

NADIA: Can't you?

OLIVER: Not if they won't help themselves. The first instinct of a sick person is to suspend judgement. Their immediate impulse is very powerful: they want to put themselves in someone else's hands.

NADIA: Is that a bad thing?

OLIVER: When told you're seriously ill, the easiest reaction is to surrender to what you think is authority. When it comes down to it, people would rather gamble than calculate.

NADIA: Well, it's an easy mistake to make, isn't it? Doctors are always telling us that they know things which we don't.

PHILIP: Aren't they just?

OLIVER: I'm a GP, remember? Behind me, the ranks of experts, waiting.

NADIA: Did you never want to be an expert yourself?

OLIVER: I was an expert. Long ago.

(*There's a silence. They expect him to go on.*)

NADIA: What happened?

(OLIVER *smiles. Then he reaches for the bottle.*)

OLIVER: I'm going to give everyone another glass of wine and then we're going to go to bed.

PHILIP: I'm going to take Nadia up Shep Hill.

OLIVER: Take her up.

(PHILIP *waits a moment. Then he gets up, picking up some dishes as he goes.*)

PHILIP: I need a jumper.

(PHILIP *puts a hand on* NADIA's *shoulder, then goes out.*)

NADIA: What a gorgeous evening.

OLIVER: Isn't it?

NADIA: What time is it?

OLIVER: Gone twelve.

NADIA: He worships you.

OLIVER: I don't think so.

NADIA: Underneath.

OLIVER: Oh no, not even underneath.

NADIA: All right, "worships" is the wrong word. But he wants to please you.

OLIVER: Not at all. He wants to get me out of the way.

NADIA: Are you sure?

OLIVER: He wants to forget me. That's why he's here. He's doing his duty. He's not doing anything more. This was never a visit of reconciliation. It's a visit of farewell. I'm enjoying your company, Nadia. But I suspect, whatever happens, I shan't be seeing a lot of you.

(NADIA *looks at him a moment.*)

NADIA: I'm beginning to see . . . I'm beginning to understand how marked Philip is by his upbringing. He still feels bad he didn't become a doctor.

OLIVER: Do you think so? I'm not sure. He was going to Newcastle to read medicine but he never took up his place. It was at a difficult time. In the family. He said he'd rather do something less ambitious but do it better. Fair enough. Far less gifted people than Philip saw bones.

NADIA: When I met him, in fact, what I liked most was his self-assurance.

OLIVER: On the surface, Philip has wonderfully high self-confidence and very modest self-esteem. It's a combination you find in all the most winning people.

NADIA: Did he inherit that?

OLIVER: I think you can say: on the contrary. Or not from me, anyway. You might say I've suffered from the opposite. Excessive self-esteem and no self-confidence. Hence.

NADIA: Hence? Hence what?

OLIVER: Hence.

(OLIVER *is thoughtful a moment.*)

Philip looked after his mother after I left. He's hard-wired. That's what he does best.

NADIA: Hard-wired for what?

OLIVER: No disrespect, but I think you could say he's drawn to difficult women. They've been a constant in his life.

NADIA: Until now, you mean?

(*The two of them are still. It's seductively quiet.*)

And you?

OLIVER: Self-evidently, yes. I'm drawn to them too.

(PHILIP *appears, silently, tense, behind them. Does* OLIVER *know he's there?*)

You'll like Shep Hill. The view is extraordinary. By day they say you can see eight counties. And by night, the panoply of the stars. Weather permitting.

(OLIVER *gets up.*)

If you hear me in the night, don't worry. I like to read. I like to read outside. I'll clear up tomorrow. Leave it for now. Good night. Good night, son.

(*This last to* PHILIP *as* OLIVER *acknowledges him on his way out. There's a few moments' silence.*)

NADIA: Well?

(PHILIP *doesn't answer.*)

Is something wrong? Do you still want to go for the walk?
PHILIP: Of course I want to go for the walk.
NADIA: Well then.

(NADIA *waits.*)

I don't understand. Why are you angry?
PHILIP: Because it's an act. It's a mask. You do know that, don't you?
NADIA: Does it matter?
PHILIP: He's not who he claims to be.
NADIA: You mean underneath?

(NADIA *smiles at the phrase.*)

PHILIP: What's funny? Why do you say "underneath" like that?
NADIA: Oh. One of my students—something—anyway, this student kept saying, People are different underneath.
PHILIP: Your student's right.

(NADIA *waits again.*)

NADIA: What's wrong, Philip?
PHILIP: He sits there so fucking reasonable, as if he were the most reasonable man in the world. He drove my mother nuts. Why do you think she was so unhappy? Anything in a skirt he fucks it. He's fucked every woman from here to Akaba.

(PHILIP *turns towards her.*)

And he killed one as well. Oh by accident, it was an accident. But he killed someone.

NADIA: A patient?

PHILIP: No. Not a patient.

NADIA: Who, then?

(PHILIP *looks away.*)

I don't understand. What's up, Philip? This isn't like you.

(*Suddenly* PHILIP *is passionate.*)

PHILIP: People aren't their views, you know. They aren't their opinions. They aren't just what they say. They aren't the stuff that comes out of their mouths!

NADIA: I know that.

PHILIP: Urbane! Civilised! It's a trick. Anyone can do that. It bears no relation to who he is. All that high-mindedness! All that principle! The love of literature!

(PHILIP *shakes his head in contempt.*)

And apart from anything else—I know you won't believe it because it's unbelievable—but he's trying to seduce you.

NADIA: Don't be ridiculous. You dope!

PHILIP: He is. He wants to remove his son's girlfriend and take her to bed.

NADIA: I don't think so, Philip. I don't think it's likely.

PHILIP: That's what he does. That's the sort of thing he does. Throughout my childhood. He smuggled a French prostitute across the Channel in the boot of a car.

(NADIA *can't help laughing.*)

You think it's funny?

NADIA: I do think it's funny yes. For god's sake. You've got to escape this stuff.

PHILIP: Oh yes? Have you escaped this stuff?

NADIA: I don't know. I'm searching for any recollection of my father putting hookers in the back of his car.

(PHILIP *shakes his head.*)

And we say trunk. In the States we say trunk.

PHILIP: What about a man who fucks some woman in the living room, while my mother's sleeping upstairs?

NADIA: Did he do that?

PHILIP: Is that funny? Is that charming?

(NADIA *concedes.*)

NADIA: All right.

PHILIP: Just look back.

NADIA: At what?

PHILIP: At the way the day has gone. Look at it! It began with him undermining. The subtle undermining. Even you must have noticed, the way he set out to subvert you. How he doesn't approve of you going to see the president.

NADIA: Oh, that.

(NADIA *smiles to herself.*)

PHILIP: How you must have sold out. How you must be some kind of raging opportunist for supporting the war in Iraq. In your own interests, he implied. For reasons of personal ambition, he implied. No integrity, he implied. Well?

(NADIA *has no answer.*)

Then calculated—I promise you—calculated, not spontaneous: The switch. Oh suddenly he doesn't dislike you. Suddenly, he makes you a meal and he thinks you're great. I've seen him do it so many times. So the woman thinks, "Oh, he's changed towards me. That's interesting. What an interesting man!" God, it's so pathetically obvious. It's Casanova Page One.

NADIA: Why does it matter?

PHILIP: It matters because it's wrong!

(PHILIP *moves away in anger.*)

And it's disgusting. My whole childhood a trail of women fucked over and spat out while my mother sat alone . . .

(*There's a silence.* NADIA *speaks quietly.*)

NADIA: And you don't think now's the time to start to get over it?

PHILIP: Of course I do. I am over it. I got over it. It doesn't matter to me anymore. I'm just pointing it out.

NADIA: Good.

PHILIP: What does "good" mean?

NADIA: What do you think it means?

(NADIA *waits a moment, taking him seriously. She's calm.*)

Where's your sense of humour? Don't say you've lost it.

PHILIP: I haven't lost it. I've mislaid it. I'll find it again.

NADIA: When? When will you find it?

PHILIP: Soon. I'll find it soon.

(NADIA *smiles.*)

NADIA: Philip, we came for a vacation. We came as a couple. I want us to leave as a couple.

PHILIP: Yes, well, that would be the definition of a successful weekend.

NADIA: I've been honest with you. I've been in a series of relationships which didn't work. One reason: I was often with volatile men. I told you that. You're not like that. Let's say, after some of my experiences, it was a very attractive quality.

PHILIP: Was?

NADIA: Is. It is a very attractive quality.

(*There's a moment's silence.* PHILIP *speaks without bitterness.*)

PHILIP: Too difficult for you? Too much trouble for you? This whole thing too much trouble for the veteran of Sarajevo?

NADIA: Just, I don't like to see people suffer over things they can do nothing about.

PHILIP: I thought those were the things in life we *have* to suffer about.

NADIA: I hope not. I really do hope not.

(PHILIP *smiles, conceding.*)

So. Tell me. What are we going to do on that hill?

PHILIP: What would you like to do on that hill?

NADIA: Good.

(*The argument is resolved. They stand in each other's arms.*)

ACT TWO

7.

(PHILIP, *alone.*)

PHILIP: Asleep. Fast asleep. And dreaming of childhood. My father, the famous physician. The memory of my mother, sitting on the side of the bed, her hair tumbling over her face. Me, alone in my room, looking up at the sound of her crying, as if the plane to America were already waiting, one day, many years later, to take me away . . .

8.

(*The middle of the night. The lawn.* OLIVER *is sitting in a dressing gown on one of the canvas chairs, reading, a small battery-powered light attached to the book. He does not hear as* NADIA *comes, sleepy, barefoot, from the direction of the house. She approaches, and he turns.*)

OLIVER: Do you know what Richard Nixon said when they took him to the Great Wall of China?
NADIA: No. No, what did Nixon say?
OLIVER: He said, "This is a great wall."

(NADIA *smiles.*)

OLIVER: It's awesome, isn't it?
NADIA: Kind of.
OLIVER: What I admire: It's majestic in its simplicity. Of all the reactions a human being could have on being shown a wall, Nixon's is the purest. The most undeniable.
NADIA: Nobody fools Richard Nixon.
OLIVER: Quite.
NADIA: He knows a great wall when he sees one.
OLIVER: I think it may just be the all-time Zen remark of politics.

(NADIA *moves forward to look at the stars.*)

NADIA: What a night! My God, what a night!
OLIVER: It's beautiful here, isn't it?
NADIA: It's very beautiful.

OLIVER: Aren't I lucky?

(OLIVER *smiles to himself.*)

I don't think my son will be very happy to wake and find you gone.
NADIA: He won't wake up. He sleeps like a log.
OLIVER: Not you?

(NADIA *doesn't answer.*)

NADIA: Did you cook the supper yourself?
OLIVER: Who else?
NADIA: Single-handed?
OLIVER: Did you think I bought it in?
NADIA: How did you do the salad? It was delicious.
OLIVER: Pomegranate seeds. It's a trick. It's a cheap trick.

(NADIA *is looking out at the night.* OLIVER *puts his book aside.*)

Politicians only speak to please. Or to preempt an argument. Or to fill an uncomfortable silence. "This is a great wall." How can you teach that?
NADIA: I'm interested in the art of settling differences. To me, that's what it's about. How do we all get along when we want different things?
OLIVER: Is that what it's about?
NADIA: I think it is.
OLIVER: Nothing nobler than that? Nothing more heroic?
NADIA: For the Vietnam peace talks, two months were spent simply deciding the arrangement of the table. It needs determination. It needs resolve. And a measure of honesty. The good people are the negotiators. The bad people are the posturers.
OLIVER: That's the secret, is it? Sitting at the table? Staying at the table? Not leaving?

(NADIA *looks at him a moment. Then she shrugs.*)

NADIA: Look, I understand the urge people have to turn their backs. Many of us, after all, escaped from Europe . . .
OLIVER: Your own family?
NADIA: My great-grandparents.
OLIVER: Where to?
NADIA: Northern California.
OLIVER: Ah . . .
NADIA: I come from a liberal background.

OLIVER: I guessed.

NADIA: Like your own, I assume. The way you think, the way you speak, they're familiar to me. Public service, public ethics.

OLIVER: Are your parents still alive?

NADIA: Why, yes.

OLIVER: Together?

(NADIA *shakes her head.*)

NADIA: Anyway—whatever—our first instinct as immigrants was to remove ourselves from your disputatious continent.

OLIVER: Fair enough.

NADIA: That's why we went.

OLIVER: You were right.

NADIA: To get away.

OLIVER: Who can blame you?

NADIA: And if you look at recent American history—World War Two, Korea, Vietnam, the Cold War—then it's hardly surprising, is it? that so many of us are happier within our own borders. What's the point of being rich if you can't enjoy your wealth? When the Soviet Union collapsed, there was to be a dividend. We would live our own lives. But the opposite has happened. We're more and more drawn into the world.

OLIVER: You weren't exactly drawn into it, were you?

NADIA: Well . . .

OLIVER: More like, you stepped into it, don't you think?

NADIA: Depends which part.

OLIVER: Barged in, I'd say. The West's been using Islam as a useful enemy for as long as anyone can remember. "Shall we go to Constantinople and take the Turk by the beard? Shall we not?" It's from *Henry V.*

(*There is a silence.* OLIVER *speaks quietly.*)

Your feet will get wet. The dew comes early.

(OLIVER's *tone is so private that* NADIA *turns.*)

NADIA: And you? You read all night?

OLIVER: I don't need much sleep. It's a doctor's trick. Snatching sleep on the wards.

NADIA: Everything's a trick to you. You use that word all the time.

OLIVER: Do I?

NADIA: Yes.

(NADIA *stands, not moving.*)

OLIVER: How was the hill?
NADIA: I'm sorry?
OLIVER: Didn't you go up Shep Hill?
NADIA: Oh yes. It was spectacular.
OLIVER: What did you do up there?

(NADIA *hesitates for only a second.*)

I'm sorry. What a stupid question.
NADIA: And the view was great.
OLIVER: It is. It always is.

(*There's a moment's silence.*)

NADIA: Philip . . . Philip began to tell me about his mother.
OLIVER: Did he?
NADIA: He began to open up. He talks very little about her.
OLIVER: Maybe there's a reason.

(NADIA *catches his tone.*)

NADIA: It was a bad separation?
OLIVER: You could say.
NADIA: He said agonizing.
OLIVER: It was.
NADIA: She lives in North London? In your old house?
OLIVER: Yes.
NADIA: She never left?

(OLIVER *shakes his head.*)

OLIVER: Long before I decided to go, there were problems. She'd become
   obsessed with a need for control. To control life.
NADIA: Her own life?
OLIVER: Certainly. And, by extension, the lives of others.
NADIA: She's a doctor too?

(OLIVER *nods.*)

What do you mean by "control"?
OLIVER: It took different forms. It's one thing to put a label on the sugar jar
   saying "Sugar." You can put the word "Tea" on the jar where you keep the

tea. But when you type the word "Fridge" and put it on the fridge, then the signs are that you're in a certain amount of trouble. Easiest to say, her world shrank. From being a woman in the world she became a woman in flight from it. Even the trip to the hospital became unbearable to her.

NADIA: Because?

OLIVER: Oh, the feeling of being seen.

(NADIA *waits.*)

The feeling of being watched.

NADIA: Was she watched?

OLIVER: Of course not. Nobody gave a damn.

NADIA: Maybe that was the problem?

OLIVER: I don't think so.

NADIA: The feeling of being neglected. Your absences.

(OLIVER *thinks a moment.*)

OLIVER: Look, you know, plainly it's clear—

NADIA: All right, I shouldn't have said that—

OLIVER: Say what you like.

NADIA: It's none of my business.

OLIVER: Philip has his own view of things, of course he does. His mother's mental state is an issue between us. She's been on medication for a number of years. Philip thinks I'm to blame.

NADIA: He didn't actually say that.

OLIVER: Didn't he? It's no secret. Philip disapproved. Philip disapproved of our marriage. Of the kind of marriage we had.

NADIA: What kind of marriage was that?

OLIVER: The open kind. The kind in which love is free.

(*There is a silence.* NADIA *says nothing.*)

Philip's also in flight.

NADIA: Flight from what?

OLIVER: Why, from me. Why did he go to live in America?

NADIA: He's never said that.

OLIVER: No, but you know Philip. It's obvious. Philip defined his life in opposition to mine. England. America. Many partners. One. Pleasure in discourse. Pleasure in silence. I like early Dylan. He prefers late. That's who he is. Sees it as a kind of strength. He's an interesting chap.

(OLIVER *shrugs slightly.*)

For as long as he could, he tried to keep the peace between me and his mother. Then at a certain point he was forced to choose. I don't hold it against him. He likes me but he'll never trust me. Who's to say he's wrong?

(*They look at each other for a moment, level.*)

NADIA: Please. I'm not taking sides. I'm simply asking.
OLIVER: It's fine.
NADIA: I wouldn't have raised the subject but after all.
OLIVER: After all?
NADIA: We're alone on the lawn. There's no-one around.

(OLIVER *smiles.*)

OLIVER: It was you who said you needed private things to stay private.
NADIA: I did.
OLIVER: So? What is it? The night? The night is changing you?

(*There's a moment.* NADIA *looks at him.*)

NADIA: In combat medicine, there's this moment—after a disaster, after a shooting—there's this moment, the vertical hour, when you can actually be of some use.
OLIVER: Of use to me?

(OLIVER *looks, disbelieving. Then he begins to speak decisively.*)

Very well. Our marriage. If you want to know. If you're interested.
NADIA: I am.
OLIVER: I've tried to understand. I've tried to understand what happened between us. Pauline began to suffer from the very thing she most wanted.
NADIA: What was that thing?
OLIVER: Freedom. She suffered from freedom.

(*There's a moment.* OLIVER *waits.*)

Pauline said to me, very early on, she said, I remember her saying, "I don't believe human beings need to practise holding on. Holding on is easy. It's letting go we need to learn."
NADIA: Really?
OLIVER: Yes.
NADIA: That's a hard view.

OLIVER: Is it?

NADIA: Certainly.

OLIVER: I don't think so.

NADIA: It's a hard way to live.

OLIVER: Excuse me, but I'm not sure anyone who makes their living as a foreign correspondent is in any position to judge.

NADIA: Why not?

OLIVER: What, rushing abroad to dangerous places?

NADIA: It isn't that simple.

OLIVER: Isn't it?

NADIA: Are you telling me I was running away?

OLIVER: I didn't say that.

NADIA: Well what?

OLIVER: All I'm saying: you didn't choose the most obvious way of life for someone who wants to invest everything in another human being.

NADIA: Maybe, but I gave it up, remember?

(*He looks a moment, but* NADIA *doesn't go on.*)

OLIVER: All right. So. Pauline arrived in my bed with no intention of staying there. We were carefree. We worked day and night.

NADIA: You worked in a hospital?

OLIVER: Yes.

NADIA: That's when you were a specialist?

OLIVER: Training. Training to be. Pauline was already living in a certain way— we were medical students, we grew up in the sixties. For God's sake, the body's our field. If you've ever worried what a doctor is thinking when he asks you to take your clothes off, you needn't worry anymore. I can tell you the answer. Never underestimate the medical professional's capacity for filthy-mindedness. Pauline had no intention of changing just because she'd met me. You may not believe this, but people of that age, we had an idea. Underneath all the bullshit, all the evasion, all the "I'll see you tomorrow" when you mean *you won't—ever*—you'd cross the road if you so much as saw the other person coming—we actually had an idea.

NADIA: What kind of idea?

OLIVER: We believed.

NADIA: What did you believe?

OLIVER: Oh. The more people you sleep with, the more you learn.

(*There's a silence.* OLIVER *is quiet.*)

The liberation of Eros. All right, it's no longer a fashionable point of view.

NADIA: You could say.

OLIVER: It went the way of smoking. But that's what we thought. The more widely you love, the wider your capacity for love becomes.

NADIA: Did you really believe that?

OLIVER: It was a different time.

NADIA: It certainly was.

OLIVER: Love's a feeling, isn't it? It's a feeling. It isn't the truth.

NADIA: Is it?

(*There's a silence.*)

Go on.

OLIVER: There was a lot of talk about ownership. About not being owned. People not being property. William Blake to his wife: "If you wish my happiness, how can you not wish me happy with someone else?"

(NADIA *grins.*)

NADIA: They're handy, these poets of yours, aren't they?

OLIVER: Well they are.

NADIA: Never really on your own, are you?

OLIVER: Not really.

NADIA: You always have a poet around.

(NADIA *shakes her head, disbelieving.*)

I must say, it does take a particular gift, it takes a particular flair—you sleep with a lot of women and somehow you want to claim it *means* something?

OLIVER: Well?

NADIA: I have to ask, this "generation" you talk about—you think it was time well spent, do you, dreaming up a philosophy to justify what anyone else would have known was simple selfishness?

OLIVER: I think it may go a little deeper than that.

NADIA: Do you? What's the idea? You sleep with a lot of people and it's an *ideal?*

OLIVER: Well, so it was.

NADIA: I mean, the obvious question, why not just fuck 'em for fun?

OLIVER: All right . . .

NADIA: That's what the rest of us do.

(*There is a moment's silence.*)

Did do. Did do.

OLIVER: Before you met Philip.

NADIA: Right.

(NADIA *smiles, acknowledging the slip. She makes a gesture of "What can you do?"*)

OLIVER: You may be right. Though it didn't feel like that at the time. For a start, we were a lot happier than our parents.

NADIA: Isn't everyone?

(OLIVER *smiles, acknowledging the truth.*)

OLIVER: As time went by, I admit, there was a burden of guilt.

NADIA: Specifically?

OLIVER: The ending of the relationship was, for one reason or another, spectacular. Has Philip never said?

(NADIA *shakes her head.*)

But also the more general question: Could I have made this woman less unhappy?

NADIA: Could you?

OLIVER: How can you tell? I'm nearly sixty.

NADIA: Does that make a difference?

OLIVER: I've learnt a little respect for mystery.

(OLIVER *smiles.*)

The fashion now is to attack Freud. He's not acceptable, is he?

NADIA: Freud?

OLIVER: Not anymore.

NADIA: I don't know. Isn't he?

OLIVER: But there he is, working away, trying to define the impossible line between what we need to suffer and what we don't. We can try to understand each other, we have to, it's our life's work, but finally, Freud comes to us and reports that people remain unknowable. It's strange, isn't it? it's typical that we're all so keen to dismiss this man—"a prisoner of his time," we say—but in their resentment, their determination he should be obsolete, nobody sees, nobody remembers: there's something beautiful about what Freud's telling us. So many scientists leave the world diminished. He leaves it enlarged. He doesn't explain life. Rather he warns us to take care because so much is inexplicable.

(OLIVER *smiles.*)

NADIA: Is that his message?

OLIVER: Among others.

NADIA: I've never really known.

OLIVER: You don't approve?

NADIA: Not that. More: one of my students . . .

OLIVER: Yes?

NADIA: . . . brought Freud up—only the other day.

OLIVER: And?

NADIA: And I did notice, it did occur to me, people usually talk about Freud when they want to get their own way. They talk about Freud because they don't like the look of the facts.

OLIVER: You mean they use him because he's convenient?

NADIA: Exactly. That's exactly what I mean.

OLIVER: In what way?

NADIA: "I don't want to fuck you." "Oh yes you do. *Underneath.*"

(*They both smile.*)

Freud's used to justify everything, isn't he? "It's not my fault. It was my mother." Hear the word "Freud" and it's like a flag. You know there's an excuse coming. I mean, wouldn't it be refreshing to restore the notion of *bad behaviour*? And people being responsible for what they do? You do something wrong, you own up, you pay the price! Wouldn't that be refreshing!

OLIVER: Goodness.

NADIA: I know.

OLIVER: Well, goodness.

(OLIVER *smiles.* NADIA *stands, slightly taken aback by her own outburst.*)

Something tells me you're winding up for a drink.

NADIA: As a matter of fact, I am. Do you mind?

OLIVER: Not in the slightest.

NADIA: What time is it?

OLIVER: Five.

NADIA: OK.

OLIVER: Five's a good time for a chardonnay.

(NADIA *pours a huge slug from a remaining bottle.*)

NADIA: I'm sorry . . .

OLIVER: No . . .

NADIA: It's ridiculous.

OLIVER: Not at all.

NADIA: I know I sound harsh . . .

OLIVER: It doesn't bother me. Nothing bothers me.

NADIA: But I travel in so many countries where all this stuff counts for nothing.

OLIVER: I'm sure.

NADIA: It counts for nothing! It means nothing!

(NADIA *has raised her voice, vehement.* OLIVER *throws an anxious glance to the house.*)

I don't know, you can't help noticing when you return . . . when I came back, last time, say, from Iraq . . .

OLIVER: Is that when you met Philip?

NADIA: Yes.

OLIVER: How long ago?

NADIA: A year. It was a year ago.

(NADIA *stands a moment, thinking.*)

What is it now? Seventy-nine journalists already dead, the most dangerous war in the history of my profession.

OLIVER: Your ex-profession.

NADIA: OK. Anyway, this last time I went to observe, not to report. I went as an academic. Not that it matters. They kill you whoever you are. And yes, it's true, I came back to my nice job at Yale, I looked at these kids, looked at my colleagues and I thought, "I know I've got to resist this feeling, I know I've got to fight it, but these people seem spoiled. They seem soft and spoiled."

(NADIA *thinks, then drinks her wine.*)

OLIVER: And so we are.

NADIA: As if nothing worried them except their jobs and their bosses and their fucking love-lives. And I remember thinking, "I have no right to despise these people, I have no right to look down on them . . ."

OLIVER: Nor have you.

NADIA: I remember thinking, "I don't like this feeling. I don't like this feeling at all. I'm not different. I'm the same. I'm not better. Just as confused.

Just as lost. Covering up by always having a purpose, always having an intention . . ."

OLIVER: But underneath?

NADIA: Exactly.

(*There is a long silence.* NADIA *shakes her head.*)

"Underneath."

(*Suddenly* NADIA's *eyes well up with tears. She stands, fighting them back. With no warning at all, she is crying.* OLIVER *makes the slightest move towards her, but she puts up a hand. Then she goes and pours herself a second, large glass of wine.*)

OLIVER: So?

NADIA: So—something I've never done—I went to the gym.

OLIVER: Well, fair enough.

NADIA: The classic response—go to the gym, make minute adjustments to the proportion of body fat to muscle, conform to social norms: Skinny! Skinny! I was in the gym. I was standing there, thinking nothing, or rather just thinking, "Live a long life! Look as much like other people as possible!" And suddenly there was Philip. Standing near me. Incredibly composed. Strong.

OLIVER: What did you think?

NADIA: I thought, "Here's someone who looks as if he knows who he is."

(NADIA *shakes her head.*)

Shaming.

OLIVER: Why? Why shaming?

NADIA: I suppose . . . I'm ashamed to say this. I'm not sixteen.

OLIVER: It was romantic?

NADIA: Kind of. Yes.

OLIVER: Say it.

NADIA: You're not supposed to like men's looks, are you? Aren't looks meant to be a sign of shallowness? They say, "He was good-looking, in a shallow sort of way." They never say, "He was good-looking and it was profound." They never say that.

(NADIA *shrugs.*)

Oh be clear, it wasn't just his looks . . .

OLIVER: Of course not.

NADIA: For a start, I liked the idea that he didn't come from my world.

OLIVER: Well, no.

NADIA: He's not bothered by things that bother me. Nothing he couldn't do. Fix a car. My car broke down. Even my roof. He knew what store to go to, he could re-tile a roof. There he was, within hours of our meeting.

OLIVER: Up on your roof?

NADIA: I remember thinking, "I've never met a man like this. A man who can actually do things." I wanted him.

(OLIVER *looks at her thoughtfully.*)

I'd always associated passion with turbulence. With upset. This was passion, only benign. That's rare. That's very rare.

OLIVER: I imagine, after what you'd been through, it came as a relief.

NADIA: It did.

OLIVER: I'm sure.

NADIA: I might as well tell you, there are so many kinds of men who don't attract me. Include in that: journalists, academics, people who talk about politics all day.

OLIVER: You mean, people like you?

NADIA: Exactly. I've never been attracted to anyone like me.

(*They both smile.*)

OLIVER: So who does attract you?

NADIA: Oh . . .

OLIVER: You have the air of someone who's had their heart broken.

NADIA: What makes you say that? Why do you say that?

(OLIVER *looks at her, not answering.*)

Out of the blue, out of the blue, you say that.

(NADIA *looks shaken. She stands, waiting for him to explain.*)

OLIVER: All right. Last night, when you were talking, when you were talking about your past, about Sarajevo, I couldn't help thinking: this is a woman who's been badly hurt.

NADIA: What, you think you can see right through me?

OLIVER: No.

NADIA: Though, of course, it's not surprising, is it, given your area of expertise? All your background, all your experience . . .

OLIVER: All right . . .

NADIA: All your women.

(*The mood has changed.* NADIA *is on the attack.*)

In fact, would you mind, can I just say something?

OLIVER: Of course.

NADIA: Earlier . . .

OLIVER: Yes?

NADIA: When you were telling me about your marriage? How difficult it was. How hard to understand. I found myself wondering: You were speaking so tenderly. With such longing. OK, it must be tempting but weren't you rather overdoing the clouds of romantic mystery?

OLIVER: Was I?

NADIA: It's one of those things. One of those gender things. Women's ears tend to get fine-tuned.

OLIVER: Fine-tuned? Fine-tuned to what?

NADIA: Lying. Men who lie.

(NADIA *looks, unapologetic.*)

You made a deal. Didn't you? Isn't that the truth? The two of you made a cynical deal. It suited you. As time went by, it turned out it didn't suit her. She grew out of it. You didn't. Are things really any more complicated than that?

(*For the first time she has reached* OLIVER. NADIA *looks at him, then almost laughs before she moves away. He speaks quietly, to himself.*)

OLIVER: I think they are. I don't think that begins to get near it.

NADIA: In fact, I can't believe it, I sat here yesterday, I was sitting here . . .

OLIVER: So?

NADIA: Eating my breakfast, you made me feel terrible, you gave me shit about going to see my president . . .

OLIVER: What shit? I don't remember giving you shit.

NADIA: As if you could judge me! As if somehow you were entitled to judge me!

(*Again,* NADIA *has raised her voice, newly confident of what she wants to say.*)

The funny thing is, I didn't even mind at the time.

OLIVER: Didn't mind what?

NADIA: My interrogation.

OLIVER: Oh come on! Interrogation!

NADIA: I didn't even notice. At the time I just thought, "Oh this is an Englishman. I've heard about this, this is the kind of guy who sits on his lawn and thinks it's demeaning to get involved in anything."

OLIVER: Is that me? Is that meant to be a description of me?

NADIA: Charming as hell. But lethal.

(NADIA *looks at him a moment.*)

If you really want to know, I didn't go to the White House because I was under any illusions.

OLIVER: Of course not.

NADIA: I wasn't going for myself. I went because I thought it was necessary.

OLIVER: Sure.

NADIA: I went because I thought it might be useful. It might be worthwhile.

OLIVER: I'm sure. I'm sure you did.

(NADIA *waits.*)

NADIA: Well? What's wrong with that?

OLIVER: I didn't say it was wrong.

NADIA: What's the alternative? We just give up, do we?

OLIVER: Of course not.

NADIA: The rest of us give up?

(OLIVER *says nothing.*)

It's easy, isn't it? It's easy, your position?

OLIVER: Do I have a position?

NADIA: Stay home, sit on your hands, look superior, say this administration's nothing but a bunch of seedy opportunists and crooks?

OLIVER: You said it.

NADIA: Yes, but like it or not, they're the party in power.

OLIVER: Of course.

NADIA: They're the guys.

OLIVER: Of course.

NADIA: Fuck their ideology, fuck their golf-cart morals and their tenth-rate business deals—but I happen to agree with them on one basic thing: it isn't a bad idea when people are suffering—when you're faced with that scale of suffering, you act. You help.

(*Again,* NADIA *has raised her voice.* OLIVER *looks again to the house.*)

OLIVER: All right, no need to jump off a building.

NADIA: I'm not.

OLIVER: Defensive or what?

NADIA: Oh, we're all defensive, aren't we? Don't we both have things to be defensive about?

(OLIVER *just looks at her, a little shaken.*)

Yeah, sure, you're the generation that talked about ideals, have I got that right?

OLIVER: Roughly.

NADIA: Everything had to be an ideal.

OLIVER: So?

NADIA: Everything was a matter of principle! You may have noticed—we are more practical. I admire the practical people. I deal with what's there.

(NADIA *nods, bitter, speaking from the heart.*)

"Ancient hatreds," that's what they always tell you. In the Balkans I got so tired of hearing that phrase. "Ancient hatreds." Whenever people tried to explain what the hell was going on. Oh yes, people love ancient hatreds, because if it's an ancient hatred, what can you do? You don't have to do anything. They tell you all the time in Israel, in Palestine, in Bosnia, in Chechnya, in Ireland, "Oh there's nothing you can do until these crazy people decide to stop killing each other. They *like* killing each other." Well it's never true. What is true is that wherever there's a history of violence you can be sure to find unscrupulous politicians looking to exploit it. But underneath there are always rational causes. And "ancient hatreds" is just the phrase they drag out when they can't be bothered to do anything at all.

(NADIA *looks at* OLIVER.)

It took America years, you could say it's taken us centuries to understand we had responsibilities. And now we've acted, nobody gives a damn about the Iraqis. They just can't wait to tell us we were wrong. "You were wrong! You lose!" Do you think I haven't paid my price on campus? Kids with four by fours and private trust funds, coming in Gucci jeans and designer T-shirts saying, "Oh it's a matter of principle. I won't take class with Nadia Blye."

OLIVER: Has that really happened?

NADIA: Yeah, interesting, isn't it? Kids coming snarling up to you, spitting, "Hey, didn't you go to the White House? Aren't you the woman who spoke to George Bush?"

(NADIA *impulsively moves away.*)

What do you think? What do you think it was like? That day I went to Washington ...

OLIVER: I can't imagine.

NADIA: It's true, I walked in that day, I thought this is the oddest thing I've ever done in my life.

OLIVER: I'm sure.

NADIA: Who are these people? What am I doing here? And then you remember it's democracy you're there to defend. So. In fact, when it comes down to it, there's only one "principle." I'll tell you what that principle is: push up your sleeves, put away your personality, and get on with the work.

(NADIA *is quieter now, her emotion raw.*)

The only reason you're there, the reason you're talking to the president is that you happen to be an expert on issues exactly like this. And isn't it better to talk to people we have nothing in common with? Isn't that better? Isn't that more useful than just talking to ourselves?

OLIVER: Yes.

(OLIVER *smiles.*)

Yes, by all means. It's better. Always assuming people are listening.

NADIA: Of course.

OLIVER: It's quite a large assumption. Isn't it?

(NADIA *just looks at him. She is apprehensive now, nervous.*)

And you have to consider another possibility, don't you?

NADIA: What's that? What other possibility?

OLIVER: It must have occurred to you. I would have thought: don't you have to take care you're not being used?

(NADIA *is quiet, no longer fighting him.*)

NADIA: Yes. Of course. I accept that. I know that. Of course I do.

(OLIVER *shrugs slightly.*)

OLIVER: After all, I don't know what you told the president.

NADIA: No, you don't.

OLIVER: I wasn't there.

NADIA: No, you weren't.

OLIVER: I can only guess. I assume it wasn't you who said, "Do it regardless of whether it's legal." I assume you didn't say, "Drop bombs where you like. Don't take field hospitals, lawyers, sanitary engineers, doctors, or any of the apparatus that any decent, resultant society might actually need. Forget those. Don't take enough troops. Just bomb and hope for the best." I can't see you saying that.

(OLIVER *waits a moment. It is now very quiet.*)

I assume you didn't say, "Be sure to have no plan for civil society. Take no notice of international opinion. Manufacture intelligence from the most corrupt and dishonest elements in the country. Sanction torture. Ignore objections. Be deaf to criticism. Somehow magically order will come out of chaos."

NADIA: No. You're right. I didn't say that.

OLIVER: You didn't say, "It doesn't matter if tens of thousands of people get killed, just so long as they're not Americans . . ."

(*They are both still,* NADIA *conceding at last.*)

NADIA: Jesus, what a mess.

OLIVER: You could say.

NADIA: We certainly made a mess of it, didn't we? Oh God, I'm so tired.

(NADIA *is vulnerable. There are tears in her eyes again.*)

It's so much easier to do nothing than something.

(OLIVER *reaches out a hand. She takes it. There is a silence, he seated, she standing, holding hands. Then, after a while,* NADIA *shakes her head, and goes and sits down at the abandoned dinner table.*)

It's true. As you guessed.

OLIVER: What's true?

NADIA: I did have a relationship.

(OLIVER *doesn't move.*)

I did. A journalist. He's Polish. I'd been with him in the Balkans. Then, as luck would have it, who's the first person I meet when I drive into Baghdad? What you might call a hard-line reporter. Meaning: fair chance he's going to get killed. Meaning also: he doesn't give a fuck about anything. Including himself.

OLIVER: That's difficult.

NADIA: It is. Or anyone else. Including me. As it turns out.

(NADIA *thinks a moment.*)

Six foot tall. Thin as a rake. A professional. Meaning: he has no opinions. Opinions are for idiots, he says. Oh he gets angry. He gets involved. But it's the job he loves. Dodging bullets. He's unequivocal. He says he couldn't live in the West.

OLIVER: What you're saying is, he's heroic.

NADIA: Yes. Heroic. Heroic. Completely oblivious of his own personal safety. And in the evening . . . he likes to get drunk.

OLIVER: What's his name?

NADIA: Marek.

(NADIA *looks away.*)

I couldn't take it. He turned me inside out. Like gutting a fish. I'd never known anything like it. I was jealous. Oh, not just ordinary jealous. But wanting to be as alive as he was. So little frightened. I thought, I can't do anything. I can't work, I can't sleep. This will kill me.

(NADIA *shakes her head slightly.*)

Anyway, I came back to America. I met Philip. You'll think me contemptible.

OLIVER: No.

NADIA: I want to tell you something. I shouldn't. You're going to hate me for saying this.

OLIVER: Please.

NADIA: I thought, if I just live quietly with Philip, then I'll get my private life out of the way.

(OLIVER *sits back, as if this is what he's been waiting for.*)

And that's what happened.

OLIVER: I see.

NADIA: It's been very peaceful. I've been at peace. I've gotten on with my work.

OLIVER: That's good.

NADIA: The students don't bother me. The stuff on campus—it doesn't touch me.

OLIVER: Good.

NADIA: Why should it? Philip's always there. He's there when I need him.

OLIVER: Does he know?
NADIA: Oh yes.
OLIVER: About who came before him?
NADIA: Certainly.
OLIVER: He doesn't mind?

(NADIA *doesn't answer.*)

What I'm asking: he can live with the difference?
NADIA: He's not second-best. If that's what you mean.
OLIVER: I didn't mean that.
NADIA: Good. He's different. Easier.
OLIVER: And easier's better?

(NADIA *hesitates.*)

NADIA: I thought so. Yes. I had thought so. Until I came here.

(NADIA *shakes her head.*)

OLIVER: Are you all right?
NADIA: I'm fine.
OLIVER: Too much to drink perhaps?
NADIA: No. Too little.

(*They both smile.*)

What about you?
OLIVER: I'm not drinking.
NADIA: No. That's not what I meant.

(OLIVER *now understands her.*)

OLIVER: Oh. Oh I see.
NADIA: I've told you what happened to me.
OLIVER: Yes.
NADIA: Well?
OLIVER: It's so long since I talked about anything. To anyone.
NADIA: Exactly.

(*He looks at her for a while, then concedes.*)

OLIVER: All right.
NADIA: Are you going to tell me about the person you killed?
OLIVER: Yes. That person. It's what ended my marriage. It was an accident.

NADIA: I hadn't imagined you killed someone deliberately.

OLIVER: No.

(OLIVER *hesitates.*)

Well, you have to understand, I don't know if you know this, the guts are distributed between various specialists. I was a nephrologist. I was very much the man. The man you went to, in that ridiculous snobbish way people have. "Who's best? Who's best for kidneys?" "Oliver Lucas for kidneys." I was very, very rich and conceited. Arrogant, in the way doctors are. I'd been in the country. East Anglia. I was driving back.

NADIA: Had you been drinking?

OLIVER: No. I'd spent an afternoon in bed with a friend. I left about five. I thought if I can be home by supper, I can avoid the inevitable scene. I was on a country road. The man was in his mid-eighties, in one of those—I don't know, we have them in England—Eastern European cars, incredibly lightweight. Not even soft skins, no skins. He went straight into me. He never even saw me. I'd signalled incorrectly.

(OLIVER *looks straight at her.*)

The police afterwards said it would have made no difference. It was what they call a 50-50. Yes, I'd signalled left, intending to go right, but this man was on the wrong side of the road.

(OLIVER *stops a moment, thoughtful.*)

You might say, all right, he was going to die anyway . . .

NADIA: He was in his eighties.

OLIVER: That's right. Sometimes at the hospital it used to occur to us we were slaving to save a human being who'd be dead in two weeks. But that's the contract.

NADIA: What's the contract?

OLIVER: Life at all costs.

(OLIVER *looks at* NADIA, *apparently casual.*)

I also killed the woman.

NADIA: What?

OLIVER: Yes. She died at my side. In the crash. I was giving her a lift back to London.

(*There is a silence.*)

She was killed instantly. We spun over and I laid her out in the road. Bad luck. She hit her head at an unlucky angle. Very little visible damage. She had a silk scarf round her neck. Soaked in blood. Very shocking. Apart from that, nothing.

NADIA: Who was she?

OLIVER: I'd met her at a party. You might say, I didn't even know her. But of course I did know her. We'd spent several afternoons together. But I didn't . . . oh God, it turned out she'd told me all sorts of lies. Almost nothing she'd told me was true. She was a fantasist. She was married. Something she'd omitted to mention. Not that I'd asked. That wasn't the nature of the venture. But still.

(NADIA *is shocked, silent.*)

NADIA: My God.

OLIVER: Exactly. From the bed to the roadside.

NADIA: How old was she?

OLIVER: Young. Younger than me. There was a husband, who was . . . lunatic. Impossible. Understandably. Wanted to sue me. A lot of stuff about the General Medical Council. But it was an accident. After all, in theory, I'd done nothing wrong.

(OLIVER *is lost in thought.*)

It was Marx, I think, who said that shame is the only revolutionary emotion. And so. I gave her everything.

NADIA: Pauline?

OLIVER: I gave her the house and every penny I had.

NADIA: You left your practice?

OLIVER: I did.

NADIA: And came here?

OLIVER: I left London. I came to live in Shropshire. I moved away to where I wouldn't do harm.

(OLIVER *shrugs slightly.*)

Of course for Pauline—for Philip also—it was a simple issue. My wife had always said I was a despicable person. So at last here was the proof. She detected the workings of justice. It was what I deserved. For myself I was tired of justifying myself to another human being. I walked out. I came here to be a GP. It felt clean, it felt refreshing to stand aside from the racket. I need enough money to live, to drink decent wine, to buy books. Why do I need money to put in the bank?

(OLIVER *is quiet now.*)

To me, you see, the lesson was different. It wasn't what Philip believes. To me the lesson was, You can't spend your life in flight. Sometime you have to stop running.

(OLIVER *looks at her.*)

I'm sorry. Perhaps I shouldn't have said that.

NADIA: No. No. Say what you want.

OLIVER: I see life for what it is: fragile. Every moment for what it is: potentially disastrous. And, at all times, I try to take care.

(PHILIP *appears silently behind them, in night-clothes. He is very quiet.*)

PHILIP: Here you are.

NADIA: Yes. I was talking to your father.

PHILIP: I can see. I was dreaming. I dreamt you weren't beside me. Then I woke up.

NADIA: Philip . . .

PHILIP: It's all right.

NADIA: We were just talking.

PHILIP: What else would you be doing? What time is it?

OLIVER: It isn't yet six.

(PHILIP *moves barefoot across the lawn, the two of them watching.*)

PHILIP: It's a beautiful morning.

OLIVER: It is.

PHILIP: Of course that's what you don't get in America.

OLIVER: What's that?

PHILIP: The softness. The softness of the dawn. Nadia's an early riser. So she's already at work when I wake. I look out the window for a moment. It's the only time of day when I do feel nostalgic.

(*There is a silence, no-one daring to speak.*)

OLIVER: Then what happens?

PHILIP: Oh. I go to make coffee and I cheer up.

(PHILIP *turns.*)

I'll make some now. Do we all want coffee?

OLIVER: I'll make it. I can make it.

(OLIVER's *beeper sounds*.)

NADIA: What's that?

OLIVER: It's probably a customer. I'm on death-watch. A patient of mine. I may have to go anyway. Excuse me.

(OLIVER *has got up, and he goes out, taking some dirty dishes with him*.)

NADIA: Are you angry?

PHILIP: Why should I be angry?

NADIA: Then good.

(*There is another silence*.)

He hasn't said one single word in any way disloyal to you.

PHILIP: Of course not. He's not stupid.

NADIA: What does that mean?

PHILIP: He has a strategy.

(PHILIP *shakes his head slightly*.)

I knew you'd get up. I didn't need to look. I knew you'd go to him.

NADIA: Were you awake?

(PHILIP *doesn't answer*.)

And as it happens, I wasn't looking for him. It never occurred to me. I simply had jet-lag. I didn't even know he was outside.

PHILIP: Didn't you?

NADIA: What's wrong? What's wrong with our talking?

PHILIP: Because I'm sure he was spinning a line.

NADIA: That's not fair.

PHILIP: Isn't it? And tell me, how would you know?

(*There's a silence*.)

NADIA: Talk to me, Philip. You use these silences. You use them against me. Tell me what's wrong.

(PHILIP *turns and looks at her*.)

PHILIP: He wants you to leave me. I know him. That's what he wants. He wants to split us up.

NADIA: Why would he want that?

PHILIP: He's jealous.

NADIA: Why is he jealous?

PHILIP: Isn't it obvious?

NADIA: Tell me.

PHILIP: Because we have something he's never had.

(*There's a silence.* PHILIP *looks at her and nods, as if knowing he's right.*)

NADIA: And?

PHILIP: And what?

NADIA: And even if that's true, why would I leave you?

(PHILIP *doesn't answer.*)

What possible reason would I have to leave you?

(PHILIP *is quiet, regretful.*)

PHILIP: I had the idea we were perfectly aligned. When we met. We both have the same way of looking at the world. What you might call, a basically helpful attitude. We'd die rather than say so, but don't we both have this thing about trying to help?

NADIA: So?

PHILIP: It's odd. You've travelled more than I have. You've seen much more. But you still believe the world's all about argument and reason. You're power-blind. It's so obvious: he's trying to exert power over you. It's like there's a dimension missing from the way you look at people. You trust their good intentions.

NADIA: Don't you?

PHILIP: When I read what you write—someone does this, so someone else does that. You simply don't see it, do you? You're an innocent.

NADIA: I'm not an innocent.

(*Suddenly* PHILIP's *anger begins to show through.*)

PHILIP: I was born to an unhappy couple, remember? I woke up every morning, my parents were tearing each other apart. I keep the peace. That's what I'm good at. The conciliator. I've done it all my life.

NADIA: Well?

PHILIP: Until yesterday evening. I warned you against him. I said, be careful. I told you to be careful. You deliberately ignored me.

(OLIVER *returns with a tray.*)

OLIVER: It's a text message. We're losing her.

NADIA: Who's that?

OLIVER: A patient. I'm losing a patient. It's been clear for a while.

(PHILIP *is firm, a new resolution in his manner.*)

PHILIP: I was just about to suggest to Nadia it might be nice if we tried to get going.

NADIA: What?

PHILIP: I think we should get going. As we're all up. Why not?

OLIVER: Philip . . .

NADIA: Can we be practical? Where are you going?

(PHILIP *has turned to go out.*)

PHILIP: I'm going to pack.

NADIA: Pack?

PHILIP: Yes. Pack. Pack now. I was thinking that way we'll get to see something we wouldn't otherwise see. The road to Harlech is spectacular at this time of day.

(PHILIP *has gone.* OLIVER *is quietly clearing the table of last night's dishes onto the tray.* NADIA *looks across, hopeless.*)

OLIVER: I'm sorry. I'm not sure how, but I know this must be my fault.

NADIA: It's so stupid. I can't take it seriously.

OLIVER: Nevertheless.

(OLIVER *waits.*)

NADIA: I should go to him.

OLIVER: Yes.

(NADIA *goes out.* NADIA's *voice is heard calling.*)

NADIA (*off*): Philip! Philip! Are you really packing? Philip! Do you have any idea of the time?

(OLIVER *stands alone. Now dawn has broken, and the sun's rays are falling across the table.* OLIVER *looks out for a few moments. Then he dials a number on his mobile phone.*)

OLIVER: Yes, it's Doctor Lucas. How's she doing? I see. It's all right. I'll be down soon. I know, but I'd like to.

(OLIVER *listens for a moment.*)

Please don't concern yourself. It's my job.

(OLIVER *clicks the little phone shut.* NADIA *returns, more amused than upset.*)

How is he?
NADIA: Not good. He's locked the bedroom door. He won't speak to me.
OLIVER: You're joking. Have another.
NADIA: No thanks.

(NADIA *looks at him, genuine.*)

You've been very kind.
OLIVER: I wish.
NADIA: I mean it. But I will have to leave.
OLIVER: You will.
NADIA: It's better.
OLIVER: Yes. Undoubtedly.

(PHILIP *reappears.*)

PHILIP: I'm ready.
NADIA: Good. Let me go and get my things.

(NADIA *goes out.* PHILIP *is apprehensive.*)

OLIVER: Philip. What is this? Explain to me. You're angry with me. But why?
It was chance. I just happened to be sitting on the lawn.
PHILIP: In the middle of the night?
OLIVER: Yes. I was reading a book on linguistics.

(*There's a silence.*)

People are beginning to feel it may be the key to consciousness.
PHILIP: And it's coincidence, is it?
OLIVER: What's coincidence?
PHILIP: That she just happens to get up from my bed?
OLIVER: That. Yes. Coincidence.
PHILIP: And you discussed me?
OLIVER: Briefly. But not exclusively. We discussed others as well.
PHILIP: Why did you talk to her? Why did you have to talk to her, Dad?

(OLIVER *looks at him.*)

OLIVER: Philip, I am not Lucifer. I don't wish you ill.

PHILIP: I didn't say you were.

OLIVER: You can spend your whole life being angry with your father. It's a
waste. Truly.

(PHILIP *is listening now.*)

Who do you want to be thinking about on your deathbed?

PHILIP: I don't want to be on my deathbed.

OLIVER: No, well nor do I. Nor does anyone.

PHILIP: So?

OLIVER: In the normal sequence of things, it's a bad sign if you lie on your
deathbed thinking about your father! That is not a sign of a life well
lived. I would say if you're still thinking about your father, you've got real
problems.

PHILIP: I won't be.

OLIVER: Good.

PHILIP: Don't flatter yourself. I won't!

(*There is a moment's silence.* OLIVER *is quiet.*)

OLIVER: You ought to plan to be thinking of her.

(PHILIP *looks, only half-daring to trust him.*)

I mean it. She's worth it.

PHILIP: All right.

OLIVER: She's worth a whole lifetime.

PHILIP: Really?

OLIVER: Yes. That's my opinion. It's my opinion. If it's of any value to you.

(PHILIP *looks at him.*)

PHILIP: You mean it? You really mean it?

OLIVER: Come on, she's a great woman. She's extraordinary. However, you're
going to find she has what Americans call issues. She has unresolved issues.
And she has some incredibly stupid ideas. But there you are. You can't have
everything.

PHILIP: What sort of ideas?

OLIVER: She thinks she can set her private life away to one side. In an admirable determination to get on with things which she regards as far more
important. I've tried it. It's not going to work.

PHILIP: You said that to her?

OLIVER: Of course not.

PHILIP: What did you talk about?

OLIVER: Oh . . .

PHILIP: Tell me.

OLIVER: Nothing much.

PHILIP: Tell me. Please. Dad.

(PHILIP *nods.*)

OLIVER: Your mother. Iraq. The woman I killed. Politics. Solitude. Love.

(NADIA *returns, calm, humorous, fully dressed.*)

NADIA: All right. I agree. We drive towards nowhere.

OLIVER: Very well.

NADIA: I'm happy. Let's do it. Let's spend the day kicking our heels and feeling remorse. Harlech.

OLIVER: Have some coffee first. Let me get the stuff.

PHILIP: Dad . . .

OLIVER: Let me. I'd like to. At least have something before you set off.

(*He goes.* NADIA *and* PHILIP *are left alone.*)

NADIA: I'm sorry.

PHILIP: No. No, it's me who should be sorry. I don't know what happened. I thought he was trying to seduce you. I apologize. We can stay if you like.

(NADIA *says nothing.*)

I feel foolish.

NADIA: Don't.

(NADIA *looks at him, then makes a decision.*)

I think you're right. We should go.

(*They move together, and kiss. They stand holding on to each other. They look into each other's eyes. Then they part. Neither knows what to do. It's resolved, but it's not. Some moments go by.*)

Philip, I didn't mean to hurt you.

PHILIP: You didn't hurt me. Really.

(PHILIP *smiles.*)

NADIA: I like your father.

PHILIP: Good.

(PHILIP *waits for an answer, but before she can,* OLIVER *returns with a tray of cups and a cafetière.*)

OLIVER: Here we are. Let's have the coffee. Then I have to go and watch someone die.

PHILIP: Really? Do you have to? Why do you have to?

OLIVER: Because I said I would.

NADIA: Seems like a good reason.

OLIVER: The best.

(OLIVER *fusses over the cups and saucers. A few moments go by, everyone struck by the strangeness of the situation.*)

Anyone take sugar?

(NADIA *holds up her hand.* OLIVER *spoons some into her cup.*)

OLIVER: Philip, you always took milk.

(*They smile at one another. He hands them both coffee.*)

Good. Excellent.

(OLIVER *looks out at the hills.*)

What a splendid morning.

(*The three stand, nervously drinking their coffee.*)

NADIA: We'll drive carefully.

OLIVER: Please do.

9.

(OLIVER, *alone.*)

OLIVER: I walked down the hill. I sat at my patient's bedside all day. She was
tougher than I thought. My beeper was going. But years ago I learnt: deal
with one thing at a time. My patient lost life sometime early that evening.
I'd told her the truth and I'd stayed with her to the end.

For some time, I heard nothing from Philip, nothing from Nadia. In fact,
next time I read Nadia's name it was in another context entirely. When I
saw what it was, forgive me, it made me smile.

10.

(NADIA's *office*. NADIA *is once more casually dressed. Opposite her is* TERRI SCHOLES, *an African American, just twenty. She has not taken her jacket off.* NADIA *is holding an essay in her hand. She is passionate, disbelieving.*)

NADIA: All right. I don't know. Really. I'm lost for a response. You're an intelligent student. You're much more than that. You're a highly intelligent person. What are you actually saying? Have you thought about it? Is this what you think? Not "I've got to do an essay, so I'd better write something," but, "I actually *believe* this. This—this is what I believe"?

(NADIA *holds the essay out, quoting.*)

"Why did Bush go to war? Because he could." What kind of a statement is that? "Because he knew he'd get away with it." Do you call that a theory? "For Bush and those like him, the exercise of power is enough in itself. America went to war for no strategic objective. Iraq was irrelevant to the war on terror and that was the reason it was chosen. The point of the action was its very arbitrariness. To demonstrate to any possible enemy of the US that no-one should ever consider themselves safe."

(NADIA *smiles and holds the pages out to* TERRI.)

Yeah, well, it's an interesting thesis, but, unburdened by evidence, maybe it doesn't quite have the impact you hope.

(NADIA *waits, but* TERRI *is not responding.*)

I mean, Terri, this isn't a talk show. This isn't talk radio. It's not "Let's go into the studio and say stupid things." This is an essay. In a serious discipline. The causes and origins of the war in Iraq. Jesus, I hear this stuff—as you do. I don't know what's happened. Suddenly everyone's a blowhard. Yale—the point of Yale University is—very simply—that it should be a blowhard-free zone.

(NADIA *quickly corrects herself.*)

By which—look, I'm not calling you a blowhard.

TERRI: Thanks.

NADIA: I understand there's such a thing as disaffection. I do. When you're young. It's great. In the 19ᵗʰ century there was a movement in Russia called nihilism. Have you heard of it?

TERRI: Sure.

NADIA: I think you have.

TERRI: I've heard of it.

NADIA: That's the irony. Of all my students, you're one of the few who would even know what it was. But truly, they should find you an application form. Do you remember what it was they believed in?

TERRI: Nothing.

NADIA: They believed in nothing! Exactly!

TERRI: Random acts of violence.

NADIA: Right. Do you?

TERRI: No, I don't. Not the violence.

NADIA: OK. Good. So just the believing-in-nothing. Terri, there's a darkness in this essay. There's a scary kind of hopelessness. Are you going to tell me what's going on?

(*There's a moment's silence.*)

TERRI: All right. I'll tell you.

NADIA: Thank you.

TERRI: For a couple of weeks now, I've been breaking up with my boyfriend.

NADIA: Say what?

TERRI: My boyfriend's left me.

(NADIA *frowns.*)

NADIA: Well, I'm sorry. I don't know what to say. I'm sorry.

TERRI: Not as sorry as me.

(*They both smile.*)

NADIA: No.

TERRI: And losing him . . .

NADIA: Yes?

TERRI: Losing him . . . it's made me think hard. It's made me realize a whole heap of things.

NADIA: About American foreign policy?

TERRI: No. No, not about that. More about—more about really, how I don't want to stay on at Yale.

NADIA: Terri . . .

TERRI: I don't want to. Not without him.

(NADIA *looks in disbelief.*)

NADIA: Oh come on . . .

TERRI: No, I'm serious.

NADIA: I know you are. That's why I'm indignant.

TERRI: It's what I feel.

NADIA: It may be what you feel.

TERRI: It is. It is what I feel.

NADIA: I can't believe someone as gifted as you is seriously thinking of quitting solely because of some boy.

TERRI: He isn't some boy.

NADIA: No.

TERRI: He's not just some boy.

NADIA: I'm sorry.

TERRI: How would you like it if I talked about someone you knew and called him "some boy"?

NADIA: I shouldn't have said that. I apologize.

(*There's a silence.*)

TERRI: I met him more or less the first day I got here.

NADIA: And?

TERRI: Just one example: every brick in this place reminds me of him.

(TERRI *is a little teary, vulnerable.*)

OK, maybe it's part of the problem, I didn't bother to make other friends. I didn't need to. And some of the people I did meet didn't exactly make me want to meet any more.

NADIA: No.

TERRI: And also—I don't want to walk out on campus and see him with somebody else. So, the point of all this: I put a lot of work in that essay. It's serious. It may be the last thing I write.

(NADIA *looks at her, thoughtful.*)

NADIA: No, it's just—look—I'm not your counsellor, I'm your teacher.

TERRI: It's fine. You can't hurt me. I've been hurt enough already.

(NADIA *takes another nervous, speculative look.*)

NADIA: Just: I have some idea what you're going through.

TERRI: You do?

NADIA: By an interesting coincidence, this summer I broke up with someone as well.

TERRI: Why?

NADIA: Why? Well, we went on a ridiculous visit to Wales—or rather the bit beside Wales. He and I had been pretty close and yet for some reason, when I started talking with his father . . . I guess I began to see the son differently. Do you think that's unfair?

TERRI: Well it is unfair, isn't it?

NADIA: I don't think so.

TERRI: Was his father trying to break you up?

NADIA: That's what my boyfriend believed.

TERRI: That's what I'd believe.

NADIA: Yeah. But I didn't feel that. I really don't think he was. I was only there one night. We sat out on the lawn. It was like I'd been revealed to myself.

TERRI: And what was revealed?

NADIA: I felt my own cowardice. He made me feel I'd been cowardly. In all sorts of ways. I'd made easy, cowardly choices. And also: I had this conviction—for as long as I stayed with Philip, I couldn't be true to myself.

(TERRI *looks at her unconvinced.*)

TERRI: Yeah, well there's a difference, isn't there?

NADIA: What difference?

TERRI: You were with the wrong man.

NADIA: I don't know.

TERRI: And I was with the right one. It does make a difference.

NADIA: Yes. Yes, it's just—reading your essay, which perhaps I now begin to understand, I have this uneasy feeling that you may have been doing what psychologists call "projecting" your unhappiness onto the subject in hand. We have to fight this, we have to make this not about ourselves, we have to fight our own feelings, we must try and be objective.

TERRI: I think I am. I'm not that stupid.

NADIA: I've never said you were stupid.

TERRI: I know we're looking at two different things. First thing—my boyfriend has gone off with a girl who looks as if she eats shit with a dirty spoon, and also—second thing—I'm deeply despairing of the direction my government has recently been taking. I think I can hold both these things in my head at one time.

NADIA: Yes, of course . . .

TERRI: Without confusing them!

NADIA: I'm not saying you're confusing them. All I'm saying is—*look!*

(*Both of them have raised their voices.*)

I suppose I feel this so passionately—it's terribly important you don't simply give up.

(NADIA *picks the essay up again.*)

You say here, "There is only one truth. The powerful exploit the powerless. Indiscriminately," you say. "And without any conscience. Rich countries are, by definition, massively self-interested and will never reach out to help anyone else. Whoever heard of a country," you ask, "which gave up power or wealth voluntarily? Nothing ever changes except by the use of force. Reason never prevails."

(NADIA *throws it down.*)

I just ask: how can you write that?

TERRI: Because I've just lived through the last five years. I read the papers. I watch television. It's what I've seen for myself.

NADIA: You're twenty, Terri. What are you suggesting? Everything's cynicism, is it—already?

TERRI: No. But why pretend? Why argue for things which aren't going to happen? Like the world getting any more sensible?

NADIA: Because we have no other choice!

(NADIA *has yelled out in anger, way beyond the demands of the situation. Realising this, she moves across the room and speaks more quietly.*)

This is what gets to me. Despair's an affectation. That's what I think. It's self-indulgence.

TERRI: I don't think so. It's more like not fooling yourself.

(NADIA *looks at her, then goes and sits down at her desk.*)

NADIA: I don't know. You must do what you think best. Please don't do it unthinkingly. All I'm saying is: just be careful. Delay any decision.

TERRI: Well I will.

NADIA: In either context. Your studies or your private life. After all, he may come back to you.

(*They both smile.*)

TERRI: Thank you. Is that the end of the class?

NADIA: I guess it is.

TERRI: I'm going to give it twenty-four hours and then see how I feel.
NADIA: Well that's sensible. Good.

(NADIA *holds out the discarded essay.*)

Take this. I don't want it.

(TERRI *takes it from her and heads for the door.* NADIA *clicks on her desk lamp to prepare to work. Then she looks up.*)

Oh, and by the way, I should tell you if you do decide to see out your time here at Yale, I'm afraid I won't be here to see it through with you.
TERRI: Are you going to teach somewhere else?
NADIA: Not exactly. No.

(TERRI *waits.*)

TERRI: Are you going to tell me?
NADIA: I don't mind telling you.

(NADIA *looks at her a moment.*)

I used to be a war correspondent. Recently I've noticed I miss it. I'm going back to Iraq.

PROPHECY

Karen Malpede

ABOUT THE PLAYWRIGHT

Karen Malpede is author of fifteen plays, short fiction, and essays on theater and human rights. Her new play *Another Life* is published in *The Kenyon Review*. Her plays *Sappho & Aphrodite, Us, Better People: A Surreal Comedy About Genetic Engineering, The Beekeeper's Daughter, I Will Bear Witness* (coadapted with George Bartenieff from the diaries of Victor Klemperer), and *Prophecy* have been performed in Europe, Australia, and the United States. Her other plays premiered in New York and include *A Lament for Three Women, Rebeccah, The End of War, Making Peace: A Fantasy, A Monster Has Stolen the Sun, Blue Heaven, Kassandra* (an adaptation of Christa Wolf's novel), and the docudrama *Iraq: Speaking of War*. Her books on theater are *Women in Theater: Compassion & Hope, Three Works by the Open Theater, People's Theater in America,* and a collection of her plays, *A Monster Has Stolen the Sun and Other Plays*. She is cofounder, with George Bartenieff and the late Lee Nagrin, of Theater Three Collaborative, www.theaterthreecollaborative.org, info@theaterthreecollaborative.org.

PRODUCTION HISTORY

Prophecy had its world premiere at the New End Theatre, London, September 8, 2008. The direction was by Ninon Jerome. The American premiere was at the Fourth Street Theater, New York City, June 1, 2010, produced by Theater Three Collaborative in association with New York Theater Workshop. Kathleen Chalfant played Sarah Golden; George Bartenieff played Alan Golden; Brendan Donaldson played Jeremy Thrasher and Lukas Brightman; Najla Said played Miranda Cruz, Hala, and Mariam Jabar; Peter Francis James played Charles Muffler. The direction was by Karen Malpede. Maxine Willi Klein designed the set; Tony Giovannetti, the lighting; Sally Ann Parsons, costumes; Arthur Rosen, sound and music.

Grateful acknowledgment is made to the Penguin Group and the estate of Robert Fagles for permission to use the Tiresias speech from *The Three Theban Plays* by Sophocles and translated by Robert Fagles. First published in 1982 by The Viking Press, Inc., Penguin Classics (New York: 1982). Copyright © Robert Fagles, 1982, 1984.

CHARACTERS

Sarah Golden, late fifties, smart, lively, actress and acting teacher

Jeremy Thrasher, twenty-one, an acting student

Miranda Cruz, twenties, acting student

Alan Golden, late sixties, Sarah's husband, executive director of the Refugee Relief Committee

Hala Jabar, twenties, and, then, in her forties, Alan's associate; a Palestinian-Lebanese human rights worker

Charles Muffler, sixties, dean of the acting school where Sarah teaches

Mariam Jabar, twenties, Alan and Hala's daughter

Lukas Brightman, nineteen, young lover from Sarah's youth

TIME & PLACE

"Prophecy" takes place in the early fall of 2006, in New York City and in the memories of Sarah and Alan Golden in 1969–72, and 1981–82.

STAGING & SET

In style, the play bridges modernist realism with something older and more classical. The setting needs to be simple, beautiful, and spare. Scene follows scene seamlessly.

A back wall has two entranceways, one to either side which serve as the *parados* of the classical theater, allowing quick and easy entrances and exits. In the middle of this wall is a bedroom alcove, inside of which is the marriage bed on a slight rake. These three openings are framed behind. Wall and floor are painted to look like light stone. Furniture, painted white, and realistic props are minimal. On stage right is a desk, with telephone and snow globe, and a desk chair. Center stage: a wooden bench. Stage left: a small wrought-iron table with two chairs. Lighting defines location as does the actors' relationship to the space.

ACT ONE

SCENE 1

(SARAH GOLDEN *has a quick and ironic sometimes self-deprecating wit; she carries a burden whose origin even she has forgotten. In a rush,* SARAH *enters from the aisle of the theater, her book bag slung over her arm.* JEREMY THRASHER *runs behind her, stopping her on the lip of the stage.*)

JEREMY: Ms. Golden! (*She startles and stops, turns to him.*) Can we talk?
SARAH: Afterwards.
JEREMY: About a word.
SARAH: After class.
JEREMY: I'm in the first semester class.
SARAH: I know. I do remember.
JEREMY: It's just, I never read out loud, or even say anything. I'm performing today.
SARAH: That's good.
JEREMY: It's Jeremy.
SARAH: Jeremy.
JEREMY: Thrasher.

(*He sticks out his hand to shake. She takes it.*)

SARAH: Jeremy Thrasher.
JEREMY: Augury.
SARAH: Jeremy Thrasher Augury.
JEREMY: That's it. You said to look it up. You told us any word we didn't know we had to look it up. You talked about that for a long time in class. How we've got to understand what we are saying before we can act. How we've "absolutely got to know the precise meaning." I looked it up. Look.

(*He fishes a precisely folded piece of paper from his jean pocket, unfolds it, and reads.*)

"Augury: the art of the augur."
SARAH: Very good.
JEREMY: "An augural observance or rite."
SARAH: Right.
JEREMY: What?

SARAH: You looked it up.

JEREMY: Yeah.

SARAH: That augurs well.

JEREMY: Sure.

SARAH: So, now, you see.

JEREMY: I don't. "An omen, a portent, a token."

SARAH: Are augurs.

JEREMY: Portent!

SARAH: It's going to happen.

JEREMY: What is?

SARAH: Whatever has been portended, or, let's say, augured. My class, for instance.

(SARAH *tries get around him to enter the room.* JEREMY *stands in front of her.*)

JEREMY: "Foreboding, anticipation, promise, indication."

SARAH: Augurs, each.

JEREMY: So which one is it?

SARAH: You can choose.

JEREMY: I can't choose because I don't know.

SARAH: Listen. Foreboding. Fore. As in be-fore. But, *bode,* that has the feeling.

JEREMY: Bad?

SARAH: Good.

JEREMY: Anticipation?

SARAH: Snappy. Short. You hardly can wait—for class to start.

(*She tries to move around him. Again, he stops her.*)

JEREMY: Look, I can't say it if I don't know what it means.

SARAH: Use it in a context. Say the word out loud, surrounded by other words.

JEREMY: Go ahead.

SARAH: Fine. (*Attempting to enter the room, again.*)

JEREMY: In a sentence. Augury. Do it.

SARAH: Right. From my place of augury I'd say Jeremy Thrasher is likely to be a good student who should speak up more during class.

JEREMY: Look, there were no books in our house. No one in my family ever read the Greeks. The Greeks ran the diner at the end of the street. They went to the wrong church. You tell me I can't say it if I don't know what it means. You tell me to look it up. I look it up. Foreboding. Anticipation. Promise. Indication. I'm confused. I'm the one who has got to act it.

SARAH: Just say the sentence in your script with the word "augury" in it when the time comes for you to say it. I promise you, you'll feel it. At least for right then. You can always change your mind.

JEREMY: Great, oh, great. You had books in your house.

SARAH: We had books, but not what you'd call literature, art. We didn't have any of that.

JEREMY: But the Greeks?

SARAH: Not the Greeks, no, definitely not the Greeks. I joined the pagan church later in life.

JEREMY: So how did you learn to feel what augury is?

SARAH: You know what, Jeremy; it's love. That's all it is. Forget about not having books. Give yourself over. The language is your lover and you are in bed murmuring to her, or him, for that matter. Once you love, the language opens itself up. You fall in. You start to vibrate with sense. Now, we're both late for class.

(*Quickly,* SARAH *moves by him and enters the rehearsal room. A young woman student,* MIRANDA, *sneaks up behind* JEREMY *and slaps him playfully on the butt.*)

MIRANDA: Ready for Ms. Thing and the Greeks?

JEREMY: I guess.

MIRANDA: Yeah, well, I'm going to rock.

JEREMY: Ain't nobody rocks my balls like you, baby.

(JEREMY *and* MIRANDA *kiss, passionately; he lifts her up, her legs around his waist; they kiss again. He lets her down.*)

MIRANDA: Just wait till you see what I do.

SCENE 2

(*The rehearsal room: there is a rehearsal mirror somewhere, depending upon the theater space.*)

SARAH: Good morning, everyone. So, who is ready to present?

MIRANDA: I'll go.

SARAH: Good.

MIRANDA: My name is Miranda Cruz. I will be doing a choral speech from *Antigone.*

(MIRANDA *takes off jewelry and jacket, picks up her scarf.*)

SARAH: Wonderful. Great. The chorus speaks in the voice of the people, for the polis, city-state, for all of us.

(MIRANDA *begins to move across the stage in some sort of a rather bad idea of a choral dance.*)

MIRANDA: Many

(*She stops close to* SARAH, *gyrating her hips.*)

the wonders but

(*She juts her bottom almost into* JEREMY's *face.*)

nothing walks stranger than man.

(*She dances suggestively across the stage.*)

This thing crosses the sea
Making his path through the waves,

(MIRANDA *falls to the floor close to* JEREMY, *writhing sexually.*)

And she, the great god of the earth—
Ugh . . . old, no, ageless
SARAH: Stop.
MIRANDA: Ageless she is.
SARAH: Stop. Please. The feeling tells you where to go. If you keep flitting about, you'll never know what you feel. Stand still. Stop looking at yourself in the mirror. Begin.
MIRANDA (*in an expressionless voice*): Many the wonders but nothing walks stranger than man
This thing
SARAH: Listen! Wonders, strange, thing. A play of opposites, people with ideas that don't go together, but they still have to live in one city. "Many the wonders / but nothing walks stranger than man." Can you feel that? Can you take that in? Again.
MIRANDA: This thing crosses the sea

(*She resumes her dance.*)

Making his path through the rolling waves.
SARAH: What kind of waves? *Roaring,* not rolling, *roaring,* so stop flitting about.
MIRANDA: Making his path through the *roaring* waves.

And she, the greatest of gods, the earth—
Ageless she is, and unwearied—he wears her away

SARAH: Wait. I can't stand it. I shouldn't be able to stand it. Not you, I mean. It's not you I can't stand. I can stand you. You're fine. You're doing well. As well as you can do without seeing or feeling one single thing you are saying. You're alive inside. Show me: the enormity. The madness driving us. Man, wonderful, strange, he wears her away. The earth on which he lives. The greatest of gods. She, ageless, unwearied, we wear her away. Why do we do such things? Greed? Rage? Is it sorrow? The death wish inside? It is very strange. Please tell. What we want from the chorus is to be made to ask the unanswerable things. Go. I'm on the edge of my seat.

MIRANDA: Look, I worked hard on this. I had a stomachache all night, I couldn't sleep. I'm sick.

SARAH: Right. We are both feeling ill. Rolling waves, a rough sea. But, let me tell you, for the next class, this is where you've got to end up: Antigone appears, right then, in chains. "My mind is split at this awful sight." Ripped, torn in half. There's the tragic dilemma: Two sets of laws. Always two choices, but what if the gods want one thing from us and the nation-state wants something else? Next class, when your tummy ache is over, when your blood starts to flow, will you let us know if we should murder this girl. (*Pause*) Who's next?

(JEREMY's *hand shoots up.*)

JEREMY: I'll go.

(MIRANDA *gives him a furious look as she starts for the exit.*)

SARAH: Wait a minute. Where are you going?

(MIRANDA *storms out.*)

Dear me. (*To the class*) Never mind.

(JEREMY *grabs a folding chair.*)

JEREMY (*nervous*): I'll be doing Tiresias's speech, also from *Antigone*.

(*He sits. His voice trembles.* SARAH *leans forward, attentive, silent, watching. The presence of this young man has moved her more than she knows.*)

JEREMY: As I sat on the ancient seat of augury,
In the sanctuary where every bird I know
Will hover at my hands—suddenly I heard it,

(SARAH *starts writing on a half of her yellow pad, but she is speaking what is inside her mind. Something has come over her she cannot control: she has been snapped back into memory.*)

SARAH: Jeremy Thrasher grabbed me, like a hand from under the earth. I saw
    Lukas the minute Jeremy Thrasher started to speak.
JEREMY: A strange voice in the wing beats, unintelligible,
    Barbaric, a mad scream! Talons flashing, ripping,
    They were killing each other—that much I knew—
SARAH: The night we lay on the rug after love, and started talking about
    the war.

(JEREMY *and* SARAH *speak in unison; their words become a contrapuntal duet.*)

JEREMY: I was afraid.
    I turned quickly, tested the burnt-sacrifice,
    Ignited the altar at all points—
SARAH: We were more frightened than either of us knew.
    We saw every night on television, flames coming
    Out of the backs of children running from the napalm
JEREMY: But no fire,
    The god in the fire never blazed.
    Not from those offerings . . . over the embers
SARAH: Whole villages burning up. Babies, charred,
    In the arms of their mothers, because of our bombs,
    Blood coming out of their mouths.
JEREMY: Slid a heavy ooze from the long thighbones,
    Smoking, sputtering out, and the bladder
    Puffed and burst—spraying gall into the air—
    And the fat wrapping the bones slithered off
SARAH: Body counts. Body bags.
    When he moved from under me,
    When he pulled himself out,
    Lukas was coated with my blood.
JEREMY: And left them glistening white. No Fire!
    The public altars and sacred hearths are fouled,
    One and all, by the birds and dogs with carrion
    Torn from the corpse.
SARAH: Blood of life, we said, not death.
    We felt we had done something sacred
    To counteract the shame in the world.

(JEREMY *gathers force, stands, trembling, as he turns to face the mirror.*)

JEREMY: And so the gods are deaf to our prayers, they spurn
The offerings in our hands, the flame of holy flesh.
No birds cry out an omen clear and true—
They're gorged with the murdered victim's blood and fat.

(JEREMY *grabs the chair and flings it at the mirror which shatters and breaks.*
JEREMY *runs from the room.*)

(SARAH *pulls the curtain across the broken mirror, in the process she cuts her hand.*)

SCENE 3

(*The hallway:* JEREMY *is eerily calm; he is split off from what he's just done.* MI-
RANDA *has been waiting for him.*)

MIRANDA: What have you got to say for yourself?
JEREMY: Nothing much.
MIRANDA: You sit there waving your hand. You just want to perform.
JEREMY: I guess.
MIRANDA: The bitch insults me in front of the whole class. You beg to go next.
You shuffle up like a house slave, like a brownnose, kissing ass.
JEREMY: I guess I'm paying good money to be able to act.
MIRANDA: The chorus doesn't stand there, duh! and talk. They dance. I'm a
dancer. A movement artist. She forgets about that. She stops me after each
word. Then she treats me like a cunt.
JEREMY: You do have your period.
MIRANDA: It's no business of hers.
JEREMY: I guess another woman can tell.
MIRANDA: I was not up all night having cramps.
JEREMY: No way.
MIRANDA: You better bottle the smell. I am not some dumb chick you fuck. I
worked hard on that dance.

(MIRANDA *storms off.* JEREMY *sinks to the ground.* SARAH *approaches. She has
bloody paper towels wrapped around her hand.*)

SARAH: Jeremy, what happened in there?
JEREMY: What'd you do to your hand?
SARAH: I was picking up the glass.
JEREMY: Glass?

SARAH: What do you think?

JEREMY: I guess I don't know.

SARAH: You threw a chair.

(JEREMY *jumps up.*)

JEREMY: At you? Not at you. I wouldn't do that . . .

SARAH: Not at me. Not at anyone, thank God. At the mirror. (*She understands.*) At your own face in the mirror.

JEREMY: Man, oh, man.

SARAH: Jeremy, you do remember what you did?

JEREMY: I was doing Tiresias's speech. I was inside it, way inside, you know.

SARAH: I do know, but, Jeremy, right now, you're in big trouble.

JEREMY: Augury was easy. I started trembling.

SARAH: Yes, that's right. It was a strong start.

JEREMY: Really? Because I didn't think you were paying attention.

SARAH: I was riveted.

JEREMY: You weren't looking.

SARAH: I was on the edge of my seat.

JEREMY: Like you were somewhere else.

SARAH: I was right there, taking notes. You've got talent, you know.

JEREMY: I felt it, just like you said.

SARAH: Yes, but, Jeremy, you threw a chair. The building supervisor notified the dean.

JEREMY: I've got talent you said?

SARAH: The dean wants to speak to each of us, separately. Tell me you remember what you did?

JEREMY: It was good?

SARAH: Look, I can't go into Muffler's office with you. You've got to sit there and nod your head. Don't disagree. Just say "I'm sorry" over and over.

JEREMY: About the mirror, you mean?

SARAH: That's right. Because you put people in danger.

JEREMY: I was frightened. Everyone was.

SARAH: You bet.

JEREMY: You insulted Miranda in front of the whole class.

SARAH: I, what?

JEREMY: You told everyone about her blood, you know. You pretended like she can't act. It's true, but it's nobody's business but ours.

SARAH: It was a figure of speech.

JEREMY: I was upset. She ran out of class. The more I said my speech, the worse it got.

SARAH: That's what you're going to tell the dean?

(JEREMY *runs out.*)

Jeremy!

SCENE 4

(SARAH *and* ALAN's *bedroom. That night.* ALAN *seems to be asleep.* SARAH *enters and begins to get ready for bed.*)

SARAH: Alan. Are you up?

ALAN: No, Sarah, I'm not up.

SARAH: Alan.

ALAN: I'm not up, Sarah.

SARAH: Please.

ALAN: I'm asleep.

SARAH: Alan.

ALAN: Sarah, honey. Stop. Let it go. Rest.

SARAH: Right. (*Silence*) You need your sleep.

ALAN: We went over this ten times tonight.

SARAH: I should have stopped him, that's what.

ALAN: I have a donors meeting tomorrow, yes.

SARAH: A donors meeting, of course.

ALAN: Good. So, tomorrow we'll talk some more, if you like. At dinner. I'll take you out.

SARAH: Right. A big day coming up. You're a success.

ALAN: Please.

SARAH: My husband, the savior. Donors arrive at his door. The executive director of the Refugee Relief Committee doesn't have time to talk to his wife.

(*She clicks on the light and sits up in bed. He reaches over her and clicks the light off. Silence. She turns on her light and his light.*)

ALAN: We talked all evening, Sarah, all through dinner. You talked to me, that is, at me, in one of your endless monologues. It's been years since I've heard that hysterical tone in your voice. Nothing I said made any difference. It never did. I know all about this, Sarah. You are obsessed by that boy. You have always been obsessed.

SARAH: This marriage is over.

ALAN: He's crude, but pretty. A pet.

SARAH: You miserable lout.

(SARAH *clicks off both lights.*)

ALAN: Fine. I have to be up by six.

SARAH: I am humiliated, Alan. Not obsessed. The fine points, as always, elude you.

ALAN: Please. I've got refugees all over the world depending on this thing tomorrow.

SARAH: Good, because our marriage is done.

ALAN: We'll talk about all of this, Sarah, after work.

SARAH: Right. Such important work as yours cannot wait. If you cut through the red tape, children will be able to eat. What do I do? It's so insanely unimportant, isn't it. A kid freaks out in my class. So what. He's not from the third world. He doesn't live in a Palestinian refugee camp. He doesn't live in Iraq. He's a white kid. He doesn't count. And my job. My job? You thought you married an actress. You thought you married a star. A woman who would look good on your arm.

ALAN: Nonsense. You weren't working when I married you.

SARAH: And thirty years into it . . .

ALAN: You were falling apart . . .

SARAH: . . . you find out I'm a wrinkled, sag-bellied failure with thinning pubic hair who speaks in monologues without end. And you need to change things, don't you, Alan? You need to make a huge difference in the world. What do I need? I need to drudge along with the wreck of my life, the wreck of my dreams. As if you never messed up our lives.

(ALAN *snaps on both lights.*)

ALAN: All right, Sarah, let's talk.

(SARAH *turns both lights off.*)

SARAH: Too late. This time it is really too late. I'm going to sleep.

ALAN: Sarah? (*No answer.*) I do love you, Sarah.

SARAH: We'll talk tomorrow. After you've massaged your donors . . . after that.

(*Long silence.* ALAN *snores. The doorbell rings.*)

SCENE 5

(*Silence. The doorbell rings, insistently this time.* SARAH *gets up, wraps herself in her robe. She goes to the hallway door of the apartment.*)

SARAH: Who's there?

(*Silence.*)

You've got the wrong door. Go away.
JEREMY: It's Jeremy. Thrasher. (*An angry knock.*) Augury.
SARAH: Jeremy. It's three in the morning. What do you want?
JEREMY: Open up.

(*They enter the living room.*)

SARAH: You didn't sit there, did you, saying "I'm sorry."
JEREMY: Look, I'm sorry about that.
SARAH: Sorry. Great.
JEREMY: I couldn't sleep.
SARAH: Neither could I. He's taken my class away.
JEREMY: No way.
SARAH: I get paid by the class. I don't have a full-time salary.
JEREMY: Look, I've got to talk. (*Looking around*) This is a pretty nice place.
SARAH: The dean spoke with your girlfriend, what the hell is her name? Anyway, she acted up quite a storm. Wept right on cue.
JEREMY: Look, I didn't mean . . .
SARAH: To say it was my fault that you threw your chair through the mirror because I said your girlfriend had her period and that got you so upset.
JEREMY: Right. You live here alone?
SARAH: Because that is what you said.
JEREMY: I guess.
SARAH: There is someone in the next room.
JEREMY: You're not alone.
SARAH: From your place of augury, you don't guess, you speak. Do you normally fuck up people's lives?
JEREMY: Look, there's no one else in the entire world I can talk to but you.
SARAH: There, you can sit.

(*She motions to the bench and sits beside him.*)

Why did you lie, Jeremy?

(JEREMY *reaches out to her.*)

My husband is in the next room.

JEREMY: You already said.

SARAH: Not for long.

JEREMY: Let me talk.

SARAH: My husband, I mean.

JEREMY: Oh, newlyweds.

SARAH: Not quite. What's up?

JEREMY: Look, I freaked out.

SARAH: You threw a chair.

JEREMY: I did.

SARAH: At your own face.

(*Impulsively, she takes a lock of his hair and puts it behind his ear.*)

It was not because I said, whatever it was that I said, to that ditsy girl, Miranda! that's it. You wouldn't risk your career to defend that girl's honor. She's a lousy actress. She's not even that interested in you.

JEREMY: Look, that's between me and her.

SARAH: You get my class taken away, the least I can do, is tell you. Watch out. Where is she right now, for example?

JEREMY: How do I know? At home, asleep.

SARAH: Right.

JEREMY: I don't care where she is. I'm not here to talk about her.

(JEREMY *reaches for her hand, holds it, and then brings it to his lips.* SARAH *snatches her hand from his and moves away.*)

JEREMY: You touched me.

SARAH: Your hair.

JEREMY: My hair, face, so what, you touched.

SARAH: I'm sorry.

JEREMY: Sorry! I guess.

SARAH: Sorry, yes.

JEREMY: That's not what I thought.

SARAH: I was thinking of someone else.

JEREMY: Great. The husband in the next room.

SARAH: Not him.

JEREMY: Good for you.

SARAH: It was a long time ago.

JEREMY: Some young guy you came on to?

SARAH: I don't "come on to" young men, Jeremy. Let us be very clear. You arrived here.

JEREMY: I don't know. I've been come on to before.

SARAH: I'm certain you have.

JEREMY: Well, it's true. By an older woman, too.

SARAH: Perhaps, but not me.

JEREMY: Sure, you were coming on to someone else. It was just my hair you touched.

SARAH (*laughs*): That's it, you know. You are finally telling the truth. Good.

JEREMY: Look, you've got to talk to the dean. He thinks, I don't know. He wants to send me to counseling. I've got to go, he says, if I want to stay in school.

SARAH: Sure. I have lots of influence, you see. I have lots of influence because you lied . . .

JEREMY: But, she has it. How did you know?

SARAH: Go to counseling, Jeremy. It might do you good. Of course, the counselors at the school are fools.

JEREMY: Listen to me.

SARAH: Otherwise, they'd be in private practice wouldn't they? Otherwise, I'd be on stage.

JEREMY: Sarah, can I call you Sarah? You said we could the first day of class. I've got to stay in school. Everything I've done I've done to get here. It's so fucking stupid. It doesn't make any sense. I'm an actor. I know it. You know what my father does? He's a butcher. Mainly he grunts and waves a knife. Now, I'm acting the Greeks. I'm acting the Greeks because you taught me how.

SARAH: Yes, Jeremy, I taught you. But, you know what, you already knew. You really can't teach anyone anything they don't already have inside. You can open them up. That's all. Your father, the butcher, was he in Vietnam?

JEREMY: Yeah, you sure opened me. Big time. So, you have to talk to the dean. You've got to tell him I'm not fucked up. I just got opened up. I don't need to talk about that. You can explain.

SARAH: It's late. We both have to get up very soon.

JEREMY: You'll talk to the dean?

SARAH: Tell me what happened in class.

JEREMY: Yeah, okay, I will tell you. I was doing the speech of the prophet, see. Tiresias's speech, the blind guy, and he's giving this prophecy when all of a sudden, he's saying that the fat isn't burning, that the altars are glutted with the fat thigh bones smoking, that the gods aren't hearing, that they won't take the offering in. And that's when it hits me, shit, fuck, like a truck, it hits. We've been cut off. We're floating free in space and even the gods aren't listening; they don't care anymore. We've gone too far. They won't take our offerings. I'm a Catholic. I was brought up to believe in forgiveness. In redemption, see. You say you're sorry. You say you've sinned. It's okay. God forgives you. You say twenty Hail Marys and you're back in. He's a forgiving god. But all of a sudden I think it might not work that way, you see what I mean? It might work another way. You might go too far. You might step off the end of the earth. There might be no way back. The altars might be glutted with flesh. And that's when I saw, like I didn't see out of my eyes. I was blind. I saw it inside my head. How it is when the gods can't bear to listen. They can't bear to hear anymore. They've already heard it all. You can't ask for forgiveness. The gods aren't hearing. They're fed up with us, sick. We're cut off. I got scared.

SARAH: And you threw the chair?

JEREMY: That's it.

SARAH: Makes perfect sense.

JEREMY: That's what I think. I'm not crazy. You see. I'm not crazy at all.

SARAH: It had nothing to do with that girl.

JEREMY: Of course not. Why do you keep talking about her?

SARAH: Jeremy, what are you frightened of?

JEREMY: Nothing. The idea, of course.

SARAH: I see.

JEREMY: You do? Because you weren't paying attention. You were thinking about someone else.

SARAH: Please.

JEREMY: Look, you've got to talk to the dean. You weren't listening to me. I threw the chair. You woke up.

SARAH: Leave. You've got to go.

JEREMY: Talk to him. Damn it!

SARAH: Quiet! My husband is in the next room.

JEREMY: Please. I've got to stay in school.

(*She nods her head "yes."*)

You will?

SARAH: I will.

JEREMY: Promise?

SARAH: Scout's honor, Jeremy Thrasher. In the morning. Go home.

JEREMY: Thank you. Really, I thank you from the bottom of my heart.

(*Impulsively, he grabs* SARAH *and kisses her awkwardly, chastely, on the cheek. She's charmed, in spite of herself.*)

SARAH (*laughing and pushing him out the door*): Out, Thrasher, out.

(JEREMY *exits.* SARAH *is confused, moved. This young man has undone her, somehow. She cares for him more than is wise. A light comes on in the hall.* ALAN's *voice.*)

ALAN: Sarah? Are you all right?

SARAH: But, of course.

ALAN: I heard something slam. Voices, too.

SARAH: There's nothing. Go back to bed.

(ALAN *comes in; he has pulled on pants and a shirt, half unbuttoned. He looks around.*)

ALAN: Entertaining the doorman because your husband's a lout.

SARAH: It was him, my student. Upset. We talked. Cleared things up.

ALAN: Well, good. (*Pause*) I'm sorry, Sarah, I am.

(*He takes her hand and leads her over to the bench. They sit. After a moment she snuggles into him, buries her head in his chest.*)

The things you say, sometimes, Sarah; I never know what's coming next.

(SARAH *kisses* ALAN *on the cheek.*)

You've hardly ruined your life. You do wonderful work with those kids. You teach them how to feel, to think.

SARAH: She was dancing like a chorus girl. That's what the word "chorus" means to her.

ALAN: That boy; he's the real thing, you said.

SARAH: A kid breaks a mirror in my class because I'm somewhere else . . . what do you call that, Alan?

ALAN: A trigger. You got snapped back to your paradise lost.

SARAH: We each have our own never was.

ALAN: Our marriage is all the more precious for that.

SARAH: More improbable, in any case.

ALAN: Our chimera of love. The odd beast we've made over time. Not of burden. That's not what I mean.

SARAH: You don't need me, do you, Alan? Not like that.

ALAN: Like what? Of course, I need you.

SARAH: You're so rational, poised, in control. You pick up the pieces; put things back together, save people . . .

ALAN: Go talk to Chuck Muffler. Tell him to give your class back.

SARAH: Chuck Muffler. That I have to bow and scrape before him.

ALAN: You can act a little superior.

SARAH: He calls himself Charles now. Sober as a dean.

ALAN: You are superior in every way.

SARAH: I ought to have stopped him before he freaked out.

ALAN: Hey, no one got hurt.

(*She takes his hand, as if to lead him back to bed.*)

I'll stay up. Do some work.

SARAH: Alan, I do hate this rug . . .

SCENE 6

(SARAH *breaks away from* ALAN, *turns, goes downstage center. By directing her comment to the audience she sets up the first of the memory scenes, which are indicated, also, by change of light.*)

SARAH: I hate this rug because of what happened here in 1981.

(ALAN, *nervous, moves a chair. Romantic music. From the memory entrance center stage right in walks a much younger woman,* HALA JABAR. *She is dressed professionally, in a slim skirt and jacket, high heels. She holds an armful of documents.*)

HALA: Where's Sarah?

ALAN: Sarah phoned. Technical rehearsal. Late night. Don't wait up.

HALA: You phoned.

ALAN: I thought, let's work here, then. You also live uptown. I'll order something in.

HALA: Fine.

(*She sits down on the chair, clutching the documents in front of her, like a shield.*)

ALAN: Can I fix you a drink?

HALA: All right.

ALAN: My God, you're beautiful.

HALA: Please . . .

(*She stands.*)

ALAN: Breathtaking. You.

HALA: Alan, we must not . . .

ALAN: Hala, you take my breath away.

(HALA *backs away, yet she does want him and his speech will win her.*)

ALAN: Hala, stop. Don't go. I'm sorry. Sometimes one has to say what's on one's mind. To clear the air. It's over now. Nothing will happen. Nothing can happen. Sarah is my wife. She was my lover before that. She was my friend. She was a girl who needed saving. She was, always, there is, will always be, Sarah. But, Hala, you are something else. Beautiful, brilliant, and so calm. Sarah is, well, Sarah is not calm. That's one thing Sarah is not, calm, that is. Brilliant, yes, in an artistic sort of way. But Sarah is not someone you can count on, really, at least not me. I was never able to count on her. I feel I can count on you. There is something steadfast in your nature. That is odd because I can see the hurt in your eyes. You have dark eyes with sorrows inside. I would like to share your sorrows, Hala. The whole of you, I would like to know. I'm making a hash of this, a mess. But Sarah is not coming home tonight until late, that is, very late. I would like to hold you, Hala, in my arms. I would like to give you what comfort I can. I can't promise anything. I can't. But I can tell you this: I will never abandon you. I will stand by you if . . . I would be there for you and a child.

(HALA *smiles lovingly at* ALAN, *then walks out the apartment door.* ALAN *remains standing, looking at the door. After a moment,* HALA *returns, without the documents in her arms. She walks forward to the rug.*)

HALA: Alan, I'm pregnant.

(ALAN *stands for a moment, without speaking. Then he goes to* HALA. *He kisses her face, her belly, gently, very gently, in awe. He gets down on his knees in front of her.*)

ALAN: A blessing. Thank you. My goddess. My darling. My precious. We make life.

(*His arms are around her feet. Carefully, she steps out of his embrace and exits.* ALAN *falls asleep on the floor.* SARAH *enters the living room.*)

SARAH: Alan? Oh, sweetie, you waited up. How adorable, my adorable, sweet husband. Come on, let's go to bed. The tech was horrendous. HORRENDOUS. The producer smokes Cuban cigars. Chuck Muffler. Sips from a flask. Made a fortune in something. Now, he wants meaning in his life.

What a profession. I do nothing for an entire year, now, all of a sudden . . . I'm not complaining. It's going to be good. Alan, I really think this one time, I will get what I deserve. I am going to be seen.

ALAN: Great, Sarah. That's great. I hope so. I really do.

SARAH: I know you do, baby. How sweet of you to try to wait up.

(*She sees something on the floor, a pair of black silk women's underwear.*)

What are these? Whose are these? Oh, shit, Alan, oh shit. Someone was here. Answer me. Were you fucking some bitch on my rug?

ALAN: I was not "fucking some bitch."

SARAH: Are you a cross dresser?

(*She dangles the underwear.*)

ALAN: Sarah, it's very late. I want you to get some sleep. I'll stay on the couch.

SARAH: What are you saying, Alan, what? The couch? So, it's true. You are not a cross dresser. I would have understood that, you know. I'm a tolerant person.

ALAN: We should speak in the morning.

SARAH: You are jealous of my success.

ALAN: Of course not. This is not about that.

SARAH: Then, why now? Why tonight? You've been faithful through everything else. Tonight, you bring some slut into my house. A ninny. Don't lie to me. Some NYU student you picked up in a bar. Who is she? Why?

ALAN: Calm down, Sarah, please. Think about your career. It is so very important to you.

SARAH: You're the one who wanted to be married to a star. Is this the day you've been waiting for all along? Obviously, you hoped to get caught.

(*She flings the underpants at* ALAN. *He catches them and stuffs them in his pocket.*)

ALAN: You won't believe me if I tell you I love you. I hardly believe it myself.

SARAH (*suddenly, perfectly calm*): All right, Alan. Tell me the truth.

(*She sits.*)

Then I'll go straight to sleep. I'll get up in the morning. I'll use all this for my work. I'll put it right into Nora. Believe me, I can do that.

ALAN: Promise?

SARAH: Yes.

ALAN: All right, then. It's Hala.

(*She rushes at him.*)

SARAH: You slimy bastard.

ALAN: You want to know, I'm telling you.

SARAH: You fucking imperialist.

ALAN: Hala is my colleague.

SARAH: She works for you, in your office, you prick.

ALAN: There is nothing wrong with me.

SARAH: No?

ALAN: My sperm count, in fact, is rather high, above average.

SARAH: You're an above average sort of guy.

ALAN: I want a child.

SARAH: Right. We'd adopt someday, we agreed, if we ever wanted that's what we'd do.

ALAN: My doctor suggested . . .

SARAH: Your doctor?

ALAN: Just to make sure. I agreed, without thinking, really. I had no idea, Sarah, believe me, I had no idea at all, none. The desire came over me so suddenly . . .

SARAH: All those sperm fighting to get out.

ALAN: When my father died.

SARAH: Oh my god, Alan, very good. Play the Holocaust card.

ALAN: It is hardly, Sarah, as you insist, in your own inimitable way, "the Holocaust card."

SARAH: I can't trump the gas chambers. You get to have whatever you want . . .

ALAN: Shut up.

SARAH: All those great-aunts and uncles you never knew.

ALAN: My father, Sarah, a remarkable person. He saved many people, worked, slaved, to bring people here, to this country, as you know very well. I do not want his story to end with me.

SARAH: Not his story, his DNA.

ALAN: I had no idea, no idea at all I would need my own child. It's some sort of biological thing. I am not in control.

SARAH: Forgive me, Alan.

ALAN: Oh, Sarah, yes, long ago.

SARAH: But, I am not able to forgive.

ALAN: You might try, Sarah. Please.

SARAH: You could have bought eggs from Hala, Alan, had them implanted in me, or in someone else, if my play runs, if it was blood you wanted to mix.

ALAN: Why does this sound so crude in your mouth?

SARAH: I can't imagine, really, I can't.

ALAN: We are not molecules but souls. I had to be there.

SARAH: Are you going to divorce me, Alan, if Hala is pregnant that is? Are you finally going to leave me then?

ALAN: It is possible to love two women at the same time.

SARAH: A harem.

(SARAH *gets up and she begins a belly dance, slowly at first, but maniacally.*)

ALAN: I don't know what to do.

SARAH (*dancing faster*): Go away, Alan. Get.

ALAN: Sarah, stop.

SARAH: First wife is tossed into the garbage . . .

ALAN: Enough!

SARAH: Shame. For being infertile.

ALAN: I still love you, Sarah.

(SARAH *stops dancing.*)

I don't know how to explain.

SARAH: And Hala, too?

ALAN: Yes, and Hala, too. We are enlightened people, let us think.

SARAH: Who thinks at a time like this?

ALAN: Then, let's get some sleep.

SARAH: Sleep!

ALAN: Come to bed.

SARAH: Go. I will stay here on this rug. "Stewed in corruption" in the seamy stink of your love.

(*She sinks onto "the rug."* ALAN *exits to bedroom.*)

I bought this rug. I picked it out so we could start fresh. White . . . The other rug, the red one where Lukas and I slept, I rolled up and stored in the basement because I cannot bear to throw it out. The night we protested the "secret" invasion of Cambodia. The night we thought the war would never end. I pulled Lukas off the street. I was forever pulling Lukas away from the police. He was always aching for a fight. I brought him up here. It was a collective apartment, then. Below, on the street there was tear gas. Lukas told me he had flunked all of his classes, except one. In English composition I gave him an "A." He would go to Canada, he said, to avoid the draft.

Or join the Weathermen, and become a real revolutionary. "Go to Canada," I told him, "Please. I'll come to you, there." I leaned down to taste him again. When finally we finished, when he lay beside me on the red rug and I cradled him in my arms, he smiled and said he had figured out what he should do. He would leave school and get himself drafted. He would join the GI resistance and organize from the inside. He sat up. He saw his destiny plain: "When the army refuses to fight the war will end." "Don't be an asshole," I said. "Kiss me," he said. I want your child, Lukas, but I couldn't say that to him. "Don't be a hero," I said. "You know how long those guys live in the jungle." "I'm working class," he said. "Those are my men." "Stay here. You can make up your failing grades. I'll talk to the dean." We lived in our grief, legs looped, sex linked. "It's okay," Lukas said, "Whatever happens to me it will be fine. There's no time for personal happiness, now." He learned to talk that way at Columbia. "Little kids are being napalmed. This shit has to stop." "I'll give up Alan for you. I'll call him in Cambridge right now." I reached for the phone. But Lukas was only nineteen. He was more frightened of me than of Vietnam.

(*She exits.*)

SCENE 7

(*The dean's office. Later that morning.* DEAN CHARLES MUFFLER *enters humming a happy tune. He is a commanding presence but beneath his bellicose good humor, he is hiding something. He sits behind his desk. On it there is a snow globe with a rural scene which he strokes with his free hand as he pushes the button on his speaker phone.*)

CHARLES: Lizzie, put that call right through when it comes.

(CHARLES *sees* SARAH *at his office door and waves her in.*)

CHARLES: Come on in, Sarah, come. What's on your mind? At ten, I've got the Ford Foundation.
SARAH: Jeremy Thrasher.
CHARLES: Quite a name. Like a character in a play.
SARAH: He does tend to make waves.
CHARLES: Sarah, I'm going to give your class back.
SARAH: Good. (*Pause, during which* CHARLES *drums his fingers on his desk.*) Thanks.

CHARLES: We all make mistakes. I've put the Thrasher boy somewhere else.

SARAH: I wish you wouldn't call him that.

CHARLES: You were quite distraught, yesterday. You seemed in over your head. Maybe things at home . . .

SARAH: Alan and I are just fine, Chuck.

CHARLES: Charles, if you don't mind. Chuck was my Broadway name. Dean Charles Muffler. Glad to hear married life is good. Sometimes one bad egg, one rotten apple . . .

SARAH: Are you speaking of Jeremy Thrasher?

CHARLES: I'm being harsh, over-harsh; I'm overstating my case. Still, sometimes, a student needs another approach. In any case, the class is yours. No need to ask.

SARAH: I want Jeremy Thrasher back. He's the best actor I have.

CHARLES: It will cost us eight or nine hundred dollars to replace that mirror. Mercifully, no one got hurt. Let me handle the Thrasher boy. You get the rest of the class.

SARAH: Jeremy, too. Trust me.

CHARLES: Thrasher's here on scholarship.

SARAH: So?

CHARLES: Working class, a bit out of his element.

SARAH: If only you could hear yourself speak.

CHARLES: Let's not wrangle, my dear.

SARAH: Right. I'll work with him privately. Independent study. Greek tragedy. I tell you, he's the real thing.

CHARLES: Bad idea. Let him do something light. Situate the narrative in another part of the self.

SARAH: You wanted to send him for counseling.

(CHARLES *drums his fingers on his desk.*)

Charles?

CHARLES: No. No counseling, no. Counseling is not a requirement anymore. I've gone over the boy's record. I'll stick him in my monologue class. We're doing Moliere and Goldoni. Both are smart, both are snappy. Counseling is not advised at the moment. Give my best to Alan. What's he up to, by the way?

SARAH: Refugee policy, the usual stuff. Why no counseling, Charles?

CHARLES: It's over and done. Best to move on. We were lucky the glass didn't fly. I shudder to think.

SARAH: It won't happen again. What is over and done?

CHARLES: He's a good man, Alan, officer material. A pity he never served.

SARAH: You know Alan was a draft resister. You know that, Charles.

CHARLES: I thought it was just an array of student deferments he got.

SARAH: Everyone got student deferments in those days.

CHARLES: Not everyone.

SARAH: No, Charles. Not you. You got medals, defense contracts, too.

CHARLES: And you got *A Doll's House* on Broadway. I apologize for nothing I've done.

SARAH: You asked my forgiveness on opening night.

CHARLES: I've been sober, now, a long time.

SARAH: You asked my forgiveness for getting drunk?

CHARLES: I don't want you fraternizing with our students, my dear.

SARAH: What did you need forgiveness for? Mine, that is. Not the forgiveness of your three wives.

CHARLES: Young men get hurt, Sarah, when they are pushed. The Greeks are too much.

SARAH: I disagree. The Greeks hold us when we can't hold ourselves. Tragedy keeps us honest, in fact.

CHARLES: Young men are vulnerable, you, of all people, ought to know.

SARAH: Chuck it, Charles.

CHARLES: Touché. Nevertheless, this Thrasher boy has had something stirred up, not, I think by the Greeks. When that happens, we are no longer effective teachers; pedagogy flies out the window . . . mirrors become shattered. Next time, a student could be harmed. Then, I could not give your class back to you, Sarah, or any class, for that matter.

(*He walks around his desk to dismiss her, but in a warm, expansive way.*)

Always good to have you stop by. Give my regards to Alan. We ought to get together sometime. Reminisce. Are you still such a good cook?

SCENE 8

(*Hallway, immediately afterward.* JEREMY *has been waiting for* SARAH *and steps in front of her.*)

JEREMY: Yeah, well, thanks a lot.

SARAH: You're welcome, Jeremy, you can skip therapy.

JEREMY: Big deal. You took me out of your class.

SARAH: I took you?

JEREMY: You told him you couldn't handle me. I'm "unruly" he said you said. I didn't need to look it up.

SARAH: Charles Muffler said I said that? This does not augur well because I never said such a thing.

JEREMY: I don't care what you said. I need you. The dean said I can't have you. Why did you tell him I came over last night?

SARAH: I did not.

JEREMY: He said you said, he asked, I thought, anyway . . .

SARAH: I have just come out of his office, as you can see since you've obviously been lying in wait.

JEREMY: So what?

SARAH: So I couldn't have said anything to him, could I, before he apparently spoke with you this morning?

JEREMY: How do I know? There are cell phones, email.

SARAH: Well, Jeremy Thrasher, contrary to your idea of yourself as the center of my life, I had other things on my mind this morning besides calling Muffler. I spoke to him because you asked me to. He's agreed not to send you to counseling. Although, frankly, I think you could use it. I argued to keep you in class.

JEREMY: Great.

SARAH: I lost. So that's the end of it. It's been a pleasure, Jeremy, I wish you well.

JEREMY: What about last night?

SARAH: I should never have opened the door.

JEREMY: Now, I'm inside.

SARAH: That was my mistake.

JEREMY: Of Tiresias, I mean. It's going to come out one way or another. You've got to be there.

SARAH: Look, you'll be doing Moliere.

JEREMY: What the fuck does that mean?

SARAH: You've been moved into Muffler's monologue class. It's an honor. You should be pleased. Don't swear at me.

JEREMY: Oh, fuck, I'm sorry. I'm so sorry, look. Please. Let me just do the speech for you, one time. I won't bother you ever again. I can pay you. I will pay you.

SARAH: Stop. Enough.

JEREMY: I'll come to your house, anytime. Anytime you are free.

SARAH: Absolutely not.

JEREMY: Something is inside of me. They put it there. The Greeks, I mean. No one can help me but you. Tonight?

SARAH: It's not possible. It's not right.

JEREMY: Right. He shouldn't pull us apart. Two of us who love the Greeks. And I do, let me tell you. I love them like you.

SARAH: Dean Muffler will tell you he, also, loves the Greeks.

JEREMY: Look, I do believe in redemption, only now there's something new. I've been thinking about it all night, ever since, last night, you know. It's something we've got to go through.

SARAH: That's right. That's it exactly.

JEREMY: So, I've got to finish that speech. I can't just leave it like that. I threw a fucking chair through a mirror. I need help. I know. With the words.

SARAH: All right, Jeremy. You win. Eight o'clock. My husband will be home.

JEREMY: Fine, okay, anything you say. It's a date.

SARAH: It's a rehearsal, that's what.

JEREMY: I'm not dangerous. I would never hurt you.

(JEREMY *exits*.)

SCENE 9

(SARAH *walks downstage to announce the second memory scene.*)

SARAH: I am a good cook. I made the pasta from scratch. Alan was leaving the next day, business trip. It was 1982.

(*She exits as* ALAN *enters from memory entrance center stage left. He hangs his jacket on the back of his chair and takes two airline tickets from the pocket. He puts the tickets on the table and sits.*)

ALAN (*calling to her in the kitchen*): Sarah, I want a child.

SARAH (*she calls back*): Fine. Good. I agree. How about Colombian?

ALAN: No coffee, thanks.

SARAH: I meant from Colombia, country of. I'll steam the milk.

ALAN: No, thanks. My stomach is upset.

SARAH: Poor dear.

ALAN: My child, Sarah.

SARAH: Ours. A girl math prodigy from China. So adorable. Or a little boy with an Afro. Sweet.

ALAN: Hala is pregnant, Sarah.

(*Silence. Then,* SARAH *enters. She is calm if nonplussed.*)

SARAH: Hala miscarried. I forgave you. Over and done.

ALAN: Hala is pregnant again.

SARAH: How Abrahamic, Alan, really, truly, how profound. I'm impressed. Ishmael, is that what you'll call it? You can start the whole cycle over again.

ALAN: It might have worked with us, Sarah, if you had tried.

SARAH: My womb rotted, Alan. Fell out between my legs.

ALAN: Don't be repulsive.

SARAH: Me, repulsive? You're the one who impregnated your office assistant.

ALAN: Colleague.

SARAH: Twice. Two times!

ALAN: Hala and I are . . . we are together all the time.

SARAH: You're having a midlife crisis, my dear. And she can have an abortion.

ALAN: Like you, and your Lukas, the only one whose child you wanted to have, the one you kept on getting pregnant with, how many times, was it, Sarah? And so when I finally got you, when I finally won you, after Lukas was dead, it was too late for us.

SARAH: I never lied to you about the abortion. One, Alan, one.

ALAN: And I'm not lying to you.

SARAH: How the fuck could you do this again?

ALAN: Because I want a separation.

SARAH: You don't mean that. You can't. We are like, always us . . . before Lukas, even.

ALAN: Stop. I promised Hala if she became pregnant again, I would be more than the father of her child. We would make a life.

SARAH: You discussed this?

ALAN: Of course.

SARAH: It wasn't a mad fit of passion, a late night when you couldn't think straight, after Sabra and Shatila, or some other horrible event? Overwhelmed, distraught. It wasn't on our rug. You had sheets. You spoke about when and where in the yellow light of late afternoon. You planned.

ALAN: Close enough, I'm afraid.

SARAH: You're leaving me?

ALAN: Yes. I am.

SARAH: But I love you.

ALAN: Sarah, don't.

SARAH: And you love me, that's what you say, Alan, right now, please . . .

ALAN: It won't be . . . oh, Sarah . . . I'll try . . . . I don't intend never to see you, again. I don't intend to put you out of my life, that is, if you can stand it. Oh, darling, I didn't want it to come to this. But I've gone and done it. It seems that I can't have both. My dearest friend Sarah, and a child and a wife.

SARAH: I feel like Medea. I feel like poisoning her.

ALAN: If you were Medea, this never would have happened.

SARAH: Right. Two sons. I am a vessel and you're trading me in.

ALAN: Stop, darling, stop. I can't take any more.

SARAH: Then, send her away.

ALAN: Away?

SARAH: Give her money; we can support it. When it's older it can come around.

ALAN: "It"?

SARAH: I'll forgive you. I promise I will. I want to kill you, too, now, of course, wring your neck, but we both know that won't last.

ALAN: "It" is my child.

SARAH: Bastard.

ALAN: Hala will be the mother of my child. I can forget you, Sarah. I can't, of course. I won't.

SARAH: All right, Alan. Have it your way.

ALAN: You understand?

SARAH: Shredding your life. It should be done every decade, I think. We were long overdue. Why, I ought to have walked out on you.

ALAN: You should never have married me, Sarah. You never loved me.

SARAH: I never loved you! I adored you, worshipped you. You taught me everything I know.

ALAN: I got you by default. After Lukas died, you came back. I thought I could live with that, I wanted you so, and maybe I could.

SARAH: What happened to Lukas in Vietnam?

ALAN: How would I know? I was 4-F, remember.

SARAH: Not a conscientious objector?

ALAN: Philosophically, yes. I had a psychiatrist's note.

SARAH: Who killed Lukas, Alan?

ALAN: Sarah, please, our marriage is falling apart.

SARAH: Lukas was murdered. He wanted me to know.

ALAN: Lukas was brain dead, Sarah. Lukas could not speak.

SARAH: Help me, Alan, with this. I won't bother you ever again.

ALAN: Help you with what? Please. I feel like I've got to throw up.

SARAH: I didn't poison you, I'm sorry to say.
ALAN: I've got to lie down.

(ALAN *exits to their bedroom.*)

SARAH: It's just your sperm count, acting up.

(*She sees the pair of airline tickets and she rips one up. She takes* ALAN's *jacket and exits.*)

SCENE 10

(*Continuation of memory scene, 1982. It's raining.* HALA JABAR *enters from the memory entrance stage right. She walks across the stage, and mimes pushing open a restaurant door. She goes inside, looks around for* ALAN, *then she sits at the table just as* SARAH *approaches.* SARAH *enters the restaurant and sits at* HALA's *table.*)

HALA: Sarah, how amazing, really.
SARAH: It is, isn't it?
HALA: Do you often come here?
SARAH: This is our favorite restaurant, Alan's and mine. He proposed to me here. At the same table at which you are sitting.
HALA: Really?
SARAH: Really.
HALA: I see.
SARAH: He's not coming.
HALA: I don't understand.
SARAH: My husband, Alan, sent me instead.
HALA: Instead? Of what?
SARAH: Let's not play games.
HALA: All right, let's not. I'm late.
SARAH: Yes, but Alan is not coming.
HALA: Then, I must go.
SARAH: Go. Where will you go?
HALA: Home, of course. It's late. I've a plane early tomorrow.
SARAH: Such dignity, Hala, I'm impressed.
HALA: I should not be dignified? Do you think so?
SARAH: I? No. Of course not. I admire you more than you know. It's just me, I suppose. My way is, well, Alan has told you all that. My husband, Alan, you know; I've known Alan for a very long time. We were students together in the sixties.

HALA: A long time ago.

SARAH: I occupied buildings; Alan got the judge to drop charges. I've watched Alan operate, so to speak. Then, in a fit of grief, I married. I rather suppose I owe Alan my life. I suppose Alan has told you all this.

HALA: Alan has told me many things; we spend many hours together, after all, at work and after. But, I really must be going. I've a lot on my mind. There is a war. I am Lebanese.

SARAH: Not Egyptian.

HALA: Palestinian and Lebanese. My people are being killed.

SARAH: Not a slave from Egypt given to Abraham, given to Sarah, in fact, by Pharaoh, given to barren Sarah, to bear the patriarch an heir.

HALA: I don't need to listen to any more. I have relatives in those camps.

(HALA *stands abruptly and exits the restaurant.* SARAH *immediately follows, stopping her on the street. Thunder.*)

SARAH: Alan wants a child, from his loins, such a strange expression that, like a cut of beef; yes, he wants a son, but Sarah is barren since Lukas's child was dug out of her, like a wad of fat cut from a lamb chop. I was half mad. I said "yes," that is, to Alan. I had the abortion. If I had not been grieving privately, so that Alan would not see, and what is more private, after all, than the blood from a woman's insides, tears, great globs of them, then, well, who knows, we went on. Our sex life became astonishingly good.

HALA: Let me give you a word of advice.

SARAH: No, Hala, that's not how it works. The other woman puts out; she does not get to talk.

HALA: It might be correct, Sarah, if I were to tell you, now, about our plans, Alan's and mine, because, I think, perhaps, he has not.

SARAH: Alan did not come here to meet you tonight because Alan is not leaving me. In some inextricable way, Alan and I are too tightly bound. We are barren, yet we do love. Alan gave me this ticket to give to you.

(SARAH *hands* HALA *the ticket.* HALA *takes the ticket from* SARAH, *and looks at it.*)

I'm sorry, Hala.

HALA: I don't think so.

SARAH: I admire you, Hala. Alan does, too. We will often speak of you.

(HALA *begins to walk away.*)

SARAH: Oh, and just one more thing. Don't wait too long to get rid of it.

(HALA *stops and looks at her.*)

HALA: Alan did tell me about your abortion. He was quite clear. You had just been hired to play Antigone, in a big important production. You could hardly play Antigone, could you, if you were pregnant? (*Pause*) And will you please tell Alan for me that I choose this child of ours. I will have a girl. I will call her Mariam. Good night. Alan need not worry about us.

(HALA *exits stage right, memory exit. After a moment,* SARAH *follows.*)

SCENE 11

(*The present. Outside bells. Eight o'clock. The phone rings, and rings.* SARAH *opens the apartment door, in a rush, dressed as she was when she went to meet* CHARLES MUFFLER *that morning.* SARAH *grabs the phone just in time.*)

SARAH: I just walked in. (*Pause*) You were going to take me out tonight. Right. Are you lying to me? Someone you "absolutely must see"? Has Hala come back, Alan, after all these years? I was thinking about her, that's all. I was, what can I say? Some things you don't forget. They pop up, like pop-up books in your head. (*Pause*) I think I can tell when you're lying, Alan. Fibbing, right. All right, I'll trust you. Later, then. Bye.

(SARAH *puts down the phone.* JEREMY *enters.*)

JEREMY: Hey, you should be careful. Who knows who could get in? Where's the husband?
SARAH: He stepped out for a minute, to pick up Chinese food.
JEREMY: Okay. Fine.
SARAH: You want to start from the beginning, of the speech, I mean.
JEREMY: Just jump into it?
SARAH: Why not.
JEREMY: What if he comes back?
SARAH: He won't . . .
JEREMY: With the Chinese food.
SARAH: . . . come back.
JEREMY: Where's he gone, Taiwan?
SARAH: Sorry, sorry.
JEREMY: Right. You were thinking of someone else.
SARAH: Something else, okay. There's a chair.

(*He takes the chair, places it in the center of the room. He looks around.*)

JEREMY: Just want to make sure there are no mirrors. (*He laughs.*) Okay. All right. Here we go.

(*He clears his throat. He begins but it sounds very flat and he has trouble remembering his lines.*)

As I sat on the ancient seat of augury,
In the sanctuary where every bird I know
Will hover at my hands—

(*He stops, stands.*)

Shit! I'm not into it. It's terrible, isn't it?
SARAH: Pretty bad.
JEREMY: Look, let's forget it.
SARAH: Fine. You can go.
JEREMY: Why? What's happened to me? Why can't I do it? I feel like I've lost it. It's gone. I had it. I knew it. Now, I don't have it anymore. What's wrong?
SARAH: You're scared.
JEREMY: No shit.
SARAH: You lost control, now you're trying to control too much. You've got to just let go.
JEREMY: I'm worried your husband will open that door, and I'll freak out.
SARAH: Don't be. He's out until late.
JEREMY: You lied?
SARAH: I didn't know.
JEREMY: No Chinese food.
SARAH: Maybe, but not with me.
JEREMY: Does he do that a lot? It's not right.
SARAH: Look, you do the speech and then I'll order us something to eat.
JEREMY: Sure. Okay. Fine.

(*She goes to him and begins to rub his shoulders.*)

SARAH: First, relax. Breathe.

(*They stand there, breathing together. And then* JEREMY *begins to speak, looking at* SARAH. *He gets better and better. He's got it, this time, and the speech is so real to him that it takes him back to the moment he's been hiding.*)

JEREMY: I was afraid,
   I turned quickly, tested the burnt-sacrifice,
   Ignited the altar at all points—but no fire,
   The god in the fire never blazed.
   Not from those offerings . . . over the embers
   Slid a heavy ooze from the long thighbones,
   Smoking, sputtering out, and the bladder
   Puffed and burst—spraying gall into the air—
   And the fat wrapping the bones slithered off
   And left them glistening white. And no fire.
   I had my gun, I took my gun. I jabbed
   My gun into that Haji's head, talk or I'll
   blow your fucking brains out. I kicked that
   bastard until he bled. Where's the Fucking IED?
SARAH: Jeremy.
JEREMY: Where's the bomb, rag head? Tell me, I'll let you
   Go. I'll let your sorry ass live. The motherfucker
   Grabs at my leg. I take my rifle, hit him hard.
   His jaw breaks. Blood spurts out and bone.
SARAH: Jeremy. Stop.
JEREMY: Stop. His wife starts to scream. She starts pulling
   At my jacket. Begging. She grabs for my gun.
   My gun starts to go off. She's screaming, stop.
SARAH: Jeremy, please. That's enough.
JEREMY: Shut the fuck up. It doesn't stop.
   I can't take my hand off. I don't know
   She's pregnant. I see pieces of baby fall
   Out. He's down on his knees, begging.
   And we're crying. We are, all of us,
   Crying. My gun is on the floor, next
   to her. Her hair comes loose from that scarf.
   Her black hair spreads out on the floor.
   He's kneeling, stroking her hair.

(*Silence.* JEREMY *is on his knees, staring at the spot.* SARAH *pulls herself together and speaks calmly.*)

SARAH: Jeremy. Jeremy?

(*She touches him gently and he jumps, crouching behind the table, screaming.*)

JEREMY: If you tell anyone anything you heard here tonight, I'll kill you I swear I will. I'll blow your brains out.

(*She is behind a chair, but, again, she speaks softly, reassuringly.*)

SARAH: Hush. I won't tell. Trust. I'm here for you, Jeremy.

(JEREMY *falls to the floor, moaning and sobbing.* SARAH *gets down next to him and she gently lays a hand on his back. Slowly, he quiets. She sits next to him, lightly stroking his back. For a time, there is only the sound of their breathing. Then,* ALAN'S *voice is heard from the hall, speaking to someone.*)

ALAN: Go on in.

(*Louder.*)

Sarah! I have someone I want you to meet!

(*A young woman,* MARIAM, *dressed in jeans, sneakers, a long-sleeved form-fitting top, with a hijab on her head, steps into the room in front of* ALAN. SARAH *shakes her head, and waves her other hand in a gesture that says "go away."*)

SARAH (*in a whisper*): Get out of here, Alan, please. With her.
ALAN (*expansive with pride*): Sarah, this is my Mariam. My daughter.
SARAH: Jesus Christ.

(JEREMY *jumps up, terrified as he sees the woman in the hijab.*)

SARAH: Jeremy, it's all right. This is my husband, Alan, and this lovely young person is his daughter, Mariam. Amazing, but true. This is Jeremy Thrasher, my most gifted acting student. We've been here tonight working on quite a difficult speech from *Antigone*. Jeremy found a whole new truth . . . (*To* JEREMY) It takes great courage to speak like that. Your work was very honest, very brave.
ALAN: Hello, Jeremy. Sarah has spoken very highly . . .
MARIAM: *Antigone* is my favorite play.

(JEREMY *is staring all the while at* MARIAM.)

JEREMY: I've got to get out of here.
SARAH: Stay. We'll have supper. I said, we'd eat.
JEREMY: Can't. My girlfriend. Got to go.
SARAH: Jeremy, come to class tomorrow.
JEREMY: Yeah, okay, sure.

(SARAH *moves very close to him.*)

SARAH: Look at me, Jeremy.
   Go straight home. Tomorrow, come to me, first thing.
JEREMY: Sure, whatever you say.

(JEREMY *exits. Silence.*)

ALAN: So, Sarah, I always imagined Lukas to look like that.

(SARAH *is too upset to respond to him. She speaks to* MARIAM.)

SARAH: You look like your mother. That's lucky, you know, you might have had
   Alan's looks. You remember what Bernard Shaw said to who was it, Mrs.
   Somebody or Other, about looks and brains. She wanted his child. My god,
   I've lost my mind. I can't think who it was. Anyway, in your case, the anal-
   ogy doesn't hold up. Hala was brilliant and beautiful. Is, I should say. I do
   hope she's all right. You can see, I suppose, why I was jealous. Here you are,
   a grown woman in our living room, standing on our rug, and it all seems
   amazing. Because, it doesn't seem to matter what happened then. None of
   that matters anymore, not after, well, it doesn't matter, now, after all. Here
   you are. I'm extremely grateful that you are here. In one piece. Look, how
   lovely, Alan, she is. With such beautiful hair. Spread out. On the ground.

(SARAH *is completely undone.*)

ACT TWO

SCENE 12

(CHARLES MUFFLER *sits behind his large desk, talking on the phone. Outside his open office door,* MIRANDA *paces, agitated; she reacts with scorn to what she overhears.*)

CHARLES: Yours is truly exceptional foresight, Mrs. Gifford, extraordinary. Jennifer is our most gifted student. I had no idea she was your niece, none, when she auditioned for us. Juliet. Who could forget? The balcony speech. I wept. A bronze plaque. Right in the center between the two doors, as you enter. "In loving memory . . ." yes, and something, a few words, a couplet, perhaps, about your late husband's love of the bard. This has made my day, Mrs. Gifford, my year. I can't thank you enough. By pure coincidence, it happens, our senior project is to be *Romeo and Juliet,* beating out Moliere and Goldoni. With our Jennifer, of course. Mark Gant adores her work. The Mark Gant, yes. He will direct. (*He laughs at something she says.*) You are very kind. And I will call her in and let her know. I'm certain she'll phone you directly after. Ciao for now.

(*He clicks the speaker button on his phone.*)

Lizzie, send the young lady back in.

(MIRANDA *has a black eye. She's full of manic energy; she shifts her weight from foot to foot.*)

MIRANDA: The "young lady" has a name. Miranda Cruz.
CHARLES: Take a seat, please, Ms. Cruz.

(*She plops onto a chair. Silence. He ignores her, jots some notes.*)

MIRANDA: I did Juliet for my audition, too. I won't be cast as her, though. My aunt works at Wal-Mart. I'm going to have a scar. And, I'm going to sue. I will need plastic surgery. And, if I want to work, I'll need a theater with my aunt's name on a plaque, "Sonia-Lynnette Cruz," in the center, between the two doors. Where the fuck is she?

(CHARLES *sees* SARAH *outside the door and waves her in.*)

SARAH: Charles, thanks for seeing me right away.

MIRANDA: Damn straight.

(SARAH *wheels around and looks at her.*)

SARAH: What happened to her?

MIRANDA: Miranda. Miranda Cruz. She doesn't even fucking know my name. No one in this place knows who I am. You will.

CHARLES: Sit down, Miranda. I'm on your side, believe me. I only ask you to control your tongue. You'll get further in life. So, Sarah, what have you to say for yourself?

SARAH: What happened to you, Miranda? Not Jeremy?

MIRANDA: What do you think?

CHARLES: I'm afraid so. The worst.

SARAH: Jeremy beat you up?

MIRANDA: She acts surprised. (*Under her breath*) The bitch.

CHARLES: Let's watch our language, please, Ms. Cruz, I don't want to tell you again. The Thrasher boy has a concussion, from a frying pan, I believe, wielded by our Ms. Cruz.

SARAH: Shit.

CHARLES: You, also, Sarah, please, your tongue.

(MIRANDA *jumps up.*)

MIRANDA: My face is ruined. Destroyed because of this cunt.

SARAH: I beg your pardon?

CHARLES: Sit, Miranda. Not another word. (*To* SARAH) You were with Jeremy Thrasher last night. We know that.

SARAH: Jeremy came to my house.

CHARLES: After I'd strictly forbidden you to see him?

SARAH: Come on, Charles. You took Jeremy out of my class. I told you that was a bad decision. He needed to finish work on that speech. Believe me, he has his reasons.

CHARLES: And what are those reasons, if I might be so bold as to inquire?

MIRANDA: I know damn well what his reasons were. Ms. Thing here is trying to break us up.

SARAH: Wrong.

MIRANDA: You slept with my boyfriend.

SARAH: Don't be ridiculous.

MIRANDA: Me? You could be his mother, his grandmother. You're his teacher. Mine, too. *Were.*

SARAH: I would never.

MIRANDA: I saw how you looked at him from the first class. You knew we were together, that's why you hated my work.

SARAH: I'm afraid that's not why . . .

CHARLES: "I did not have sex with that woman," excuse me for quoting our former president.

SARAH: Stop this nonsense.

CHARLES: I spoke with the boy by phone from the emergency room.

MIRANDA: He came home at four A.M., drunk, smelling of sex. We had a fight. What do you think? He told me he was with you.

SARAH: At my house . . .

MIRANDA: The bitch admits.

CHARLES: Silence, Ms. Cruz. Sit.

(MIRANDA *sits.*)

SARAH: He worked on his speech.

MIRANDA: I'm suing your ass. I want you out of this school.

CHARLES: Miranda, you have crossed the decency line too many times.

SARAH: Jeremy left by nine, nine-thirty at the latest. I begged him to go straight home. He told me he would go to his girlfriend's, you, Miranda. He did. My husband came in with his daughter. Amazing, but true. I have witnesses. Alan's daughter. Charles, I must speak with you alone.

MIRANDA: Blame the victim. It's illegal what she's done.

CHARLES: Well, ill-advised. And prohibited at this school.

SARAH: You can't believe this . . . Miranda, I did not do what Jeremy has said, if he even said it, that is. Jeremy is disturbed. He's lying to protect himself. I can't believe you hit him on the head.

MIRANDA: The prick had a gun.

SARAH: Fuck.

CHARLES: Ladies, enough.

MIRANDA: I love him. He tried to kill me.

SARAH: You saw the gun?

MIRANDA: That's why I grabbed the pan. I love him.

CHARLES: No gun was found.

MIRANDA: He threw the gun out the window; I told the police

SARAH: Charles, we must talk, alone.

MIRANDA: He was kissing me. Then, he grabbed my hair. He was acting so wild. Saying dumb things about the war.

SARAH: I see. Miranda, why not wait outside, for a minute, please.

MIRANDA: I've been sitting outside the whole morning. I'm not rich, but I've got an uncle on the force.

CHARLES: I have great respect for the NYPD.

MIRANDA: New Jersey.

CHARLES: Miranda, take a seat outside.

MIRANDA: They talk . . .

(MIRANDA *glares at them through her tears and goes out. Silence.*)

SARAH: Charles, Jeremy Thrasher was in Iraq.

CHARLES: We know that.

SARAH: I did not know that until last night.

(CHARLES *does not respond.*)

> Charles! You might have told me. After the mirror incident. That's what they call them, don't they, "incidents," "regrettable incidents," in fact. We regret the loss of each civilian life. But, they are all civilians, aren't they, until they sign up. Jeremy did it for the tuition money, so he could get out of his godforsaken life and come to this school. The Tiresias speech became the minefield he had to walk through.

CHARLES: More matter, less art.

SARAH: Right. Jeremy Thrasher killed someone in Iraq.

CHARLES: Naturally, my dear, it's a war.

SARAH: He murdered a woman.

CHARLES: Innocent people get killed. Regrettable, always, of course.

SARAH: I see.

CHARLES: We go on.

SARAH: Is that what "we" do?

CHARLES: Did you have sex with the Thrasher boy or not?

SARAH: Stop this. Jeremy flashed back during the speech.

CHARLES: Jeremy Thrasher should not have been at your house.

SARAH: Did he threaten that girl with a gun?

CHARLES: A little provocateuse, that one.

SARAH: Did Jeremy have a gun?

CHARLES: Absolutely not.

SARAH: Are you certain of that?

CHARLES: The gun story is hers.

SARAH: She made it up?

CHARLES: Trust me. (*Pause*) Thrasher got the thrashing he deserved. Nevertheless, Jeremy Thrasher is out of this school.

SARAH: Don't be ridiculous, Charles; you can't throw him out.

CHARLES: No? We're a conservatory, not a mental hospital. I might as well expel that foul-mouthed little tart, also.

SARAH: This is the wrong approach. The worst idea . . .

CHARLES: I believe your class starts at ten.

SARAH: You must not expel Jeremy Thrasher.

(CHARLES *picks up the snow globe and appears totally lost in it.* SARAH *pulls up a chair and sits facing him, waiting.*)

Charles?

CHARLES: I cannot tell you what comfort it is to get lost in a snowstorm for a bit. It takes me back to my boyhood on the farm. Mother would send me out first thing in the morning to gather the eggs. The whole world was new, sparkling with frost. Icicles tinkling in the wind. The chickens would be hunkered down, feathers plumped up, a brown egg hidden under each one. They'd flap their wings and screech, trying to scare me away. It was a loss, of sorts. My fingers were stiff from the cold but the eggs were warm. I'd have my pockets full. There'd be snowflakes on my nose.

SARAH: I see.

(CHARLES *"comes back."*)

Charles, did you know Lukas Brightman in Vietnam?

CHARLES: I had many young men in my command.

SARAH: You asked me to forgive you on opening night.

CHARLES: Enough. This Thrasher fellow was honorably discharged. There's not a stain on his record. It's a pity. What can I do? We're an acting school. In the long run, we may be doing him a favor by asking him to go. Adversity builds character, it's so.

SARAH: I don't believe you, Charles.

(*He stands to usher her out.*)

CHARLES: No more, now. No more of this. I know a good man at the VA; I'll send the boy to him. Thanks, Sarah, for dropping by. Your class awaits. A great source of satisfaction, our students. Go, give them your best. Lose your cares, Sarah, in art.

(SARAH *looks hard at him and then leaves.*)

SCENE 13

(*The hospital:* SARAH *enters an empty room.*)

SARAH: I visited Lukas at Walter Reed in 1972. The place was full of young, beautiful bodies with unlined faces, only they were missing one or two of everything: arms, legs, private parts, and a few, like Lukas, were missing themselves. They lay about like detritus on a beach . . . "Urns with ashes that once were men."

(SARAH *walks closer to the chair where she imagines* LUKAS *to be sitting.*)

He was alone, in his own room. So as not to upset the others, I suppose. He was tied to a chair. "Lukas?" His glorious hair was all gone, his scalp wrapped. His head hung like it was barely attached to his neck. But, his eyes were open, with a faraway look. Lukas was breathing through a plastic tube in his nose. I started to cry. Then, I thought, what if he can still see? I closed my eyes; I saw Lukas, the beauty he was. I sat down on the stool next to him.

"Hi, Lukas. I'm here."

(*She sits on the bench next to the empty chair.*)

I took his hand. His flesh was soft, moist. He smelled sweet. He gripped my fingers like a baby does. He held tight. We sat for a long time like that.

"Lukas, can you hear me? Let me tell you . . . Please, can you hear? Yesterday, there was a great protest, Lukas, the best. The vets took their medals and they threw them over a chain-link fence back at Congress, right into the faces of those smirking, self-righteous bastards. One by one, the vets ripped their medals off of their chests and heaved them over the fence. It was on television, Lukas, on Walter Cronkite. The whole world watched it. Your friend, John, he had your Purple Heart. He said into the microphone, 'This one is from Lukas, who hated this mother-fucking war, and who is in fucking Walter Reed because he was going to talk about what he saw,' and he threw your Purple Heart back. I asked John what he meant. 'What the fuck difference would it make?' But it does matter, Lukas, doesn't it.

"Lukas, what did you see in Vietnam? What were you going to say? Who did this to you, Lukas? Please, tell me."

Lukas tightened his grip. He jerked himself straight. I felt him tremble. I heard him roaring inside like the ocean. A wave rushed through him.

And, then, there was nothing. Lukas slumped in his chair. His fingers fell from mine. Lukas was gone.

I couldn't tell him I carried his child. If I had . . . never mind. Two weeks later, Lukas was dead. Lukas used himself up trying to speak. Lukas wanted me to know.

(JEREMY *comes in the door. A white bandage wound around his head.* SARAH *startles.*)

JEREMY: Jeeze, Ms. Golden, you're here.
SARAH: Jeremy, what happened to . . .

(JEREMY *paces as he unwinds the gauze from around his head. There is another smaller bandage underneath.*)

JEREMY: Wounded. See. Took a hit. Discharged. Ready to go. Said I'd talk to a shrink; they took the cuffs off. (*Pause*) You know what the shrink said? (*He paces, laughs nervously, and says in a mocking voice*) "Well, young man, you are not a risk to yourself or to anyone else." So, that's that. Fixed me right up. Stitches. X-ray. Had counseling, too. "Not a risk." Fine. Inside and out. Good as new.
SARAH: Jeremy, stand still.
JEREMY: Look, I don't have a gun if that's what they said.
SARAH: How do you know they told me that?
JEREMY: She starts screaming. I yell back.
SARAH: Be honest with me.
JEREMY: I stopped to have a few drinks. She throws a frying pan. If I'd had a gun, I'd a blown her head off. I smacked her, instead.
SARAH: Very smart.
JEREMY: Ms. Golden, Sarah, look, I can control this stuff, if I can act. I know I can. Trust me. Please.
SARAH: Jeremy, Muffler has thrown you out of school.
JEREMY: Right. Sure. Fucking dickhead. Jerk.

(JEREMY *slumps into the empty chair.*)

It's over. See. I fucked up.

(SARAH *sits on the bench next to him.*)

SARAH: It was war, Jeremy.
JEREMY: Sure. That's what it was.

SARAH: You can tell me. Anything. Anything at all.

JEREMY: Help me. I've got no one else.

SARAH: I promise.

JEREMY: Stop looking at me.

SARAH: Trust me, Jeremy. I will help. I know how hard . . .

(*She reaches out to him. He flies into a rage.*)

JEREMY: I told you not to talk about that. Never, I said. Shit. Fuck. You know what: just get out of my life. Stop following me around. Asking me stuff. Pretending you know. That's right. Give up and leave us alone. Miranda and me.

(JEREMY *storms out the door.* SARAH, *stunned, waits a moment and then leaves.*)

SCENE 14

(*The desk phone is ringing in* ALAN's *office, later the same day. He enters, nervous and excited, he speaks into his phone.*)

ALAN: Yes, I'm free. Send her right up!

(SARAH *enters, carrying several large shopping bags from an expensive boutique.*)

ALAN (*surprised, not altogether pleasantly*): Sarah!

(*She kisses him.*)

SARAH: Surprise, sweetie. Give me a minute. I'll slip into something smashing, cashmere, décolletage. You'll take me some fabulous place. We'll drink, fuck.

ALAN: Sarah, it's two o'clock.

SARAH: I'll forget.

ALAN: My afternoon's booked.

SARAH: Everything was on sale.

ALAN: I'm certain it's lovely.

SARAH: I can't take anything back.

ALAN: Sarah, truth is . . . I've a meeting.

SARAH: Whenever I get near a hospital, my life falls apart . . .

ALAN: Darling, later, I promise, my head will be clear.

SARAH: I see. What exquisite timing. Isn't it amazing how life works? All our ghosts.

ALAN: Don't say that.

SARAH: Alan, help me. I'm afraid.

(*He goes to her and holds her.*)

ALAN: Don't be, darling, I'm here, with you.

(MARIAM *opens the door. She clutches a large leather lady's handbag to her chest and stands awkwardly.*)

MARIAM: I'm sorry, I'll . . .

(ALAN *moves quickly away from* SARAH.)

ALAN: Mariam, please, come in. I'm so happy you're here.

(*He moves to hug her, but she steps away. Everyone stands in awkward silence.*)

SARAH: Is your mother in town?
MARIAM: My mother?

(*Silence.*)

My mother is in Beirut.
ALAN: Sit down, everyone, please. Coffee? Tea? I've cleared the whole afternoon just for us.

(*He points out the two chairs around the table, and he holds one out for* MARIAM. *The women sit.* ALAN *sits on the bench. He is effusive.* SARAH *is distracted.* MARIAM *tenses.*)

Here, everyone. Good. Now, how long will you stay in New York?
MARIAM: Long enough.
ALAN: Great. I'll show you the city. We will, won't we, Sarah? What would you like to see? Do you like opera, museums, food, we have the best restaurants, shopping, do you like to shop? Read? Hip-hop? There are mosques. We have quite a few Arab neighborhoods. There are so many people I'd like you to meet. You'll stay for a while, I hope. You could think of studying here, at Columbia.
MARIAM: I won't stay that long.
ALAN: No?
MARIAM: I don't think you know why I've come?
ALAN: I had hoped to see me.
MARIAM: That's true. I want to know about you.
ALAN: You do? Sure. That's so nice. Well, what's to know? I'm still executive director here.

SARAH: Your mother's office was right next door.

(SARAH's *cell phone rings; she fishes for it.*)

ALAN: Yes. Well, I'm rather overwhelmed at the moment. We're trying to figure out how to get some aid into Tyre, then, of course, there's Gaza. There's
always Gaza, as we say around here. Not to mention Iraq.

MARIAM: It's an overwhelming moment, yes.

(*Silence.* SARAH *is listening, intently, to the voice on her phone.* ALAN *and* MAR-
IAM *lock eyes.*)

SARAH: Yes, Jeremy, of course, I know just where it is. Right away.

(SARAH *gathers her things, getting ready to leave.*)

ALAN: It's fine, Sarah, stay.

SARAH: Can't.

ALAN: Tonight, then. Be careful, will you.

(ALAN *kisses her.*)

SARAH (*to* MARIAM): I leave Alan to you.

(SARAH *exits.*)

ALAN: Well, then, good. Sarah stopped by out of the blue . . . I had planned
for us to be, well, here we are, now, just we two. (*Pause*) I will work hard,
Mariam, to become a real father to you.

MARIAM: There's no need. I'm grown.

ALAN: Even for a grown-up, a father is . . . I miss my own father quite a bit.
It went so fast, your growing up. I thought about you every birthday, what
you'd be wearing, where I would take you. I always wanted you to ride the
merry-go-round in Central Park. I never knew the actual date.

MARIAM: June 27.

ALAN: Close! I always thought the first of July. Somehow, I think, I was not
surprised to see you as you are now, in the hijab, too. A father knows his
daughter, somehow, even if . . .

MARIAM: I never felt I knew you.

ALAN: You look so much like Hala.

MARIAM: I have your nose.

ALAN: Sorry, that was a mistake.

MARIAM: Don't be sorry about that.

ALAN: Does Hala ever speak about those years? (*Silence*) All right, Mariam, look, I will tell you. I never intended to leave your mother while she was pregnant. It was Sarah. By the time I had sorted things and Sarah was, well, resigned, your mother didn't want me anymore. How is she? How is Hala?

MARIAM: Hala was traveling the road north from Tyre with a convoy of women and children when the road was hit. The first ambulance, clearly marked, it could be seen from the sky, was destroyed. Deliberately targeted, Hala says.

ALAN: We heard. (*Pause*) Hala would be in the thick of it all.

MARIAM: Everyone, now, is in the thick of it, I think.

ALAN: True. Does she know you're here? That you've come?

MARIAM: It was a beautiful summer in Lebanon, Alan. Our house on the Corniche overlooks the sea. In the morning there were birds, at night music. So many friends had come home. We were laughing all the time. Hala made me leave, to go to London, she thought. I never left Heathrow. I got on a plane for New York.

ALAN: I'm very glad.

MARIAM: I am glad, too.

ALAN: I'm happy about that.

MARIAM: Happy?

ALAN: Thrilled, I'd say, yes.

MARIAM: I don't think you know why I've come.

ALAN: I had hoped to see me.

MARIAM: Yes, to see you at work. I wanted to be here in this building with you and all these good people, all these innocent civilians, at this particular time, when so many innocent civilians in my part of the world . . . You do good work, all of you. You send aid to people like me. You send protein bars and bottles of cooking oil, not olive oil, of course, vegetable oil, but still, we can cook up the dried chick peas, and rice, if we have clean water, that is. If the water purification plants have not been bombed, if crude oil has not been dumped in the sea, killing the fish. Never mind. You send ready meals, if you have to, dump them on us from the sky. And you send little pieces of paper telling us to leave our houses before they are bombed. That is very kind. The good people in the United States continue to think they are good because of the work you do here helping refugees. The more refugees your country makes, the more people like you try to help.

ALAN: That is one way of looking at it, I suppose.

MARIAM: Do you look at it another way?

ALAN: I try. There is always evil in the world, and there is always good.

MARIAM: True.

ALAN: I do what I can to tip the balance our way.

MARIAM: That is admirable, Alan.

ALAN: Thank you. Your mother, too, Hala feels the same way. Felt. I'm certain, still does.

MARIAM: Oh, yes. My mother thinks exactly like you. But let me ask you, Alan, one thing. I have come here just to ask you. Why when you tip the balance, as you say, why is it always Muslims who must die? Why does the balance never tip the other way? There is a bomb ticking right now inside my bag. Please answer soon.

ALAN: Don't talk like that. Not even inside my office. It's fine to be outraged, of course. I am, also, outraged. But someone might overhear you, even here. That would put you at risk.

MARIAM: I understand.

ALAN: Fine, then, okay. We all know what's going on. What do you think I do day in and day out? But I want to tell you something else: My father, your grandfather, he lived in times worse than these, and he never gave up. He wasted not one instant on revenge. He got people out. Snatched from the Nazis. He saved lives. Often, of course, it does feel useless. I feel hopeless . . . but I learned from him, from what he did, individuals can make a difference to other individuals. That may be all we can do. But we must do that much.

MARIAM: That is true.

ALAN: My father left a legacy to me. I intend to pass his legacy to you. I have letters to you, Mariam, a drawer full, returned by your mother, unopened. I wanted to know you. I tried to imagine what you needed to hear at every time, every age. You can read them. Tell me if I got anything right.

MARIAM: That would be nice.

ALAN: I sent money, too.

MARIAM: Naturally. Of course.

ALAN: I wanted you to have the best. Be the best. Your mother and I spoke about a new race. It was foolish, romantic talk, of course. But we believed it in those days, and we still do, Hala, too, I am certain of that, in peace, somehow, in justice, in living together, side by side, that someday clearer heads will prevail. We believed in you, too, Mariam. We believed that in making you from our flesh we were going to give something beautiful not just to ourselves but to the world. I am so sorry I wasn't there to see you grow up.

MARIAM: In Lebanon for the Civil War? In East Jerusalem? Where?

ALAN: I am sorry, Mariam. I have a great deal to be sorry for. But, please know, how thrilled, how blessed I feel, truly, I don't use that word lightly, that you came to find me. Amazing at this time in my life to have one more chance.

MARIAM: One more chance?

ALAN: I might live to know my grandchildren, a wonderful thought. I am a fortunate man, Mariam, because you've come.

MARIAM: I see. I thought it would be nice if you knew me, if you understood everything in your last minutes, if your whole life flashed before you, and you got to know at the very last moment that this child who was supposed to bring in the new world, only you never got to watch her grow up, unfortunate, that, but there was always a war on, after all, and how could you leave your important job to go there, anyway. It was always so unsafe. But, I wanted you to know, now, at last, about the new world you made with your big dreams, your empty words, and the murderous actions they cover up, the peace plans, the road maps running every which way, they have to bulldoze so many houses to get there, and put up such a big wall, build a fence around Gaza, such a nice prison they built, to keep the fishermen from being able to fish, and there is nowhere to run, you get blown up if you go to the beach, if you leave, you can't get back in, and, then, why not send Lebanon back to the stone age, the people, after all, are so primitive. But none of that matters, now, at all, because most of all I wanted to see your face at the moment you understand it is your own flesh who is going to blow you up.

(*At this,* ALAN *makes a lunge for her, and he grabs her bag.*)

I wouldn't open the clasp.

(*He lets go of the bag and takes a step back.* MARIAM *laughs.*)

We are all terrorists, after all.

ALAN: Forget about me. I'm an old man. Don't ruin your life.

MARIAM: Get ready, Alan. I'm going to give you a treat. Parents are always already dead. They don't get to hear this:

(MARIAM *begins to recite the Kaddish, the Jewish prayer for the dead.*)

Yeetgadal v'yeetkadash sh'mey rabbah
B'almach dee v'rah kheer'utey
V'yanleekh malkhutei, b'chahyeykhohn, uv' yohmeykhohn
Uv'chahyei d'chohl beyt yisrael

(ALAN *is frozen in terror; he doesn't want to believe her, yet he does.* MARIAM *opens the bag and dumps its contents onto the floor: lipsticks, pens, her passport, a diary, a wallet, keys, the usual stuff, a book.* ALAN *feels like a fool, but he relaxes.* MARIAM *picks up the book.*)

See Under Love *by David Grossman. A great Israeli novelist. A great Holocaust book. And do you know that David Grossman had a son, Uri. He was a tank commander in the ground invasion. His father had just signed a petition with other Jewish intellectuals calling for an end to the fighting. This war could have ended before Uri Grossman got killed by a Hezbollah rocket. He was twenty years old. And you think we are the only ones who love to make martyrs? Do you think we are the only ones who love death?*

(*She trembles.*)

Like an ocean, like two seas crashing together between the rocks and that is my bloodstream, that churning is always my heart. You cannot imagine the power with which my heart beats. How does my heart not jump from my chest? How does my blood not rush out? You wanted something else. I believe you wished for a son. In your mind I would be a great man. I would have had a bar mitzvah. I would have done good. I would have figured out how. Like your father, like you.

ALAN: No, Mariam. It was you I wanted. All the time, I wanted you.

(ALAN *goes to her and he holds her and comforts her.*)

MARIAM: It's too hard.

ALAN: I know that, believe me, my dear one, my daughter, my child, I do understand.

(ALAN *helps her up and they walk out together.*)

SCENE 15

(*That night.* SARAH *is in bed.* ALAN *enters the bedroom.*)

SARAH: I'm awake.

(*He kisses her head.*)

I can't sleep.

(*She sits up and turns on the light.*)

Poor kid . . .

(ALAN *sits on the bed.*)

ALAN: She pulled quite a stunt.

SARAH: He was crying when he called. I met him in the park at Strawberry Fields. He got down on his knees and apologized.

ALAN: Well, good for him. Mariam threatened to blow me up. She said she had plastic explosives in her bag.

SARAH: You didn't believe her?

ALAN: She was quite convincing.

SARAH: You believed her.

ALAN: For an instant.

SARAH: It's your guilt.

ALAN: Afterwards, I felt like a fool. Worse than a fool. Some kind of criminal. At least, I didn't show her how angry I was.

SARAH: He promised me he doesn't have a gun.

ALAN: A gun? Sarah, stay away from that kid.

SARAH: He would never hurt me.

ALAN: Don't be so sure.

SARAH: He never threatened to blow me up.

ALAN: He's not your flesh and blood.

SARAH: Right.

ALAN: I looked for them, Sarah, more than once. Hala was good at covering her tracks but it wasn't Hala by then I cared about.

SARAH: We went to a stupid movie to clear our heads, stuffed ourselves. We laughed, Alan, like kids. I won't let that boy go off on his own. I promised I'd get him back into school.

ALAN: Somehow the pain dulled over the years. Days would go by when I wouldn't even feel the ache.

SARAH: Alan, what have we done?

ALAN: Abraham rode twice to Egypt to see Ishmael, Sarah, did you know that? He could not get off his white horse. Sarah forbade his feet touching the ground, still, she let him go.

SARAH: I let you.

ALAN: He left signs for his son to interpret so the boy knew he was loved.

SARAH: Mariam found you.

ALAN: Daughters are impossible, it turns out.

SARAH: You deserved a fright—look at it from her point of view.

ALAN: She recited the Kaddish.

SARAH: Really?

ALAN: Perfectly, yes.

SARAH: You couldn't do that. I suppose she can do it, someday, for you.

ALAN: It was ghastly, really, I thought. I know, it's ridiculous. That beautiful, brilliant girl . . . to think such a thing.

SARAH: Like Hala, really.

ALAN: Quite.

SARAH: I always liked Hala, actually. I thought of having an affair with her myself.

ALAN: No.

SARAH: Yes. It's a line from a Pinter play. Robert says to his wife, "I always liked Jerry rather more than I liked you. I should have had an affair with him myself."

ALAN: Something else happened to me when I thought I was about to die.

SARAH: What?

ALAN: Lukas.

SARAH: Lukas, of course. I've never been unfaithful to you, Alan, not since.

ALAN: That's something, I suppose.

SARAH: It most definitely is. All our friends had open marriages, then.

ALAN: Then.

SARAH: Well, that's how it was.

ALAN: Years after the war, a man, he said he was in Muffler's command, came to see me. He was having nightmares. His therapist suggested we talk. He knew Lukas, Sarah.

SARAH: Was his name John?

ALAN: John, yes, that was his name. I talked to the guy. He was pretty distraught. Paranoid I thought.

SARAH: You didn't believe him?

ALAN: It's not that I didn't believe him. I was no longer practicing law.

SARAH: You believed him. John was Lukas's friend.

ALAN: After that, I went to see Muffler.

SARAH: To accuse the bastard.

ALAN: Not exactly, Sarah, I needed to hear his side of the story.

SARAH: His side!

ALAN: Muffler was a mess. Incoherent. Drunk. Shortly after we spoke, he dropped out of sight.

SARAH: You'd always been jealous of Lukas. Perhaps, you were grateful to Muffler, in your heart of hearts.

ALAN: Nonsense. He canceled the play you were in.

SARAH: *Uncle Vanya.* I was the Yelena.

ALAN: Right. You were pretty upset.

SARAH: I loved the part.

ALAN: I felt I had undermined your career for no reason. It would have been impossible to prove, and what would have been accomplished after all? Muffler had disappeared.

SARAH: But, today when you thought you were going to lose your life in a terrorist attack carried out by your own flesh and blood, this scene in your office with John flashed through your head and you decided that you don't want to go to your final destination, however hot that may be, Alan, without making a clean breast, so you decided to tell me tonight that I owe my career to the decorated war criminal who shot Lukas in the head.

ALAN: We don't know that.

SARAH: I ought to have known, Alan, all along. But, I didn't want to know, did I? I wanted to act.

(SARAH *looks at him. She takes her robe and leaves the bedroom.*)

SCENE 16

(*Split scene:* SARAH *enters her living room. Her cell phone is in her hand. A phone rings. Day in Beirut and* HALA's *living room is drenched in Mediterranean light.* HALA *enters, her cell phone in her hands. Both women use ear-pieces and hold their phones, allowing them mobility. The scene has a strange sort of physical intimacy; though the women cannot see one another and never look in the other's direction, their movements indicate a growing synchronicity of feeling.*)

SARAH: Hala?

HALA: Hala, yes.

SARAH: It's Sarah.

HALA: Sarah?

SARAH: Alan's . . . you know . . .

HALA: Ah, Sarah! Hello.

(*They laugh a bit nervously; then, they begin to speak at the same time.*)

SARAH: How are you?

HALA: How are you?

SARAH: You're well?

HALA: As usual. And you?

SARAH: I'm fine.

HALA: You are?

SARAH: I am, yes.

HALA: I'm glad.

SARAH: I'm glad you're all right. Mariam is in New York.

HALA: I sent her out of here to England. I had no idea.

SARAH: She's a wonderful young woman. Amazing, really.

HALA: I'm glad you think so.

SARAH: I do. She's ballsy, if you know what I mean.

HALA (*laughs*): I do.

(*Pause*)

I don't want to speak to Alan.

SARAH: Alan's asleep.

(*Pause*)

Hala?

HALA: Yes, Sarah, what?

SARAH: Something has happened. Not to Mariam; she's fine. Really. Lovely.

HALA: Has she taken off the headscarf in New York? Tell me, yes. She started that at boarding school in England, not in Beirut. Here she was disco-dancing. Here, before, I worried about sex, drinking, usual things. Now, who knows what to fear. The young are putting on the scarves. If my mother were alive, she'd . . .

SARAH: Something's happened, Hala, to someone else. To me, too, I think. I couldn't sleep. I haven't been. Sleeping, that is.

HALA: I know.

SARAH: You do?

HALA: I don't sleep.

SARAH: Oh, my god, of course not. I'm . . . what can I say?

HALA: The bombing has stopped. The truce might hold.

SARAH: I hope so.

HALA: We are relieved.

(*Pause*)

SARAH: Hala, I have something in my head. A woman. I had to tell someone. You. I thought: Hala, I could tell. You've been to Iraq.

HALA: I was there, yes. At the start. Afterwards, there was no room for the UN.

SARAH: How can such things happen? This war, I mean, we let it, not you, we, here, and, now, well.

(HALA *puts her head into her hands.*)

I teach, you remember, do you? A talented young man in my class. She was pregnant, Hala. I don't know what I'm asking. He can't forget. That's good, I think, he shouldn't. But now? I mean, I know. I see. It's an indelible image, really. (*Pause*) I don't know. What do you do?

HALA: Do?

SARAH: With such things? With the things you've heard, things you have seen, I mean. How do you?

HALA: Go on?

SARAH: I suppose. I don't know. You go on. Obviously, you do. But it's in my mind. Like a scene in a play. I didn't see it, firsthand, like you, like I suppose you have seen, and worse things, still, I can't forget. I cannot stop looking. Sometimes I feel I am her.

HALA: I see.

SARAH: You do? Because I'm afraid I'm completely unhinged.

HALA: There's a concept the therapists have, secondary traumatization, it happens from the things you hear, things that the people tell you. They tell you, and you see it all in front of you. You take their story into your body. It happens to everyone, everyone who listens, that is. Is this what you wanted to hear?

SARAH: What do you do?

HALA: Do?

SARAH: Yes, Hala, please.

(HALA *gets up and as she does* SARAH *sits down and gently rocks herself back and forth.*)

HALA: You weep with them. You hold them, if you can. If they let you. If they are not so stiff they can't be touched. You try to hold them, until, you hold them until they can start to shake. You want to know this?

SARAH: I know it, yes . . .

HALA: Sometimes they bury their heads in your lap, even if they are men, sometimes, often, if a wife has been killed. They cry. Or if their children . . . Grown men. They tremble in your arms. They were not home when the house was bombed. They come home. Everyone they love is gone. They dig. They find, maybe, a hand. I can't tell you, Sarah. I will not do it, not over the phone, not in your West Side apartment with all those white walls.

SARAH: But I know, I mean, I read, I watch the news, we do see, but, please, it is this boy I have, he was a soldier.

HALA: A soldier.

SARAH: A boy, innocent, really, then all of a sudden . . . he shot a pregnant woman, Hala, many times. (*Silence.*) Hala?

HALA: I will tell you about the survivors, the ones who remain alive, after soldiers like yours. Let me tell you about their eyes. Their eyes have a look you do not see in anyone else. They are looking, trying to look, from very far away. They cannot believe themselves what they tell you that they've seen. They do not anymore know how to believe.

(*Silence. Both women are very still.*)

Sometimes, I think we are held here by threads, each one of us, by threads slim as the web of a spider, to the people we love, to our children. How easy it is for someone to walk through our web without seeing, to wipe it away with one move of the hand, without ever knowing what they've done. If you cut a person's threads, they go spinning, all by themselves. They are whirled out to the other side of a divide, to a place where there is no one they can touch; there is nothing to hold them. They are a long distance from us. (*Pause*) Here, in my part of the world, family is so important. Now they have no one. "I am no more a man." "I am no more a woman." They do not, anymore, know how to be. This frightens me. It should frighten us all. They look at us with dead eyes from very far.

(*Long pause in which both women walk closer.*)

Sarah, I am sorry that I took your husband. That from him I had my child, my Mariam, with her headscarf, and her rage. I didn't want this life. I wanted, yes, of course, my child, I wanted her, and Alan, I wanted him. I did. We wanted, he and I . . . We forgot the moment, the present in which we lived. I forgot the thread connecting me to you. We had no idea, then, what would come. We wanted to weave . . . I wanted strings, Sarah, threads.

(HALA *turns toward* SARAH *who turns around to face her.*)

I am glad you called, Sarah, I have wanted to tell you this.

(*It is almost as if they can touch.*)

SARAH: Thank you, Hala.

HALA: Thank me?

SARAH: Yes.

HALA: I am to be thanked?

SARAH: Not for taking Alan, not for that. For making Mariam, for making threads to keep you, to keep us, you and me, attached. For telling me what you have. Somehow, it helps. It does.

HALA: Good morning, then, Sarah, it must be very early.

SARAH: It is. Good afternoon, Hala. Take care.

(*They each listen, for a moment, to the other's breathing in the phone, unable to hang up.*)

HALA: Your country has caused a great shame with this war.

SARAH: I believe that, too, Hala. I don't know what to do.

HALA: Shame drives people mad. (*Pause*) Good luck, Sarah.

(SARAH *goes toward her bedroom stage right.* HALA *exits stage left.*)

SCENE 17

(SARAH *and* ALAN's *living room, the following evening.* JEREMY *is alone and is busy going over his lines.* SARAH *enters from her kitchen.*)

SARAH: You know what, Jeremy, get up.

(*He stands.* SARAH *takes the chair away.*)

For the audition with Muffler tomorrow let's cut the chair.

JEREMY: "I sat," he says. He's sitting down.

SARAH: No. He appears; he comes, led by a small boy, to confront Kreon. Jeremy, have you read the whole play?

(JEREMY *hangs his head.*)

Wonderful. How can you act, if . . . never mind. Read the play, Jeremy. It's good for you.

JEREMY: He's sitting there talking to the general.

SARAH: No, he's on his feet in front of King Kreon, yes, general, too.

JEREMY: The commander-in-chief.

SARAH: Close enough. This is the big moment, the turning point. The highest spiritual authority confronts the temporal . . . it's like the Pope coming from Rome to say "stop the war."

JEREMY: The Pope would sit down.

SARAH: Well, you're going to stand. Look, I had quite a talk with Muffler today. He just needs to see . . .

JEREMY: If he thinks I'm good.

SARAH: You are good.

JEREMY: At least, you think so.

SARAH: Well, that's what you've got to go on so far. My word. Plus what you feel, inside. Are you good enough Jeremy?

JEREMY: Good enough?

SARAH: As an actor, I mean.

JEREMY: Are they two separate things?

SARAH: Sometimes, yes. Sometimes, usually, in fact, I would say all the time, we are better in our art than we are in our lives. After all, we get to rehearse. So, let's begin.

(JEREMY *stands.* SARAH *sits.*)

JEREMY: Okay, here goes. (*Pause*) You'll catch me?

SARAH: I most certainly will.

(JEREMY *tosses his head so that his hair falls down around his eyes.*)

JEREMY: As I sat on the ancient seat of augury . . . (*He stops.*) See! "Sat."

SARAH: "As," Jeremy. As in "when I sat."

(*The doorbell rings.* SARAH *shrugs, goes to the door.*)

MARIAM: Sarah, hello.

(*There's an awkward moment, then* SARAH *hugs* MARIAM. MARIAM *is wearing a headscarf, jeans, and a form-fitting, long-sleeved shirt.* JEREMY *stares at them.*)

SARAH: Come in. (*To* JEREMY) You've met Alan's daughter, Mariam. (*To* MARIAM) He's held up. Crisis at work. No time to talk. And we're just in the middle . . .

JEREMY: Salaam, Mariam.

MARIAM: Salaam.

SARAH: We're rehearsing, Mariam.

MARIAM: I'm sorry. I'll go.

JEREMY: Stay. It's good. An audience, you know . . .

SARAH: Fine, then, sit. You can start at the top, if you like, or anywhere.

(MARIAM *sits.* JEREMY *stands, smiling at her.*)

JEREMY: Hey, the Arabic worked.

SARAH (*a bit annoyed*): Whenever you're ready. I'm here.

(*Split scene:* CHARLES MUFFLER *enters and sits in his desk chair, opposite. He's attentive to* JEREMY's *audition and disturbed by it.* SARAH *sits between* JEREMY *and* CHARLES. *There are two time periods here: the confrontation between* SARAH *and* CHARLES *earlier that day and the rehearsal at* SARAH's *house that night. As the scene unfolds, there will be a third,* JEREMY's *audition in front of* CHARLES *the next morning.*)

JEREMY: They were killing each other—that much I knew.
 The murderous fury whirring in those wings
 Made that much clear!
 I was afraid,

(*Freeze:* JEREMY *is completely committed to the speech and* MARIAM *is paying complete attention.*)

(*Action:* SARAH *turns toward* CHARLES's *desk. They are in the midst of the confrontation they had earlier that day.*)

CHARLES: You're correct in one thing, Sarah, one. Lukas Brightman was on that patrol. He volunteered. It's a village, he said, those were his words. It's a village full of women and children, old men. There are no Vietcong. Well, they shot him point blank in the head. His brains blown away by someone's little, old grandmother in black pajamas.

(*Action on the other side of the stage:* JEREMY *continues with his speech, becoming strong and angry, he speaks directly toward* CHARLES.)

JEREMY: And it is you—
 Your high resolve that sets this plague on Thebes.
 The public altars and sacred hearths are fouled,
 And so the gods are deaf to our prayers, they spurn
 The offerings in our hands, the flame of holy flesh.

(CHARLES *is becoming undone.*)

CHARLES (*the scene in Vietnam playing out in his head*): Stop! Why should I be made to watch? I see the whole thing in my head. I give the order to open up. I use overwhelming force, yes. I use everything I have. Lukas is the only soldier I lose on that patrol.
SARAH: Lukas was going to blow the whistle on you.
CHARLES: Enough. I know about that man who rants about massacres. Poor devil, he's not in his right mind. He came after me, stalking. Proof of what? He made a grab for me right on the street, screaming obscenities, threaten-

ing. A passerby called 911. I was supervising the men putting up the signs for our *Uncle Vanya*. I blame Alan. Putting absurd ideas into a crazy vet's head. I was afraid for my life. A murderer, believe me, I'm not.

SARAH: Right, Charles, have it your way. But if you don't let Jeremy back into school, I will not be able to stay.

CHARLES: Don't push me, my dear.

(SARAH *turns back to* JEREMY *as the speech continues to build. He is still speaking as if directly toward* CHARLES *who drums his fingers during the speech, then puts his head into his hands, visibly shaken.*)

JEREMY: Take these things to heart, my son, I warn you.
    All men make mistakes, it is only human.
    But once the wrong is done, a man
    Can turn his back on folly, misfortune, too,
    If he tries to make amends, however low he's fallen,
    And stops his bullnecked ways. Stubbornness
    Brands you for stupidity—pride is a crime.

(MARIAM *begins to applaud energetically; she's completely taken with him.*)

SARAH: Well done, Jeremy. It gets better and better.

MARIAM: You are very, very good. You will put some truth into the world.

JEREMY (*to* MARIAM): Ma'am, I'm not good.

SARAH: It was, Jeremy, really. Very fine.

(*He steps closer to* SARAH *and hits his heart.*)

JEREMY: What do you think I see when I talk?

SARAH: You got through it. You used it. The speech will hold you. The words become your container. You can pour your heart in.

JEREMY: I never don't see it; that's the thing. But he says you can get up, no matter how low.

SARAH: Sophocles was a general; his actors had all been soldiers. You're not alone, Jeremy. Stay, both of you. I'll order in.

MARIAM: No, it's fine.

JEREMY: Me, too, got to go, home, read the play, you know.

(JEREMY *smiles at* MARIAM.)

    I can walk you to the train.

SARAH: Jeremy, call me, if you need anything. Call me, anytime, tonight, tomorrow morning before the audition. Call me the minute you hear.

(SARAH *kisses* MARIAM. JEREMY *exits with her.* SARAH *reenters the earlier confrontation scene with* CHARLES.)

I don't push, Charles. I'm telling you. I will be forced to resign, quite publicly, in fact. I know what happened to Lukas in Vietnam.

(CHARLES *is shaken; he is humbler, more fragile than we've ever seen him. This is the memory that haunts, and he has never told anyone before.*)

CHARLES: You think I never think about that night? You bet. There's Lukas and all the rest of it, too. Over and over it plays. A film in my head. Machine guns. Grenades. Blood-curdling yells. Wings beat the sky, shatter the rays of the sun. Birds squawk, trying to fly. Flesh drops to the ground. Feathers flying like snow. A boy falls out the door. Two eggs in his hands. Yolk breaks on black dirt. Eyes roll in his head. A white feather lands on his nose.

(*Pause*)

So, I am aware, yes. I see. I ask myself: Did I let Lukas volunteer to go first because I hated the little commie bastard? If true, I'm not saying it is, if unconsciously, that's what I felt, well, that was a good decision, wasn't it? Lukas was turning my men against my command. He was a fifth column. You don't take prisoners in a jungle. We needed bodies.

SARAH: Come, Charles, we are members of one another. Lukas, me, you, Jeremy, too. For your own sake, as well, Jeremy Thrasher should come back to school.

CHARLES: I have done you some good, Sarah, have I not?

SARAH: True. Now, you can help Jeremy, too. *You will* help him—for all of our sakes.

(*He's had it; he stands to usher her out.*)

CHARLES: Enough. We've spoken our minds. I'll take a good, hard look at the boy.

SARAH: Thank you, Charles.

(SARAH *exits the office.* JEREMY *enters, stage left, where he was standing before. He is at the very end of his audition, full of the force and fire he displayed in* SARAH's *living room. He finishes his audition speech.*)

JEREMY: Stubbornness
Brands you for stupidity—pride is a crime.
No, yield to the dead!

Never stab the fighter when he's down.
Where's the glory, killing the dead twice over?
I mean you well. I give you sound advice.
It's best to learn from a good advisor
When he speaks for your own good.

(*The words hit* CHARLES *like a blow to the thoracic.*)

CHARLES: Well, well. (*Pause*) That's . . .

(*He clears his throat; he's undone by the words and force of the speech. It's all too much for him. He struggles to pull himself together.*)

Thank you very much, young man.
JEREMY: Sure. I mean, thank you for the opportunity, sir.
CHARLES: That's enough, then.
JEREMY: I could do it again. If you have . . . I could try . . . anything, you want.
Do you want anything else?
CHARLES: No need to do it again.
JEREMY: It was okay? It felt good, I mean.
CHARLES: Yes, yes. We'll give you a call, Jeremy.

(*He looks at his watch, in a hurry to end this.*)

I've got . . . something else. Young man, you can go.
JEREMY: Yes, sir.

(*Awkward pause.* JEREMY, *defeated, exits.* CHARLES *stares, terrified, into space as if in the middle of his recurring flashback—he sees it all again, the little boy falling out the door, and* LUKAS, *being shot, blood bursting out of his head. He exits.*)

SCENE 18

(*Split scene: That evening, after* JEREMY's *audition.* SARAH *enters her living room. She looks nervously at the phone, which has not rung, and sits on the bench.* JEREMY *and* MARIAM *enter stage left into a Japanese restaurant and he pulls her chair out. They sit.* MARIAM *wears the hijab, a pretty top, jeans.* ALAN *enters the living room and begins to massage* SARAH's *back. They become increasingly loving;* JEREMY *and* MARIAM *are flirtatious.*)

SARAH: Alan, how kind.
ALAN: My heart feels light for the first time in years.

(*Silence. Both couples smile at each other. The two conversations alternate.*)

JEREMY: I'm glad you like Japanese food.
MARIAM: I do.
JEREMY: You eat the raw stuff. I can't do that. I like this steak teriyaki. I'm a
   red meat sort of guy.

(*He laughs, nervously.*)

MARIAM: I suppose you are.

SARAH: Amazing, really. The absence of hurt.
ALAN: I've passed through something with Mariam.

JEREMY: How did you learn to eat with chopsticks?
MARIAM: Maybe in London, maybe Beirut, probably not East Jerusalem.
JEREMY: Wow. You've seen plays in London?

SARAH: There's a dreadful staying power to grief. Suddenly, we've loosened its
   grip.
ALAN: I wish she'd stay here, go to school.
SARAH: Jeremy's good. I hope Muffler saw it that way. Jeremy's raw. Muffler
   likes crusted over, as he says, "in control."
ALAN: Muffler liked you.
SARAH: I'll blow the bastard's cover if he doesn't let Jeremy back into school.

MARIAM: You were quite wonderful the other night.
JEREMY: Thanks. (*Pause*)

ALAN: She learned Hebrew, this Lebanese-Palestinian girl with a headscarf
   when she found out who her father was.

JEREMY: I think you're pretty wonderful, too.

SARAH: Proof that she has a good mother.

MARIAM: I began to applaud. That's what you liked.
JEREMY: It sure sounded great. I thought just wait till that sound of two hands
   clapping is multiplied by a thousand, you know, like on Broadway.

ALAN: I thought Hala would refuse. Instead, she said, "If you wish to find him, go ahead."

SARAH: I think Hala might have been pleased.

JEREMY: It's hard being an actor you know. It's harder than . . . (*He stops.*) It's the hardest thing I've ever done. It's terrifying.

SARAH: I told him I'd quit.

ALAN: You should audition, again. Act.

MARIAM: When you want something very much, it's always difficult. There is so very much to lose.

SARAH: Right.

JEREMY: After the speech, my audition, I mean, the dean, he didn't applaud.

MARIAM: I don't think the dean would.

SARAH: I stopped by his office; he'd left. He didn't return my call.

ALAN: Relax. He's pulling rank.

SARAH: But why hasn't Jeremy phoned?

ALAN: Jeremy has a date, with Mariam, in fact.

SARAH: I see.

(*Both couples are silent.*)

MARIAM: I only came to meet my father. To confront him, I thought . . . finally, to get it all off my chest. And then I find out that I like him, despite myself. That he listens and understands, that, in many ways, we think the same.

JEREMY: My old man . . . forget it, you don't want to know . . .

SARAH: Hala is an extraordinary woman.

ALAN: I thought so. I still do.

SARAH: It must have been hard, very hard.

ALAN: I also think so about you.

SARAH: You forgave.

JEREMY: I wanted us to celebrate tonight, wanted to, except the dean, he hasn't called.

MARIAM: He will.

JEREMY: I don't know . . . it was like he didn't like . . . (*Imitating* CHARLES's *pompous voice*) "Thank you very much, young man."

(MARIAM *laughs.*)

I swear to you, that's how he talks.

ALAN: We must, in order to live. Forgive. Ourselves, too. That's the one thing we must do.

JEREMY: Look, I'm a Catholic. I haven't been to Confession for years. I feel like, I don't know. There are things no one forgives.

MARIAM: God does.

JEREMY: Maybe, but you're talking to priests.

(*They sit in silence;* JEREMY *reaches for* MARIAM's *hand and they toy tentatively with one another's fingers, smiling into each other's eyes.*)

SARAH: Alan, come to bed.

(ALAN *and* SARAH *exit to their bedroom.* MARIAM *carefully removes her hand from* JEREMY's. *Something about the way he is looking at her . . .*)

JEREMY: I thought only married women wore that scarf. I mean I like it, it's pretty, it looks nice on you and all that, but I would like to see your hair. I bet you have beautiful hair.

MARIAM: That's why I wear the scarf. So I don't have to talk about my hair.

JEREMY: I could talk about your hair for a long time. I could say all sorts of wonderful things. I could talk about it a lot longer if I could see it. If I could wind a curl around my finger . . .

MARIAM (*pulling back*): I'm certain you could.

JEREMY: Hey, don't get upset. You are a beautiful woman. I'm a guy. It's only natural, that's all. We can talk about something else. (*Pause*) We can talk about London.

MARIAM: London, fine.

JEREMY: Look. Can I tell you something? Can I just talk? There's something about you, not just that you're pretty, beautiful, like I said. There's something in your eyes, some deep thing, a sadness, that's what I see. You remind me of . . . you look so much like this woman I saw in Iraq. Someone I didn't even know, but she was beautiful, like you. Met. Ran into, I guess. Someone who, well, she had black hair. Her scarf came loose and her hair spilled out all over the floor. How beautiful, that's what I thought, how beautiful.

MARIAM: Please, don't say any more.

JEREMY: They tell us everyone is armed and dangerous. They tell us all the women have bombs under those robes; they just look pregnant. That they'll blow themselves up just to kill us. They tell us not to trust.

MARIAM: I can't listen to this.

JEREMY: Please, forgive me. Just forgive me, please.

MARIAM: I must go. Excuse me.

JEREMY: Please, I'm so sorry, really I am. I'm so sorry, goddamn it. I'm telling you. You're beautiful. You're smart. You're gorgeous. I think. I thought. The minute I saw you, I thought you were perfect. Then you applauded. You clapped for me, for something I'd done. It was the most amazing feeling. I think I fell in love with you then.

MARIAM: Stop. You come on to me because I wear a headscarf. You know nothing of my life. Then, you use the word "love."

JEREMY: I'm sorry. I'm telling you that. You can't go. Not like this.

(JEREMY *roughly grabs her from behind; they struggle.*)

You've got to. Damn it. Let me.

(JEREMY *pulls off her hijab.*)

You're beautiful.

(JEREMY *runs his hands through her hair.* MARIAM *frees herself from him, stands her ground.*)

MARIAM: I won't listen. I don't want to know. Go to your priest if you need forgiveness. Go ask your government for help.

(MARIAM *pulls the hijab out of his hands.*)

Why is it an Arab who must forgive?

(MARIAM *exits.* JEREMY *becomes completely undone.*)

JEREMY: Forgive, please. Fore, but *bode,* that has the feeling, Foul, yes, deaf. Splatter and burst. Cut off. Gorged on the flesh. With such beautiful hair. Cracked jaw bones glisten. Please. Stop. No, not listening. Glutted with blood. Not good. Not good enough.

(JEREMY *runs out.*)

SCENE 19

(*Early morning.* SARAH *comes out of the bedroom. She is still halfway inside a dream. This is her memory of the boy she loved.*)

SARAH: Before he shipped out we went away for a weekend. The last weekend, really, of Lukas's normal life. A history professor lent us his cabin on the beach on the North Shore of Long Island. The idea was Lukas and I would spend the weekend writing one paragraph we could duplicate many times on strips of paper telling why the war was wrong and how the enlisted men could organize on the ground to stop it. Lukas could hide them inside cigarette packages, hand them out, palm them to guys. Oh, how we argued, cut and pasted, reworked and reworded to get it all into one paragraph. Basically, we just wanted to tell them to say "no," just to say no and to stop. I think he was a little bit excited, intoxicated, somewhat; Columbia had felt like a betrayal to him. His people were car mechanics, waitresses. We fell asleep on the floor in front of the fire. Early the last morning we got up and decided to walk along the shore. It was late summer, the early morning was cool and the sun was just coming up from under the sea. One of us began to sing:

(SARAH *begins to sing.*)

> Morning has broken like the first morning
> Like the first morning

But we didn't know the rest of the words. So we began to make things up:

(LUKAS'*s voice is heard.*)

> . . . praises to be.

(LUKAS *walks forward, he's a lovely, young, long-haired boy dressed in jungle fatigues in the style of the sixties, a bandana around his curls.*)

> The mist is rising, like the first morning,
> Like the first morning, praises to be.

(SARAH *stops singing, and* LUKAS'*s voice grows stronger.*)

> All hearts are open, like the first morning.
> All hearts are open, praises to be.

(*They sing together, almost holding hands. But they never touch. They are gentle, tender with one another, aware this may be the last time. Their love and sadness are palpable.*)

Praise to ocean, praise to the tides.

Praise to the new sun, red in the sky.

SARAH: Our feet were wet and caked with sand. I had gone off the pill while Lukas was in basic training but I hadn't told him and he didn't know.

LUKAS (*singing, directly into her eyes*): Morning has broken, like the first morning.

Like the first morning, praises to be.

SARAH: When we got up from the little beach, I was pregnant. I felt the collision, the blasting apart of what was. I felt like Lukas felt, intoxicated, everything up in the air, my life at risk, suddenly, too. Lukas could have had no idea, but he was smiling at me like he knew.

LUKAS (*singing*): Black bird has spoken like the first bird.

(LUKAS *vanishes.*)

SARAH: And now, after all these years, Jeremy Thrasher walks into my life, asking me if he's good enough. I would so like to hand a new morning to him.

ALAN: Sarah, my love.

(SARAH *turns.* ALAN *looks at her, unable to speak, and she begins to intuit something is terribly wrong.*)

SARAH: No. Don't, Alan.

ALAN: I am so sorry, my darling. That was the police on the phone. Jeremy Thrasher shot himself this morning . . . A note pinned to his shirt: "I am not good enough. Forgive."

(ALAN *holds* SARAH *while she cries, and she writhes in his arms, her face an agony. She is like a mother animal whose cub has been taken.*)

SARAH: No. No. No.

ALAN: My darling, my dearest, hush, now. I'm here.

(SARAH *struggles.* ALAN *quiets her a bit and holding her up, they exit.*)

(MIRANDA *enters, from the stage left door, and walks to the center of the space. She is speaking at a classroom memorial service for* JEREMY. *She says her name and then she speaks the final chorus simply and feelingly.*)

MIRANDA: Miranda Cruz.

Numberless are the world's wonders, but none

More wonderful than man.

We have all done this thing. Not one
    Young man with a gun
    or a bomb strapped to a chest.
These things are in the hands of men.
So, let the weeping start. Let
Mourning come, dawn will break.
    The Divine inside
    hallow this ground.

9 CIRCLES

Bill Cain

ABOUT THE PLAYWRIGHT

Bill Cain's widely produced play *Stand-Up Tragedy* debuted at the Mark Taper Forum before its 1990 Broadway engagement where it received the Joe A. Callaway Playwriting Award. His play *Equivocation* received its world premiere production at the Oregon Shakespeare Festival and was produced at the Geffen Playhouse, Seattle Repertory Theatre, Marin Theatre Company and in New York at the Manhattan Theatre Club. It was the recipient of the 2010 Harold and Mimi Steinberg/ATCA New Play Award. *9 Circles* was awarded the 2010 Sky Cooper New American Play Prize and received its world premiere production at the Marin Theatre Company. His extensive television credits include his work as the cocreator and writer of the ABC series *Nothing Sacred* for which he received the Writers Guild Award and the George Foster Peabody Award for excellence in television broadcasting. Cain is the founder of the Boston Shakespeare Company, where he was artistic director for seven seasons, directing most of the Shakespeare canon. His work has been developed by the Ojai Playwrights Conference, South Coast Rep's Pacific Playwrights Festival and TheaterWorks in Palo Alto.

PRODUCTION HISTORY

9 Circles was developed at the Ojai Playwrights Conference, Robert Egan, Artistic Director; and South Coast Repertory's Pacific Playwrights Festival, Martin Benson and David Emmes, Producing Artistic Directors.

It is the winner of the 2010 Sky Cooper New American Play Prize at Marin Theatre Company, where it received its world premiere under the leadership of Jasson Minadakis, Artistic Director, and Ryan Rilette, Producing Director. It was directed by Kent Nicholson.

Cast

Reeves . . . . Craig Marker*
Man. . . . . James Carpenter*
Woman . . . . Jennifer Erdmann*
Understudy . . . . Aldo Billingslea*

Designers

Set & Lighting Design . . . . Michael Palumbo
Costume Design . . . . .Callie Floor**
Sound Design . . . . Cliff Caruthers**

Stage Manager. . . . . Angela Nostrand

* Member of Actors' Equity Association
** Member of United Scenic Artists

CHARACTERS

Private Daniel Edward Reeves, nineteen to twenty years old, an American sol-
   dier in Iraq and the U.S. afterward
All other roles are played by a man and a woman as indicated.
Lieutenant (male)
Young Female Lawyer
Army Attorney (male)
Pastor (male)
Lawyer (male)
Shrink (female)
Prosecution (female)
Defense (male)

The male roles could be divided between two male actors.
The cast members will announce changes of place and time throughout.

CIRCLE 1: HONORABLE DISCHARGE.

(PRIVATE DANIEL EDWARD REEVES—*an army private for less than a year—Texan—enters. Lean. Intense. Standing at rigid military attention. This young man desperately wishes to remain a soldier. An army lifer* LIEUTENANT—*thirty—enters with* REEVES'*s orders in his hand.*)

LIEUTENANT: Private Reeves.
REEVES: Sir!
LIEUTENANT: Your orders.
REEVES: Sir.

(LIEUTENANT *opens orders. Reads. Then—*)

LIEUTENANT: Honorable—discharge.

(*A* WOMAN—*one of the cast—announces—*)

WOMAN: CIRCLE 1: IRAQ.

(*As the* LIEUTENANT *goes to sign the orders—*)

REEVES: Honorable discharge? I don't like the sound of that, sir.
LIEUTENANT: You like the sound of "*dis*honorable discharge" better?

(LIEUTENANT *goes to sign.*)

REEVES (*don't sign*): At least it means something, sir. You know something happened and it wasn't good. "Honorable discharge" sounds—bad.
LIEUTENANT: Bad? In what way?
REEVES: Sexual.
LIEUTENANT: "Honorable discharge."

(LIEUTENANT *considers that.*)

REEVES: Sounds like what your biology teacher'd say 'cause he's not supposed to say "cum."
LIEUTENANT: A euphemism.
REEVES: Is that where the words mean the opposite of each other?
LIEUTENANT (*no*): That's oxymoron. Military intelligence. Euphemism. Like somebody who wouldn't say shit if he had a mouth full of it.

REEVES (*wildly gung ho throughout*): Yes, sir. That's it exactly, sir. Sir, I want to stay here until we win this war, SIR.

LIEUTENANT: Son, if we could of won this war, we would have won it at the Battle of Lepanto.

REEVES: When was that, sir?

LIEUTENANT: Before your time. (*Preempting objection*) Private, you've got no say in the matter.

(*He goes to sign the orders.*)

REEVES (*unable to restrain himself*): I'll desert. I'll learn their language. I can already count to ten. I'll join them. I'll become their leader. Like in that movie.

LIEUTENANT (*intrigued*): *Lawrence of Arabia?* Peter O'Toole.

REEVES: *Universal Soldier*, sir. Jean-Claude Van Damme.

(*Then—*)

LIEUTENANT: Son, you know why you're being discharged?

REEVES: I know what the form says, sir. It says I have a personality disorder, sir.

LIEUTENANT: And what do you think of what the form says?

REEVES: I think—I think it's a euphemism, sir. (*Then*) I'm no expert, but I think a personality disorder can be an advantage in certain circumstances.

LIEUTENANT: Such as?

REEVES: Some things don't bother me the way they bother other people.

LIEUTENANT: Like?

REEVES: The basics, sir. Killing people. It bothers some people, sir.

LIEUTENANT: It doesn't bother you?

REEVES: Sir, we came here to kill people, sir.

LIEUTENANT (*gung ho*): Soldier, we came here to help build a nation. That is our mission. Operation Iraqi Freedom. And that's a very unusual expression because it's both a euphemism AND an oxymoron. You don't see a lot of them but when you do, run, because it means there are no words to describe the unspeakable fuck-up you are in.

REEVES (*even more gung ho*): Sir, I don't mean we're here to kill *all* the people. Just the ones who hate freedom. Whoever is left when the killing stops— that's the nation.

LIEUTENANT: Son, I don't know why they're sending you home. Seems to me you're everything we want in a soldier. (*Checking his file*) Your home's Texas, right?

REEVES: Wherever these men are is home for me. They're my brothers, sir.

LIEUTENANT: You know the French Foreign Legion? They take an oath, but they don't take it to their country.

REEVES: That's because the French are fucked up, sir.

LIEUTENANT: They take their oath to the Legion—to one another—they kind of avow themselves to one another. This isn't that.

REEVES: No?

LIEUTENANT: No.

REEVES: Army of One, sir?

LIEUTENANT: What do you think of that, private—army of one?

REEVES: Army of *one*? It's an oxymoron, sir.

LIEUTENANT: You know, for a grunt, you're pretty smart.

REEVES: That was not the consensus of opinion of the faculty at my high school, sir. I'm not smart, sir, but I can learn if someone will show me.

LIEUTENANT: It says here you sought help—

REEVES (*twitch/wince*): That was the mistake, wasn't it, sir?

LIEUTENANT: Maybe not. You've seen some terrible things. You've seen people die.

REEVES: That doesn't bother me, sir.

LIEUTENANT: No?

REEVES: No, sir. People are *supposed* to die, sir.

LIEUTENANT: Bodies like meat don't bother you?

REEVES: No, sir.

LIEUTENANT: No?

REEVES: I mean "No, not like meat, sir." Meat gets cut on the joint.

LIEUTENANT: Hamburger then.

REEVES: No.

LIEUTENANT: Like what then?

REEVES (*a moment, then—*): Like a couch. (*Then*) A leather couch in a nice house. And they took good care of the couch.

LIEUTENANT: Who?

REEVES: The people who live in the house. (*Then*) It cost more than they could afford. It cost more than anything they ever bought. Maybe it cost more than their car. But one night while one of them was sitting on the couch—

LIEUTENANT: Who?

REEVES: Doesn't matter, sir, we're talking about the couch—one night somebody breaks in and stabs the person on the couch.

LIEUTENANT: Who breaks in?

REEVES: A freedom-hating raghead breaks into the house and stabs her and she's surprised.

LIEUTENANT: She?

REEVES: She/he—doesn't matter, sir. What matters is that he didn't have time to get off the couch. *He* stayed on the couch until *he* bled out. And even though they do everything they can to make the house clean again, the realtor can't sell it because something bad happened in the house.

LIEUTENANT: On that couch.

REEVES (*no*): The couch is gone. The couch gets put in a lot. A vacant lot. Vacant except for the couch. It's a good couch, but not even junkies will sleep on it.

LIEUTENANT: Because of the blood.

REEVES: Because of the blood dogs come and tear it apart.

LIEUTENANT: What kind of dogs?

REEVES: You're right. Coyotes, sir.

LIEUTENANT: You've got quite an imagination, son.

REEVES: They think the couch is meat because it has blood in it, so they tear into it but they can't find the living part. They tear into it every time it rains because, every time it rains, the blood gets wet and it's like the couch is trying to come to life but it can't because it isn't anything anymore. Not even a couch. That's what it looks like, sir.

LIEUTENANT: You're right. That's what it looks like.

REEVES: And you look at your friend's legs and you're embarrassed because they don't even look like meat anymore. He's torn open but you don't see the inside of his body. You see the inside of the insides. Not muscles, the inside of muscles. Not bone, the inside of bone. And that's very private stuff. Not even God ever saw stuff like that. But your friend he's waving it around like he's got no shame and he's screaming and crying and you're sort of embarrassed because this guy—this guy who'll never be anything anybody will ever want again—not even as much as somebody wants a good couch in a nice house—he doesn't know enough to die? *That* bothers me.

(*Silence.*)

LIEUTENANT: You know Jackson? His legs got torn apart. Just like you say. Torn right off and a hunk of his arm gone like a shark bite. Just like a shark came up and took a piece out of him. (*Then*) He's back. It took courage, but he's back.

REEVES: Yes, sir, I know. That's what makes me so—.

(REEVES *can't speak.*)

LIEUTENANT: Talk to me.

REEVES (*torn between rage and sorrow*): So you're telling me a guy who was torn to pieces—*he* can get back here—and stay here—and you're telling me what's *IN HERE—*

(REEVES *points to his head.*)

WHAT'S—INSIDE—HERE—(*fighting tears*)
—is in WORSE SHAPE—than a guy who was TORN TO FUCKING PIECES BY A PACK OF DOGS AND A SHARK? Is that what you're telling me?

(*Compassionate silence. Then—*)

LIEUTENANT: No, son. Nobody's saying that. What's wrong with you—it might be something small. But whatever it is—all they're saying is—it can't be fixed. (*Then*) Dismissed, soldier.

REEVES: Sir! I took an OATH, sir. It's not just the French Foreign Legion. We take oaths too. (*Then, truth—*) I, Daniel Edward Reeves, do SOL-EMNLY SWEAR I will SUPPORT AND DEFEND the Constitution of the United States AGAINST ALL ENEMIES, FOREIGN AND DOMESTIC; that I WILL BEAR TRUE FAITH and allegiance to the same; and that I WILL OBEY THE ORDERS OF THE PRESIDENT OF THE UNITED STATES and the orders of the officers appointed over me, according to regulations and THE UNIFORM CODE OF MILITARY JUSTICE. SO—HELP—ME—GOD. So help me God the first time I said it—(*moved*) I knew it was the truest thing I ever said. Do not make me break my oath.

LIEUTENANT: A minute ago, you were going to join the enemy.

(REEVES *works on it. Then—*)

REEVES: Infiltrate.

LIEUTENANT: Infiltrate.

REEVES: Infiltrate. Not join. I'll volunteer to be a suicide bomber. I'll strap on a vest and in the middle of my going-to-Allah party, I'll pull the pin and blown them all to hell. (*Then—*) Joking, sir.

LIEUTENANT: You're an articulate son of a bitch. I'll give you that.

(REEVES *laughs.*)

What's funny?

REEVES: Nothing, sir. Things come together in my head sometimes and I laugh inappropriately, sir.

LIEUTENANT: What was funny?

REEVES: Me—articulate, sir.

LIEUTENANT: What's funny about that?

REEVES: My job description, sir.

LIEUTENANT: What's that?

REEVES: I'm a GRUNT, sir.

LIEUTENANT: Not any more. You're discharged. Honorably. (*Signs*) Your war is over, son.

(LIEUTENANT *signs the form. He leaves.* REEVES *leaves the army and the army leaves* REEVES, *taking all military dress.*)

(*As the uniform comes off, it's almost as if* REEVES *loses his bone structure along with the clothes. And his will to live. But that might be the fact that he is coming off a very committed three-day drunk.*)

(*He ends up in a police station—T-shirt and flip-flops—out cold.*)

(YOUNG FEMALE LAWYER [YFL]—*business suit—sits across a cold metal table from* REEVES. REEVES *is out cold.*)

YFL: Mr. Reeves. (*Nothing.*) Mr. Reeves.

(*A* MAN *from the cast announces—*)

MAN: CIRCLE 2—UNITED STATES OF AMERICA. SOME MONTHS LATER. JAIL.

CIRCLE 2: DUI.

YFL (*losing patience*): Mr. *REEVES.*

(REEVES *starts awake. Looks around.*)

REEVES: Man, I hate waking up and not knowing where . . .

(*Completely hung over, he looks around at his surroundings.*)

Oh. (*Then*) I want a lawyer.

YFL: Mr. Reeves, I am a lawyer.

REEVES: I mean a *real* lawyer.

YFL: I am a real lawyer.

REEVES: Really? You *look* like a public defender.

(*Amused at his joke, goes back to sleep.*)

Nothing personal. It's just—tell you the truth—I've been through this before.

YFL: Well. To tell you the truth—I haven't.

REEVES: Great. Fucking great.

(REEVES *farts satisfyingly. Shrugs.*)

YFL: I am fully competent to get you through the arraignment. Then you're done with me and you can hire whatever lawyer you want.

REEVES: I got five thousand dollars and a beat-up car. How can I hire any lawyer I want? You. You're my lawyer. You're my—defender.

YFL: Tomorrow, Mr. Reeves—Mr. Reeves?—Mr. *Reeves,* all you have to do tomorrow is watch for me to nod my head and, when I do, say in a loud clear voice—Not Guilty.

(*She starts out. When almost gone—*)

REEVES: Hey, defender. Defender! I can't lose my license.

(*He's embarrassed about needing the car. Not-giving-a-shit-entirely would be real freedom. However—the truth is—*)

I *need* the car.

YFL: Mr. Reeves. In all probability—you will never drive a car again.

(*Silence. Then—*)

REEVES: That's a mean thing—just—what a *mean* thing to say. (*Then, getting it*) OK. I'm sorry for what I said about public defenders. OK? Now—worst case. *Worst* case. What kind of time am I looking at?

YFL: You are looking at the death penalty. Mr. Reeves.

(*Silence. Then—*)

REEVES: For a DUI? (*Then*) Even a public defender—even a *lame* public defender—ought to be able to get less than the *death penalty* for a DUI.

(*She does not respond.*)

This isn't a DUI, is it? (*Then, amused*) What did I do? Did I get in a fight? Did I black out? I didn't hit somebody with the car, did I? (*No*) Whatever.

I was drunk. I had the right to be. I don't know why *everybody* isn't drunk. You know why I was here?

YFL: You were here for—for the funeral. (*Impressed*) I understand you served with him?

REEVES (*bragging*): Him? *Them.* I "served" with all *three* of them. Funerals in Texas, Oregon and Arlington. (*Shaking off the hangover*) Can't go to them all. I thought—Arlington ought to know how to do a funeral. Don't get me wrong, it was nice, but—

YFL (*with some awe*): Texas.

REEVES: You saw it?

YFL: On the news.

REEVES: People every twenty feet. Everybody holding flags. For miles. Not bad for a dropout who pumped gas. He just got married. You know that? He didn't tell his folks. Just us.

YFL: Eighteen. She was—

REEVES: Eighteen. Hell, he was—. (*Bizarrely bragging*) It's—*my*—*fault* he's dead. Hell, it's my fault *all three of them* are dead. If I had been there . . .

YFL: You think you could have protected them?

REEVES (*not exactly*): I make people nervous. People get—careful—when they're around me. (*Then*) You feel a little careful around me? Don't you? (*Silence, then*) Well, they *needed* to be *careful.* If they'd let me stay over there, those soldiers would still be—. (*Twitch-wince, then—*) What the hell. GUILTY. I was drunk. I was driving. Whatever happened, it's my fault. Plead me guilty.

(*The professional emerges in our* YFL.)

YFL: Mr. Reeves, there are only two words I want to hear from you and "my fault" are not those words. Say "my fault" to the judge tomorrow and you will make me look like I didn't do my job—like I didn't defend you—for a public defender, that's *bad.* Two words. (*Cuing*) Not—???

(REEVES *is getting to like her.*)

REEVES: Not guilty. OK? (*Yes*) Hey, what did I do? What am I "not guilty" of?

(*A moment. Reluctantly, she takes out paperwork.*)

No. Just—your own words—that's all.

YFL: You should hear the charges again.

REEVES: Again?

YFL: *Listen* this time. (*Then*—) 1. *On or about March 12, 2006, outside the United States, to wit, in Iraq—while a member of the United States Army—*

REEVES: Wait . . . Iraq? (*Yes*) Iraq? (*Very puzzled*) I didn't have my car in Iraq.

YFL: Would you like me to start over? (*No*) *While a member of the United States Army subject to Chapter 47 of Title 10 of the Uniform Code of Military Justice—the defendant, Daniel E. Reeves, did, with malice aforethought, unlawfully kill a person, an Iraqi man by shooting, an offense punishable by more than one year if committed in the special territorial jurisdiction of the United States, all in violation of Title 18, Section 7 and 3261(a) (2).*

(*Silence. Then*—)

REEVES: Hell—they're not going to take my car away for that.

(*Silence. Then—with a building edge*—)

YFL: 2. *On or about March 12, 2006, outside the United States, to wit, in Iraq*—

REEVES: *Iraq*—did I kill people over there?

YFL: —*while a member of the United States Army*—

REEVES: You bet I did.

YFL: *Subject to Chapter 47 of Title 10*—

REEVES: How many?

YFL: —*of the Uniform Code of Military Justice*—

REEVES: Nowhere near enough.

YFL: *The defendant*—

REEVES: You want to know what I plea?

YFL: *Daniel E. Reeves did*—

REEVES: Guilty.

YFL: —*with malice aforethought*—

REEVES: Kill people?

YFL: —*unlawfully kill another person. An Iraqi*—

REEVES: *THAT'S WHAT I WAS SUPPOSED TO DO.*

(*Then*—)

YFL: *An Iraqi woman.* (*Then—from memory*) *An offense punishable by more than one year if committed in the territorial jurisdiction of the United States in violation of Title 18, Section 7 and 3261 (a) (2).*

(*Silence. Then*—)

REEVES: You're not a regular public defender, are you?

YFL: Federal.

(*Silence. Then—*)

REEVES: How can what happened over there be a crime over here?

YFL (*no clue*): Like I said—I've never been through this before. (*Then*) 3. *On or about March 12, 2006*—

REEVES: Cut to the—

YFL: *Daniel E. Reeves did unlawfully kill—an Iraqi child.*

(*A moment. Then—sobering up—*)

REEVES: I made a mistake over there. Fisher. Fisher did it right. I should have done what Fisher did.

YFL: Fisher?

REEVES: Oregon.

YFL: What did he do?

REEVES: He *died* over there. (*Then*) You know what they did to him? You see the video?

YFL: Yes, I saw the video.

REEVES: They cut off his head.

YFL (*enough*): I saw the video.

REEVES: THAT's why people are lining the streets. That's what makes him a hero. He got his head cut off. The mistake I made was coming home alive.

YFL: Well, you may get your wish yet, Mr. Reeves. People are most definitely out for your head.

REEVES (*realizing*): Fuck. *Everything* we did over there is a crime over here.

YFL (*becoming personal*): Mr. Reeves? We're at war. Terrible things happen in a war. I know that.

REEVES: You know that?

YFL (*even more personal*): Terrible things happen. Yes, I know that. I believe— under the right circumstances, anyone—*anyone*—is capable of terrible things. I think that's why I became a public defender.

REEVES: No, that we're at war. You know that?

YFL: Yes.

REEVES: How? How do you know *that*?

YFL: How do I—

REEVES: I mean it could be like the moon landing. Couldn't it? Do you think we landed on the moon? Really. Do you?

YFL: Mr. Reeves. Daniel—

REEVES: Do you?

YFL: Yes, we landed on the moon.

REEVES: We landed on the moon? *We* did?

YFL: Yes.

REEVES: You think *YOU*—any *PART* of you—landed on the moon?

YFL: Well . . . no.

REEVES: So *WE* didn't land on the moon. You're pretty sure of that? You pretty sure you didn't land on the moon. (*Yes, then, violently*) Then how can you be SO FUCKING SURE *we're AT WAR? YOU'RE* about as much at war as you are on the *FUCKING MOON.*

YFL: I mean the country is at—

REEVES: The *Marines* are at war. The *Army* is at war. The country? You know what this country is fighting? (*She doesn't.*) An obesity epidemic! (*With vast contempt*) Now what fucking Iraqi accused us of—

(REEVES *grabs the papers from her.*)

Who wrote that? Who—(*reading*) *S.O.I.1 was interviewed and explained that*—(*then*) S.O.I. 1? Who the hell is—

YFL: S.O.I. Source of Information. It was in a stress debriefing.

REEVES: A stress debriefing? Iraqis don't get—

YFL: It was an American soldier. Talking to a counselor.

REEVES: An American? Soldier? Said?

(YFL *takes the papers.*)

YFL: *S.O.I.1 explained that S.O.I.2, S.O.I.3, PFC Daniel E. Reeves and K.P.1*—

REEVES: K.P. 1?

YFL: Known Participant 1 . . . *were conducting duties at T.C.P.2*—

REEVES: Traffic Control Point 2—

YFL: —*two hundred meters from the residence where the crime occurred.*

(YFL *creates the event.*)

Prior to departing T.C.P.2, S.O.I.1—

REEVES: IN YOUR OWN WORDS.

YFL (*this is hard*): Well—it says Private Daniel Reeves and several of his squadmates—currently in the brig in Iraq—went to a house. There Private Reeves herded an Iraqi man, woman and child into the bedroom where he shot and killed them. Then he went into the living room where two of the soldiers were holding a woman down and he raped then killed her. Afterwards, they set her body on fire. (*Then*) I don't know why they call her a woman. She was fourteen.

(*Silence. Then—*)

REEVES: Do you think we did this? Is that what you think?

YFL: Terrible things happen.

REEVES (*astounded*): YOU THINK WE—? WE don't DO things LIKE THIS. *In-sur-gents* did this. We *investigated* it. That report—it's *nothing* but *lies*.

YFL: Perhaps. Still, there is something to be learned from it. (*A moment, then—*)
There is only one name in this report. In this whole report, there is only *one* name.

REEVES: Daniel E. Reeves.

YFL: Exactly, (*with some sympathy*) Daniel, you are going to need a lawyer—not only a real lawyer, an extraordinary lawyer—to get you through this—but for tomorrow, you are innocent until proven guilty.

(*As she goes—*)

REEVES: You're going to help me, aren't you?

YFL: I'll get you through tomorrow.

REEVES: Tomorrow? Tomor—?

YFL: A lawyer will be appointed for you, Mr. Reeves.

REEVES: By who?

YFL: The government.

REEVES: Wait a minute. Who wants me dead?

YFL: The government.

REEVES: Well, that's not good. Is it?

(REEVES *laughs out loud. Whoops loud.*)

YFL: Be careful what you say tomorrow. Two words. "Not guilty," Mr. Reeves. "Not—"

REEVES (*fuck you*): Two words. "HONORABLE—DISCHARGE." You think they give honorable discharges to people who—

(*A name is called.*)

VOICE (MAN): Daniel Reeves.

(*At the sound of his name, she leads* REEVES *into court.*)

How do you plead? (*No response.*) Mr. Reeves—guilty or not guilty?

(YFL *looks to* REEVES. *Nods.* REEVES*'s brain jams with a thousand things he could say. He shakes them off one after the other.*)

REEVES: Huh?

(YFL *nods again. Nothing. Then—*)

YFL: Mr. Reeves will not enter a plea at this time.
VOICE: Are you represented by counsel? (*No response.*) Mr. Reeves?

(REEVES *laughs inappropriately. Then—*)

REEVES: Judge, do you think we went to the moon?
VOICE: Counsel will be appointed.

(*Gavel.* YFL *moves for the exit.* REEVES *is stripped of his civilian clothes and is redressed in an orange jumpsuit. Before she leaves—*)

YFL (*to audience*): CIRCLE 3—A HOLDING CELL—PRIOR TO TRANSFER TO FEDERAL PRISON.

(*She exits.*)

CIRCLE 3: OPTIONS.

(REEVES—*now in orange jumpsuit—is pissed off at himself and the world in general.*)

REEVES: GUILTY! GUILTY! I meant to say, "*Hand me over* to the Iraqis. *Let them* bury me up to my neck in sand and *stone* me to death. *Televise* it. I'll sing "God Bless America" till I'm dead and people will see what I'm made of and who those fucking people are.
ARMY ATTORNEY: Tell me, Mr. Reeves—does that work for you?

(ARMY ATTORNEY—*military uniform—enters. Rank: Captain. Presentation: Military perfection. Education: Princeton. Third generation military.*)

REEVES: What? Does what work for me?
ARMY ATTORNEY: That act.
REEVES: Act? What act?
ARMY ATTORNEY: "Let them bury me up to my neck in sand and stone me to death." Does it work for you? Because it will *not* work in your trial.

(REEVES *looks him over, then—*)

REEVES: Who the hell are you?

ARMY ATTORNEY: Someone who would very much like to represent you in your trial, Mr. Reeves.

REEVES: An army lawyer. How stupid do you think I am?

ARMY ATTORNEY: I'm a good lawyer, Mr. Reeves. I have won cases against the government. (*Be impressed*) I got a man out of Guantanamo.

REEVES (*not impressed*): Yeah, whose side are you on?

ARMY ATTORNEY: Yours. If you'll let me be.

(REEVES *is unsure. So—nonchalant bravado—*)

REEVES: Well, between you and me, I've decided not to worry too much about the trial. Innocent until proven guilty, right?

ARMY ATTORNEY: Mr. Reeves, you have already been tried and convicted.

REEVES: What?

ARMY ATTORNEY: The only thing still in question is the sentence. Not even the sentence—only the manner of its execution. *Your* execution, Mr. Reeves.

REEVES: What . . . ? What'd I miss? They've had me locked up pretty tight here and I—. Did I miss something?

(ARMY ATTORNEY *puts hat, briefcase on chair. Surveys room while schooling* REEVES.)

ARMY ATTORNEY: You were arrested the third—

REEVES: Thursday.

ARMY ATTORNEY: The next night—July 4th—the President of the United States went on television and spoke to the nation about you.

REEVES: He did? . . . About—

ARMY ATTORNEY: He said you were a stain on the United States' honorable image.

REEVES: Well, that's not right.

ARMY ATTORNEY: The next morning—

REEVES: Yesterday.

ARMY ATTORNEY: General Pace went on television—

REEVES: Who?

ARMY ATTORNEY: You used to work for General Pace, Mr. Reeves. He's the head of the Joint Chiefs of Staff. He said 99.9% of America's fighting men and women serve with honor. You were a dishonorable exception. (*Preempting* REEVES) There were "allegedly's" in all the right places, but everyone knew what they meant. They meant you're guilty, Mr. Reeves. Of capital crimes.

(*A moment. Then—bravado—*)

REEVES: Anybody else talk about me?

ARMY ATTORNEY: The President of Iraq wants you handed over to Iraqi justice.

REEVES: Iraqi justice. (*Showing off*) Oxymoron.

(REEVES *impresses himself. But—*)

ARMY ATTORNEY: You're a bit of a disappointment to me, Mr. Reeves. I was expecting someone smarter.

REEVES: I'm smart. People are always telling me how smart I am.

ARMY ATTORNEY: Would you like to know what you are, Mr. Reeves? (*Then—*) You are a Texas boy brought up in a single-parent home. Your father split early so you grew up alone with your mother in The Back of Beyond, Texas.

REEVES: Is that in my file?

ARMY ATTORNEY: Just a guess. Stop me when I'm wrong. You did what you could for her—your mother. You tried to help out. My guess is that she relied on you as the man of the house.

(*Silence. Then—*)

REEVES: Maybe.

ARMY ATTORNEY: That's a kind of incest, Mr. Reeves.

REEVES: Are you saying—are you saying I slept with my—

ARMY ATTORNEY: It doesn't matter. Either way, she made you her Man. Because you were confident of your Manhood at an age when everybody else was learning to tie their shoes—nobody could get to you. Am I right, Mr. Reeves?

REEVES (*yes, so, defensive—*): Didn't anybody teach you not to talk about somebody's mother?

ARMY ATTORNEY (*thought so*): Teachers, coaches, cops—they all tried to wake—you—the—hell—up before you did something destructive of self and others but they couldn't because you thought you were The Man when all you were—all you *really* were—was your mother's anger at men.

(*Silence. Then—*)

REEVES: Well, that ought to be worth something in a court of law.

ARMY ATTORNEY: I would never bring that into court.

REEVES: Then why are we talking about it?

ARMY ATTORNEY: Because I want you to know I know who you are. I want you to know that you are not going to manipulate me like you manipulated those men—good men probably—in your squad. You got them to kill and to rape—

REEVES: Allegedly.

ARMY ATTORNEY: —and you did it easily—

REEVES: *Allegedly.*

ARMY ATTORNEY: —because that is what you were trained to do—

REEVES: *ALLEGEDLY.*

ARMY ATTORNEY: —by basic training that was a lot more basic than anything the army could devise.

(*Silence. Then—stone cold anger—*)

REEVES: How did you do at basic? No, don't tell me. Let me guess. You sucked up everything the army threw at you and asked for more. I bet you were great. Look at you. You ARE the army. You know what, Army? You know how *I* got here. You TOOK me. It was you or jail and you fucking took me. (*Bitter, driven truth*) You know what the recruiter said to me? He said, "Son, this will be a new start for you." You know how much I wanted to hear that? I thought fuck—maybe they can *beat* something new into me. Maybe they can nail me onto a tank and drive me into battle. You know what they did in basic? They *advised me of my rights. RIGHTS?* I didn't *WANT* any fucking *RIGHTS.* I wanted somebody to fucking tell me there was no way but their way. (*Then*) Fuck! THIS—(*the cell*)—is what the ARMY was *supposed* to keep me *out* of. Well, FUCK THAT. *I kept MY END of the BARGAIN.*

(*Silence. Then—*)

ARMY ATTORNEY: *That . . .* That's what I mean. Does *that*—work for you?

REEVES: WHAT?

ARMY ATTORNEY: That—*act.* Do you ever drop it or are you West Texas bullshit to the core?

(*Consideration. Then—*)

REEVES: It got me where I am today.

ARMY ATTORNEY: And where is that?

REEVES: Heads of state are fighting over me.

(*Silence. Then—*)

ARMY ATTORNEY: Good-bye, Mr. Reeves.

(*Gets hat, briefcase. Leaves.*)

REEVES: Bye. Tell the army I fell for their bullshit *once* and I won't—

ARMY ATTORNEY (*stopping*): Oh . . . No . . . The army didn't send me. Officially I'm not even here.

REEVES (*confused, then—*): Huh?

ARMY ATTORNEY: I'm here on my own, Mr. Reeves. On a hunch.

REEVES: Hunch? What hunch?

(ARMY ATTORNEY *almost speaks. Thinks better.*)

ARMY ATTORNEY: You aren't what I was expecting, Mr. Reeves. And it was a long shot at best.

(ARMY ATTORNEY *sees* REEVES *as a lost kid for a moment.*)

(*Sincerely*) Good luck.

(*Then, as he leaves—*)

REEVES: You know I got baptized? During basic.

ARMY ATTORNEY (*checking watch*): No. I didn't.

REEVES: No act. No bullshit about it. I prayed. I prayed to be a soldier. (*A moment*) Fuck. I prayed to be you.

(*A moment. Then—*)

ARMY ATTORNEY: I'm not the answer to a prayer, Mr. Reeves. I have a very ordinary life. Wife-house-kids.

REEVES: Ordinary, huh? You're fucking clueless.

(*A moment.*)

ARMY ATTORNEY: Everyone has a destiny. You have yours.

REEVES: Right.

ARMY ATTORNEY: Mr. Reeves—(*with respect*) you scared them.

REEVES: Say what?

ARMY ATTORNEY: You scared them, Mr. Reeves. (*Then*) The Supreme Court doesn't scare them. Congress doesn't scare them. The death of the young does not scare them. I would have said nothing could, but you, Mr. Reeves, you put the fear of God in them.

REEVES: Who?

ARMY ATTORNEY: Heads of state.

(REEVES *wonders if he's being mocked.*)

REEVES (*absurd*): You think that a general is scared of a fuck-up from Midland, Texas?

ARMY ATTORNEY: Yes, but not you.

REEVES: Of who?

ARMY ATTORNEY: The other fuck-up from Midland, Texas. (*Then*) And I think that *other* fuck-up is afraid—very afraid—of you. (*Then*) If this had happened in Midland, Texas, they wouldn't have cared. But it didn't. It happened in the middle of their war and you have scared them, Mr. Reeves. You tore the war open. You did the unimaginable.

(*Clueless. So—*)

REEVES: I got a good imagination.

ARMY ATTORNEY (*indeed you do*): You performed an act so unimaginably cruel that—for a second—you made them feel the pain of the enemy. It scared them and rightly so. If you were to do that for the country, you could end the war.

REEVES: If this war could end, the battle of Lepanto would have ended it.

ARMY ATTORNEY (*surprised*): What do you know about the battle of Lepanto?

REEVES: Not much. It was before my time. Go on.

ARMY ATTORNEY: They don't want this war to end, so they need to make you go away and they usually get what they want. So, take your pick, Mr. Reeves, lethal injection or stoning.

(*A moment. Then—*)

REEVES: *Those* are my *options*?

ARMY ATTORNEY: There might be another. (*A moment, then—*) Mr. Reeves— I would like you to consider reenlisting.

(*Consideration. Then—*)

REEVES: Man, the army must be having some *serious* trouble meeting its quota *this* month.

ARMY ATTORNEY: I need to know if you're willing. It effects the options for your trial, Mr. Reeves.

REEVES: You're not kidding. Are you?

(*No, HE does not kid.*)

ARMY ATTORNEY: If you reenlist, you would be tried by a military court.

REEVES: The army threw me out.

ARMY ATTORNEY: An honorable discharge isn't getting thrown out. The military can return a soldier to active duty.

REEVES: Why would they?

ARMY ATTORNEY: There are some in the military who feel this war is a brutal misuse of resources. They might be willing to accept you to get jurisdiction in your case.

REEVES: But why—

ARMY ATTORNEY: There is a question about the war that should have been asked before this war began. They would like to ask it now in the only way they can—in a military court. A federal court won't tolerate it.

REEVES: What question?

ARMY ATTORNEY: "Is it worth it?"

REEVES: The war? Is it worth—? (*Offended*) WE WERE ATTACKED. People—people got KILLED.

ARMY ATTORNEY: Yes, they did. Do you know how many?

REEVES: What does it matter how many?

ARMY ATTORNEY: Three thousand.

REEVES: OK, three thousand. *THREE THOUSAND AMERICANS GOT KILLED*. *Somebody* has to pay.

ARMY ATTORNEY: *FORTY* THOUSAND Americans get killed in *traffic accidents* every year.

REEVES: So?

ARMY ATTORNEY: Based on your logic, we should be bombing car dealerships. To avenge three thousand deaths, we have lost five thousand soldiers. It makes no sense. There are those in the military who would like to point that out.

(*OK, so—*)

REEVES: What would you say?

ARMY ATTORNEY: No more than what you said a moment ago. The army knew what it was getting when it took you. You have drug convictions. No high school diploma. No employment record. They had to lower every requirement they have to get you in. They had to give you a morals waiver. In most states you wouldn't be allowed to own a gun and yet—

REEVES: Wait a minute. You're going to say the army is fucked up because I'm *IN* it? (*No response.*) You're going to say I never should have been in the army?

ARMY ATTORNEY: I think I can get you life, Mr. Reeves.

REEVES: Everything I did before the army? Everything since? Shit. The army was my life. I had ten months of life. What's the point of getting "life" if I can't hold on to the only part of it I ever cared about?

ARMY ATTORNEY: Mr. Reeves, life matters to *everyone.*

REEVES: Your life, maybe. Lethal injection. Have the doctor put me to sleep and then—sweet dreams.

ARMY ATTORNEY: No doctors are involved, Mr. Reeves. In fact, no medical personnel. They take an oath to do no harm.

REEVES: So who—?

ARMY ATTORNEY: Amateurs. It isn't pretty. And it is entirely possible that death by lethal injection is excruciating. But nobody knows, because—well, who can you ask? (*Then*) Sodium thiopental puts you to sleep and then pancuronium bromide paralyzes you so everything that follows *looks* peaceful, but? If you are not actually asleep—and who's to know after the paralysis sets in—or if the amateur crew injects the potassium cloride into a muscle rather than a vein—you might be awake—trapped—unable to move for the rest of it. Some doctors feel that it is like being crushed to death from within. You are completely aware, but unable to move or communicate. You smile. For—what?—ten minutes. Half hour? You have a good imagination. Imagine that. Or. You could end a war. What do you think about that?

REEVES: I'm not even sure this is a war. I think it's just—violence.

ARMY ATTORNEY: I may have underestimated you, Mr. Reeves. (*Then*) There is a very narrow window for making this happen. I need your answer. (*No response.*) Mr. Reeves, you have antisocial personality disorder. Be aware of that. Don't let it destroy what hope there is.

(*Then,* REEVES *at his best*—)

REEVES: My squad. We were traffic cops. Our sergeant goes out to stop a car. Puts his hand out. Guy in the car shoots him. I don't know—the guy in the car—maybe he had antisocial personality disorder. What do you think? 'Cause I think—yeah, probably. Me? I stayed with my sergeant till the end. I looked in his eyes all the way. You can tell a lot from a person's eyes.

ARMY ATTORNEY: Yes, you can.

REEVES: Well, he never looked away from mine. I think he liked what he saw. I guess I wasn't feeling all that antisocial that day. And that was no fucking act.

(ARMY ATTORNEY *respects that. Then*—)

ARMY ATTORNEY: Did you tell the psychiatrist about that?

REEVES: You—you know about that?

ARMY ATTORNEY: Tell me about it.

REEVES: No. It's confidential.

ARMY ATTORNEY: Tell me.

REEVES (*duuuuuh?*): It's *confidential.*

ARMY ATTORNEY (*confused then—amused*): The confidentiality applies to the shrink. *He's* not supposed to tell what *you* say.

REEVES: *She* told me *I* couldn't tell what *SHE* said.

ARMY ATTORNEY: Mr. Reeves—I think we might have a case here. (*Then*) Well, Mr. Reeves?

(*A moment. Then—*)

REEVES: You didn't tell me.

ARMY ATTORNEY: What?

REEVES: Is it worth it?

ARMY ATTORNEY: I just want to be the one to pose the question.

REEVES: You think—you think I might have the answer?

ARMY ATTORNEY: Who can tell? You might *be* the answer. Who can tell? The answer can be anything. A flag at Iwo Jima. A naked girl burning with napalm running down a highway. For this war—who knows?

(*A moment. Then—*)

REEVES: Maybe that little girl didn't want to be covered in napalm.

ARMY ATTORNEY: She's now a housewife with two children in Ontario, Canada. She ended a war.

REEVES: Would you have to say I did it?

ARMY ATTORNEY: I will say you did no more or no less than what you thought necessary to stay alive over there.

(*Consideration. Then—*)

REEVES: I thought you didn't want the act.

ARMY ATTORNEY: I don't think that part of it is an act.

REEVES: No?

ARMY ATTORNEY: I believe in you, Mr. Reeves. It's as simple as that.

REEVES: I'm important?

ARMY ATTORNEY: Yes, Mr. Reeves. That is why I am here. There are two people in the world who think you are important. I'm the other one.

REEVES: All because I made the enemy feel pain?

ARMY ATTORNEY: Anyone can do that. You made them feel the pain of the enemy. That isn't the end of a war. That is the end of war. It is unendurable. (*Then*) Did you feel it?

REEVES: There's a lot I don't feel. I got. I got this—disorder.

ARMY ATTORNEY (*understood, then—*): Mr. Reeves?

REEVES: If I say yes . . . will you be back? (*A moment, then—*) 'Cause not that many people—talk with me.

ARMY ATTORNEY (*understood, then—*): Is that a yes? (*It is.*) I will be back, Mr. Reeves.

(*Before he goes—*)

REEVES: Hey . . . How long ago was the battle of Lepanto?

ARMY ATTORNEY: 1571. Christendom versus the Ottoman Empire. Our God versus theirs. Winner take all.

REEVES (*oh, yeah—right—then*): Who won?

ARMY ATTORNEY: We did.

REEVES: Then how come we're still at war?

ARMY ATTORNEY: Maybe we were waiting for you.

(ARMY ATTORNEY *exits.* REEVES *tries to reclaim his best military self. His basic training. His military drills.*)

REEVES (singing): MINE EYES HAVE SEEN THE GLORY OF THE COMING OF THE LORD . . .

(*He washes himself. When he is clean—the* PASTOR *enters.*)

CIRCLE 4: SELF-POSSESSION.

(*The* PASTOR—*folksy, with serious resolution under—carries a Bible.* REEVES *waits for* ARMY ATTORNEY *to come back. He's not coming back.*)

PASTOR (*to audience*): Circle four. Federal prison. Some weeks later.

(*The* PASTOR *is uncomfortable in a prison cell.*)

If you *did* what they *say* you did—son, you *need* Jesus.

REEVES: And if I didn't?

PASTOR: Well. (*Then—*) You still need Jesus.

REEVES (*OK, then—*): So it doesn't matter what I did.

(*Silence.*)

PASTOR: I'm in over my head here, aren't I?

REEVES: You're just the wrong tool for the job. I don't need a pastor. I need a lawyer.

PASTOR: Son, the *last* thing you need is a lawyer.

REEVES: I talked to a lawyer. He said he'd come back.

PASTOR: Did he?

REEVES: Not yet. He made sense out of everything. Can't remember how.

PASTOR: He made it not your fault.

REEVES: How do you know that?

PASTOR: It's what lawyers do.

REEVES: Well, that's a good thing as far as I'm concerned.

PASTOR (*really?*): Son, you raped a girl, led others to do the same, and then you killed her and her whole family.

REEVES: You're sure I did that?

PASTOR: I am. Then you set fire to that girl's body and tried to put the blame on others. If you swore while you were doing it, you broke all ten of the Lord's commandments at one crack and broke 'em hard. Son, that *lawyer* was the wrong tool for the job. You need Jesus. (*A smile*) And I'm going to take you to him.

(REEVES *looks at the* PASTOR *with anger. Thinks better of it. Smiles.*)

REEVES (*self-containing*): I'm not going to get mad at you. I'm not going to shout. I'm not going to do that anymore. Fuck the act. (*Then, matter-of-fact*) You want to talk about breaking commandments? You know what they did to my friends after I left? They cut off their dicks, put them in their mouths, cut off their heads, and then took pictures of themselves— laughing. That's what those people are like.

PASTOR: All of them?

REEVES: Close enough so it doesn't matter. (*Then*) One day there was a kid— walking towards us. Couldn't have been more than eleven. Hot *hot* day and the kid is wearing an overcoat.

PASTOR: You shoot him?

REEVES: We don't do things like that. We got him to take off the coat.

PASTOR: You speak Arabic?

REEVES: Enough to make ourselves understood. And so he took off his coat, then his shirt, and there he was—in his underwear—covered in explosives. They strapped munitions onto an eleven-year-old boy.

PASTOR: I never met an eleven-year-old boy didn't have munitions strapped to him . . . I suspect you had more than most strapped on you.

REEVES: Look, why don't you go over there and bother them. If *anybody* needs Jesus, *they* do.

PASTOR: They aren't baptized. The minister from the base called me when he saw your picture in the papers. He told me he baptized you.

REEVES: Well, it didn't work.

PASTOR: Maybe he should have held you under longer.

REEVES: A few seconds more and it would've been water-boarding. Didn't work.

PASTOR: Worked on me. Made you my responsibility. (*Then*) Speaking of lawyers. Your father hired a lawyer. It was in the paper.

REEVES: Really? (*With growing hope*) Now why didn't anybody tell me that?

PASTOR: Why should they? The lawyer wasn't for you. He hired a lawyer to speak for him. Somebody he went to school with.

REEVES (*fuck it*): Wouldn't have done me any good anyway.

PASTOR: Not a good lawyer?

REEVES: Good enough if you're buying a house.

PASTOR: Son, I don't know who you have at this point *but* Jesus.

REEVES (*restraint failing*): *Fuck* Jesus. OK. *Fuck* Jesus. Where I was—the Tigris and Euphrates?—that's *Bible* land and there was no sign *anywhere* that *anybody* was one BIT *better* for the *Bible*—and they had it *first*, OK? (*Then*) No. I'm not going to shout.

PASTOR (*I understand. In fact—*): I was like you once. Didn't even believe Jesus lived. Till I read one verse. One verse changed my life.

REEVES: God is love?

PASTOR (*no*): "Back off, you Syrian bitch."

(*Silence. Then—*)

REEVES: I don't recall ever hearing that one. And I had the book read to me when I was little.

PASTOR (*admittedly*): It's a loose translation . . . Woman comes up to Jesus. Says, "My daughter's dead. My little girl's dead. Can you bring her back to life?" And Jesus says to her, "Get away from me, you Syrian bitch." (*Then*) At least, that's the sense of it.

REEVES: You are one fucked-up minister.

PASTOR: Actually, he says, "You don't give the master's meat to the dog under the table." Called her a dog. A female dog. It's in the book . . . I expect that Arabs had been calling Jesus names for a long time and this Syrian woman asking him to perform a miracle for her—that was his limit.

REEVES (*what the fuck?*): Out of ALL the verses in the Bible—ALL the miracles—all the HEALINGS—*that* saved you?

PASTOR: Who said I was saved? I'm a recovering alcoholic with an Internet porn addiction I'm working on. Sometimes I think I walk through life just exchanging one addiction for another. I'm a weak and shallow vessel but I believe in Christ Jesus the Lord.

REEVES: Because he said, "Back off, you fucking Syrian bitch?"

PASTOR: See, the thing is—(*serious thought*)—nobody would put words like that into the mouth of their Savior and Lord. Would they? (*Then*) I mean who would dare add his own darkness to the Savior's blinding light? (*Then*) *Nobody* would make that up. Nobody could.

REEVES: Guess not.

PASTOR (*exactly*): He had to be *real* to say that. And if he was real, why—there is hope for us all.

REEVES: You know, you're the first pastor I ever met I might be able to talk to . . . Maybe we should go back and start over with our area of common interest.

PASTOR: And what is that?

REEVES: Internet porn.

PASTOR (*with kindness*): Son, read the book and prepare yourself for the shit storm that is about to hit you. There is a fair amount of shit repellent in here. It'll help when the storm comes your way.

(REEVES *takes the Bible. Then*—)

REEVES: The girl—she wasn't dead.

PASTOR: The paper said you shot her dead.

REEVES: No, not her. The Syrian girl. In the story. I know that story. She wasn't dead.

PASTOR: No—matter of fact—she wasn't.

REEVES: Girl in the story was possessed by a demon. The mother asked Jesus to drive the demon out. You changed that part of the story.

PASTOR: Yes, I did. Out of respect for you.

REEVES: You think I'm possessed, Pastor?

PASTOR: It would be a comfort to me to think you were. Otherwise—we're just talking about plain I-don't-give-a-fuck human evil and even God himself is helpless before that. Are you?

REEVES: Am I what?

PASTOR (*takes courage to ask*): Are you evil, son?

REEVES (*amused*): Well, I'm not possessed. No voices in here. No distractions and 20/10 vision. I think I could have been a sniper. (*Pointing to his head*) It's quiet in here. Lonely sometimes. Might be good to have a voice or two to talk to.

PASTOR: Voices in your head aren't interested in conversation. I knew a young man killed himself.

REEVES: Voices?

PASTOR (*yes*): There was some discussion as to whether he should be buried in consecrated ground or not.

REEVES: Well?

PASTOR: What?

REEVES: Was he? Buried in consecrated ground?

PASTOR: Do funerals interest you, son? . . . Maybe that's where I should've started. Maybe *that's* our area of common interest. Paper says you came here to see a funeral.

REEVES: I don't want to talk about that.

PASTOR (*understanding*): Because those three men who just got buried—they died for you.

REEVES: Well, that's a funny way to put it, but I believe—had I been there— they'd still be alive. I. (*Then* —) I don't want to talk about them.

(*The* PASTOR *takes that in. Decides not to pursue it. Yet.*)

PASTOR: Would you care to talk about the rape?

REEVES: It's the rape that interests you, isn't it?

PASTOR: It doesn't bother me unduly. Tell you the truth, I'm not sure I believe in consensual sex. I mean somebody always wants it more, right? It's rare that need and desire are equally matched.

REEVES: You are the god-damnest minister.

PASTOR: I suspect I am.

REEVES: You're enjoying this, aren't you?

PASTOR: Tell the truth, you scare the shit out of me. I'm scared to be here with you. Scared to say what I have to say. Still, it's my duty to bring you to the Lord. Even at the end.

(*Then, with new seriousness—*)

REEVES: I don't want a funeral. When I'm dead, leave my body on a couch in a vacant lot. Let dogs come and eat it. I'd like that.

PASTOR: Really?

REEVES (*no, then—for real*): I'd like to get shot and go out on a hummer hood.
PASTOR: You don't have to punish yourself, son. God will do that for you.

(REEVES *appreciates this. Amused—*)

REEVES: He already has.
PASTOR: Yes, he has. More than you know.

(*A moment—*)

REEVES: What don't I know? (*No response.*) What?
PASTOR (*a risk*): They're saying now—it was done for revenge.
REEVES: Really?

(REEVES *laughs.*)

Well, that's a relief. I knew somebody would figure that out. See, we all figured some hajis—they killed her for revenge. Maybe an honor killing. That's what they do over there. Nothing but revenge.
PASTOR: I wasn't talking about the girl.
REEVES: Who then?

(*Very careful. Very delicate.*)

PASTOR: Your friends. The ones just got buried. They're saying now that *they* were killed for revenge.
REEVES: Revenge? For what?

(*Silence. Then—*)

PASTOR: *For the rape of a young girl.*

(*Silence. Then,* REEVES *laughs with relief.*)

REEVES: Now that just shows your ignorance. They would never have anything to do with something like that.

(*The* PASTOR *lays this out carefully.*)

PASTOR: Maybe it didn't matter. (*Then, feeling at risk*) Maybe the family of the girl wanted revenge. (*Then*) That's how they are, after all. According to you. (*Then*) Maybe they saw your friends—three American soldiers in a hummer—unprotected. They weren't the soldiers they wanted—they *wanted* you—but maybe any Americans were close enough so it didn't matter.

(*Silence. Then—getting what the* PASTOR *is laying out—*)

REEVES: Are you saying—?

PASTOR: I am.

REEVES: Are you saying it was because of me they got killed?

PASTOR: If you killed that family. Did you, son?

REEVES: No. (*Then*) And you're a sick fuck to make that up.

PASTOR: But I didn't make it up.

REEVES: Where'd you get it then?

PASTOR: Internet.

REEVES: You know, there's a lot of bullshit on the Internet.

PASTOR: True enough, but I believe this.

REEVES: Yeah? Why?

PASTOR: Because it's like that story.

REEVES: Which?

PASTOR: Of the Syrian woman. (*Then*) It's one of those stories you just couldn't make up. (*Then*) Don't think anybody could.

(*The implications begin to hit* REEVES.)

They were killed for you, son. They died for your sins. Somebody had to and you wouldn't let Jesus do it for you.

REEVES: I don't believe it.

PASTOR: I didn't either. At first. But it makes sense, doesn't it, when you think about it. I mean, the violence of their deaths—that feels *personal.* The kind of thing oh a father might do—

REEVES: I want a lawyer.

PASTOR (*pleased*): Wrong tool for the job.

REEVES: They did *not* die for me.

PASTOR: The thing that worries me is—what were they thinking as they were dying—your friends. Did they think they were dying for their country?

REEVES: They had their parade. Nothing can hurt them now.

PASTOR: Or did one of the Iraqis know enough English to make it clear what they were dying for? Did somebody make it understood to them that they were dying for you. For Daniel Reeves and his demons. (*Then*) The only thing I can think of worse than knowing that you were dying a terrible death for nothing is the pain of knowing you were the one caused it.

REEVES (*deep denial*): You'll say anything—anything at all—to get me to come to Jesus.

PASTOR: Have I disturbed the quiet of your mind?

REEVES: Is that what you wanted?

PASTOR: Yes, I believe so.

REEVES: Jesus drove demons out. He didn't drive them *in*.

PASTOR: No, he didn't. But there's no confusing me with Jesus, is there? (*Then*) Well, I'll be going now. I'll just leave the Bible in case you want to take a look. I've marked that story.

REEVES: You want voices—you want voices telling me to kill myself like that boy in your story, don't you?

PASTOR: Oh, the voices didn't tell him to kill himself.

REEVES: No?

PASTOR: The voices told him to kill his family . . . That's why he killed himself. So when they asked if that boy should be buried in consecrated ground, I said there was no worry there. Wherever that boy was buried would be consecrated ground. He was a hero in death. And that's what I want for you, boy. Same thing you want for yourself. You want to be a hero, don't you, boy?

REEVES: Man, why are you doing this?

PASTOR (*truth*): The girl.

REEVES: I thought that didn't bother you.

PASTOR: Not so much the rape, terrible as that is.

REEVES: What then?

PASTOR: The fire. You set fire to her body. See, that's where your sin comes face to face with my addiction. I can't stand to see beauty vandalized.

REEVES (*powerful truth*): I didn't do that.

PASTOR: Don't deny it, son.

REEVES (*very strong and sure*): I told them not to. I—didn't—do—that.

(*A moment. Then—*)

PASTOR: No, you probably didn't. The man who did that was ashamed of what he did . . . But you did the rest, didn't you, son?

(REEVES *grows increasingly agitated as the* PASTOR *prepares to leave.*)

Don't lose heart, son. Let it be a call. Even Jesus needed a call. The woman said to him, "Maybe I don't get the meat from your table, but even dogs can have a crust of bread." And he threw her a crust. He drove out the demon. There is hope. For us all.

(PASTOR *exits.* REEVES *paces in his cell. The pace of his pacing increases and becomes self-harming frenzy. When the frenzy becomes suicidal,* GUARDS *subdue* REEVES *violently and put him in restraints—wrists and ankles—in a chair that is bolted to the floor. After a moment, a* CIVILIAN LAWYER *enters.*)

CIRCLE 5: THE DOG OFF THE ROOF.

(CIVILIAN LAWYER. *Forties. Smart. Professional. Dishevelled. Definitely not military. His full attention is on* REEVES, *even when it does not seem to be.* REEVES— *fierce military bearing over self-hate and exhaustion.* REEVES's *eyes are fixed. Unblinking.* REEVES *is in restraints throughout.*)

MAN: CIRCLE 5—SOME WEEKS LATER.

(*Immediately*—)

LAWYER: Mr. Reeves. I will be representing you in your trial. (*No response.*) They did tell you I was coming, didn't they?
REEVES: SIR, YES, SIR.

(*The* LAWYER *is taken aback by this. Then*—)

LAWYER: Before you entered the army, you went through several trials, didn't you, Mr. Reeves, for some petty crimes?
REEVES: SIR, YES, SIR!
LAWYER: Mr. Reeves—
REEVES: SIR?
LAWYER: Mr. Reeves, we're going to be having *many* conversations and a great deal is going to have to be accomplished in a *limited* amount of time. I suspect our work will be *more* productive if we could lower the volume.
REEVES: SIR, I DOUBT THAT, SIR.
LAWYER: That quieter might be more productive?
REEVES: THAT WE'LL BE HAVING MANY CONVERSATIONS.
LAWYER (*a moment, then*—): Go on.
REEVES: PEOPLE SEEM TO SPEAK TO ME ONCE AND THEN NEVER RETURN, SIR.
LAWYER: OK. Say this is the *only* conversation we are ever going to have. Say that when I leave this room I am hit by a beer truck and die. It would *still* be easier on me if we could make the tone a little more civil. A little more—*civilian.*
REEVES: *Sir, yes, sir!*
LAWYER: Mr. Reeves, you know you're not in the military, don't you?
REEVES: You don't have to be in the army to talk this way, *SIR.*
LAWYER: But if you aren't, why would you?
REEVES: To get off the medication they have me on, I have to be on an emotional even keel. Talking this way helps, sir. I've been through trials in civilian life, sir. Three. Drugs, alcohol, fights.

LAWYER: But you've always pled guilty, so you've only ever seen *half* a trial. In a trial a story is told twice. In the first version you are guilty. In the second—same story—you are innocent.

REEVES: SIR, I'm guilty, SIR.

LAWYER: Doesn't matter. At least not to me.

REEVES: Sir—if I'm being tried for a crime I'm guilty of—shouldn't it *especially* matter to you?

LAWYER: There's a jury to decide that. I have one job. And that job is to defend you. Do you know what that means?

REEVES: Proving I didn't do what I did. I'm not going to let that happen, SIR. I'm guilty, SIR.

(*Silence. Then—*)

LAWYER: What's harder these days, Daniel? Not eating or not sleeping?

REEVES: *Cramps,* sir. I can't *shit,* sir. It's the medication. I killed the hajis, sir. We went to their shack and I killed them. I'm *guilty.*

LAWYER (*a moment, then—*): Prove it.

REEVES: Sir?

LAWYER: Prove it.

REEVES: I was *there,* sir. I *know* what I *did.*

LAWYER: Mr. Reeves, if I wanted to know what you did, you would be the *last* person I would ask. We know very little of ourselves.

REEVES: Maybe you don't know *your*self, sir.

LAWYER: The one thing I am certain of is that we are not who we think we are.

REEVES: SIR, I was warned about you. You'll turn everything upside down. You're a lawyer, SIR.

LAWYER: Who warned you about lawyers?

REEVES: A preacher, sir.

LAWYER: Preachers usually turn things upside down. Did he? (*A nod.*) Well, then, I'm just putting things back.

REEVES: Don't play with me, sir. People always play with me. They say they'll come back and they don't. They say, "Say 'not guilty,'" then they throw me in jail. They swear me in and then throw me out. I think it's driving me insane. SIR.

(*Silence. Then—*)

LAWYER: Mr. Reeves—I'll plead you guilty.

REEVES: Thank you, sir.

LAWYER: —if you will just give me one shred of evidence that you were involved in a crime.

REEVES: Like what?

LAWYER: Spent cartridges, semen stains, blood samples, a murder weapon. A dead body would help.

REEVES: SIR, you may not have NOTICED, SIR, but I am in RESTRAINTS in a CELL in a FEDERAL PRISON. Where am I going to get any of that SHIT?

LAWYER: Where is *anybody* going to get any of that shit? That's what I'd like to know. There is no case—at least not in the conventional sense—against you.

REEVES: I'm *guilty,* sir.

LAWYER (*OK, then*—): There is one thing I think I *can* prove you guilty of.

REEVES: Sir?

LAWYER (*in his notes*): There was an incident with a dog.

REEVES: A dog?

LAWYER: You threw a dog off a roof?

REEVES: Fuck the dog, sir.

LAWYER: A surprising number of people *saw* you do that. If you want to be guilty of something, I suspect I can prove you guilty of that.

REEVES: *Fuck* the dog.

LAWYER: The dog—

REEVES: *FUCK THE DOG!*

LAWYER: OK, if it upsets you. (*Then—more serious*) Let's talk about the girl you killed.

REEVES (*easy with that*): All right.

(*Puzzled by* REEVES*'s lack of upset*—)

LAWYER: It doesn't bother you to talk about her?

REEVES: Sir, no, sir! I don't give a fuck about the girl.

LAWYER: That surprises me. I thought that's what you were guilty of. (*Preempting*) I'm not playing with you. This is the crime. What happened with the girl. That's what this trial is about. What you demand to be guilty for. And yet you don't feel bad about her?

REEVES: She ruined a lot of good men's lives, sir.

LAWYER: *She* did.

REEVES: By her, I mean all of them in their fucked-up country, sir. She fucked up a lot of good men's lives.

LAWYER: She was fourteen.

REEVES: She doesn't *matter.* She really doesn't *matter.*

LAWYER: Well, if she doesn't, who does? Who are you so anxious to give up your life for?

REEVES (*looking him over, then*—): You were never in the military, were you, sir? (*No*)

Then you wouldn't understand.

LAWYER: The brotherhood. The camaraderie.

REEVES (*his deepest belief*): Sir, yes, sir.

LAWYER: You feel bad for the men you left behind. The ones who were beheaded and mutilated—because of what you did to the girl.

(REEVES *can scarcely bear hearing this. He struggles against his restraints.*)

Mr. Reeves—*they* don't matter.

REEVES: *The fuck they don't.*

LAWYER: You are not being tried for their deaths.

REEVES (*violent bottom line*): I'M GUILTY. I will tell them I'm guilty!

LAWYER (*violent bottom line*): I will NOT let you testify AGAINST YOURSELF. Not in COURT.

Not in HERE.

(*Puts finger on* REEVES's *forehead.*)

And not in *here.*

(*A long moment of contact.* REEVES *takes that in.* LAWYER *removes his finger.*)

REEVES (*simple and sad*): I did it, sir. I'm guilty.

LAWYER: One remarkable thing about a trial is—even if a person is guilty, if his story can be presented in such a way as to make the *reason* for his actions comprehensible—no matter how strange they might seem in the cold light of day—if they can be shown to have made sense at the time to the person doing them—people tend to understand. (*Then*) I think that's wonderful.

REEVES: A sympathetic reaction.

LAWYER: Yes, exactly.

REEVES: I've had them, sir. Twice.

LAWYER: Just twice?

REEVES: Sir, I think that's more than most.

LAWYER: Well, we only need *one.* One member of the jury who understands your story. But to tell the story in that way—I will have to know who you are—exactly who you are—in the story—what you did—why you did it. (*Then*) Now, would you like people to understand what you did?

REEVES: I'd like to understand it myself.

LAWYER: Just answer my questions, OK? (*A nod, then, seriously*) Tell me about the dog.

REEVES (*instantaneous*): *Fuck* the DOG.

LAWYER: Why did you throw the dog off the roof?

REEVES: FUCK! THE DOG!

LAWYER: YOU WANT TO BE GUILTY ABOUT SOMETHING? START *HERE*. You DID this. Why? *WHY DID YOU THROW THE DOG OFF THE ROOF?*

REEVES: I thought it was—(*what?*)—funny.

LAWYER: Funny. (*Then*) Funny? Killing a dog? Did other people find it—

REEVES: Other people *freaked*. That's funny, right?

LAWYER: Not to the dog.

REEVES: Really? You know what a dog thinks? *You* do? You can *prove* the dog *didn't* think it was funny? Who knows—maybe the dog thought it was funny. Dogs think *everything* is funny. Maybe the dog thought it could *fly*—*what* the *fuck* are we *talking* about? Look, am I being charged with *cruelty to animals?*

LAWYER: You and your buddies are being charged with rape and murder. Capital crimes.

REEVES: How are they pleading?

LAWYER: Guilty.

REEVES: How come they get to plead guilty and I don't?

LAWYER: Because they got a deal. Plead guilty and live.

REEVES: Get me the same deal.

LAWYER: I can't.

REEVES: Then get me a new lawyer.

LAWYER: It doesn't have to do with me. You can't do what they're doing.

REEVES: What?

LAWYER: They're testifying against you, Daniel. (*Silence, then*—) They are *lining up* to testify—they are *falling over themselves* to testify against you. They're going to nail—your—hide to the barn door, Mr. Reeves, your brothers-in-arms. See, they know who *they* are in the story. They're the ones who are out on parole in ten years—all because they are willing to throw you off the roof, Daniel.

(REEVES *struggles with his restraints*—)

It doesn't have to be that way. (*Then*) All they have are fifteen photographs of the crime scene. That's *all* they have and those photographs were used as proof that the killings were the work of insurgents. *Everyone* up and down the line signed on to that. Fifteen photos and the testimony of your squad mates—every single one of whom is seriously and repeatedly *perjured.* They've got *nothing.* There is no evidence against you.

REEVES: You want evidence against me—dig up the girl.

LAWYER: Daniel—

REEVES: *Dig up the girl.*

LAWYER (*with sudden edge*): Please don't talk about "the girl." She has a name. Khorsheed. It means "sun."

(*Sensing his sympathy for the girl—*)

REEVES: You know I'm guilty. Don't you?

LAWYER: I am trying to understand what happened *inside* you.

REEVES: I don't know.

LAWYER: OK. Let's figure it out. You walk into the room and you see "the girl" being held down on the floor. Was she struggling? Was she crying?

REEVES: Crying. Screaming. It was embarrassing.

LAWYER: Why were you embarrassed? What did she scream?

REEVES: I don't know.

LAWYER: You know some Arabic. You talked to the locals in it. What did she—

REEVES: I don't know. "Fuck you, Americans."

LAWYER (*driving*): I don't think so. You would have understood that. What was she saying?

REEVES: *How am I supposed to know?*

LAWYER: Well, what did you *feel? That's* the important thing.

REEVES: I have a personality disorder. I *don't* feel things.

LAWYER: Of course you do.

REEVES: *I DON'T FEEL—*

LAWYER: Mr. Reeves, you feel so many things, they had to restrain you. You are pumped full of pharmaceuticals just to keep you functioning. You walked into a room and saw a girl struggling. Two people, your brothers, are holding her down. A lovely fourteen-year-old girl. You look at her and you felt—

REEVES: *Nothing.*

LAWYER: Did you think it was funny?

REEVES: Are you sick?

LAWYER: You thought killing the dog was funny.

REEVES: Killing the dog wasn't the funny part.

LAWYER: What was?

REEVES: FUCK THE DOG! IF YOU WANT PROOF AGAINST ME—DIG—HER—UP.

LAWYER: Even if Islamic law allowed it, I don't think it would prove anything.

REEVES: I WAS THERE. What happened *happened*. We *raped* and *killed* a girl.

LAWYER: Prove it. (*Then*) Source of Information 3 isn't sure about what he did. He says he attempted to rape the girl but—(*his notes*)—"*he was not sure if he had done so.*" (*Then*) SOI2 says the same. I am not saying this wasn't horrific, but I do *not* think it is what it seems to be. What happened? Are you *sure* you raped that girl?

REEVES (*enough of this*): I'm sure I killed the bitch.

LAWYER (*enough of this*): But then again—(*the heart of the matter*)—you're also sure you caused the deaths of three men at a checkpoint.

REEVES: SIR, YES, SIR.

LAWYER: Prove it.

(*Brief moment. Then—*)

REEVES: Huh?

LAWYER: PROVE—IT. Prove one event had any connection whatsoever with the other. (*Then*) That's what you really feel guilty for? That's what you want to die for—not the girl? OK, I get that. Just *prove* it.

REEVES (*baffled*): Sir?

LAWYER: At the time they—your buddies—at the time they were killed, when their bodies were put on display—when the videos were made and shown? Nobody said a word—not a word—about the girl or her family. The story didn't come out for weeks. Then Al-Jazeera combined the two stories and created a propaganda bonanza. Why would they sit on a story that was *that* good if there was *any* truth to it *at all*? People believe it because it is a *terrific* story. (*Then*) You believe it because it flatters your ego. It makes you important—tragic even. It gives you something easy to confess to.

REEVES: Easy? EASY?

LAWYER: It's always easy to be guilty of something you *didn't* do. It makes YOU the victim instead of the girl—but there is *no proof* the events are *related*. I do *not* believe that they are or we would have heard about it the *instant* it happened.

(REEVES *takes a moment. Then—*)

REEVES: Are you lying to me?

LAWYER: I'm a lawyer, Mr. Reeves. That is an awkward question.

REEVES: DO NOT PLAY WITH ME.

LAWYER: The good news is—I do *not* think you are responsible for the deaths of your squad mates at the checkpoint. The bad news is your other squad mates are shopping you for reduced sentences. The simple *truth* is you are what you have always been—an individual human being with a story to tell. Now tell it to me. There is nothing to hide. Tell me, Daniel. You walk in and you see her on the floor, you look in her eyes—

REEVES: They're testifying against me?

LAWYER: Yes, Daniel. I am sorry, but they are.

REEVES (*with growing anger*): I am not the dog.

LAWYER: Good.

REEVES: I am NOT the dog! I AM NOT—

LAWYER: Tell me about the dog.

REEVES: We were up to our asses in *dead bodies.* We were wearing *full body armor,* carrying *automatic weapons* walking around looking for people to kill and everybody went NUTS when I threw a *DOG* off a *ROOF.* (*Amused*) "He killed the dog! There's something wrong with him—he killed the dog." (*Then, laughing*) The *dog.*

LAWYER: Go on.

REEVES: And it's *funny.* I mean, all this shit is going on—bombings and body parts—and they point at *me* and say, "Look at *that*! What *he* did? *That's* wrong. He killed a *dog.*" *It's funny.* But it's not. Is it? I mean, not to the dog. You think I'm the *dog* off the *roof* AND IT'S NOT—FUCKING—FUNNY!

LAWYER: Daniel, please believe I never thought that. You are not the dog.

REEVES: Who am I then?

LAWYER (*with growing enthusiasm*): That's the other thing I can prove. I can *prove* that you are the person—the *only* person in this whole affair who said, "Something is wrong here." You are the *only* one who sought help—*before* the event—to get out of this mess. You sought help and they said—Well, we don't know what they said because the psychiatrist you went to won't say *what* she said. She won't testify.

REEVES: She won't?

LAWYER: Not without a grant of immunity.

REEVES: What does that mean?

LAWYER (*driving forward*): It means she thinks she did something *very* wrong. Something that she *does—not—want* on the record. But you went on the record. In a culture in which seeking help is the *last* thing you do, you sought help. And I need to know what went on in that conversation. What did she say?

REEVES: It's confidential.

LAWYER: What did she say that was so terrible?

REEVES: It's confidential.

LAWYER: I need to know, Daniel, or there is no second story to tell at your trial.

REEVES: Dig her up. I'm guilty. DIG—HER—UP.

LAWYER: There would be no point, Daniel. She's dead. Her family is dead. All that's left of that girl is in here. All that's left of this whole incident is in here.

(*Indicating* REEVES'*s head.*)

REEVES (*wild*): I—AM—THE—DOG. I—AM—THE—DOG.

LAWYER: What did you tell the shrink, Daniel?

REEVES (*wilder*): I TOLD HER I WANTED TO KILL EVERYBODY.

LAWYER: And what did she say?

REEVES (*wildest*): SHE SAID I WAS NORMAL!

(*Immediate blackout. Lights return almost instantaneously on* REEVES *in uniform.*)

CIRCLE 6: SYMPATHETIC REACTION.

(REEVES—*in uniform—three months before all the shit hits—faces the* SHRINK— *also in uniform. She's tired of dealing with inarticulate nineteen-year-olds. Most of what she does is push paper and dispense medication. Given a chance, she'd do more.* REEVES *tries to contain himself, but inside he is a horse in a burning barn—incapable of the move he must make.*)

MAN: CIRCLE 6. IRAQ. A YEAR EARLIER.

SHRINK (*immediately, mid-scene*): Well, do you want to kill *me*?

REEVES: No.

SHRINK: So you don't want to kill *everybody*? (*Then*) Go on. What's on your mind?

REEVES: I say I want to kill everybody. You tell me I don't. What is there to talk about?

(*A moment. Then—*)

SHRINK: Are you trying to get out of the service?

REEVES: *NO, MA'AM.*

(*No response. Then, too casual—*)

Man, a shrink in the army—that's just—crazy.

SHRINK: This isn't about me.

REEVES (*immediate and* not *casual*): Well, I'm not ready for it to be about me.

(*Silence.*)

SHRINK: Have you ever seen a shrink before?

REEVES: School counselor. Social worker. Parole officer. I know the drill. Aren't you supposed to ask me some questions?

SHRINK: You want me to ask you some questions?

REEVES: Whatever.

SHRINK (*from a form/almost by heart*): Have you experienced a traumatic event where your or someone else's life was in danger or you thought that your or someone else's life was in danger?

REEVES (*is she serious? then—*): You're joking, right?

SHRINK (*sort of*): How did you react to the trauma?

REEVES (*enjoying this*): You got some choices there?

SHRINK (*the form*): Were you frightened or horrified? While it was happening did it seem like things were unreal, like a dream? (*No response.*) Did it seem like your body or some part of your body was somehow changed, not real, or detached from you?

REEVES: No, but if a body part does become detached, I'll come back and discuss it with you.

(REEVES *starts out.*)

SHRINK: One word, private. Give me one word and I'll do my best. (*Preempting*) Not "whatever."

REEVES: "Whatever" covers a lot of territory.

SHRINK: You're a smart guy. You ought to be able to come up with one word.

REEVES: What makes you think I'm smart?

SHRINK: You're here. And nobody made you come and you're here. (*No*) Private, everything that happens here is confidential.

(REEVES *laughs.*)

You don't believe that.

REEVES: Never had a confidential conversation that what I said wasn't public knowledge before I got home. You'll tell *somebody.*

SHRINK: And you'll go back to barracks and tell everybody how we did it on the desk until the desk broke and we still kept doing it and you've got another appointment not because you need it but because I do.

(*Silence. Then*—REEVES *laughs. She sees an opening. What the hell. Takes it.*)

A shrink in the army. It's crazy. Crazy I'm here, crazy you're here, the whole thing is crazy.

REEVES: Not so crazy—defending our country.

SHRINK: You think?

REEVES: You don't?

(*Easy back-and-forth. A dance.*)

SHRINK: Doesn't matter what I think.

REEVES: Matters to me. I need to talk. I need to know I can trust who I'm talking to. I tell you I want to kill everybody and you tell me I don't. I think that's fucked up.

SHRINK: What do you want me to say?

REEVES: Maybe you should say what you think?

SHRINK: Doesn't matter what I think.

REEVES: Matters if you want to hear what I'm thinking.

(*A moment. Then*—)

SHRINK: I think maybe wanting to kill everybody is a deviation from the norm in Texas—maybe—but over here—under the circumstances—very unofficially—yeah—that's pretty normal. Is that what you wanted to know—if you're normal?

REEVES: You tell me wanting to kill everybody is normal. Makes me wonder what kind of a home you came from. I think you're a fucked-up shrink in this fucked-up war. I'd like to know what you think of that.

(*A test?*)

SHRINK: Confidential? (*A nod from* REEVES.) I don't think this is a war.

REEVES: No?

SHRINK: I think this is just—violence.

REEVES: Wars are violence.

SHRINK: Violence *for* something.

REEVES: This *isn't* for something?

SHRINK: What do you *think*?

REEVES: What do *you* think?

SHRINK: I think this is just a mistake.

REEVES: A mistake?

SHRINK: We invaded the wrong country and—ever since—everything's fucked up. And the puzzle is—once we knew it was the wrong place, why we didn't pull out. That's what I think of this fucked-up war.

(REEVES *is lost in his own thoughts. A moment.*)

That was my best shot at honest. Your turn.

(*Silence.*)

OK, you come back when you're ready. We're done here.

(*Deeper silence. Then—*)

REEVES: So—you think he was an idiot, right?

SHRINK: Who?

REEVES: The sergeant.

SHRINK: What sergeant?

REEVES: Ortiz.

(*Silence. Then, with new seriousness—*)

SHRINK: Why would he be an idiot?

(*Silence.*)

REEVES: Cause he thought he was over here fighting for his country. But this is all just a big mistake, right? That's what you think.

(*New start.*)

SHRINK: Were you there?

(*He was.*)

REEVES: He died under me.

SHRINK: He was the sergeant. You were under him.

(*Shrug. Then—*)

REEVES: They grabbed Sergeant Ortiz. Tossed him on the hummer hood. I jumped on him. Don't know why. Held him on the hood all the way back to base. We were going fast, but I never looked where we were going. I just looked at him and held him on the hood. I was on top of him. All the way. On the hood. He died *under* me.

(*A moment. Then*—)

SHRINK: Soldier, just to clarify, I don't think the sergeant was an idiot for being here.

REEVES (*instantaneous painful reversal*): He was an idiot. He had no business
being here. Fighting for his country, shit. It wasn't even *his* country. He
wasn't even a citizen.

SHRINK: He was what—an alien?

REEVES: An—an *alien*?

SHRINK: Resident alien.

REEVES: Ma'am?

SHRINK: "Resident alien." It's an oxymoron. "Non-dairy creamer." Something
that means its own opposite.

REEVES (*done with this*): Ma'am, I don't have a clue what you're talking about.
(*Rising to go*) Well, this has been *very* therapeutic, but I think that maybe I
came to the wrong place—like we invaded the wrong country—so maybe
I should just leave like we should have.

SHRINK: Sit down, private.

REEVES: No, ma'am.

SHRINK: You afraid of talking to me, private?

REEVES: No, ma'am.

SHRINK: Then what are you afraid of?

REEVES: *I'm afraid of killing everybody, ma'am. But you don't want to hear me
say that, ma'am. You're AFRAID to hear me say that. That's what YOU'RE
afraid of.*

(*Silence. Then*—)

SHRINK: How about Sergeant Ortiz? What would he do if you told him you
wanted to kill everybody?

REEVES: He'd do what he always did. He'd put his hand out with a big smile.
Like at the roadblock. (*Then*) He walked up to the car like he walked up
to everybody. (*Then*) Even in cammies and kevlar, that's all you could see
when he came up to you. A smile and his hand out. He had his daughter's
name tattooed on his wrist so you could see that too. The guy in the car
smiled back at him. Put his hand out. There was a gun in it. He shot him.
Just like that. (*Then*) He shot Timmons too. Timmons fell down dead.

(*Silence.*)

Sergeant Ortiz was alive. Most of the way. Looking at me. He never looked
away. I never looked away from him. Never once.

(*He holds his look at her for a while. Then can't. Then—*)

SHRINK: Did he say anything?

REEVES: No, ma'am. He was dignified. Never complained. Not a word.

SHRINK: Did you say anything?

REEVES: Oh, yeah. I was real poetic.

SHRINK: What did you say?

REEVES: I said "Sergeant Ortiz. Sergeant Ortiz." See, I got a way with words. (*Then—*) "Sergeant Ortiz." (*Then*) Fucking stupid thing to say.

SHRINK: That was his name.

REEVES (*fuck you*): That was his *job*. His *name* was Rudy. At least I could of said Rudy. He was fucking dying. You think you'd say his name.

SHRINK: Anything else?

REEVES: No, ma'am.

(*Silence. A thought. Dismissed.*)

SHRINK: What?

REEVES: Well—

SHRINK: What?

REEVES: I drooled on him. Pretty great, huh? I wiped it off. (*Then*) Like it mattered. (*Then*) He wouldn't care about a little spit.

SHRINK: It mattered to you.

REEVES: He was *dying*. And here I am—*drooling* on him. I could have—

SHRINK: What?

REEVES: He liked jokes. He told jokes. You know when you been in Iraq too long? Ask me. Go on. Ask me.

SHRINK: How do you know you've been in Iraq too long?

REEVES: You know all the lines in the fourth season of *Sex in the City*.

(*He nods for her to ask again.*)

SHRINK: How do you know you've been in Iraq too long?

REEVES: You start thinking of building a house for your family someplace nice—like the Green Zone.

(REEVES *laughs.*)

SHRINK: How do you know you've been in Iraq too long?

REEVES (*laughing*): You're in the Army and you start saying Ooorah . . . Or in the Marines and you start saying Hooah. Or the temperature drops to 102 degrees and you put on a jacket.

(*Silence.*)

(REEVES *is about to cry.*)

(*Silence.*)

SHRINK: You didn't tell him a joke.

(*Silence.*)

REEVES (*then, no, then—*): I rubbed his chest. I said "Sergeant Ortiz." He
    died. And that's the trauma, right?
SHRINK: If it bothered you, it is.
REEVES: If it *didn't* bother me, it is too, right?
SHRINK: You're a smart guy.
REEVES: Nothing smart about it. It's a trick. You just say the opposite of what
    people say to you—it confuses them.
SHRINK: Why are you letting me in on the trick?
REEVES: I suppose one of us shouldn't be confused.
SHRINK: Are you confused about what happened?
REEVES: No, ma'am, I am not. It did *not* seem like a dream. I did not leave my
    body. (*Amused*) He left his though. (*Not amused*) He surely did.

(*Silence.*)

(*Then, with hard, sincere compassion—*)

SHRINK: I think you did a very hard thing. I think you accompanied a man to
    his death. I think you called his name to make sure that he knew he wasn't
    alone. You touched him with gentleness. You eased his passing. I think you
    did a great thing. I think he did a great thing being the kind of man you
    could look up to. Maybe that's what this is all about. Maybe that's why we
    came here. For that to happen.

(*Silence.*)

(*Then, with extreme focused anger—*)

REEVES: That's the *most* fucked-up thing I've ever heard.

(*Silence.*)

SHRINK: Tell me about it.

(*Then—with violent anger—*)

REEVES: No, ma'am. I got *nothing* to say to somebody who thinks this war is about letting Sergeant Ortiz die so I can see it. I think that is fucked up.

SHRINK: You mad? (*No response.*) How mad?

REEVES: Ask me *now* if I'd like to kill you.

SHRINK (*hard ass*): Private Reeves, you say you want to stay in the service?

REEVES: YES, MA'AM.

SHRINK: Well, there are certain things I *cannot* hear. If you tell me you want to kill everybody or kill yourself, I have to warehouse you. If you *don't* want to go home, do NOT tell me that you want to commit MURDER or SUICIDE.

REEVES: Then it seems to me that there's AN EXTREMELY LIMITED RANGE of things that are OPEN for DISCUSSION.

(*Silence. Then—hard, fast, diagnostic—*)

SHRINK: If a bullet came through the tent and I were bleeding here on the floor, would that bother you?

REEVES: No, ma'am. Would it bother you if that happened to me?

SHRINK: Yes, it would.

REEVES: Why?

SHRINK: You see somebody die, it's disturbing.

REEVES: Why?

SHRINK: It's a sympathetic reaction. You forget it's happening to somebody else. It feels like it's happening to you.

REEVES: Does it, ma'am? You're sure of that.

SHRINK (*yes*): It's an emotional thing. It confuses the brain. It's what makes us human. Even in a movie. You have a sympathetic response. Watching a football game, you take sides—you feel you win when your team wins.

REEVES: I've never been much of a team player, ma'am.

SHRINK: You were on Sergeant Ortiz's team.

REEVES: Yes, ma'am.

SHRINK: Did his death bother you?

REEVES: No, ma'am.

SHRINK: What did?

REEVES: That I didn't KILL the FUCK who SHOT him BEFORE he had the chance.

(*A moment. Then—*)

SHRINK: Soldier, you couldn't have saved him.

REEVES: No?

SHRINK: The way you tell it, not enough time to aim and fire.

REEVES (*sure there was*): If I had him in my sights.

SHRINK: You going to keep them all in your sights all of the time?

REEVES: You think we're not in their sights all the time? Could've shot him as soon as he got out of the car. Hell, before he got out.

SHRINK: Without cause?

REEVES: Plenty of cause.

SHRINK: What?

REEVES: HE *SHOT* SERGEANT ORTIZ.

(*A moment.*)

SHRINK: You had no way of knowing—

REEVES: I did. (*Fuck, terrible pain*) I KNEW. I knew it would happen. We all knew.

SHRINK: How?

REEVES: He never looked out for himself. It was just a question of time. We should've been looking out for him. *We knew.*

(*Then—*)

SHRINK: So you should have shot anybody who got out of a car? You think Sergeant Ortiz would have approved of that?

REEVES: He would have been mad, but after he found the gun? He would've thanked me. Put his hand out. Smiled. He'd know I was watching out for him.

(*A brief moment.*)

SHRINK: You see this in your head a lot.

REEVES: Like that movie you were talking about? Yes, ma'am. It's a good movie. A feel-good movie. You ought to catch it sometime.

(*Silence. Then—*)

SHRINK: You want to kill everybody.

REEVES (*amazed!*): Oh, you figured that out, huh? God, you're SMART. That's how you got to be a shrink in the army, right? Because you're so SMART and can figure things like that out. I want to kill everybody—everybody but you—and what I *do* want to do to you—well, I suspect that falls into the normal category too.

(*Then*—)

SHRINK: OK, we're done here.
REEVES (*leaving*): Yes, we are.

(*He moves. Stops.*)

SHRINK: We're done.

(*Then*—)

REEVES: This is confidential, right?
SHRINK: No, not right. I told you what I could hear and what I couldn't.

(*Silence. Then*—)

REEVES: If I had a bullet in my head and I were lying here, you'd feel bad for me.
SHRINK: I would.
REEVES: Do I have to have a bullet in my head to qualify?

(*Silence.*)

If I were laying here on your floor bleeding from the head, *how long* would you feel bad for me? (*No response.*) Because—out there—they put a bullet in me—they'd celebrate for a month. A year. Fuck. Forever. They kill me, they get to go to God, directly to God, do not stop at any checkpoints. When those construction workers got killed—they hung their body parts from the bridge and they danced their asses off for days. Now you want to talk about sympathy—I've got all kinds of sympathy for that because that is *exactly* how I feel about them. We want each other dead. Now you—you've got all the sympathy in the world for a dying sergeant—fuck—ANY-BODY CAN FEEL SYMPATHY FOR THE GOOD GUY. He doesn't *need* your sympathy. He's got a wife and a kid for that. But that guy who shot him—I want to fucking kill him over and over. That's what goes on in my head and you've got no sympathy for that. "Don't tell me that. You're on your own with that" and you know what that means? You've got no sympathy for the one thing that NEEDS it here and I don't want to make him an excuse. I think I've *always* wanted to kill everybody. Him dying just makes me think I'm finally going to do it.

(*Brief, brief moment. Then, pissed*—)

SHRINK: You're a killer.

REEVES: Yes, ma'am. I have killed.

SHRINK: And it didn't bother you?

REEVES: No, ma'am, it did not. That's who I am.

SHRINK: A killer?

REEVES: Yes, ma'am.

SHRINK: Well, killer, did it bother you that you drooled on the sergeant?

(*Silence.*)

REEVES (*stung*): I wiped it off.

SHRINK (*escalating*): Why? It didn't bother him.

REEVES: I *wiped* it *off*.

SHRINK (*escalating*): Why? Did it *bother* you?

REEVES: YOU GONNA MAKE FUN OF ME FOR THAT?

SHRINK: ARE YOU GOING TO ATTACK ME FOR TRYING TO HELP YOU?

REEVES: NO, MA'AM. HELP ME.

SHRINK: HELP ME AND I WILL.

(*Silence. Then—*)

REEVES (*wild*): SHIT!

(*Silence.* REEVES *weeps. Weeps till he drools.* SHRINK *watches. Then—*)

SHRINK: How old are you, soldier?

REEVES: I'm a fucking baby.

(*Silence. Then—*)

SHRINK: Do you think. Do you think the sergeant might've been thinking of his daughter as he was dying?

REEVES: He thought about her all the time. He had her name tattooed on his arm.

SHRINK: So—maybe the drool made sense to him.

REEVES: Ma'am?

SHRINK: I mean, she's a kid, right. Kids drool on their fathers. Maybe it made sense to him. Maybe he thought it was her.

(REEVES *takes that in.*)

REEVES: I wish it was. (*Then*) Till he turned into a sack of shit and blood. (*Then*) Then it was good it was me there and not her.

(*Silence. Then—*)

SHRINK: I think that's what I was trying to say before. (*Then*) Sorry.
REEVES: I get it. (*Then*) It's hard sometimes to—
SHRINK: I get it.
REEVES: I—

(*They both get it. Then—*)

SHRINK: When was the last time you felt that?
REEVES: What?
SHRINK: That it was good that you were there.

(*No response.*)

You felt like you were part of his family.

(*Silence.*)

REEVES: No.
SHRINK: No?
REEVES (*no*): I felt I was part of him.

(*And this is painful, glorious, and shameful. Silence. Then—*)

SHRINK: When was the last time you felt that?
REEVES: Like I said—when he died.
SHRINK (*no*): Before that?

(*Silence.*)

You can look at me. (*Nothing*) Soldier. (*Nothing*) Eyes.

(*He looks at her.*)

Have you felt that way before?

(*Silence. She holds his glance throughout.*)

You never felt that way before.

(*Silence.*)

You always felt alone?
REEVES: I always figured I felt pretty much the way everybody feels. (*Then*)
That's not right. Is it? (*Then*) What I felt on the hummer hood—that's nor-
mal. Right? (*No response.*) I'm one of those morons you were talking about.

SHRINK: Morons?

REEVES: Things that are the opposite of themselves.

(*Silence. Then—*)

SHRINK: Soldier.

REEVES: Ma'am.

SHRINK: I think you've been in Iraq too long.

REEVES: Ma'am, do NOT—do not send me home. (*Then*) I am begging you.
    Let me stay.

SHRINK: Why? So you can kill everybody?

(*No.*)

Why then?

(*Truth.*)

REEVES: Ma'am, I think being here is my one shot at normal. (*Then*) What
    happened? I want that to happen again. (*Then*) I'd like to feel that a—(*then,
    deeply embarrassed*) look, let's just forget I ever came in here. Nobody knows
    but us. OK? Please. Let's just forget it.

SHRINK: You want to forget this conversation?

REEVES: No, ma'am. (*Then*) At least not all of it. That thing you said about
    the. The drool? That was a nice thing to say. Even if it wasn't true. I'll think
    about that later.

(*She needs a commitment from him. Laying it out—*)

SHRINK: Kids drool on their dads. They cry on them too. Kids cry a lot. Cry till
    somebody comes to pick them up. Some kids don't get picked up. Crying
    doesn't do them much good—so they stop. Some start again. Some don't.
    Doesn't matter much one way or the other. (*Then*) They can't stop crying—
    we send them home. (*Then*) They can stop—that's good for me—because I
    get to recycle them. Either way's OK, but I got to know which way is the
    soldier's way so they don't end up fucking everybody up. (*Then*) Are you
    going to fuck everybody up?

REEVES (*honest/amused*): Well—I always have.

(*Wrong answer. She goes to write him out of the army.*)

Can I try that again, ma'am?

SHRINK: Are you going to—

REEVES: No, ma'am. (*Then*) How about this? I don't want to kill everybody. Just the bad people. Is that normal enough?

(*She nods. Enter the* LAWYER *from the 5th Circle.*)

LAWYER: Did you ever go back?
REEVES: Told you. I never saw anybody twice till you. (*Then, to the* SHRINK) I picked a bad time to go normal, didn't I?
SHRINK: Here. This might help.

(*She offers him a bottle of pills.*)

REEVES: What are these?
SHRINK: Seroquel. Something to take the edge off.
REEVES: Ma'am, the last thing I want is for the edge to be taken off.

(*He takes the pills from her anyway.*)

LAWYER: What happened then?
REEVES: She told me to get a good night of sleep.
SHRINK: Try to get a good night of sleep.
LAWYER: When did you see the shrink again?
REEVES: Different shrink. After the dog. See—

(REEVES *switches his focus to the audience.*)

It was the dog that got them upset.

(*A* WOMAN—*professionally dressed*—*and the* LAWYER *from Circle 5 flank* REEVES. *A moment. Then*—)

REEVES: CIRCLE 7. THE TRIAL OF DANIEL EDWARD REEVES. (*re: the* MAN—) Lawyer for the Defense. (*re: the* WOMAN—) Lawyer for the Prosecution.

(REEVES *sits between them during*—)

CIRCLE 7: A COTTON DRESS AND A CHANGE OF CLOTHES.

PROSECUTION: A cotton dress. (*Then*) I want to speak to you about a cotton dress. (*Then*)
    Young girls need protection. The girl we are concerned with—living in a war zone—needed more than most. She had a cotton dress. (*Then*) She *had* had another defense—her family.

(*Then*) But a soldier deprived her of the protection of her family when he herded her father, her mother and four-year-old sister into the family bedroom and murdered them in cold blood.

(*Then*) This soldier then proceeded from the bedroom to the living room where two of his fellow soldiers were holding the girl on the floor and—against them—against him—the protection of a cotton dress was not sufficient.

(*The* DEFENSE *speaks.*)

DEFENSE: The crime we are discussing only *ended* in Iraq. (*Then*) It began in a recruiting office in Texas. (*Then*) There—a recruiting officer met a deeply troubled nineteen-year-old with convictions for alcohol, drug abuse, violence. He had a personality disorder and everybody in town knew it. (*Then*) To make his quota, this recruiting office obtained a morals waiver for him, and this disturbed young man was soon strapped up with world-class weaponry to fight in a war so lacking in popular support that an army could not be assembled to fight it—without candidates like this young man.

PROSECUTION: The war is not on trial here. A man accused of a specific crime is.

DEFENSE: OK. Let's investigate the crime. Starting with the murder. (*Then*) Let's look at the weapon.

(*He looks around. Finds none.*)

We cannot. (*Then*) Let us investigate the rape. Let's examine the DNA evidence.

(*He looks around. Nothing.*)

None . . . OK, then. Let's—Let's take a look at that cotton dress. (*Then*) No dress? (*To the* PROSECUTION) Do we even know if the dress was cotton?

(*A moment. Then—*)

PROSECUTION: There are photographs.

DEFENSE: Without a single bit of evidence to back them up—for all we know they could have been taken on a studio back lot. (*Then*) Strange trial in which there is absolutely no evidence.

PROSECUTION: There is testimony.

DEFENSE: There is a flood of testimony. (*To the audience*) Every bit of it coming from men and women who outrank my client placing every bit of the blame on him—the lowest ranking man involved in this incident. (*Then*) A ritual was invented in the ancient near east—not far from where the events we are discussing took place. For terrible crimes, all blame was placed on an animal and the animal was driven into the wilderness to die. (*Then*) We are more enlightened now. We would never allow an animal's life to be sacrificed. And yet. Our government—from the president on down—is calling for the scapegoating of a young man—the lowest ranking man involved in this admittedly horrifying event.

PROSECUTION: What we are discussing did not take place in the mythic past, but in the nearly immediate present. It was not a symbolic action. It was not an "event" or an "incident." It was a crime. Very real. Very brutal. And, in it, rank is absolutely immaterial. Nuremberg made that quite clear. A solider of any rank is responsible for his moral choices.

(*A moment. Then—*)

REEVES: He's my lawyer, but I like her.

(REEVES *rises. While the attorneys continue their cases,* REEVES *goes upstage, strips out of his uniform, washes himself and dresses in clean white T-shirt, distinctive underpants, new institutional shirt and pants. From this point forward, the words— though very important—are less important than the physical, ritual transformation of* REEVES.)

PROSECUTION: The testimony. Though much of the testimony in this case is compromised, there is one unimpeachable witness—the accused himself. He *told* people he was out to kill. To *murder*.

DEFENSE: No dispute there. (*With some enthusiasm*) Daniel Reeves told anyone who would listen he intended to kill. He wanted to kill everybody. More specifically, all Iraqis.

(*Then*) To his everlasting credit, he sought help. He went to an army psychiatrist, asked for help, was given unrecorded medication, told to get a night's sleep, and was recycled the next day to patrol the area known as The Triangle of Death. With disastrous consequences. What were his superiors expecting?

(*A moment. Then—*)

PROSECUTION: I want to be careful here. (*Then*) I too, think it is admirable that a troubled soldier sought help. And the army was remiss in not providing more help than it did. No question. However. There is a conclusion to this seeking for help that the Defense does not draw. (*Then*) The Defense has—condescendingly—portrayed Mr. Reeves as an animal. A goat and that is not fair. Mr. Reeves is a man, a smart young man. He may have been undereducated when he was inducted into the army, but he educated himself along the way. He learned. (*Then*) He learned some Arabic. Leadership skills. Even moral virtue—loyalty—brotherhood—self-sacrifice. He availed himself of his opportunities and, troubled by his desire to kill, he—sought—help. And the logical conclusion of this is—unfortunately— (*then*) He knew what he was planning on doing—was *wrong.* (*Then*) He *knew* it was wrong. (*Then*) And he did it *anyway.* (*Then*) And this was no act of passion committed after the death of a beloved sergeant. No. It happened three months later. It was not an act of war against the people who killed the sergeant or anyone else. It was a premeditated, cold, brutal attack on the people he was assigned to defend. (*Then*) And, regardless of his rank, he was the leader in this attack. If he had not been there, it would not have happened.

DEFENSE: If *we* had not been there, it would not have happened.

PROSECUTION (*insistent*): The war is not on trial here.

DEFENSE: Frankly, I don't know what *else* TO try?

PROSECUTION: I have an admission to make. (*Then*) Given the history of war, I like this war. Sixty years ago, in a war remembered with considerable nostalgia, fifty million people were killed. (*Then, honest and simple*) What we have now is a war-in-miniature—in which we can see what has never been visible before—the faces of the victims. Which is why we must get this right. The rape murder of a young girl by a man who knew better must not be ignored. It deserves—it demands—judgment.

(REEVES—*redressed*—*returns to his chair and sits between them.*)

DEFENSE: Let's say it does. Who then can judge this man? (*Then*) And it is at *this* point that Nuremberg becomes instructive. Who were the judges then? Who was the jury? (*Then*) They were the ones who said "no." Not in casual conversation, but with the commitment of their lives. (*Then*) Not the ones who financed the war with their obedient taxes. Not the ones who have not said no to this insane useless violence. (*Then*) Who has the right to judge this man? (*Then*) Anybody who stood in front of a recruiting center and said, "No." "You can't have them." "Not if this is what you are going to do with them." "This is not what we do with our young." (*Then*) If that's who you are—judge. If not—don't. Not even in the secrecy of your thoughts.

You—no—We—We haven't the right. How could we? We hired him. We paid his salary. We were his employers.

(*As he completes his case,* DEFENSE *moves upstage.* PROSECUTION *takes stage.*)

PROSECUTION: This is not—*not*—about the war. This is about a young girl. (*Then*) The Defense wants to tell you who you are in this case, but you already know. You are the rule of law. You are a young girl's last line of protection. What her family could not do—what a dress could not do—you can. The law is in your hands. Her final fate—is in your hands. (*Then*) And if anyone ever asks you again, "Did you say no to insane violence?"—do the right thing now and you will be able to say forever, "Yes—as a matter of fact—I did." (*Then*) The choice is yours. Guilty. Or not? Consider your decision.

(PROSECUTION *moves upstage.* REEVES *stands for a long moment. Long enough for the audience to make a decision. Then—*)

MAN: CIRCLE 8. THE LAST WORDS OF DANIEL EDWARD REEVES.

(*Other cast members listen as we enter—*)

CIRCLE 8: A LEARNING EXPERIENCE.

(REEVES—*terrified—attempting to appear confident—stands before the audience at his execution.*)

REEVES: I've had a good life. Can't complain. I had my war. It was a learning experience. For example—
The Battle of Lepanto was fought in 1571. I have learned that.
Shrinks fuck up your head; lawyers talk; soldiers—they can't keep a secret.
Even if you've got nothing, people still try to take things from you.
I've met a couple of good people, but I don't know how they do it.
In the story about Jesus and the woman? I wonder. I wonder where that demon went when he got driven out.
I suspect I'm about to find out. If I wake up and there's sand, I'll know I'm in hell.
Nobody can tell my story because nobody knows it.
How can they?
Nobody ever asks the right questions.

They asked me what I wanted for my last meal. Like I'm thinking about food.

They should've asked me what I wanted to wear.

I did not want to die in a diaper.

This is my story. I did it. I raped her and I killed her family. I wish I didn't but I thought about it and I honestly don't see how anything could have been different.

I don't have a daughter.

I regret that.

I think I could've given better than I got, but I learned how a little late.

That also seems to be the story of my life.

The Battle of Lepanto took place in 1571 but somehow I fought in it.

Seems to me that people do not learn a lot.

Seems to me that I have learned more than most.

(*After some thought*) That's about it.

(*Silence. When the silence becomes awkward,* REEVES *sits. Then—*)

WOMAN: CIRCLE 9. INFERNO.

(*All other cast leave.* REEVES—*for the first time—is alone. We sit in silence long enough to experience our solitude with* DANIEL EDWARD REEVES. *Then—*)

CIRCLE 9: INFERNO.

(*Quietly. Body—perfectly still.*)

REEVES: Where am I?

I hate waking up not knowing where I.

No sand.

Well.

That's good.

(*Noticing.*)

People. Looking at me.

Where am?

On a couch. Can't move. Strapped down. Am I in a hospital? Did I. Did I wreck the car?

I need the car.

Mr. Reeves, in all probability you will never.

(*Remembering where he is.*)

Oh.

So that's.

They didn't find the vein. Stuck me five times and they still couldn't find the vein. What was it? Potassium chloride right into the muscle. Fucking amateurs. I knew this would happen. I fucking *knew*. Fucking knew I'd wake up. I.

(*Silence.*)

No. No act. Go like him. Quiet.

(*Silence.*)

Anybody asks does it hurt?

(*Silence.*)

Hurts.

Sharks.

Coyotes.

Don't cry.

Pointless.

(*Perfect clarity and tears.*)

Nobody's coming.

If my head was cut off, they'd come. Go ahead. Do it. Hell, bury me up to my neck in sand and stone me to. No. No act. He was right. No act. Go like him.

(*Beat.*)

He looked at me. Saw something. Something good.

(*Beat.*)

That was my life. Not twenty years. Not ten months. Five minutes on a hummer hood. That was enough. Go like him. No words at all.

(*Silence. Then—terrible pain—*)

Muscles inside out.

Don't fight it. Give in to it. People are supposed to die. Die.

(*Silence.*)

Can't.
One more thing I can't.

(*To audience—*)

Help me.

(*No one moves.*)

Don't cry. She cried. Don't go like her screaming and crying. Eyes, soldier.
He saw. In me. Something.

(*Beat.*)

She saw. Lifted her head and saw. Saw me come in. Last person in the
world.
Sa'dny. She said Sa'dny.
How am I supposed to know what that meant.

(*His own pain.*)

Christ help me. Help. Me.

(*Silence.*)

Cavalry isn't coming.
The cavalry isn't coming, darling. You know what I came to. Sa'dny. Sa'dny.
What did I feel? Not much. Very little. She felt—very little. Very. Soft.
Felt her. No munitions strapped on.

(*Beat.*)

Got to do it. What I came to do. I got people looking at me. Got to get it
done. Help me, darling.

(*His pain.*)

Don't fight. Oh, Christ. Don't fight. She fought. Fought them. Fought me.
Looked in her eyes.
That was my mistake. Wasn't it.
Her eyes.
Saw.
I knew.
Right away.

Wrong place.
Should've left.
Couldn't.
Can't now.
People watching.
Got to do it. Put your head down and do.
Head down.
Eyes closed.
But I knew. Knew then. Right away.
No.
No hummer hood for me.
Army of one.
Forever.
What would he say if.
Felt tears.
On my face.
Not crying but.
Tears.
In my eyes.
Her tears.
In my eyes.
Pain of the.

(*Unendurable.*)

War over.

(*A moment.*)

Dishonorable discharge.

(*A moment.*)

She saw.
Me.
Last one in the world.
Who could. Help.
Sa'dny.
No act. I knew. I knew what she said. I'm smart. Sa'dny. I knew what she said. Help me. Help me. She said—Help. Me.

(*To her—*)

Show me. Show me how.

(*She speaks.*)

"Ana ayaz a'sh."
What?
"Ana ayaz a'shhhhh."
And I thought no. You don't want that. That's not what you want. Your family is gone.
Ana Ayaz A'shhhhhhh. Let me live.
You've been with me. No one will touch you.
Ana Ayaz A'sssssssssh. Let me live.
Even if they don't stone you, you'd always be alone. You don't know what that's like. You don't want that. You've never been. No, it's better this way.

Ana Ayaz A—

—Bang.
I ended it.
Sympathetic reaction.

(*Then—terrible pain.*)

This is it. This is death. Has to be. Can't get worse.

(*Silence. Then—*)

Worse.

(*Then—*)

Won't shout.
Feel it. Feel what she.

(*Silence.*)

Don't shout.
Be him.
For once.
At the end.
No more words.
Won't speak again.
Silence.

(*Silence.*)

(*Against his will—her voice—*)

Ana Ayaz A'sh.
Oh, God.
Let.
Me.

(*Blackout. A breathing out of a spirit into the darkness.*)

NO SUCH COLD THING

Naomi Wallace

Grief melts away
Like snow in May,
As if there were no such cold thing.
—George Herbert

ABOUT THE PLAYWRIGHT

Naomi Wallace's work has been produced in the United Kingdom, Europe, the Middle East, and the United States. Her major plays include *One Flea Spare, In the Heart of America, Slaughter City, The Trestle at Pope Lick Creek, Things of Dry Hours, The Hard Weather Boating Party,* and *The Fever Chart: Three Short Visions of the Middle East.*

Her work has received the Susan Smith Blackburn Prize, the Kesselring Prize, the Fellowship of Southern Writers Drama Award, and an Obie Award. She is also a recipient of the MacArthur "Genius" Fellowship. Her award-winning film *Lawn Dogs* is available on DVD. Her new film, *The War Boys,* cowritten with Bruce McLeod, will be released in 2011.

Wallace is writing new plays for the Public Theatre, Oregon Shakespeare Festival, and Clean Break of London. *One Flea Spare* was recently incorporated into the repertoire of La Comédie-Française.

PRODUCTION HISTORY

No Such Cold Thing was commissioned by the Tricycle Theatre of London in 2008, as part of *The Great Game: Afghanistan.* It received its world premiere at the ReOrient 2009 Festival, produced by Gold Thread Productions and directed by Bella Ramazan-Nia.

Poetry quoted from *Ghazals of Ghalib*, edited by Aijaz Ahmad (New York: Columbia University Press, 1971): "Ghazal 111," translation by W. S. Merwin, p. 77; and *The Rebel's Silhouette*, by Faiz Ahmed Faiz (Salt Lake City: Peregrine Smith Books, 1991): "A Night in the Desert," translation by Agha Shahid Ali, p. 95.

CHARACTERS

Alya, a young Afghan, thirteen years of age
Meena, a young Afghan, fifteen years of age
Sergio, U.S. Army soldier, Chicano, twenties

TIME

Late Autumn, 2001

PLACE

Just outside Sar Asia at the edge of a possible desert, near Kabul, Afghanistan.

(*Lights up on an almost empty stage/desert. Night. Two sandbags, one slightly smaller than the other, lie upstage, some distance apart.* ALYA, *wearing a burka, stands center stage, looking up into the sky.* ALYA *carries a small, hard, old-fashioned suitcase. Suddenly her sister* MEENA *appears.* MEENA *is wearing a headscarf covering her hair, and a long coat, covering her more Western-style dress.* ALYA *is startled to see* MEENA. *They stare at one another for some moments in silence.*)

MEENA: Hedgehog? Is it you, hedgehog? Alya, is it you?

ALYA (*quotes*): "He is the lord of sleep/lord of peace/lord of night."

MEENA (*quotes*): "on whose arm your hair is lying"

(MEENA *claps her hands with joy.*)

You still have a good memory for verse!

ALYA: Ahmed Faiz gets sentimental when it comes to his Lord. Allah doesn't like sentiment. He likes lemons, hard rain, and hedgehogs.

(MEENA *takes a small book of verse from her coat.*)

MEENA: I've still got the book.

(MEENA *holds it out to* ALYA *but she doesn't take it.*)

ALYA: You stole it when you left. That was our one book of verse that Uncle Khan brought back from his studies in Pakistan.

MEENA: What do you care if I took it? You don't like Faiz.

ALYA: But I like to read. Mother taught us from that book.

MEENA: Show me your face.

ALYA: Not here. I'm not supposed to be out of the house.

MEENA: Look at my hair.

(MEENA *pulls her scarf off and shakes her hair free.* ALYA *gasps and looks about her nervously.*)

ALYA: I can see your ankles. They'll kill you.

MEENA: They're on the run. The Americans have sent them running.

ALYA: Not all of them are running.

MEENA: Let me see your ankles.

ALYA (*backing away*): No.

MEENA: Please.

ALYA: It is forbidden.

MEENA: Let me see your hair.

(ALYA *shakes her head "no."*)

All right. But I can see your shape through the cloth. The little hedgehog has become a woman. (*Beat.*) That's your suitcase then? It's not much. I've so many things now I would need six suitcases. But we have to go. The taxi is waiting at the end of the road.

ALYA: We have no one to travel with us. If the Taliban see us traveling alone, they'll beat us.

MEENA: I told you they've left the area. It's all clear.

(MEENA *moves to take* ALYA's *suitcase but* ALYA *won't let it go.*)

ALYA: I can't go to England with you.

MEENA: Don't be silly. Father is waiting for us at the airport. They wouldn't let him pass but he is waiting. The airport is in the hands of the Americans. It's safe.

ALYA: I can't speak English. They'll laugh at me.

MEENA: You're speaking English now.

ALYA: Mother still pulls me out of bed at two A.M. I try to bite her because I am so tired. We do math, geometry, English.

MEENA: If my exams are good I'll go to university. I'm going to write a brilliant essay on Faiz Ahmed Faiz and—

ALYA: the idea of hell and heaven. You already wrote us about that.

MEENA: Oh. (*Beat.*) The taxi won't wait for long. He warned me. Father is anxious.

ALYA: Mother says she'll follow us soon. I don't believe her. She limps. In England they won't like a limp.

MEENA: Don't be stupid, everyone limps in England.

(ALYA *suddenly eyes* MEENA.)

ALYA: You've lost your tarbia.

MEENA: No. I haven't lost my manners.

ALYA: You go without the burka.

MEENA: Father agrees. In England no one cares. I wear the hijab. Sometimes just a scarf.

ALYA: What size bra do you wear now? When you left you only had buds. I see melons now.

MEENA (*delighted*): Not melons. Maybe oranges, yes. But I think yours are bigger and I'm older than you. Can I see them?

ALYA: No. Do you let men touch you?

MEENA: Of course not. But I make a noise when I walk.

(MEENA *opens her coat and walks in a circle, purposely clicking her heels as she walks.* ALYA *is nervous.*)

ALYA: Shhh. Shhhh. Someone will hear you.

(MEENA *just laughs and makes louder clicks as she walks.*)

Remember Fauzia?

MEENA: Fauzia with the black, black hair.

ALYA: Black as oil.

MEENA: I think I'm prettier than she is now.

ALYA: Fauzia was walking with her father to see family. It was two years ago. She had on her best shoes and they made a click, click, click. Not loud but too loud. The Virtue Police heard Fauzia clicking and they shot her.

(ALYA *watches* MEENA *walk. Then* MEENA *stops "clicking."*)

It's true. Now you are prettier than she was.

MEENA: Let's go.

ALYA: We've been alone, Mother and I, and outside, the Taliban. We cannot leave the house. Mother had to stop her teaching; she is forbidden to work. Uncle Khan keeps us alive with scraps from his table. Our cousin Nargis laughed too loud at the market and the police hit her and now she is missing three front teeth and is ugly. Girls are not allowed to go outside at all. I'm forbidden to learn to read and write. There is no one to collect the water. Uncle brings it. And all this. All this and you and Father are far away in England, clicking.

MEENA: The plan was for Father and I to get out first. You know that. We couldn't get back here till now.

ALYA (*calmly*): Pig. I want to slap you.

(MEENA *steps close to* ALYA, *within her reach.*)

MEENA: Then slap me.

(*The two sisters just regard one another.*)

ALYA: Does it rain in England all the time?

MEENA: It rains. But it's not hard rain.

ALYA: Then Allah doesn't like England. Will you take me to buy earrings?

MEENA: Yes.

ALYA: Mother says they have hedgehogs there. But with little ears, not like here with the long ears.

MEENA: You can buy a bird at a shop on the high street and teach it to sit on your finger. You can't do that here.

ALYA: Do the English like their hedgehogs?

MEENA: There is a hedgehog society. You can join.

ALYA: But they'll laugh at me. All the children in the new school will laugh at me.

MEENA: You're just a girl. That's not so funny. No one will laugh.

ALYA: Liar. I'm not just a girl. My back hurts. It hurts so much I can hardly move.

MEENA: What's wrong with your back?

ALYA: Quills. I'm growing quills.

(MEENA *laughs but* ALYA *is serious.*)

Along my spine.

MEENA: Let me see.

(MEENA *grabs at* ALYA *but* ALYA *dodges her.*)

ALYA: No! You might cut yourself. The quills are sharp. I can't go with you.

MEENA: You're just scared. Take my hand.

(MEENA *holds out her hand but* ALYA *doesn't take it.*)

ALYA: Don't tell anyone. It's a secret.

(ALYA *thinks she hears something, whispers.*)

Shhh. Footsteps!

(*Both of the girls listen, alert.*)

MEENA: It's nothing. The streets are clear tonight. We're safe. Alya, I have a secret too.

ALYA: Tell me.

MEENA: I've been held in the arms. Of a man.

(ALYA *slaps her sister's face.* MEENA *touches the sting with her hand.*)

ALYA: You are dirty. You are disrespectful. You shame me. You shame Father.

(MEENA *just stares at her sister.*)

Tell me more.

MEENA: It was night. Dark. I couldn't find my way home. I got lost. Such a big
city. I was tired and he put his arms around me, and carried me.

ALYA (*eager*): Did he squeeze your boobs?

MEENA: Now you are dirty! No. He just carried me and then put me down
again. His hands were warm. He touched my neck.

ALYA: You've been touched by a man not of your family. That's a death sentence for you here. Whore. Whore. I have missed you every hour. I smell
your clothes to remember you. Your bed is quiet and your pencil cold on
the table. (*Beat.*) We'll come back here when we're teachers?

MEENA: Yes. And we'll teach in the daylight. And girls will be allowed to go
to school.

ALYA: And we'll scrape, scrape the paint from the windows.

MEENA: And we'll open our doors, skip out anytime,

ALYA: and we won't need a man to be with us.

MEENA: And we can click and shout as loud as . . .

ALYA: cannons! And we can eat till our bellies are round . . .

MEENA: as buckets!

ALYA: And we'll have radio and singing

MEENA: and so many apples we can fill our mouths

ALYA: till they burst!

(*The girls are enjoying their reunion, but then suddenly they find their composure
again.* ALYA *glances around nervously, fearing their discovery.*)

Shhhh. Okay. I'm ready to go with you, sister. My back hurts and I can't
move but my shoes are strong.

(MEENA *notices now that* ALYA's *shoelace is hanging loose.*)

MEENA: Your shoelace is untied. Let me tie it.

(ALYA *doesn't move for a moment. Then she slowly lifts the hem of her burka to reveal that she is wearing U.S. Army boots, far too big for her.*)

MEENA: Oh my.

ALYA: That's what I said when I found them. But at least they're warm on my
feet.

(*The sisters continue to stare at* ALYA's *shoes. Elsewhere onstage* SERGIO *wakes on a
small bed that has no mattress. He's been sleeping on the springs but he doesn't seem*

to notice. A sandbag is his pillow. The bed is rusty and old. SERGIO *is wearing boxer shorts and is barefoot. He shakes his head and moans, confused.*)

SERGIO: Fuckin' Kubick. Jeez that guy can put 'em away. Put 'em away. Kubick. And Tony, and Mike, and . . . Shit. We were all there at . . . Joe's Place, yeah bunch of drunks and I didn't even drink that much.

(SERGIO's *words roll steady out of him.*)

And I said I'm going to have one of those dogs Yeah I'm going to eat one of those dogs That one Yeah I was hungry and my gut hurt. I'm still hungry and my gut hurts. Mama's gonna make me French toast when she gets up. What time is it? . . .

(SERGIO *rubs his head and eyes.*)

Give me one of those jumbo-sized hot dogs I said last night they all laughed Fuck you I said and your mother and your sister even if she is only ten the hot dogs were turnin' and turnin' the heat lamp burnin' them almost black and then. She was there, alone at the bar.

(*He runs his hands out along what he thinks is a mattress.*)

And she was so pretty and her mouth was . . . Her hair was so . . . Her neck was so . . . What? What? I can't remember. Her hair was . . . Her mouth was . . . And then she was gone.

(*He suddenly feels the metal of the springs. He jumps up.*)

What the . . . fuck—

(*He suddenly looks around him and then under the bed. He finds his pajamas and starts to put them on. He still seems to be missing something.*)

Shit where are they? Where are they? (*Shouts*) Must have been one hell of a night hell of a night at Joe's Place.

(SERGIO *is now dressed in his pajamas. He surveys his bed. He notices something odd about his pillow. He takes a closer look.*)

Kubick, Tony, Mike, and . . .

(SERGIO *discovers that the pillow is a sandbag. He pulls it off the bed and holds it, his arms outstretched. It strains him to hold it like this.*)

Fuck this for a pillow. (*Calls out*) Mama? Mama you up yet?

(*Hearing no answer from his mother,* SERGIO *flings the sandbag away. It lands at the feet of the girls. Now the girls look at the "pillow" that has landed between them. Then they simultaneously see* SERGIO *and he sees them.*)

God damn.

(SERGIO *speaks in a rush of words to the sisters.*)

I wasn't I forgot I didn't I'm sorry but I must have been too drunk but hey it's all right it's all right. (*Beat.*) Two, huh. Two of you? Man I must have been wasted cause I can't remember picking you up. I can't remember bringing no chick home. Chicks home.

MEENA: We are sisters.

SERGIO: Hermanas. Jesus, sisters. (*Laughs.*) Wait till I tell Kubick, Tony, Mike, and—they won't believe it.

(SERGIO *notes* ALYA's *suitcase.*)

Uh. I guess you need a ride home?

ALYA: We have a taxi, thank you.

MEENA: Waiting at the end of the road.

SERGIO: Great. 'Cause I don't got a car.

(SERGIO *looks hard at* MEENA.)

Now you I kinda remember your face.

(*He looks at* ALYA *in her burka.*)

Don't suppose I'd remember yours anyway. But hey, to each his own. To each his own, yeah.

ALYA: The airport is safe now? Meena says it's safe?

SERGIO: Last time I checked. I flew Delta home. Did my mama see you come in last night?

(*The sisters are confused by his question but shake their heads no.*)

Good. Good. I mean my mama she's open minded and she knows I got needs but she just doesn't want me fillin' them in her house. How 'bout you go out the back door?

(ALYA *looks around perplexed.*)

MEENA: We're going to England.

ALYA: We're going to get our diplomas.

SERGIO: Even better, would you mind going out the window? I think the back door's locked.

(*The sisters glance around, uncertain.*)

ALYA: Where is your uniform, soldier?

SERGIO: Mama has it at the dry cleaners. Hey, hope you don't mind but I forgot your names.

MEENA: I am Meena. This is my sister, Alya.

ALYA: Put on your uniform please. We are young women. We don't want to see your feet.

SERGIO: You want me in my uniform? A little kink? I like a little kink. We going to do it again then?

ALYA: Do what again?

(SERGIO *just grins.*)

SERGIO: Sisters, huh? I never did two at a time before. How did I do?

MEENA: Where is your gun?

SERGIO: I mean you came home with me so you must think I'm hot.

ALYA: Where is your helmet?

SERGIO: I mean I kinda hope you think I'm a little bit hot . . .

MEENA: How many Taliban did you kill today?

SERGIO: Hey. Don't get personal.

ALYA: Can you read?

MEENA: Can you write?

SERGIO: What do you think? A year at the U of Indiana but then I joined. Thought they'd make me a pilot. Ha. No fucking luck 'cause they put me on the ground.

MEENA: But you're American.

(SERGIO *now really looks at the sisters for the first time, as though his hangover is clearing.*)

ALYA: We'll be able to work now. We'll be able to read and write

MEENA: and calculate, because of you.

ALYA: But if they see Meena's hair they will kill her.

SERGIO (*to* ALYA): Let me see your face, honey.

(ALYA *steps back.*)

Come on. I seen more than that last night.

(MEENA *steps in front of her sister.*)

MEENA: Pick up your suitcase, sister. We must go now.

(ALYA *emits a sharp scream, and puts her hands to her back. Then she's just as suddenly still.*)

SERGIO (*panicked*): Shush. Shush. Shush. Shush. Shit.

ALYA: My back hurts.

SERGIO: If my mama hears you and comes in here, I am fuckin' toast. Out the window. Both of you. Now.

(*Both sisters look around.*)

MEENA: What window?

SERGIO: The only fuckin' window in my bedroom.

ALYA: There is no window. Do you have quills?

SERGIO: What?

ALYA: Quills.

SERGIO: No, no, no. I don't do the hard stuff. A little dope. Jack on the weekends. But no quills.

ALYA: They're growing on my back.

MEENA: You said it was a secret.

ALYA: He's just an American. He won't tell anyone. Will you?

(SERGIO *is uncertain but shakes his head "no."*)

SERGIO: Nah. Where you girls from?

ALYA: We were born here.

MEENA: Our father was born here. And his father's father.

SERGIO: Huh.

ALYA: Same piece of land.

MEENA: Grapes, mulberries, pomegranates.

SERGIO: Pomegranates? Shit. You grow pomegranates here?

MEENA: Our pomegranates are famous in India and Iran.

SERGIO: Bullshit, chica. Only thing that grows in Gary, Indiana, is unemployment.

ALYA: Who is Gary Indiana?

MEENA (*to* ALYA): I think it's a movie about temples of doom. (*To* SERGIO) Are you married?

SERGIO: No . . .

MEENA: Engaged?

SERGIO: No . . . Now wait just a minute. If you two are trying to trick me it won't work. I use a wrapper. When I hose a girl I wrap up real tight so no babies. No babies from me.

ALYA (*looking at* SERGIO'*s toes*): Oh my. It's a shame to say it but you have ugly toes. Doesn't he, Meena?

MEENA: Well, they're almost as ugly as Uncle Khan's.

(*All three look at* SERGIO'*s feet.*)

SERGIO: Well, I'm sorry about the feet but last night, as you most likely re-member, I lost my boots.

ALYA: I don't think you are a good soldier.

SERGIO: You watch your mouth. I did my service. Got a purple pulling a buddy out under fire.

MEENA: You shouldn't lose your boots. It's bad luck.

SERGIO: Shit.

MEENA: Don't you like being a soldier?

SERGIO: I didn't say that. Army's paying me to finish school. I started last week. I'd lick their ass if they ran out of toilet paper.

ALYA: You have bad tarbia.

MEENA: She means manners. A man without good tarbia won't find a wife.

SERGIO: Great. 'Cause honey I don't want to marry. Certainly neither of you.

ALYA: Then you're still chaste?

SERGIO: Yeah. Chaste as the fuckin' dew.

MEENA: That's my favorite verse in the book, "There's no dew/anywhere, so/strange that there's no dew/anywhere"

ALYA (*quotes*): "not on the forehead/of the cold sun,"

SERGIO: Huh?

ALYA: She's got a thing for Faiz Ahmed Faiz.

SERGIO: Well if he thinks he can move in on my chick, my chicks, without talking to me first, I'll take out his lights.

MEENA (*quotes*): "And the roses of your hands, the—"

ALYA (*quotes*): "the decanter and the glass,/were like the outline/of a dream."

SERGIO (*to* ALYA): Baby, baby.

MEENA (*stomps her foot*): Stop doing that, Alya.

ALYA: What?

SERGIO: I like the way you talk to me.

MEENA: Finishing the lines. I hate it.

(ALYA *sticks her tongue at her sister and continues.*)

Stupid Hedgehog.

ALYA: See, I'm not even in England yet and already they're calling me names.

SERGIO: Who's calling you names?

ALYA (*to* SERGIO): Everyone. Because of my quills. Down my spine, I only have three hundred and twelve of them. But the hedgehog has seven thousand. I have a long way to go. They're ugly but I need them. They're not solid, the quills. Each one is filled with a complex network of chambers, so they're lightweight and strong, so they won't buckle and break.

MEENA (*to* SERGIO): All she knows is quills. (*To* ALYA) You ignorant brat.

(*While the girls face off,* SERGIO *moves around the stage curiously, uncertain now as to his surroundings.*)

ALYA: You shit English girl who leaves her sister and mother behind, with nothing but a fart and a smile.

MEENA: You're right. They won't like you in England. Your mouth is full of dirt.

ALYA: Your head is full of worms.

You left us to rot. Father left us to rot.

MEENA: I'll pull out your hair.

(*The girls raise their fists at each other, ready to fight.*)

ALYA: I'll tell the village you're a whore.

MEENA: I'll tear out your quills!

(*Suddenly* SERGIO *is between them, pushing them apart.*)

SERGIO: Stop it! Both of you. There will be no ass-kicking in my space. You should be ashamed.

(*The sisters quit, but turn their backs to one another.*)

You don't fight family.

(*The sisters remain with their backs to each other, angry.*)

Hey. Hey! You two make up now.

ALYA/MEENA: Never!

SERGIO: Listen you guys. When it's la familia. The family. You never say never.

(SERGIO *takes* ALYA'*s hand. She tries to pull away but he holds on. She calms. Then he takes* MEENA'*s hand.* MEENA *resists less but it's still strange to hold a man's hand.* SERGIO *squashes the sisters' hands together.*)

Because when there's no one else there anymore. Not even a sound. Nothing. Nada . . .

(*For a short moment all three of them are holding hands but then* SERGIO *quickly lets go, uncomfortable.*)

Okay, you two are good again? Right.

(MEENA *and* ALYA *glance furtively at each other and nod.*)

So as Rafael Nadal the king of clay would say: Vamos. As Sergio Vasquez, that's me, would say as nicely as possible: Please, Get. The. Hell. Out. Of. My. House. Now.
ALYA: We're not in your house. How dare you suggest it?
    This is a desert.
SERGIO: Well, yeah, there's not much here sure, but who needs more than a
    bed, right?
ALYA: Let's go, Meena. I don't like his mouth.

(ALYA *turns to leave.* MEENA *is reluctant.*)

MEENA: But Alya, we must have compassion for his bad tarbia.
SERGIO: Just get going now and haul ass out my window.

(SERGIO *looks around but can no longer see his window.*)

Hey. Where's my window?
ALYA: In our home we had to paint the windows because it's forbidden for
    men to look inside the house and see us.
SERGIO: It was right here.

(SERGIO *is disorientated.*)

MEENA: This is the desert. We are in the desert.
ALYA: Bye-bye, soldier.
SERGIO: I could see the oak tree from my bed.
MEENA: There are no trees here.
SERGIO: Hey, where the hell am I?
ALYA: I don't think I like you. Do you like him, Meena?
MEENA: Only a little. Maybe. But I'm glad we won't have to look at his toes
    anymore.
ALYA: Let's go then. But Meena, my other shoelace is untied. Help me.

(MEENA *bends down to tie* ALYA'S *other shoelace.* ALYA *lifts the hem of her burka.* SERGIO *sees his boots.*)

SERGIO: Hey. Those are my boots!

MEENA: Don't be stupid.

SERGIO: I been lookin' for them all over.

ALYA: Finders keepers.

SERGIO: That's U.S. Army property.

ALYA: Not anymore.

SERGIO: Where did you get them?

MEENA (*finishes tying*): Good-bye, soldier.

ALYA (*chants to* SERGIO): Watch your back. Watch your back.
    Taliban, Taliban might come back!

(MEENA *makes a "whooo" scary sound, then* ALYA *continues chanting at* SERGIO, *taunting him.*)

    Taliban, Taliban, Taliban
    Come to chew you
    Come to swallow you

(*The sisters laugh and chant together, staggering the song, as though this song were their childhood "row, row, row the boat," but far darker.*)

MEENA/ALYA: Taliban, Taliban, Taliban
    Will take your eyes
    And make apple pies.

(ALYA *and* MEENA *move to leave.* SERGIO *purposely steps on the hem of* ALYA'S *burka to stop her.* ALYA *can't walk further. She strains against the cloth to walk forward but can't.* SERGIO *picks up the hem and slowly pulls the burka off of* ALYA. *When* ALYA *is revealed, it is as though she is waking from a dream.* ALYA *is dressed in slacks and a long-sleeved shirt. She looks down at her "nakedness" and as she kneels she cries out in fright, as though she is falling.* MEENA *rushes to her side but it's as though* ALYA *can't see her.*)

MEENA: Alya? What is it? Alya?

(*Now* ALYA *begins to chant again, as though to comfort herself.*)

ALYA (*whispers*): Will come to chew you
    Come to swallow you.

MEENA: Alya!

ALYA (*chants*): Will take your eyes
  and make apple pies.

SERGIO: Don't ever separate a man from his boots.

(SERGIO *moves to pull the boots off* ALYA's *feet but* MEENA *gets there first and takes the boots.* ALYA *does not resist.* MEENA *clutches the boots to her chest defiantly.* SERGIO *moves towards her, she evades him.*)

MEENA/ALYA (*chant*): They'll slip into your home
  and eat you to the bone

SERGIO: Come on, honey. Don't tease me.

MEENA/ALYA (*chant*): They'll slip into your bed
  and hump you till you're.

(ALYA *finishes the chant by herself, now alert to her surroundings.*)

ALYA: Dead. Dead. (*Beat.*) Dead.

(MEENA *turns and starts to walk away.* SERGIO *no longer acts like he's in pajamas but in a battle zone. He flips the bed on its side so it's a barrier he's standing behind. He starts out speaking calmly but then gets more frenzied.*)

SERGIO: Stay where you are. All of you. Hey. Get back in line. That's right. Get back in line. Hey. Stop right there, kid. Hey. I mean you.

(SERGIO *has no gun but he seems to be holding something in his arms, perhaps the memory of a gun. All the while he shouts at* MEENA, *she keeps slowly walking away.*)

  Stop. I'm warning you. I'm warning you! You stop. You stop! Hey. Fucking stop or I shoot!

(MEENA *now stops walking and stands very still for some moments. As though she were suspended. Then* MEENA *turns around and looks first at* SERGIO, *then at her sister. The boots fall from her arms.*)

ALYA: Soldier, soldier.

(SERGIO *comes out of his "state," and looks himself over.*)

SERGIO: I don't have a gun.

ALYA: But you did today.

MEENA (*to* ALYA): Where, Alya?

ALYA: In the yard.

MEENA: Where on my body do you think he shot me?

ALYA: In your neck.

SERGIO: No, no, no.

(SERGIO *violently kicks the bed out of the way.*)

I fucked you I didn't shoot you. Right here in my bedroom.

(*The sisters ignore* SERGIO.)

MEENA: I don't believe you, Alya.

ALYA: Okay.

SERGIO: Well you better believe me.

MEENA: This is one of your stupid tricks. Isn't it, hedgehog?

SERGIO: Yeah. This is one of her stupid tricks. I got drunk last night. In my hometown bar. In Gary. In Indiana. With Kubick, Tony, Mike, and. With Kubick, Tony, Mike, and . . . (*Shouts*) Mama? Wake up. Come in here.

ALYA (*to* SERGIO, *calmly*): Meena was running in the yard. Everyone was standing in line. You told us to stand in line.

SERGIO: Be quiet. (*Calls*) Mama!

ALYA: There were twenty of you, maybe thirty. We raised our arms. My mother, my father.

SERGIO (*calls*): Hey!

ALYA: My father's arms were trembling and he was ashamed so he raised his arms higher. And you were in command.

SERGIO: You're out of your mind.

ALYA: You said

SERGIO (*in Dari*): Raise your arms. Don't move.

ALYA (*translating*): Raise your arms. All of you. Don't move.

(MEENA *raises her arms in the air.*)

SERGIO (*in Dari*): And keep them up or we'll shoot.

ALYA (*translating*): And keep them up or we'll shoot.

(ALYA *looks at* MEENA *as she speaks.*)

Meena broke out of the line and ran.

SERGIO: I told her to stop.

ALYA: She didn't stop.

SERGIO: I was scared.

ALYA: She was scared.

SERGIO (*to himself*): Fuck.

(*While the sisters continue to speak,* SERGIO *very softly talks to himself and to his mother in Spanish as he sits on the bed, gets up, sits again, trying to force himself into another reality, trying to make himself believe he is at home.*)

MEENA: I was afraid. Because . . .

(MEENA *slowly lowers her arms, trying to remember.*)

ALYA: You were afraid because I broke out of the line. I ran so fast the soldiers couldn't stop me. I ran round the back of the house.

MEENA: You ran round the back of the house?

ALYA: I could not breathe. (*Beat.*) I cannot breathe. Father tells us not to move. Mother is shushing us. All of us in line. The whole village. You grip my hand so tight, so tight and tell me to be still. You hum my favorite song to keep me quiet.

(ALYA *hums the song* MEENA *hummed to her.*)

That's how it goes. But your throat is dry with fear and the tune will not come out. So I pull. I pull and pull 'til my hand comes out from your hand. And then I run. I run so fast you almost can't see me. But I trip and fall, down the well. And as I fall I grow quills so quick because while hedgehogs are skilled climbers, they are not good at getting down. When they come across a drop they roll into a ball and just. Drop. The quills cushion the fall. To keep the quills from being damaged, the thin stem just above the skin flexes on impact. Wild hedgehogs have been seen to drop twenty feet with no apparent signs of injury. (*Beat.*) Down the well I fall and when I hit the bottom, because I don't have enough quills, my back breaks. Crack. I cannot move. I lie on my back in three inches of water.

MEENA (*remembering*): You ran first. Yes. I was afraid for you so I ran after you. Didn't I?

(ALYA *doesn't answer.*)

MEENA (*shouts*): Didn't I?

ALYA: Yes.

MEENA: So it's your fault I got shot.

ALYA: I had to run. I couldn't stand still.

MEENA (*angry*): It's your fault. It's your fault! You let my hand go.

ALYA: From where I lay on my back in the well I could see a round circle of sky above me. (*To* SERGIO) And then I heard you fire. And then I heard my sister—

SERGIO (*interrupts, to* ALYA): I gave her warning. I had to stop her. I gave her half a dozen warnings. But she kept on running. She dropped so fast to the ground. I couldn't believe how fast she dropped. I knelt beside her. I picked her up and carried her into the shade.

MEENA: You carried me?

SERGIO: Yes.

MEENA: How?

SERGIO: How? What the hell does it matter?

MEENA: It matters to me. It matters to me!

(SERGIO *looks around, locates a sandbag, and picks it up in his arms. He adjusts his arms to hold the sandbag better.*)

You held me in your arms like that?

SERGIO: Yeah.

ALYA: He touched your neck.

MEENA (*to* SERGIO): You touched my neck?

SERGIO: I tried to stop the bleeding but

ALYA: there was too much of it.

SERGIO: There was too much of it. I'd never shot someone before. Your neck was so small and. So small and. My bullet was in there. My bullet was in there, inside, and I couldn't get it out. I couldn't get it out. Your skin. Your skin was so—

ALYA (*interrupts*): Don't you shame my sister!

SERGIO: Your mouth was so—

ALYA (*interrupts*): Don't you talk about Meena like that.

MEENA: Let him speak.

SERGIO: Your hair lay across my arm, black and—

ALYA: Shut your mouth!

MEENA: Alya, please!

SERGIO: Your hair lay across my arm, black and . . .

MEENA: My hair was black and what? What, soldier?

(SERGIO *now turns away and will not answer.*)

My mouth was what? Speak! My skin was what?

(SERGIO *can no longer remember. For a moment he just looks at* MEENA.)

SERGIO: You were alive when I carried you.

(SERGIO *and* MEENA *regard one another.*)

MEENA: I was alive? (*To* ALYA.) He says I was alive, Alya, so I didn't die. I didn't die!

ALYA: You are alive, Meena. Right now. For a few more minutes. And I am alive for this same time. And the soldier too. For a few more minutes.

SERGIO: Hey. Hey. This is your shit, don't bring me into it. I got out. I got out.

ALYA: Yes. You and your buddies get out. You get out fast because the Taliban have circled back and Kubick, Tony, and Mike are with you and you're gunning the truck and spinning away from our village and then BANG, guess what?

SERGIO: Guess what? Guess fucking what? I'm going back to bed. I ate a hot dog long as my leg last night.

ALYA: Indigestion.

SERGIO: Like you wouldn't believe.

ALYA (*loud*): Bang!

SERGIO: I'm going back to sleep.

ALYA (*louder*): Bang!

SERGIO: I was out drinking last night. With Kubick, Tony, Mike, and. Kubick, Tony, Mike, and.

ALYA: You. Kubick, Tony, Mike, and you. Hit a land mine. Your friends are unharmed but you fly up in the air, high, high and your boots fly off your feet, one with a foot still attached and Uncle sees your boots lying a hundred feet from your body. He throws your boots in the well to hide them. He is afraid the village will be blamed. He doesn't even know I'm down there.

SERGIO (*threatening*): You are a dirty girl.

ALYA: Yes. At this very moment I am covered in dirt and slime at the bottom of a well and I'm dying. And my sister Meena is in the yard and she is also dying. And you are lying on the road and Kubick, Tony, and Mike are leaning over you and you are dying.

SERGIO (*fiercely*): No. No way. I'm in bed.

ALYA (*shrugs*): I think we got caught in each other's . . .

SERGIO (*interrupts*): I'm in bed and my mother's making French toast in the kitchen and I can smell it burnin' at the edges, just the way I like it.

(ALYA *starts to laugh. She laughs and laughs. Then she points to the largest sandbag.*)

And I'm in my pajamas. I'm in my pajamas. (*Shouts*) I'm in my fucking pajamas and I'm home. In Gary, Indiana. I made it home!

(*Now they are all silent some moments.* ALYA *just stares at* SERGIO *till he looks away. Now he knows he didn't make it home.*)

MEENA (*quietly*): Alya, I'm sorry to say this but you are a liar. I went to England. I studied Faiz Ahmed Faiz.

ALYA: You didn't go to England. We can't even speak English.

MEENA: But we are speaking English.

ALYA: Yes. Father and Mother would be impressed.

MEENA: Father is waiting at the airport. We've come back to get you. We're going to university!

ALYA: We've never left our village.

MEENA: But the taxi is waiting.

ALYA: There is no taxi.

(*The sisters regard one another some moments.*)

MEENA: If we were dying, I would remember. I don't remember.

ALYA: But you do. You just don't want to. (*Beat.*) What is real is that we are usually hungry. We are usually afraid. We are usually more hungry than afraid for years now. And we don't grow pomegranates anymore. Father sells scraps. Me and you, we can't leave the house so we dream of apples. Of clean water. Of the sweetness of meat and rice.

MEENA: No.

ALYA: We dream of electricity, of our fingers moving on pages, of baskets full for picnics.

MEENA: No.

ALYA: We dream of escaping the Taliban, of going to England,

MEENA: No.

ALYA: of you and Father leaving first, of your coming back to get us.

MEENA: No! It's that simple: to you, Alya, I say no. (*Beat.*) Where is my body?

(ALYA *hesitates.*)

Where is my body?

(ALYA *points to the medium sandbag.*)

That's me?

(ALYA *nods "yes."* MEENA *stands over the bag, looking at it for some moments. Then suddenly she kicks it.*)

Get up.

(*She kicks it again.*)

Get up!

(*She kicks it again and again.*)

Get up, girl! You will live. You will be a teacher. Do you hear me? You are free now. You will travel. Get up! You will write a brilliant paper on Faiz Ahmed Faiz. Get up! You will kiss a man. Get up. Get up! You will live! You will live!

(MEENA *kicks the bag till she's worn out, then she quits. The three of them are silent some moments.*)

ALYA: It's not your fault, Meena.

MEENA: Why did you let my hand go? I held on to you so tight, so tight I was afraid I'd break your bones.

ALYA: But I pulled and pulled and finally we came apart.

(ALYA *looks at her own hand.*)

You used to draw the alphabet on my palm under the table when we sat with the elders. (*Beat.*) I'm sorry, Meena.

(*The sisters are silent some moments.*)

MEENA: It's all right now, hedgehog. Listen. My throat's no longer dry.

(MEENA *now hums the song that* ALYA *hummed earlier. Now* MEENA *hums it clear and strong.* ALYA *listens with delight. Then the two of them hum the song together. When it's over they just stare at each other.*)

SERGIO: How much more time do we got?

ALYA (*calmly*): Just a few seconds, I think. I'm going now. I'm the first to go.

(ALYA *approaches her sister, takes* MEENA'S *hand, and kisses it.*)

Meena.

(*Then* ALYA *releases* MEENA'S *hand and takes a sandbag by its corner.* ALYA *begins to drag the sandbag behind her as she exits. But then she stops and looks at the bag, and speaks matter-of-factly.*)

Oh. This isn't mine. I'm the small one.

(ALYA *now takes hold of the smallest sandbag and drags it away. She glances back once, just for a moment, at* MEENA, *then disappears offstage.* MEENA *and* SERGIO *watch her leave in silence. Then* MEENA *realizes her sister is truly gone. She calls for her.*)

MEENA: Alya? Alya!?

(MEENA *listens for a reply. No reply comes.*)

SERGIO: Well, I guess I'm next. Damn it's cold.

(SERGIO *starts to drag his sandbag back to his bed.* MEENA *is still watching the place where her sister disappeared. She hears the sound of* SERGIO's *sandbag dragging and now regards him.*)

MEENA: Soldier.
SERGIO: Yeah?
MEENA: Wherever Joe's place is, you shouldn't have left it.

(SERGIO *just looks at* MEENA.)

MEENA: Soldier.
SERGIO: Yeah?
MEENA: If you were not dying, I would wish you dead. (*Beat.*) Are you sorry?
SERGIO (*sincerely*): I wish I had the time to be.

(SERGIO *drags the sandbag.*)

MEENA: Soldier.

(SERGIO *stands still.*)

SERGIO: Yeah?

(*The following is hard for* MEENA *to ask but she makes herself ask it.*)

MEENA: Am I pretty? (*Beat.*) Were we pretty? My sister and I.
SERGIO: You were just kids.
MEENA: But if we had grown up?

(SERGIO *studies* MEENA *some moments, trying to figure out what she wants.* MEENA *straightens her shirt, shifts her hair. Then they stare at one another.*)

SERGIO: Well, I wouldn't have kicked you out of bed, that's for sure.
MEENA: Bastard. (*Beat.*) Thank you.

(SERGIO *nods to* MEENA, *then lays the sandbag on his bed as a pillow and lies down on it and closes his eyes. He is shivering badly.* MEENA *watches him shiver. Then she picks up the burka and nears* SERGIO. *She looks down at* SERGIO. *Then she slowly pulls the burka over* SERGIO, *completely covering him like a shroud.* SERGIO *stops shivering and is still.* MEENA *returns to "her" sandbag. She nudges it gently with her foot. No sign of life.* MEENA *looks around her, sees the suitcase. Calmly, surely, she picks the suitcase up, feeling that it fits well in her hand. Then she stands on the sandbag, holding the suitcase to her chest, readying herself for her journey. She closes her eyes. She hums clearly, strongly the lines of the song she hummed earlier. Then suddenly* MEENA *opens her eyes, no longer humming but looking straight out over the public. Blackout.*)

A CANOPY OF STARS

Simon Stephens

ABOUT THE PLAYWRIGHT

Simon Stephens's plays include *Bluebird* (1998, Royal Court); *Herons* (2001, Royal Court); *Port* (2002, Royal Exchange); *One Minute* (2003, ATC/Sheffield Theatres/Bush Theatre); *Christmas* (2003, APE/Bush Theatre); *Country Music* (2004, Royal Court); *On the Shore of the Wide World* (2005, Royal Exchange/National Theatre); *Motortown* (2006, Royal Court); *Pornography* (2007, Deutsche Schauspielhaus, Hamburg); *Harper Regan* (2008, National Theatre); *Sea Wall* (2008, Bush Theatre); and *Punk Rock* (2009, Lyric Theatre and Manchester Royal Exchange). Additional productions include *Marine Parade* (written with Mark Eitzel) at the Brighton Festival 2010; *The Trial of Ubu* at the Toneelgroep Amsterdam and Schauspielhaus Essen 2010; and with Robert Holman and David Eldridge, *A Thousand Stars Explode in the Sky* at the Lyric Theatre, 2010. Several of his plays have been performed throughout Europe, the United States, Asia, and Australia.

He was awarded the Pearson Award for Best Play for 2002, for *Port. On the Shore of the Wide World* won Best New Play for 2005 at the Manchester Evening News Awards and the Olivier Award for Best New Play in 2006 and joint–Best International Play in Theater Heute, Germany, in 2006. *Motortown* won Best International Play in Theater Heute in 2007. *Pornography* was invited to the Berlin Theater Treffen in 2008, as one of the best productions in the German-speaking world in that year. It also won Best International Play in Theater Heute in 2008, making Stephens an unprecedented three-time winner. *Pornography* was voted Best Play in the 2008 Critics' Awards for Theatre in Scotland. *Punk Rock* won Best Play for 2009 at the Manchester Evening News Awards. His plays are published by Methuen.

Stephens was the Arts Council Resident Dramatist at the Royal Court, London, in 2000. He was the Writers' Tutor at the Young Writers' Programme between 2001 and 2005 where his students included Lucy Prebble, Laura Wade, Chloe Moss, Mike Bartlett, Leo Butler, and many other writers who went on to considerable professional success. He was the Resident Dramatist at the National Theatre in 2006 and since 2009 has been Artistic Associate at the Lyric, Hammersmith.

PRODUCTION HISTORY

A Canopy of Stars was first produced by the Tricycle Theatre, London, on April 19, 2009. It was directed by Nicolas Kent with the following cast:

Sergeant Jay Watkins, 31 . . . . Tom McKay
Richard Kenfall, 20 . . . . Hugh Skinner
Cutty . . . . Rick Warden
Murray . . . . Danny Rahim
Lloyd . . . . Daniel Betts
Medic . . . . Jemma Redgrave
Cheryl, 27 . . . . Jemima Rooper

CHARACTERS

Jay Watkins, 31
Richard Kendall, 20
Cutty
Lloyd
Murray
Voice on Radio
Cheryl Watkins, 27

SETTING

The play takes place in the present.
Act 1 is set in an underground mud and wattle bunker on the peripheries of the Kajaki dam.
Act 2 is set within the walls of Mazdurak.
Act 3 is set in the front room of a house in Levenshulme, south Manchester.

I.

(*Sergeant* JAY WATKINS, *31, infantry soldier of Helmand, Afghanistan, and Private* RICHARD KENDALL, *20, share a room in a belowground mud-and-wattle-walled bunker on the peripheries of the Kajaki dam.* RICHARD *is on watch. He glances very occasionally through infrared glasses that look out of a hole in the upper rear of the bunker.*)

(*It's 4:20 A.M.*)

(*They speak quietly. There is the sound of a generator throughout quietly but present.* RICHARD *looks through the glasses.* JAY *watches him watch.*)

JAY: I like them.

(RICHARD *looks at him briefly, says nothing.*)

> The terry.
> The flies.
> The shits.

(RICHARD *goes back to his watch.*)

> I respect them.

(*There is some time.*)

> I'd shoot every last one of them in the mouth as soon as look at 'em, mind you.

(JAY *smiles to himself.* RICHARD *continues to watch. Says nothing.*)

> But you can't knock 'em.

(RICHARD *looks at him. Half smiles. Looks away.*)

(*A pause.* JAY *thinks.*)

> I don't think my two positions are mutually exclusive, by the way.

(*There is some time.*)

> How long they been here?

(RICHARD *thinks. Before he has time to answer,* JAY *continues.*)

(*There is some time.*)

We'll never beat 'em.
Fucking impossible.

(RICHARD *looks at him. Says nothing. Looks away again to watch.*)

These hills.
All that good brown.
Can't stop 'em shifting it. Watch 'em go by, fucking convoys of it and there's nowt we can do. Burn the fuck out of it and it only sends the fucking price up, yeah? Yes, Kendall?
RICHARD: Yes, searge.
JAY: All that money.
Be buying Man City next. No bother getting Kaka then, eh?
Making money from selling smack down Cheetham Hill and hold a gun against his head until he signs the fucking contract.

(RICHARD *half smiles at this idea.*)

Just you watch.

(*Some time.*)

You know what this is, don't you?
RICHARD: What's that, searge?
JAY: This is the new Northern Ireland, Kendall. We'll be here for fucking years and years.

(*Some time.*)

You mark my words.

(RICHARD *looks again through the glasses.*)

Nothing?

(RICHARD *looks back. Shakes his head.*)

(*And now there is a longer time.*)

Best get set then, lad.

(RICHARD *looks at him. He comes down from his watch. Checks his pack. His rifle.*
JAY *remains rather relaxed looking.*)

They know it's the end of our tour and all.

(RICHARD *continues to prepare.*)

And they properly loved the blue on blue. Believe you me. Fucking lapped it up.

(RICHARD *continues to prepare. Says nothing. He checks his watch.*)

How long?

RICHARD: Fifteen minutes.

JAY: Do you mind me doing this?

RICHARD: Searge?

JAY: Talking like this to you.

RICHARD: No, searge.

JAY: It's one of the things I do. You'll get used to it. People do.

RICHARD: Yes, searge.

(JAY *nods.* RICHARD *returns to his pack. He starts dismantling and cleaning his rifle.* JAY *gestures out of the small exit of the bunker.*)

JAY: See, fuckhead. He's one hell of a shot.

(RICHARD *looks. Pauses in his cleaning. Thinks.*)

RICHARD: With Private Higgins, sir?

JAY: Peeyowng! Bullseye. Yer gotta hand it to the boy, Kendall, eh?

(RICHARD *isn't sure how to respond to this.*)

RICHARD: I'm sorry about Higgins, sir. The other lads told me he was a good man.

JAY: Oh fuck, yes. Goes without saying. He did your job for the last three tours, Kendall. On the lookout. Listening to me gabbing on.

RICHARD: I heard he was a good soldier.

JAY: Bit of a whining fuck.

(RICHARD *doesn't know what to say.*)

His shit never stank, eh?

(RICHARD *looks away. Returns to cleaning his rifle.*)

(*Some time.*)

Bet they don't need life insurance. Bet they're not getting emails from the Prudential.

(JAY *fixes on* RICHARD *cleaning his rifle for a while.*)

Your second innit?

RICHARD: Yes, sir.

JAY: It gets better.

Last time I was back home I was properly, what?

(RICHARD *looks up at him, he chooses his word with care.*)

RICHARD: Bored, searge?

(JAY *clocks him for a beat.*)

JAY: Yes. Properly fucking bored. All them lot.

Our Mam gave us a bit of a party. I says to her "Mam. Don't." All me mates. Our kid. Rabbiting on. Cheryl. Billy. Fucking giving it.

He's six. Billy. Very, what, mouthy?

(RICHARD *smiles at him.*)

Oldham in't yer?

(RICHARD *nods, working again on the rifle, which, cleaned, he now begins to reassemble.*)

Bet Oldham's a bit quiet after a night out in downtown Musa Khel, eh?

(RICHARD *finishes his reassembly and then looks at* JAY.)

RICHARD: It can be.

JAY: Full of wogs?

(RICHARD *smiles.*)

You get a kind of instinct for it, don't yer? Your hand reaches for your AK 47.

Stick an onion bhaji on this one, you fuck.

(JAY *enjoys the joke for a beat.*)

Do you miss it?

RICHARD: What's that, searge?

JAY: Fucking Oldham, you dense get.

RICHARD: Sometimes.

JAY: Do you?

RICHARD: Yeah, I do.

JAY: Well that's us fucked then.

RICHARD: How come?

JAY: If the calibre of infantry we've got sitting up at the front is the calibre of soldier that misses Oldham, then what hope have we got against these hard-assed mother fuckers?

(RICHARD *smiles at the joke.*)

What do you miss about it?

RICHARD: You what?

JAY: If you could bring one thing, one bit of Oldham out here, what would you bring?

(RICHARD *thinks.*)

RICHARD: My bird.

JAY: Yeah?

(RICHARD *thinks a bit more.* JAY *approaches his own kit and rifle and effortlessly, with the kind of expert proficiency that means he can appear more carefree, gets himself ready for his tour.*)

RICHARD: There's a chippy at the bottom of our street that I quite like.

JAY: Fuck yes.

RICHARD: Chips and gravy.

JAY: Ha!

RICHARD: If I have one more ready-made beef stew, I'll take my bayonet and smash it up Dexter's arse.

(RICHARD *waits for* JAY's *response. It takes a beat and then* JAY *breaks into a broad grin.* RICHARD *laughs with relief.*)

JAY: How old is she?

RICHARD: Who?

JAY: Your bird?

RICHARD: 19.

JAY: What, blind is she?

Special needs. Bit of a spacca.

(RICHARD *smiles, ignores the tease.* JAY *is ready.*)

What's she called?

RICHARD: Gillian.

JAY: Gillian?

RICHARD: Yeah.

JAY: Sounds like a right slapper.

(RICHARD *laughs. Takes the joke.* RICHARD *is ready.*)

How's it going for you, Kendall?

RICHARD: What, searge?

JAY: Tour 2. Of a series of eight thousand and fifty, I promise you.

(RICHARD *goes to answer then changes his mind. Some time.*)

RICHARD: You know.

JAY: No. That's why I'm asking you.

RICHARD: It's easier than the first.

JAY: Up Helmand, weren't you? 2nd Division?

RICHARD: Yes, searge.

JAY: Captain Winslow.

RICHARD: That's right, searge.

JAY: Was he as much as a fuck as Dexter?

(RICHARD *smiles.*)

RICHARD: It wasn't what I was expecting at all. One bit.

(*Some time.*)

When I was a kid I used to have these little toy soldiers. Second World War soldiers. First World War some of them. They had bayonets and all. There were nothing different between them and us.

JAY: They probably had better helmets.

RICHARD: It took me by surprise a bit.

JAY: Yeah. (*Beat.*) I quite like that about it.

RICHARD: I'm not saying I don't.

JAY: It's quite old-fashioned. Screw the bayonet on. Here y'are, Osama, yer fuck. Get this under your rib cage. Twist.

(*Some time.*)

How much you on this tour round?

RICHARD: £1050 a month. After tax.

JAY: Thirteen grand a year?
RICHARD: Yeah.

(JAY *examines* RICHARD. RICHARD *is aware of being examined. He plucks up the courage to say something.*)

I've got a mate working security in the Trafford Centre gets paid five grand a year more than me. He doesn't have this kit, either. Last time I was at home I went out with him and a couple of his pals. You should have seen the looks on their faces. They asked me if I'd met Saddam Hussein. Straight up. They haven't got a clue, you know?

(JAY *smiles.* RICHARD *looks at his watch.*)

JAY: What time is it?
RICHARD: Twenty to five.
JAY: Ten minutes. Did Dexter tell you lot where we're going tonight?
RICHARD: No details, sir.
JAY: No. Safer, eh?
RICHARD: Yes, sir.

(*A silence. Both men are waiting now to move.*)

JAY: There's a village half a fifty miles north northeast of Ghereshk called Mazdurak. It's deserted as far as we've known but is now considered a possible insurgent base. It's been unconfirmed for two weeks. We get in. We check it. We clear it. We get backup with air strike if we need it. We claim it. We get out.
   Yes?
RICHARD: Yes, searge.
JAY: They all ready?
RICHARD: Sorry, searge?
JAY: Everybody ready for that, do you think? We up to the scratch of 2nd Division? In your opinion?
RICHARD: I reckon, sir.
JAY: How are they all keeping up do you think, Kendall? From your perspective?

(RICHARD *looks at* JAY *before he confesses something.*)

RICHARD: I think well, sir. I think some of them are keen to get back to base, sir.

JAY: That makes sense.

RICHARD: I just want a shower, me.

JAY: Fuck, well, yes. Fair dos.

(*A short time.*)

RICHARD: I didn't think we'd get 9 T-4s, sir. In one regiment. That took me by surprise.

JAY: Was Cracknall your first of our lot?

RICHARD: What?

JAY: Danny Cracknall, was he your first T-4 from our troop?

(RICHARD *looks away before he answers.*)

RICHARD: Yes, searge.

(*Some time.*)

I was a bit surprised that his helmet came off.

JAY: Yes.

RICHARD: That his legs were bare, he'd lost his fucking trousers, searge.

(JAY *laughs a touch at this idea.*)

The bruises on his chest, by the way. Blue.

JAY: That's his ribs broken.

(RICHARD *nods.*)

RICHARD: They're closing in, aren't they? On the dam?

JAY: Seems it.

RICHARD: Think we'll stop 'em? Push the FLET back?

JAY: Maybe.

RICHARD: Think it'll make any difference?

(JAY *thinks.*)

JAY: If we keep it safe, it will. If they can get the fucker working, it'll sort out the lecky for the whole of the fucking south. You'll see their funny little faces light up then, believe you me. They'll be sending their daughters over to us for a bit of a thank you chomp.

(RICHARD *smiles.*)

(*Some time.*)

I'm going on a lilo.

RICHARD: Sorry, searge?

JAY: Clarkey's got a lilo. I'm gonna borrow it when we get back. Go and have a bob about on the dam.

Catch a few rays. I'll lend you a go after I'm done.

(*They smile at this idea.*)

RICHARD: Reckon we'll gab to 'em, searge?

(JAY *looks at him.*)

JAY: Who?

RICHARD: Taliban.

(JAY *looks away. Broods for a second or two.*)

JAY: We better hadn't.

RICHARD: That's what they're saying though, innit?

JAY: I'm not going to any road. No matter what Dexter says. They can all be sitting round having a fucking blather. A fucking Shura. I'll still be killing the twats. I'll charge their meetings. Fucking Rambo style.

(RICHARD *smiles.*)

Get this down your throat, yer lollipop raghead.

(*Pause.*)

It'd break my heart.

(*Pause.* RICHARD *looks at him.*)

If we can gab to 'em, then what are we shooting them for? Yer ever think on that?

(RICHARD *thinks.*)

RICHARD: I'm fighting for my mates. I don't really care much about the, what? The queen? No. The Government? No. I'm fighting to stop that lot from killing our lot.

JAY: That's not enough.

RICHARD: You what?

JAY: It's not. That's, forgive me for saying this and everything, Kendall, lad, but that is one of the stupidest things I've heard in my whole life, lad.

If the only reason you're killing them is because they're killing us lot then, then fucking hell, Kendall, let's just all join hands and stand in a big circle and go one, two, three stop and we can all fucking stop, yeah?

You want to know what I'm here for? I'm here 'cause I want to take the face of every single last Taliban and grind it into the rock of the desert.

(RICHARD *looks at him.*)

RICHARD: All of 'em, searge?

(JAY *glares at* RICHARD *for doubting him.*)

JAY: Some of the things that they do! They'll fucking breaking yer hands if yer trying to fucking, to read. They'll take a schoolteacher. They'll skin the fucker alive. They'll hang him on a telegraph pole. They'll set fire to his school.

As long as there's that then, no, I don't think we can just say "no ok tery here yer go. Fair play to yer son."

What they do is wrong. What they did is wrong. I am gonna draw a line.

(RICHARD *watches him some more.*)

Give the dumb arsed ragheads a vote. Bob 'em t'internet. Bit of YOUPORN'd sort them cunts out good and proper. Bit of Jenna Jameson. Nice bit of smack. Sun's out. Have a bit of a swim. Everybody's happy. That's what I'm fucking here for.

(RICHARD *smiles.*)

I am a little unusual in that respect I have to confess. Have you ever heard of moral relativism?
RICHARD: No, searge.
JAY: It's the new rock and roll. I'm getting it printed on my helmet.

(RICHARD *looks away. There is some time.*)

Three minutes.
RICHARD: Yes, searge.
JAY: Remembered your lines, Kendall?
RICHARD: Oh, yes.
JAY: Best get into fucking character, eh?

(*Some time.*)

RICHARD: I like this bit.

JAY: Yeah?

RICHARD: You can taste it. I always get.

JAY: What?

RICHARD: Very nervous.

JAY: My heartbeat goes like a fucking drum.

RICHARD: Yeah?

(JAY *looks at* RICHARD. *Nods.*)

JAY: Best give 'em the beginner's call, Kendall.

RICHARD: Yes, sir.

JAY: Two minutes to the stage.

(*The two men look at one another. There is a brief time.*)

II.

(The stage is suddenly completely dark. It must be pitch black. There is very sudden, very loud machine gun fire. There are men's voices from the darkness. They should be almost indistinguishable from one another. Maybe there are one or two red torch lights but extreme darkness and extreme and sudden noise should dominate the stage. One of the men's voices is JAY's. *One is* RICHARD's.)

CUTTY: Air strike in thirty seconds.
LLOYD: Fire
JAY: Go five zero.
RICHARD: Firing

(A louder machine gun blast from closer proximity.)

JAY: Keep down.
    Keep down.
LLOYD: Remainder, let's go.
MURRAY: Clear the alleyway.
RICHARD: Clear the fucking alleyway.
MURRAY: Get out of the fucking alleyway.
JAY: Come on.
RICHARD: Grenade
JAY: Just get the gun in there yeah?

(A grenade blast is incredibly loud and incredibly close by. It should be deafening and sudden.)

JAY: Cutty, what's going on with the air?
RICHARD: Grenade

(There's another immensely loud, immensely close grenade blast.)

CUTTY: Twenty seconds, sir.

(Another blast of gunshot from slightly further away. The men clearing the alleys are being shot at.)

JAY: Fuck that's—
RICHARD: Compound clear.
MURRAY: Fucking hell

JAY: Keep low

(*More machine gun fire from the troop. More shots fired at the troop.*)

   Just get your eyes to the right

LLOYD: Keep down

VOICE ON RADIO: 4 pax enemy to the north positive ID.

CUTTY: Air strike ten seconds, sir.

JAY: Watch the tracer

VOICE ON RADIO: 4 pax enemy to the north positive ID.

LLOYD: Get up there

(*There is the sound of a rocket being launched. This has the familiar whiz and scream of a firework rocket but the noise of its launch is ferocious and close and casts some light on parts of the stage.*)

VOICE ON RADIO: 4 pax enemy to the north positive ID.

LLOYD: Rapid Fire

      Rapid Fire

      Rapid Fire

JAY: Move forward

MURRAY: Go go go go

CUTTY: Five seconds till air

JAY: 50 Cal Go

(*They are shot at again. This time the shots are closer and more unsettling than they've been before. In the darkness we struggle to make out that there is a man shot. It is* MURRAY.)

LLOYD: Over run!

      Over run!

      Over run!

RICHARD: Searge. Man down

JAY: Who is it?

RICHARD: I don't know yet.

JAY: Get him to me now.

(*There is the sudden massive noise of an air strike from above. This should be far louder and far more sudden than you think you can get away with.*)

RICHARD: Through there

JAY: Get the casualty to me.

      Get the casualty to me now

RICHARD: It's Murray.

JAY: I want morphine. Suppressive fire! Get some fucking suppressive fire now!
Where's he hit?
Come on.
Get his kit off him.
Get it off of him.

RICHARD: He's gone. T-4.

(*More machine gun fire from the unit and shots at the unit. Two more rockets are fired out of the base.*)

JAY: No. He's alive.
Right get him back.
Get him back.
Leave his kit, Kendall.
Get him back.

(*More shots at the unit.*)

CUTTY: Support!

JAY: Just go. Just go.

(*More shots at the unit.*)

Needs to be quick.
Come on.
Where's his body armor?
Get me his body armor now.

LLOYD: Let's go! Two section
Extract!
Fast extraction

JAY: Where's the morphine?
Where's the fucking morphine?

KENDALL: It's here.

JAY: I want him.

(*He's still breathing.*)

KENDALL: Yes, searge.

JAY: I fucking want him.
You hear me?

(*The scene should end as suddenly as it began.*)

III.

(*The front room of* JAY WATKINS's *house in Levenshulme, South Manchester. He is sitting on a sofa with his feet up in front of him. He is watching television. He is drinking from a cup of tea.*)

(*We watch him for a while.*)

(CHERYL, *27, his girlfriend, enters. She's wearing pyjamas. She takes him by surprise.*)

JAY: Hiya.

CHERYL: Hi.

JAY: What you doing up?

CHERYL: Couldn't get to sleep.

You gonna be long?

JAY: Don't think so.

CHERYL: What you watching?

(*A beat.*)

JAY: It's Belgian football.

(*A beat. He smiles at her. She doesn't smile back.*)

CHERYL: Billy's asleep.

JAY: At last.

CHERYL: He's just excited to see you home.

JAY: Yeah.

CHERYL: I am too.

JAY: That's good.

(*She doesn't move. Stays looking at him in her pyjamas.*)

What time is it?

CHERYL: I've no idea.

JAY: Do you want a cup of tea? I made a pot.

CHERYL: I'm all right.

Shouldn't drink tea at this time. Keeps you awake.

You rang your mum?

JAY: I'll ring her tomorrow.

CHERYL: You better.

(*A brief pause. He glances at her.*)

JAY: You all right?
CHERYL: I don't know.

(*A beat.*)

JAY: What's wrong?
CHERYL: It doesn't matter.

(*Some time. He looks at her.*)

JAY: He's got bigger, hasn't he?

(*She nods her head.*)

He looks like you.
CHERYL: He doesn't. He looks like you.

(*He looks at her for a beat. She still stands looking at him.*)

JAY: You're being.
CHERYL: What?
JAY: I don't know. You keep looking at us. You're being a bit—
CHERYL: You could talk to him.
Billy.
JAY: You what?
CHERYL: Your son. You could talk to him. Or just, you know, look at him a bit. If you looked at him a bit you might clock how much he looks nothing like me at all and is basically so much the spit of you he's practically your mini-me.
JAY: I did talk to him. I do talk to him.
CHERYL: You didn't, Jay. You talked about him. You talked to me. You talked to the television. You looked right over his head, mate.
JAY: Where did this come from?
CHERYL: He was so excited to see you.
JAY: Chez, I'm a bit tired for this.
CHERYL: Well why don't you come to bed then? If you're a bit tired for this. If you're a bit tired for it, Jay, why don't you come to bed with me instead of sitting down here drinking a pot of flipping tea and watching Belgian flipping football?

(*He looks at her, slightly stunned.*)

I had this idea.

You could not go back. You could stay here. You could hand in your notice. You could come back home and you could live with me and with Billy and it could just be normal again.

(*Some time.*)

JAY: Are you being serious?

CHERYL: Doesn't it look like I'm being serious?

JAY: I don't believe this.

CHERYL: No.

JAY: I've not slept for thirty-four hours. I've barely had time for a fucking shit—

CHERYL: Don't you swear at me.

JAY: I'm sorry.

CHERYL: You should be.

JAY: I am. All right?

CHERYL: I watched you giving him a kiss. You didn't even look at him when you were doing that. I tried to give you a hug and it felt like I was hugging a bit of just wood, Jay.

JAY: I'm not listening to this.

CHERYL: No. Course you're not.

JAY: What's that supposed to mean?

CHERYL: You should just stick your fingers in your ears. Stick your fingers in your ears and sing "God Save the Queen." That'll make it a bit easier not to hear me, Jay, eh?

JAY: Chez. Please. Can we talk about this in the morning?

CHERYL: We won't.

JAY: What?

CHERYL: We never do, Jay, do we? No. Not really we don't. It's been six years of you going out to those places, Jay, and I think you've done enough and I hate it and I want it to stop.

JAY: And you need to tell me this at two o'clock in the morning?

CHERYL: What are you even doing out there?

What are you even doing out there?

What are you even doing out there, Jay?

JAY: You wouldn't—

CHERYL (*she roars at him*): Don't tell me I wouldn't understand, Jay, really don't. You don't have the slightest idea of the things that I understand only too flipping well.

Nobody thinks you should be out there. Not anymore. I can't turn the television on without somebody telling me that you should be coming back home. The place is a mess. It's always been a mess. It always will be a mess. But you're making it a thousand times worse.

And if all you're doing is shitting on the place and its shitty people, then I want my husband back and Billy wants his dad back and we want him back now, please.

(JAY *looks at her.*)

Can we have him back now, please?

(*Some time.*)

Can we have him back now, please?

JAY: There's a village about 80 kilometres west of Kandahar called Pir Zadeh.

CHERYL: Can we have him back now, please?

JAY: It was south of the dam that I spent most of my time on the last tour trying to protect it from Taliban insurgents.

CHERYL: Can we have him back now, please?

JAY: There's a school in the village. Which in itself is frankly amazing. I spent a few days on patrol there. You take your helmet off. You wander round a bit. Take the shades off. Hand out a few sweets. Got to know, actually, we got to know some of the kids.

CHERYL: Can we have him back now, please?

JAY: One of the kids that I met there was a girl called Delaram.

She was ten.

CHERYL: Don't.

JAY: And what was just astonishing about Delaram was that she was going to school.

CHERYL: Don't, Jay. I don't want to hear this story. I don't want to know this.

JAY: She was learning to read. And she was able to learn to read and to write and to do sums because we were there stopping anything from happening to her. Or to her school or to her teachers.

CHERYL: This is just stupid sentimental—

JAY: On our last afternoon there she was coming home from school when a forty-year-old man stepped from out of one of the houses in the west of the town near where the school was with a water pistol in his hand and he sprayed it at Delaram. Laughed a bit. Giggled a bit. Sprayed the water pistol in her face. And it might have looked a bit strange because here was this forty-year-old giggling and spraying a water pistol at a ten-year-old kid. Only what was in his water pistol, of course, wasn't water, was it, Chez, it was acid. He burnt her eyes out because she was ten and she was going to school.

Don't you dare tell me that I'm making that a thousand times worse.

(*Beat.*)

CHERYL: Do you think that doesn't happen here? Seriously, Jay, do you, mate? You want to go up Moss side, Jay, it's an initiation rite for thirteen-year-old girls that up there.

JAY: If we leave now then that'll be everything fucked.

CHERYL: Everything's already fucked. There's nothing you can do about that.

JAY: There are people in that country who are vicious bastard monsters and they're full of just hate and they need to be stopped.

CHERYL: There are people on our street like that.

JAY: And the ones over here are creaming a fortune selling smack from a Helmand Poppy farm that we can burn down.

CHERYL: It won't change anything.

JAY: We can open up the power supply. We can protect the water supply. We can oversee the infrastructure. We can build roads there. We can build accommodation there.

CHERYL (*talking over him*): What the fuck is it about that place that means that my husband can wander off five thousand miles away and shally around like he's some kind of action hero when he's not got the courage to come home and look his own son in the face?

You are changing nothing, Jay. You can change nothing. All you're doing is making yourself feel better about how useless you all are.

JAY: Don't.

CHERYL: You're a coward, Jay. You think you're being a hero. You're not. We're so way beyond that now. It's gone on for too long. We're not helping. We're just smashing it all up. And every time you try to make it better, you do the absolute opposite.

JAY: Stop it, Cheryl.

CHERYL: Or what? Or what, Jay? Come on. People shouldn't survive in places like that. People shouldn't survive in heat like that. On land like that. It makes no sense. Everybody gets so upset about people dying. It's stupid. People die all the time. It's one of the things we do. It's good. There are too many of us in the first place. We just need to decide where. And that's a good fucking place to start if you ask me. It's a hole in the bottom of the world. You should let them burn. They deserve it.

(*Some time. He looks at her. The football continues to play.*)

JAY: You should go to bed.

CHERYL: I don't want you to go back there. Every day I think that it's going to be you they talk about on the radio as being the person the Ministry of Defence are informing the family about. I hate that feeling. It exhausts me.

JAY: You. You should do. You'll be knackered in the morning.

(*She doesn't move.*)

(*The television carries on playing.*)

(*Sudden black.*)